Information Management in New Millennium

Opportunities and Challenges for Library Professionals

INFORMATION MANAGEMENT IN NEW MILLENNIUM

Opportunities and Challenges for Library Professionals

Edited by
Ashok Kumar Sahu

Ess Ess Publications

4837/24, Ansari Road, Darya Ganj,
New Delhi-110002
Tel. : 23260807, 41563444
Fax : 011-41563334
E-mail: info@essessreference.com
url:http://www.essessreference.com

Ess Ess Publications
4837/24, Ansari Road,
Darya Ganj,
New Delhi-110 002.

Tel.: 23260807, 41563444
Fax: 41563334
E-mail: info@essessreference.com
www.essessreference.com

Rs.1250/-

First Published - 2008

ISBN: 81-7000-531-0 (10 Digit)
978-81-7000-531-5 (13 Digit)

Published By Ess Ess Publications and printed at Salasar Imaging Systems

PRINTED IN INDIA

Acknowledgements

First and foremost, I would like to thank all the contributors of this book. The book is an outcome of an effort of all contributors who are from eminent institutions nationally and internationally. I would also express my gratitude to Dr.Kamlesh Misra, Director, IIMT Dr.U.Venkatesh, Dean, IIMT, for their support and constant encouragement throughout this study. I would also like to thank Dr.Vinnie Jauhari, University Relations Manager-India, Hewlett Packard India for her inspiration and advice throughout this study.

I am also very grateful to my Ph.D.guide Dr.Rabindra Kumar Mahapatra for his insights and innovative ideas from time to time at all stages of the work. My grateful acknowledgements to Manjit Singh, Amit Saxena, Dr.Mirdula Dwivedi and other colleagues for their support from time to time and help at all stages of the work. My sincere thanks to my wife Sujata, little daughter Suhani and my parents whose inspiration and wishes have led to the completion of this work.

I would like to thank to Mukesh Graphics for typing, formatting, and editing of this book and bearing inconvenience on account of working long hours. Last but not the least, I thank Mr.Sumit Sethi, Managing Director, Ess Ess Publications, New Delhi who has taken lots of pains to publish this book.

Ashok Kumar Sahu

Acknowledgements

Contents

Preface

Present society has moved to knowledge-based society for which information is of primary importance. In 21st century, Information plays an important role into the cultural, political, social, scientific, and technological development of a society. Information is the key resource for productivity and growth of any orgainization. In this changing context, library professionals are facing lot of challenges to capture, process, store, and disseminate the information for society. The Information Communication Technology (ICT) revolution in the last decade has had a drastic and far-reaching impact on all aspects of professional endeavour particularly in the knowledge and information sector. By the late 1990's when information was regularly disseminated across computers and other electronic devices, information managers found themselves tasked with increasingly complex devices. Information Management (IM) is characterised by the phrase 'Getting the *right information* to the right person at the right place at the right time'. Due to revolution of technology, the information services have increased their variety and quantity and refined in their quality.

Information Management (IM) is a crucial job for the library professionals in the new era. Library professionals are now being challenged by the new environment which demands changes in their styles, attitude and skills towards information handling. The traditional aproaches to information processing and organisation are undergoing transformation due to rapid advances in the area of information technologies, electronic resources and telecommunication. Information Technology has tremendously changed the role of library to information centre and Librarian to Information Manager.

The book is organized into four parts – Information and Society, Information Management, Digital Library and Electronic Resources, Future Trends including 29 Papers. The papers of first part "Information and Society" discusses about the impact of information on information society and how the present society depends on the information. The information is the backbone of knowledge society. The papers of second part "Information Management" discuss about the managing and marketing of the information. And also explain about quality management in information services. The papers of third part "Digital Library and Electronic Resources" discuss about the concept of digital library, security problems, digitalize the documents, and electronic resources. The papers of fourth part "Future Trends" explain about the future generation of the library and expert systems.

This book helps the library professionals to better understand how to manage the information in the new environment. The book would be a valuable resource for the librarians, academics and professionals involved with managing information. It would also be immensely useful for students pursuing master degrees and doctoral work in the area of information management. The book is an edited book, which compilation of 29 papers in different areas of information management. The papers are contributed by renowned writers both from India and abroad. The book is an outcome of an effort of contributors who are from very eminent institutions nationally and internationally. I would like to thank all the contributors to the book. The book caters to a wide audience of academicians, researchers, students. It provides an insight into information management in digital era.

Ashok Kumar Sahu

List of Contributors

Amitava Pani
Professor, Institute of Management
Bhubaneswar, Bhubaneswar, Orissa

Ashok Kumar Sahu
Librarian, Institute for International
Management and Technology, Gurgaon, Haryana
Email : *aksahu@iimtobu.ac.in*

Atul M. Gonsai
Sr. Assist. Prof., Department of Computer
Science Saurashtra University
Rajkot-360005
Email : *atulgosai@yahoo.com*

B.A.Rajeev
Librarian, HMS Institute of Technology,
TUMKUR-572 104, Karnataka
Email : *rajeev_bidare@yahoo.co.in*

Bambang Setiarso
Center for Scientific Documentation and
Information-Indonesia Institute of
Sciences (PDII-LIPI)
Jakarta 12710 - INDONESIA
Email : *setiarso@pdii.lipi.go.id*

Chinmayee N. Bhange
Librarian, St. Francis Institute of
Technology (Engg. College) Borivali (W),
Mumbai 400103, Maharashtra
Email : *chinmayee_bhange@rediffmail.com*

Constantine Matoke Nyamboga
Senior Librarian/Lecturer,
Egerton University Library, Njoro, Kenya
Email : *constantinebu@yahoo.com*

D.B. Patil
Reader, Dept of Library and
Information Science, Gulbarga University,
Gulbarga: 585 106
Email : *db_patil@rediffmail.com*

Hafizi Muhamad Ali
Department of Information Science,
Faculty of Information Science and Technology,
University Kebangsaan Malaysia, Malaysia
Email : *hafizi@uum.edu.my*

K Rajasekharan
Librarian, Kerala Institute of Local
Administration Mulagunnathu Kavu P O,
Thrissur - 680 581
Email : *librariankila@hotmail.com*; *rajankila@hotmail.com*

K. Praveenkumar
Assistant Librarian, Gulbarga University,
Gulbarga: 585 106
Email : *kumbargoudar@rediffmail.com*

K.M.Nafala
Computer Operator-Library,
Kerla Institute of Local Administration,
Mulagunnathu Kavu P O, Thrissur - 680 581

M. Purushothama Gowda
Senior Asst. Librarian,
Mangalore University
Mangalagangotri-574 199
E-mails : *gowda_mp@yahoo.com*

Mahendra Kumar Rawat
Librarian, IIMT Gruop of College,
Greater Noida, U.P. 201306, India
Email : *rawat1321@rediffmail.com*

Mamata. Mestri
Assistant Librarian, Gulbarga University,
Gulbarga: 585 106
Email : *mamatapk@rediffmail.com*

Neha M. Joshi
Librarian , Thakur Institute of Management
Studies and Research, Kandivali (E),
Mumbai- 400 101, Maharashtra,
Email : *sakhineha@yahoo.co.in*

Prativa Acharya
Librarian, Institute of Management Bhubaneswar,
Bhubaneswar
Email : *lali_imb@yahoo.co.in*

R.K.Mahapatra
Reader, Sanjay Memorial Institute of Technology,
Ankushpur, Orissa
Email : *mahapatrark_1962@rediffmail.com*

Raymond Wafula Ongus
Research Scholar, Department of Library and
Information Science, Bangalore University,
Bangalore 560 056, Karnataka
Email : *raymondongus@yahoo.co.uk*

S. Jayaprakash
Army Institute of Hotel Management &
Catering Technology
Bangalore-560007, Karnataka
Email : *chinnujp@indiatimes.com*

S. Parameshwar.
Research Scholar, Dept of Lib & Inf. Science,
Gulbarga University, Gulbarg
Email : *ajay_p04@rediffmail.com*

Sanjay Kataria
Librarian, Jaypee Institute of
Information Technology, Noida
Email : *lib_scholar@rediffmail.com*

Shaliendra Kumar Rawat
Associate Manager (IT) , Rap Magnum
Adlabs Multiplex Cinema, Meerut, U.P. India
Email : *rawat1231@rediffmail.com*

Shashikanta Jena
Graduate Trainee, Central Library, Indian
Institute of Technology, Madras, Chennai
Email : *shashi_jena2001@yahoo.com*

Sibsankar Jana
Asst. Librarian II, Department of Physics,
Jadavpur University, Kolkata-700032
E-mail : *sibs_jana@yahoo.com*

Subarna K Das
Dept. of Library and Information Science,
Jadavpur University, Kolkata-70032
E-mail : *skd_ju2002@yahoo.co.in*

Sujata Padhy
Jr. Librarian, Munadamarai Science college,
Mundamarai, Orissa
Email : *Padhysp@hotmail.com*

Sujata Santosh
Senior Consultant, Fidelity Information
Services India Pvt. Ltd, Chandigarh
Email : *sujata_san2@yahoo.com*

Sunil Karve
Director, Abhinav Seva Mandali's School
of Management, Education & Research, Mumbai
Email : *dr_karve@rediffmail.com*

Sunil Kumar Satpathy
Sr. Librarian, C.V.Raman College of Engineering,
Bhubaneswar, Orissa.
Email : *Satpathy_dr@yahoo.co.in*

T. D. Kemparaju
Professor and Chairman, Department of
Library and Information Science,
Bangalore University, Bagalore, Karnatak
Email : *tdkv2000@rediffmail.com*

Tariq Ashraf
Deputy Librarian, Delhi University Library System
University of Delhi. Delhi,India
Email : *tariq22@gmail.com*

Vibha Gupta
Research Scholar, Department of Library &
Information Science, Aligarh Muslim University,
Aligarh, Uttar Pradesh
Email : *vibha_amu@yahoo.com*, *vibhaamu@gmail.com*

Vrushali Rane
Librarian, NMIMS University, Mumbai
Email : *vrushalir@rediffmail.com*

Zawiyah Mohammad Yusof
Department of Information Science,
Faculty of Information Science and Technology,
Universiti Kebangsaan Malaysia, Malaysia
Email : *zmy@ftsm.ukm.my*

1

Information Society: A New Challenge for Libraries and Library Professionals

Ashok Kumar Sahu

INTRODUCTION

The advancement of science and technology has made a tremendous improvement and change almost in all walks of life. Especially, the magnetic word Information Technology has been chanted in all corners of the global arena and been incorporated in organizational, managerial, developmental and marketing sectors. Technological advances, changes in social structures and institutions, methods of communication, and cultural values have provided some evidence of change that are not only increasingly pervasive and predominantly in the industrial nations but is increasingly apparent in the rest of world as well. A recurring explanation for these changes is that information and communication technologies (ICTs) are somehow related. Increased economic growth, improved social conditions, and the spread of democracy are changes that have been observed and credited to the rise and growth of ICTs. The observed effects have suggested that we are living in an age of social transformation that is characterized by change in our global mode of production, from one of industrial manufacturing to a society where information and knowledge are the fastest growing sector of economy (Dordick and Wang, 1993).

In the knowledge age, or the information age, information and intelligence become the raw materials as did iron and coal in the Industrial Age. In the new situation, as the pressures of global competition and the use of information and communication technologies increase, we find that the libraries and the way they work with people are changing. Re-engineering, a flattening of hierarchies, networking, total quality management, part-time working and teleworking are all part of the same inevitable process of re-adjustment to a new environment. Libraries tend to be more and more organised as a network and to be decentralised, distributed, collaborative, and responsive. The development of high-speed networks and advanced services will bring about a new distribution of national and international labour. Library will no longer consider distance as a barrier to providing their services. Libraries, being a most important part of the information society due to their immense information resources, have to collect, organize and disseminate in the new information market. An extremely important role falls to library professionals who are becoming carriers and pushers of the new ideology (Ershova, 1998).

INFORMATION SOCIETY –A NEW ERA

The advent of information society can be traced to 1960s when a sift occurred from the industrial processes to a service based economy. The growth of information society is becoming pivotal for creation of resilient economies. Knowledge is empowering. Knowledge innovation is core of information society. In the knowledge era, the management refers to effectively identify, acquire, develop, resolve, use, store, and share knowledge, to create an approach to transforming and sharing tacit and explicit knowledge, and to raise the emergency and innovation capability by utilizing the wisdom of a team. So, information has become the driving force for social development (Wang, 1999).

Machlup (1962) first pronounced the United States economy as a knowledge economy, rather than an industrial economy. This heralded the debate of whether the changes in the US economy were indicative of a new developmental phase, i.e. Information society, or just a next step in industrialized society. Despite the debate, it soon became clear that not all economies in the world were shifting at the same pace, and the gap between rich and poor countries was first recognized. In order to understand the significance of what it means to be an information society, it is useful to review information science theories as they pertain to development. Webster (1995) provides a useful framework for examining the various information society theories. He groups the theories into five categories that broadly emphasize the primary perspectives including technological, economic, occupational, spatial, and cultural. Webster describes the technological phase as "the most common definition of the 'Information Society'" and suggests that its primary premise is that "information processing storage and transmission have led to the application of information technologies (IT) in virtually all corners of society".

INFORMATION RESOURCES AND INFORMATION SOCIETY

In information society, the quality of life as well as prospects for social change and economic development depend increasingly upon information and its exploitation. In the new digital divide, all nations in world are benefiting economically and socially from the new economy based on technology, knowledge and information innovation (Chopra, 2001). Information Communication Technology (ICT) is the driver of the knowledge society. ICT is providing new and faster ways of delivering and accessing information, innovative ways for real time communication. The Internet has had a major impact on modern life by facilitating direct interaction between the individual and government, businesses, organizations and other people. The direct nature of this communication has bypassed many of the traditional intermediaries in a multitude of human interactions. Technology and economics tend to be seen as the dominant forces driving us towards a world of relentless pressure to do more with less, but political and socio demographic issues are also having a significant impact on service provision (Bavakutty, 2003).

As ever more communication and delivery of services takes place within a digital environment, there is increasing pressure for citizens of those nations that would like to describe themselves as information societies to be prepared to interact with this medium. This can be empowering, but it can also be bewildering. The online environment is a relatively new phenomenon, which continues to evolve. Martin describes the current state of online interactions as being in transition but as moving towards becoming mainstream, everyday "e-activities" (Martin, 2004). To operate effectively in this online environment, to be able to learn, work, communicate with others, interact with government, shop and for entertainment, we will need a set of skills that will allow us to function with sufficient competence to achieve our goals (Wallis, 2005).

However, the IT skills are required by the citizen of the information society to use networked communication technologies, digital media, and online and traditional information resources. The IT skills are needed to use information and communication technologies (ICTs) effectively, and to access appropriate digital information resources.

ROLE OF LIBRARIES IN INFORMATION SOCIETY

Libraries have played an important role in preserving the history of civilization since the invention of writing. Alexandria, Egypt, was the site of the most comprehensive ancient library, where scholars could study manuscripts in Greek, Ethiopian, Persian, Hebrew, and Hindi. In Rome, educated citizens maintained personal libraries, and there were 28 public libraries in Rome by the beginning of the fourth century A.D.

During the Middle Ages, the libraries of monasteries preserved copies of Greek and Latin classics. During the Renaissance, collectors, kings, and noblemen preserved many works of literature and philosophy in their personal libraries. These collections became the foundations of some of Europe's great scholarly libraries.

Books received a larger circulation after Johannes Gutenberg invented the printing press in the mid-1440s. Prior to this invention, manuscripts were written by hand, an inefficient method. In addition, few members of the public were literate or had the leisure time to read books until the Industrial Revolution and other social changes in the eighteenth and nineteenth centuries. Because of these advances, libraries changed from institutions that preserved valuable works with a limited sphere of elite users to educational facilities for the common people.

As the twentieth century came to a close, new libraries are being built, stocked with print materials and connected to the Internet. Electronic information services began to play an increasing role in serving library users. Massive amounts of information were contained on database systems, and people used the library as their primary source for health, employment, financial, educational, as well as entertainment needs.

The following computer-related services were available to the public in a majority of the centers: CD-ROM databases, remote database searching, microcomputers, software, and online public access catalogs (OPACs). Increasingly, libraries offered access to the Internet, enabling libraries to serve those who do not otherwise have computer access—by providing information as well as instruction in the use of computers and other equipment.

The Internet brought the biggest change in libraries as during the 1990s saw the rapidly increasing availability of access to computers generally, and to the Internet in particular. The World Wide Web became a significant vehicle for distributing information. The growing universe of digital content was at the heart of discussions about how libraries would change as they became increasingly virtual, offering content to a larger, more geographically dispersed user base that demanded instant access to information. Many leading book and journal publishers began offering their content in both print and electronic versions. Computers are increasingly important in the library as networks linking public, college and university, school, and special libraries have expanded. Librarians maintain records on computers, and card catalogs are now nearly all replaced by computer terminals that allow online access to the library's holdings, as well as data, abstracts, and texts contained in periodicals and journals. The electronic network enables libraries to economically facilitate interlibrary loans, thus expanding their collections, controlling cost, and improving service to users. The use of libraries as a prime source of access to the Internet for those who otherwise do not have access continues to grow. Electronic resources will continue to enhance the information available to library users. Online mediated searching, CD-ROM, and various databases provide references that were previously unavailable. Online searching is the most common electronic option and was the first electronic reference service to be offered by research librarians in the 1970s. In this scenario, librarians' roles would become more consultative and advisory than ever before.

CHANGING THE ROLE OF LIBRARY PROFESSIONALS

The direct access to the complex information environment described above necessitates a change in the role of librarians and information professionals, from gatekeepers to guides. Given the demands of the knowledge society the librarian must support learning at all levels. The need for all citizens to develop a skill set of technological and media literacy means that librarians will have to be incorporated into learning programmes to teach these abilities. Librarians can teach generic skills in how to access information through a variety of media whilst emphasizing an understanding of issues around its validity, authenticity and currency. Information literacy programmes can inculcate good principles in the fundamental skills of information use in the knowledge society (Wallis, 2005).

The proliferation of electronic information resources has required library professionals to assume greater responsibility for keeping pace with technology. As the library becomes the provider of information in variety of formats to meet the different needs of users, it is essential that library professionals must be familiar with new technology to access the information in new formats. Librarians must keeping pace with changing technology has become a matter of necessity rather than choice. Presently, librarians must often be familiar with both print and electronic versions of resources to help and serve the information needs of users (Felco, 1997). Visualizing the growing trends in the context of "technology", storage and transmission capabilities it is expected that the professionals have to have e-competencies along with some managerial skills, which are essential in present context (Fallis and Fricke, 1999).

The complexity of the information environment, and of cyberspace as a cultural and emotional experience, presents library professionals of the 21st century information society with particular challenges. Vast amounts of finance are poured into the development of new technologies for delivering information and communication in ever more sophisticated ways. To manage all sorts of information resource, effectively and cope up with the ever growing information and multifarious needs of the users and to survive in the changing environment the information professionals require certain sets of essential skills and competencies. The skills which are required by the information professionals during the period prior to the information to information age, are enumerate following way and the more relevant to present society also (Ward, 1999).

1. Institutional Knowledge
2. Specialist subject Knowledge
3. Source knowledge and curiosity
4. Communicating knowledge effectively
5. Technological skills

Library professionals involved in assessing the value of electronic resources should consider the complexity of educational training programs needed to make these resources available.

The information society of twenty-first century offers the opportunity for libraries to play a central role in the academic and research community, but it will be require bold and confident leadership among the way. Information Management has become a powerful tool for promoting innovation and realizing reengineering the various walks of life. How for the library professionals to meet challenge of knowledge economy and to build knowledge management system of libraries. The effective utilization of emerging advanced new technologies has become inevitable for survival and successful management of modern libraries in a dynamic turbulent technological environment and global knowledge society.

ABOUT THE BOOK

The book consists of 29 papers in the areas of Information Society, Knowledge management, Marketing of information product, Quality management in libraries, Digital library, Electronic resources, etc.The book is divided into four different parts. The papers focus on mainly the following areas in library and information management: Information and Society, Information Management; Digital library and electronic resources, and Future Trends.

S.K.Satpathy in his paper "*Public Library: The Vehicle For Information Dissemination In A Democratic Society*" describes about growth and development of libraries in a democratic society. In new era, library and society are inter-linked and inter-dependent. This paper is critically analyses the role of public libraries in democratic society. Both library and society are two sides of a coin and one cannot exist without other.

Vibha Gupta's paper '*Impact Of Information Technology on Societal development and E-Governance*' discusses the IT revolution, impact of IT on society. Information technology is taking central stage of global economy. IT revolution is creating chaos, numerous social problems and a reorganization of human life. Economy, society, education, religion, psychology, science, and technology are all changing by IT revolution. It has transformed the whole world into a global village with global economy.

M.K.Rawat and S.K.Rawat in their paper, "*LIS distance education: A snapshot of digital resource organization, design of information services and management in networked environment*" have discussed on E-education and importance of Information Communication Technology (ICT) on education. E-education is basically the online delivery of information communication, training and learning. And also discussed the emerging role of Information Technology in distance education. Internet is play major role in e-learning, e-education.

H. M. Ali and Z. M. Yusof in their paper, "*Knowledge-Based Organisation: An Overview on the Existing Knowledge Management Models*" provides an overview of various knowledge management models with particular emphasis on the varied definition accorded to knowledge management, the types and components of existing knowledge management models. As the result of the overview, an integrated business model to facilitate knowledge creation, knowledge sharing, and knowledge discovery is suggested to serve as a basis and generic guide particularly for adoption by banks and also for future research. This model is generated after taking into consideration the limitation that all the available models possess.

B. Setiars's paper, "*Knowledge Sharing and Digital Libraries in Indonesia: Facing lot of Constraints and Challenges to Disseminate the S&T information for the Society*" discussed about Knowledge sharing and digital libraries with a new paradigm covers a wide range of functionalities and support different sets of activities. The aim of this paper is to gain a better understanding of how some factors are critical for the successful application of knowledge sharing and digital libraries. And also study in this paper about development of digital libraries among academic and research institutions in Indonesia.

M.P.Gowda in his paper "*Levels of Knowledge*" discussed about knowledge production, knowledge use and knowledge dissemination. The present century is known as knowledge century. The knowledge century is totally depending upon knowledge. And also described about transparent knowledge, relative knowledge, and independent knowledge.

S.K.Satpathy's paper "*Knowledge Management: The New Challenges for Libraries in Digital Era*" discuss the issue knowledge management. Today library professionals are facing great challenges to collect, organize, disseminate the knowledge in present society. This paper critically analysis the concept of Knowledge Management in libraries. Knowledge management has emerged as a new challenge area for libraries and a rational design of the organizational structure and business procedures of libraries is required for proper knowledge management.

The study of P.Acharya , "*Information Management*" discusses how to manage the information in new era. The aim of information management is to promote organization effectiveness by enhancing the capabilities of the organization's scope with the demands of the internal and external environments in dynamic as well as stable conditions. It includes organization, development and maintenance of integrated, systems and services, optimization of information flow, functional requirements of end users.The basic elements of information management include accessing, evaluating, managing, organizing, filtering and distributing of information in such a manner that the information should useful for end users. So information management is a logical extension of the information society.

The paper of A.K.Sahu "*Perceptions of Service Quality in Academic Library: A Case Study*" determines the perception of the users of the Jawaharlal Nehru University (JNU) Library, New Delhi, India, with regard to the quality service provided by JNU Library. Service quality is essential to change the work culture among the employees for their involvement in the services of the library to provide quality service and customer satisfaction. It focuses on continuous improvement in products and services, with greater employee involvement and an increased emphasis on customer needs.

N.Joshi's paper "*Total Quality Management: Implication on Library Services*" gives an overall view of how TQM principles can be applied in library services and how it can improve the functionality of any library. The factors for success will definitely be determined by maintaining quality in all respects including resources, services, use of management skills, creation of local content etc.

The study of Sujat Santosh "*Marketing of Information Products and services*" discusses the various issues related to marketing of information products and services at the same time highlighting its importance. Various factors like prerequisites for marketing, barriers to marketing, factors inhibiting marketing orientation and marketing plan and guidelines for preparation of marketing plan are discussed in detail. In view of the fast changing information scenario, mainly due to multifaceted developments in information technology, the realization is now dawning that a coherent marketing programme needs to be integrated into a library's organizational structure. It is extremely important to understand what the users want and how they think and then to design and market the products accordingly.

The paper of A.K.Sahu, R.K.Mahapatra, S.Padhy "*Application of 4Ps to Marketing the Information Product / services in Academic Libraries*" discusses the marketing of library and information services in 21st century on the basis of traditional concept of marketing. The aim of this study to attempt to correlate marketing as a concept to the provision of library services. In view of the social, economic and technological changes, Library and Information centers have begun to realize that marketing of information products and services is an integral part of administration. It helps to provide right service at right time and the right price to right users in the right place with support of quality staffs.

S.Karve and V.Rane in their paper "*Getting out to help Students Where They Learn: Marketing Library Services to Distance Learners*" understand the distance learner's needs and how a library can fulfill them & create marketing awareness among librarians than to report any exhaustive findings. Distance learners are a unique target population for marketing of library services and resources. Distance learners are a unique target population for marketing of library services and resources. The main objectives of the study are:

* To understand the information seeking behaviour of distance learning students.

* To gauge their awareness and level of their library use.
* To determine their needs for information resources and library use instructions.
* To identify how the library can improve its services to distance learning students

T.Ashraf's paper "*Implications for Library and Information Services: A Study of India's IT Revolution and Public Policies*" describes the role of Information, Information Technology (IT) and discusses the infrastructure, human resources, telecommunication, research and development in IT in Indian context. It Highlights the features of liberalization policy of the Indian government; software policy; development in networking and growth of IT industry in the country, and documents the proliferation and focuses on the relationship among policies and outcome in terms of its impact on various fields of life specially library and information services . It describes the limitation of Indian digital revolution in reaching out to the general masses and the various factors responsible for the lopsided character of information revolution.

The study of S.Jana's paper "*Concepts and Architecture of Digital Library With Special Reference to the Creation of Digital Library Through Institutional Repository by Using Dspace*" provides an overview of digital library, institutional repository, open source software and Dspace software. Enumerates differents steps and prerequisites to create digital library through institutional repository by using the open source software "Dspace". Different types of architectural approaches and components of digital library are described.

D.B.Patil, K.Praveenkumar, and S.Parameshwar in their paper "*Establishment of Hyderabad-Karnataka Institutional Repository at Gulbarga University Library: A Development Plan*" examined the development of Institutional Repository. The paper contained a detailed plan to design an institutional repository using Open Source-DSpace. The Institutional Repository should established using Dublin Core metadata for metadata storing and conversion. The hardware and software requirements and technical details related for establishing Institutional Repository are also discussed. The Institutional repository is beneficial to faculty, research scholars, scientists and students, which provide them an opportunity to access, communicate and publish their research findings online and also develop their career future.

M.K.Rawat, and S.K.Rawat in their paper "*Digital Libraries Development- Using RFID Methods Information Tools and Techniques*" attempt to study about the RFID technology and its advantage and disadvantages. RFID is used for item tracking and access control applications. It is mainly used in library for security purpose. This paper is also discussed about how to install RFID system in libraries. It is very helpful for stock verification, circulation of books, and security.

B.A.Rajeev, and S.Jayaprakash in their paper "*Library Security: Barcode, RFID*" discusses about the library security and how to implement the RFID and barcode in libraries. The security of library collections is major problem for all libraries. In new era, lot of new technologies (RFID, Barcode, electronic surveillance etc.) are developed for solve the security problems.

The paper of S.Jena, and S.Kataria "*RFID Technology in Library Management: Concept to completion*" provides details about, What is RFID? and how does it work? What are the applications of RFID in Libraries? This paper also aims to clarify each and every aspect of RFID Systems and how does it organize electronic library services.

M.P.Gowda in his paper "*Digital Library*" discusses concept of the digital library, provides the meaning and definitions, process, key elements distinguish features, advantages and challenges, preservation of digital library materials etc. Digital libraries offers new levels of access to broader audiences of users and new opportunities for the library and information field to advance both theory and practice. They contain information collections predominantly in digital or electronic form electronic publications have some special problems of management as compared to printed documents the include infrastructure, acceptability access restrictions, readability, standardization, authentication, preservation, copyright, user interface etc. But still the advantages are more and therefore, the importance of digital libraries has been recognized widely both in the developed and developing countries as well. Development of digital library is the new opportunity to meet the new and diversified challenges of the user community.

The paper of A.M.Gonsai "*High-speed Network Model for HiTech Libraries*" presents model for high-speed library networks for the multimedia rich high bandwidth intensive library applications. The paper is divided in three parts describing low-level network setup, middle-level network setup and finally high-speed network setup for the library. Each setup has some functionality, pros and cons for handling and managing library resources with cost and speed elements in consideration. The depicted models indicates that scalability in the increasing processing capabilities of digital computing of workstations and servers providing services to the clients, larger and larger storage needs and effective management of storage and increasing requirements of network bandwidth and high speed data transfer are the prime issues to the scientists of information technologies.

The paper of K Rajasekharan & K M Nafala "*Creating Digital Document Archives with Winisis & Genisisweb Software*" discusses step by step the application and installation of Winisis and create database, installation of Apache server and installation of Genesis Web. Very easily described installation process of above software packages with screen shots in libraries. This paper will be helpful to library professionals to use of these software packages in their libraries.

The paper of S.K.Das "*Fundamentals of Semantic Web in the Changing Context of Digital Information System in Cyberspace*" discussed about semantic web and its technologies. The semantic web is not a separate web but an extension of the current one, in which information is given in well defined meaning, and better enabling computers and people to work in cooperation. With Semantic Web technologies, organizations can provide a single, unified view of data across their applications, which allows for precise retrieval of information, simplifies enterprise and SOA integration, reduces data redundancy, and provides uniform semantic meaning across applications.

S.Jana's paper "*Anatomy and Embedded Mechanism of Web Search Engine: A Birds Eye View*" described brief history of web search engine that are some how relevant to the present context. Search engine is basically a program, which works in the back end to help to retrieve relevant information. Present study emphasizes core elements of search engine and their operations to organize, update and retrieve or present so called relevant web sites to the users screen. Discusses complex anatomy and mechanism of search engine in a very simple way, so that every one can understand the actual embedded operations. In the last portion, efforts are given on the mechanism of Google, the large hypertextual web search engine.

R. W. Ongus, T. D. Kemparaju, and C. M. Nyamboga in their paper "*Evaluation of University Websites Targeting English Speaking Users: A Comparative Analysis of Selected Sites in Developed and Developing Countries*" attempt to evaluate and compare the educational websites which are hosted in different parts of the world. The aim of this study is to compare and accessibility and user friendliness of the respective websites; evaluate the quality of information available in the websites etc. The paper has attempted to demonstrate the application of prototype website evaluations process which information professionals may employ. Information professionals empowered with the basic systematic skills of objectively distinguishing the quality of information services would be a real asset to the Internet user.

M. Mamata, K. Praveenkumar, and S.Parameshwar in their paper "*Development of Virtual Libraries in India:Problems and Prospects*" explain about the development of the Virtual libraries. The developed countries all over the world are developing virtual libraries faster and compared to the different countries, there is slow development in Information and Communication Technology applications in India. To improve the use of Information Technology applications and to fill the Digital Divide gap, the Government of India and different state government already initiated certain policies and projects. The paper also discussed the policies and projects of Central and different State Governments to increase the use of Information Technology applications in administration.

K. Praveenkumar, D.B.Patil, and S.Parameshwar in their paper *"Expert Systems: Impact on Library Services"* explained about information management techniques using emerging Information and Communication Technology (ICT) and Artificial Intelligence (AI). Artificial Intelligence is emerging technological discipline, which included advanced applications such as Natural Language Processing, Automatic Programming, Robotics, Expert Systems and such other advanced mechanized applications. It is also discussed about the structure of an Expert System, which included Knowledge Base, Knowledge Acquisition, Inference Engine, User Interface, Explanation Facility and External Interface. It highlighted the use and application of expert systems in providing different library services such as Library Cataloguing, Subject Indexing, Database Search Service, Reference Service and Collection Development. It concluded with remarks that how technology plays an important role in providing specialized library services to the users.

C. N. Bhange in her paper, *"Emerging Libraries"* explained about changing dimension of the libraries in 21st century. It also describes about the future development of library systems. In new era, libraries have begun to transfer from manual operations to an automated system.

REFERENCES

Albright, K.S.(2005)'Global measures of development and the information society', *New Library World,* 106:1214/1215, 320-331.

Bavakutty, M., Veeran, M.C.K., and Salih, T.K.M (2003) *Information access, management and exchange in the technological age,* New Delhi, Ess Ess Publication.

Corrall, S. (1995) 'Academic libraries in society', *New Library World,* 96:1120, 35-42.

Dordick, H.S. and Wang, G. (1993) *Information Society: A Retrospective View,* Newbury Park, Sage Publications.

Ershova, T. (1998) 'The Information Society: a new challenge for management', *Library Management,* 19:5, 327-332.

Felco, M.B (1997), *Electronic Resources: Access and issues*, London, Bowker,

Fallis, D. and Fricke, M (1999) 'Not by library school alone', *Library Journal*, 124:17, p.44

Kumbar, B.D., and Hadagali, G.S. (2006), 'Trends in information resources and need for rethinking in professionals preparedness: A Case study of Indian University libraries', *Library herald*, 44: 4, 295-311.

Libraries - Background and Development (online) (cited 10th Sept.2007) Available from <http://www.allbusiness.com/3780177-4.html>

Machlup, F. (1962) *Production and Distribution of Knowledge in the United States*, Princeton , Princeton University Press.

Shanhong, T. (2000) 'Knowledge Management in Libraries in 21st Century', *paper presented at the 66th IFLA Council and General Conference* 13-18, August, Jerusalem, Israel

University of Glasgow (2004) What is eLiteracy? (online) (cited 10th Sept. 2007). Available from <URL: www.iteu.gla.ac.uk/eliteracy/whatiseliteracy.html>.

Wang, Yunhua (1999) "Knowledge economy and the development of the library", *Library Work & Research*, 6, 17-19.

Ward, S.(1999) "Information professionals for the next millennium", *Journal of Information Science*, 25: 4, 239-247.

Wallis, J.(2005) 'Digital directions: Cyber space, information literacy and the information society', *Library Review*, 54:4, 218-222

Webster, F. (1995) *Theories of the Information Society*, London, Routledge.

2

Public Library: The Vechile for Information Dissemination in a Democratic Society

Sunil Kumar Satpathy

ABSTRACT

Library and society are inter-linked and inter-dependent. Society without libraries has no significance and also a library without society has no meaning. This paper describes about the growth and development of libraries & concept of library in a society. Discusses the characteristics of a public library. Critically analyses the role of public libraries in dissemination of information in a democratic society. Concludes with the remark that high position of library in a society should be maintained to perform its noble functions.

1. INTRODUCTION

Man is a social animal and the society is the web of social relationship. Being a social animal, man wants to communicate ideas from generation to generation through various medias like clay tablets, palm leaves, manuscripts, books, magazines, journals and more recently through non-print medias like CD-ROM, Floppy, DVD, online etc. These thought contents of people of various generations are preserved and stored by libraries for future use, otherwise the valuable ideas of people of various ages would have been destroyed.

Library and society are inter-linked and inter-dependent. Society without libraries has no significance and also a library without society has no meaning .The library is a product of cultural and social maturation of the society. From the very beginning of the society, library has been a product of social organization and a handmaiden of scholarship.

The Library has been created by actual necessities in modern society and is now a necessary unit in the social fabric. Library is the product of society for cultural advancement and acts as a social agency. Thus libraries not only conserve our culture but also act as agencies of communication by collecting, organizing and disseminating required information to the people. It serves as a vehicle of social progress and therefore plays many vital roles.

2. GROWTH AND DEVELOPMENT OF LIBRARY

Library is the product of "cultural maturation" of human being. It is essentially a response to the total communication patterns of modern society. The advent and advance of democracy; the extension of the horizons of education; the intensification of research, and the knowledge and information explosion etc have resulted and necessitated a well organized and up-to –date library.

Out of the main three types of libraries, public library is the nucleus of the community' s intellectual attainments, academic library is the heart of an educational institution, and special library is the main hub of concerned organization/ government organization/bodies. Therefore library can be termed as the web of social relationships; the hub of research activities; the crowning glory of education, and an education, and an agency for educating the massage in the values of democracy – Justice, Liberty, Equality and Fraternity.

3. EVOLUTION OF LIBRARY CONCEPT

The word 'library' has been derived from Latin word

'Liber' means 'book' which refers to a collection of books gathered for study, research, reference and recreation. Doubtlessly, since times immemorial libraries have preserved man's priceless acquisitions of knowledge, but this definition conveys only the meaning of the library – repository of various forms of recorded information. Thus it only conveys the custodial function. But more appropriately, library houses an organized collection of documents to preserve them and also make them available for use. Probably, the most important word in it is 'use', for which libraries have become indispensable in this modern world. As knowledge becomes more extensive, It is highly essential that it must be properly organized and processed for its easy retrieval, In addition to their vital role in the academic world, libraries serve all branches, government and civil life, supplying information needed by individuals and organization.

Rangnathan defines the term "Library" as: "A library is a public institution or establishment charged with the care of a collection of books and the duty of making them accessible to those who require use of them" [1]

Ranganathan's definition indicates towards two major functions of libraries. First, "The care of a collection of a books". This means protection the collection from the ravages of the four enemies of books—fire, water, vermin, and human beings. Librarians engineered techniques for the due discharge of this function. Naturally, the spirit dominating in them was janitor ship or caretaker ship.

The second function of libraries in his definition is "The duty of making the books accessible to those who require the use of them". This function is in direct opposition to the age-long tradition of caretaker librarians in which library was considered a place where the books were preserved for study, reading and reference. But with the advance of democracy coupled with the Acts of compulsory education in the countries like U.K. and U.S.A., the librarians took it as their moral obligation to help the common man across the street from ignorance to knowledge. From a passive stance they assumed an active role in helping man to educate himself. The often unarticulated aims of the total library were social: illiteracy was to be removed, readers were to be told what was best for them to read, and is the process the moral fiber of the nation was to be done by building large collections, indicating to readers how they might use the books for raising their standards, enlarging their intelligence, deepening their perceptions through the simple process of reading . The librarians began to feel their obligation even answering necessary questions which might help the reader in his pursuit of self - improvement and self - fulfillment. But it took practically the whole of the nineteenth century to reconcile Ranganathan's two functions of library.

Modern Concept of library

The modern libraries are service agencies that welcome users and are organized to facilitate the of graphic records. In the opinion of Pierce Butler "the basic elements of Librarianship consist in the accumulation of knowledge by society and its continuous transmission to the living generation so for as these process are performed through the instrumentality of graphic records"[2] and that "the fundamental phenomenon of Librarianship is the transmission of the accumulated experience of society to its individuals members through the instrumentally of the book"[3]. Probably keeping this new view Richardson defined library as an institution where books are acquired for use, and it is the use which is the prime motive of the libraries. However, Carl M White who stated that "modern Librarianship is concerned with assuring the continuance and full use of power to retain, organize, and use the accumulated heritage of all generations of all mankind in all it forms-the written word being only one"[4]. A library thus be defined as a collection of both print and non-print materials such as graphic, acoustic and holistic materials such as book, periodicals, manuscripts, newspapers, maps, charts, recordings, motion pictures, slides, filmstrips, magnetic tapes, art reproductions and still pictures, phonographs, records, music scores, and microforms (micro-filmed materials). Besides Public libraries often serve as cultural centres, with facilities for meetings, lectures, concerts, exhibits, and film presentations. This gives the feeling of the modern library, though some secondary activities are put at a per with primary functions. Therefore it can be said that for centuries together, the physical care of books was the primary function of libraries. So dominant was the conservation function that the early writers on the organization and management of libraries devoted much attention to the custody of book as physical entities, as artifacts. The library as a museum fulfilled a social need. Library accumulated and preserved the records of its scholarship against ravages of time and the depredation of man because graphic records were both useful and scares, as well as highly prized. But the intellectual content, of the culture, Its scholarship, had to be actively transmitted from generation to generation as well as preserved. Because of this historical necessity the two function: preservation of book and making them accessible to people who want to read them merely for the pleasure of reading or to satisfy intellectual curiosity had to coalesce.

4. CHARACTERISTICS OF PUBLIC LIBRARY

The public library should be "free" in the sense that the user should not be required to make payment for the service they use. If a man has the right of using the mine of knowledge or information, he must not be deprived of it because of his financial disabilities, keeping in view that many of those library users who would most benefit are just those most hesitant to pay. Moreover, no librarian can do his duty of disseminating knowledge with dedication if he is at the mercy of subscribers. The only one admissible and satisfactory method of financing public libraries is that they must be reared at the expanse of whole community.

A public library is a dynamic, living force and the intellectual nucleus of the community it serves. It is an institution of the public and for the public. Therefore, they must be open to all, without any let or hindrance. They must be quickly and highly accessible. This principle implies that there must be appropriate public library services points available to every one in the community. It requires the provision of urban as well as rural libraries. That the public library keeps its door open for free and equals use by all members living in area of its operation distinguishes it from an academic or a special library.

A public library must provide to its users the world's best thought giving reliable information, in an unbiased and balanced way, on as wide a variety of subjects as will satisfy individual's personal, professional, or political aspirations. It means that our libraries must be unfettered, impartial and serving no ulterior purpose, it is useless expecting a man to think for his intellectual development if he is given censored, limited, and pre-digested material to conform with someone's idea of what he should know and believe. When this is the case, library services will not only be ineffective but also constitute a gross denial of a vital human right. They will fail to safeguard democracy and prevent people from falling a pray to anti-social, anti-national, and anti-cultural forces. Thus public libraries are vital for individual's liberty, and freedom of thought—the bedrock of modern democracy.

It can be summarized that a public library is open to all and has a stock of books other print and non-print materials adequate for the educational, recreational, informational, and research needs of its public. It must never be the instrument of political propaganda, or of proselytism, religious or anti-religious. The basic characteristics of public libraries can be summarized as follows.

(i) It collects, organize, preserve, socialize and serve all expressed thought embodied in the form of manuscripts, books, periodicals, their constituent documents and also in the form of non-book materials like CDs, DVDs, etc.

(ii) It preserves and transmits the knowledge of people of different ages from generation to generation and thus helps in the contemporary development of knowledge.

(iii) It serves as a center for arousing and stimulating intellectual curiosity and the desire to learn among people by offering materials and Programmes to satisfy their desire for knowledge. It has moral obligation to educate people through self-education, informal education and continuing education.

(iv) It stimulate reading habits among people of the society through planned reading Programmes, book talks and reviews, booklists and specialized bibliographies, displays and exhibits, browsing areas, open access and teaching the use of specific library tools. Library must encourage readings at all levels and for different purposes such as reading for education, information, seeking status, emotional release, self-realization and spiritual emancipation. Library must in calculate the minds of people that reading has greater significance for the creation of intellectual, moral, aesthetic, social and political values.

(v) It help in the advancement of research in the society which is the life blood of modern society, as the economic standard of living, culture, and progress of society depends on it. To perform this noble functions, the basic services performed by libraries are to identify the areas of research, to collect, process and disseminate the right information in quickest possible time and also cheaply.

(vi) It acts as an effective repository of cultural heritage and can be referred to as live depository of the cultural past that anticipates future. Preservation and conservation of knowledge is the basic fundamental role of library. Therefore library collection must be carefully built and conserved for the present and future benefit of the community.

5. ROLE OF PUBLIC LIBRARY IN A DEMOCRATIC SOCIETY

5.1. Providing Library Materials

Being a social institution, the public library has to perform multi-faceted functions. But the function remains constant i.e. to provide and service materials for enlarging the mind and dispelling prejudice and ignorance. It implies the necessity of making access to the truth easy and rapid for anyone who seeks it. For the overwhelming majority, the quickest and easiest access to the world's best thought is through the public library. It means very recent facts and ideas as the wisdom of the ages; the library must be current as well as retrospective. Its materials are provided:

(i) to facilitate informal self-education of all people in community;

(ii) to enrich and further develop the subjects on which individuals are undertaking formal education;

(iii) to meet the informational needs of all;

(iv) to support the educational, civic, and cultural activities of groups and organizations;

(v) to encourage wholesome recreation and constructive use of leisure time.

In essence, the public library provides materials and services to promote the general diffusion of knowledge and information; to simulate freedom of expression and a constructive critical attitude towards the solution of social problems; to educate man to participate in a creative manner in community life and to promote a better understanding between individuals, group and nations; and to extend the activities of the centres of learning, offering new educational possibilities to the people. The basic principle underlying the library service is that is exists for the training of the good citizen. It must aim at providing all that printed literature can provide to develop his intellectual, moral and spiritual capabilities.

5.2. Educational Functions

Convinced of the fact that books and reading have a powerful influence on society, the public library under dynamic leadership can become an active and effective education centre. Of course, L. Stanley Jast warned: "The librarian should carefully avoid trespassing the ground of the educationalist"[5], but he has contradicted by Carl Thomsenwho said: "public libraries cannot fulfill their responsibilities in isolation from educational work"[6]. J.H.Shera was also in the opinion that Library is the handmaiden of universal education. With the aim of bringing enlightenment, improvement and happiness to one and all. In the word of Ranganathan, "libraries are social institutions charged with the duty of providing the means for the perpetual self-education of one and all" leading to material happiness, mental joy, spiritual delight and the spread of mass literacy. Books remain the sole comprehensives and proven method of self –teaching; and public library being the repository of our cultural heritage provides opportunity and encouragement for children, and woman to educate themselves continuously.

It is the duty of the public library to co operate with the school in its endeavor to awaken in the children an inspiration to make the most of his power, to give him the alphabet of learning and activity, to train his power of thought and expression, and to supply him with him with the implement with which he may attain culture. Apart from its connection with the school, its chief unction is to serve as the lifelong university for the individual , in which he may find freely, without money and without price, an opportunity for the continuous development of all his power. This point needs further discussion

5.3. Adult Education

The idea of adult education lay embedded in the realization that education is a life –long process, and that universal education is the very life-blood of modern society.

In India, the concept of adult education has been broadened. Maulana A.K Azad, the then Union Education Minister of India gave a new orientation a new life, and later on a new name to this concept by enlarging its base and giving it he aptitude of Social Education –an education for complete man. "The real aim of Social Education", Say Human Kabir," is to create an educated mind among the adult literate," for helping them to evolve a philosophy of life to develop interests which Will enrich their leisure. It is an attempt to salvage a generation by giving it the minimum of education needed to improve its way of life, its health, its productivity and its social, economic and political organization.

From the aim of the adult education or social education as given above, it is clear that many social agencies will have to work in unison to provide adults the means for educating them-selves continuously. But as adult education is varied, informal and practical, library is the most appropriate agency of adult education in so far as it provides both the requisites reading material and environment for informal reading. Probably, it inspired Alvin Johnson to hail the public library as a People's University and assigned it a vital role in fighting illiteracy and helping people in their intellectual, cultural and material advancement. He commented that as education is needed from cradle to the very end of life, "library is so obviously its proper centre that not even the purest of the pure librarian can be against it"[7]

As an agency of adult education, the public library has used various instruments of mass-communication, with increasing use of audio-visual materials for disseminating knowledge.

An integral part of the library's educational function is to supply motives for reading. Lectures, study circles, dramatic clubs, book review groups and exhibitions have been purposively organized and programmes of work planned to serve the interest of special groups, like women's club, association of parents and teachers, and church groups. The libraries themselves have helped in the formation of many other groups, viz., among young adults, old adults, rural folks and lobour groups. Group discussions have judiciously been devised and forums encouraged and run with the premises of the library to enhance intellectual interest and afford valuable educational experiences. Today, many groups flourish under the library's leadership. Opportunities to discuss critical issues of the day, community problems, burning problems, great books of the past and thought provoking books of the present draw people together in community-wide meetings and small neighborhood groups. It may, however, be added that the library is not the sole agency engaged in adult education, nevertheless, it forms a permanent nucleus around which such activities can easily grow. And Dan Lacy defining the objectives of library says "perhaps the greatest opportunity for expanding library usefulness lies in closer identification with all the manifold wealth of groups discussion and informational activities which we loosely call adult education"[8]. It is maintained that the public library is not so much a place where adults get education as where educated adults get books. It is not Robert D. Leigh states that "the people's university"as stated by Johnson but "a library of people's university"[9]. As the library is the people's University, one of the functions of the public library is to follow-up mass education Programmes by providing books of all types (v.z., books for the neo-literate, semi-literate and the literate)so that what has been learnt in adult education classes is not immediately forgotten again through lack of reading materials.

Disheartening enough, the Govt. of India has not appreciated the role of the Public Libraries in adult education. The National Adult Education Programmes launched by the Central Government through Ministry of Education and Social Welfare on 2nd Oct.1978 could have worked much effectively through the efficient public library services. Their due recognition in NAEP would have given an opportunity to public libraries to educate people to learn to be useful citizens by developing their abilities, individual judgement and sense of moral and social responsibility.

5.4. Community's Information Service

Public libraries that are entrusted with the basic duty of preserving the recorded knowledge of past and present for future use are also responsible for providing required information to the surrounding communities. Besides, in changing situation of society, public libraries are facing new challenges. On one hand there is tremendous pressure due to information explosion, development of new information technologies etc for acquiring latest information on all fields of knowledge, on the other hand there is an increasing demand for pinpointed exhaustive and accurate information in quickest possible time. Thus in the changing library environment, public libraries have no way other than to shift towards information based community oriented libraries rather than repository centers of books and other documents. Failing which, the existence of these libraries will reduced to the status of a store house of books and other printed documents.

5.5. Recreation

The term 'recreation' in library discussion denotes "such use of leisure time as will promote personal happiness and social well-being". In pursuance of its recreational function, the chief role of the public library is to provide material for relaxation, entertainment, adventure and escape. This has led to the division of library materials into two categories: fiction and non-fiction.

The new generations of library users are of leisure strongly oriented toward audio-visual materials. It, therefore follow that libraries must not be concerned only with books, they should contain all the principal media of communication.

The logic of this "cultural" interpretation of recreation is also under planned by extension activities undertaken by the public libraries: exhibitions, lectures, book-weeks, talks, films, gramophone recitals. Library also organizes cultural activities for the entertainment of the public. The Public Library and Museum Act of 1964 (U.K.) allowed "the holdings of meetings and exhibitions, showing of films and slides, the giving of musical performances and holding of other events of an educational nature and increase leisure matched by greater educational opportunity comes a leadership that requires access to information and to recorded knowledge on a greater scale than before.

5.6. Strengthening Democracy

The public library is a product of modern democracy and a practical demonstration of democracy's faith in universal education as a life long process. By throwing open the mine of recorded knowledge for effective use, critical evaluation and exploration library encourages individuality, variety and dissent within a climate of tolerance – the anti-thesis of authoritarianism.

Through the diffusion of education, the library strives to enhance equality and social justice, to promote intellectual freedom and advancement of knowledge, to generate in the young generation a sense of purposefulness and maximum dedication, confidence an themselves and faith in democracy's future.

The strongest threats to democracy come from ignorant classes who vote wrongly because of their "untutored choice" or by the influence or unscrupulous politicians. In democracies every thought and deed affect the socio-economic mechanism of the whole, it becomes the duty of whole to educate its parts to have an informed body of voters for the success of democracy. And we shall not have a democracy until we have a well-educated people: the library can play a vital role in the spread of education. Thus paving the way for the success of democracy. The public libraries disseminate works of all kinds calculated to promote the life-long education of one and all; to serve books where no good library exists. Doubtlessly, books written by zealots and propagandists, and newspaper which tend to be sensational, can be potent weapons of subversion. But a good library service providing materials in open, balanced, many sides collections on policies, mass movements, economics, citizenship, and government can help to make democracy safe, informed, stable and real.

It may be conclude with Ranganathan that public libraries generate 'material happiness, mental joy and spiritual delight; they are social institutions charged with the duty of providing the means for the perpetual self-education of one and all; and then contribute to the circulation of ideas, the harnessing of leisure, the demands of democracy, the spread of library literacy, and the success of commercial and industrial organization.

6. CONCLUSION

Library is an indispensable organ of society. Both library and society are two sides of a coin and one cannot exist without other. Library being the 'community intellectual center has certain moral obligation of collection, preservation and dissemination of human knowledge and ideas stored in various forms. To perform this noble function, library has to change itself with the social changes and the changing needs of people of the society in terms of its structure, collection, staff, services etc. therefore to maintain this high position of library in society and to keep the sociological foundation of libraries and Librarianship intact, impediments arising in the process should be removed by taking appropriate necessary measures.

REFERENCES

1. RANGANATHAN (S.R). Reference Service. 1961.Asia Publishing House;Delhi. p.63.
2. BUTLER (P). Introduction to Library Science.1933.Chicago University Press; Chicago.p.29

3. *Ibid.*p.84
4. WHITE (J L) and GOLDHOR (H) .Practical Administration of Public Libraries,1962, Harper; New York.p.4
5. Library and the Community, 1939, Nelson; London.
6. THUMSEN (C) et.al. Adult Education activities for Public Libraries, 1950 ,Unesco; Paris.
7. JONSON (A), The Public Library- A Propels University,1939. Amer.Asso for Adult; New York.
8. LACY (D), Thc Adult in changing Society.*LQ*.27;1957,292
9. *Op.Cit.*

3

Impact of Information Technology on Societal Development and E-Governance

Vibha Gupta

ABSTRACT

Information technology is the most pervasive force influencing virtually all spheres of human activities all over the world. It has transformed the whole world into a global village with a global economy. IT revolution and network evolution leading to an emergence of global information society. The enormous advantages it has in easing the delivery of information around the world, as well as the central role of information in the new global economy, means that information technology will shape the dynamics of the new millennium. This paper discusses what the impact of information Technology on society is.

1. INTRODUCTION

The present society is, in fact, transforming in a fundamental way, but the Information Revolution is only part of a more general phenomena involving multiple and interdependent causes, including human values, ways of life, culture, science, politics, and economy. This wholistic revolution is creating chaos, unrest, numerous social problems and a reorganization of human life. Economy, society, education, religion, psychology, science, and technology are all changing, since they are all reciprocally interconnected.

A popular theory and explanation of the contemporary changes occurring around us is that we are in the midst of a third major revolution in human civilization, i.e., a Third Wave. First there was the Agricultural Revolution, then the Industrial Revolution, and now we are in the Information Revolution. Information and communication technology and a world wide system of information exchange has been building growing for over a hundred years and physical technology and industry is not slowing down in growth - rather it is accelerating. (Kelly, 1994) Perhaps, the fundamental change is from a Newtonian Clock Model of the universe, technology, and human society to a Mental/Computational Model. (Ackoff, 993).

2. INFORMATION TECHNOLOGY

Information technology is playing a crucial role in contemporary society. It has transformed the whole world into a global village with a global economy, which is increasingly dependant on the creative management and distribution of information. Globalization of world economies has greatly enhanced the values of information to business organizations and has offered new business opportunities. Today, IT provides the communication and analytical power that organizations need for conducting trade and managing business at global level with much ease. To coordinate their worldwide network of suppliers, distributors and consumers, organizations have developed global information system that can track orders, deliveries, and payments round the clock. This has been possible because of the development of IT in its present form. In the broadest sense, information technology refers to both the hardware and software that are used to store, retrieve, and manipulate information. At the lowest level you have the servers with an operating system. Installed on these servers are things like database and web serving software. The servers are connected to each other and to users via a network infrastructure. And the users accessing these servers have their own hardware, operating system, and software tools.

3. DEFINITION

UNESCO defines IT as, "Scientific technological and engineering disciplines and the management techniques used I information handling and processing information, their interaction with man and machine and associated social, economic and cultural matters". Librarian's Glossary defines IT as," a development of information sources handled by computers and communication by electronic channels; database can thus be accessed telephone and television links and computer output can be transmitted in an electronic format directly to a remote receiver". Glossary of Academic Information Technology Terms, San Diego State University "Information Technology includes matters concerned with the furtherance of computer science and technology, design, development, installation and implementation of information systems and applications".

Kathleen Guinee wrote, "By information technology, I mean the tools we use to perform calculations, to store and manipulate text, and to communicate. Some of these twentieth century tools include: the adding machine, slide rule, and calculator for performing calculations, the typewriter and word processor for processing text, and the telephone, radio, and television for communicating."

4. COMPONENTS OF INFORMATION TECHNOLOGY (IT)

Information technology is a broad term that encompasses wide range of sub-technologies. In the broadest sense, information technology refers to both the hardware and software that are used to store, retrieve, and manipulate information. In particular, the use of computer and computer software to convert, store, process, transmit, and retrieve information. IT is undergoing rapid revolutionary developments. In Information technology we primarily concentrate on the following technologies:

* Computer Hardware technologies consist of input devices, central processing unit, main memory, secondary storage etc.
* Computer Software technologies include operating system software, web browsers, software productivity suits and software for business applications.
* Telecommunication and Network Technologies include telecommunications media, processors and software needed to provide wire-based and wireless access and support for Internet and other networks.
* Data Resource Management Technologies include database management system software for the development, access and maintenance of the databases of an organization.

5 EMERGENCE OF INFORMATION SOCIETY

The information society has passed through four transformational stages of development, the most radical stage started with the tail end of the twentieth century, which has brought a never-ending revolution, particularly with the introduction of information and communication technologies (ICTs). During this period, there have been unprecedented developments, profoundly affecting the social structure – the decline of manufacturing sector as compared to the prospering information-rich service sector is one example of such developments.[11] India is moving fast towards becoming an information society as the Government of India is paying due attention to the use of information technology (IT).

The Prime Minister of India constituted a National Task Force on IT and Software Development in May 1998 with the purpose of formulating a long-term National IT Policy to convert India into an IT software superpower. These steps are helping India to shift from an "economy of goods" to a "knowledge economy" or "knowledge driven economy". The beginning of the knowledge society has been made through creation of parks and corridors, and the Prime Minister has given a mission of converting India into a "knowledge society" by the year 2008... Today, India is one of the largest exporters of knowledge workers'

6. IMPACT OF INFORMATION TECHNOLOGY ON SOCIETAL DEVELOPMENT

A society can also refer specifically to any group of people, other animals and/or plants and the interactions within that group. This can be anything from a small neighborhood to the entire global community. Religion, ethnicity, interests, political opinions or other relating factors may group a group of people.

Society can be defined as "a community, nation, or broad grouping of people having common traditions, institutions, and collective activities and interests." The report will examine how the technological developments which have occurred in information technology have influenced a "broad grouping of people" in their "common traditions, institutions and/or collective activities". This broad grouping of people will primarily be those in the industrialized world of where "information technology" is commonly available.

As previously shown society can be defined as "a community, nation, or broad grouping of people having common traditions, institutions, and collective activities and interests. Therefore we shall use the common traditions, institutions and collective activities and interests as the basis for our examination of the impact information technology has had on society. We shall also integrate this examination with the impact of how information technology has changed the "way we work". This integration will occur in two areas of the analysis of society, first the institutions and second the collective activities of the society.

6.1 Common Traditions

To answer this question in the context of this report it is helpful to highlight a difference between "traditions" and "activities/interests". Tradition can be defined as the following:

"An inherited, established, or customary pattern of thought, action, or behaviour (as a religious practice or a social custom). Cultural continuity in social attitudes, customs, and institutions."

The influence of information technology on religious practices has mainly been to the effect of making information about them more accessible. The most relevant question though is whether the developments in information technologies have influenced the continuity of social attitudes, customs or institutions.

6.2 Cultural Continuity

Social attitudes have changed with the effect that citizens of a society now expect the various elements of that society to be better informed than previously. They also expect to be able to access more information about a specific product, service or organization so that they can make informed decisions with regard to their interactions with that entity.

6.3 Institutions

The word institutions can incorporate a wide variety of organizations. For the purposes of this report the institutions we will examine will be:

* Governments,
* Commercial businesses,
* News & Media organizations,
* Educational organizations.

The influence which information technology development has had on these areas will be mainly focused on how the technology has "improved" the processes by which the institution accomplishes its task or goal.

6.3.1 Governments

The "government" of a nation will be comprised of many varied institutions. However developments in information technology have helped governments to improve their "service" to their citizens. Information Technology has also had a major impact on the defense capabilities of governments. This covers both a government's capability towage war and their intelligence gathering capability. Advances in weapons technology and weapons design have increased the effectiveness of various governments' armed forces. For example it would have been impossible to design aeroplanes such as the B2 Bomber if it were not for the advances made in information technology. The B2 bomber relies on a "continuous curvature" design to minimize radar signature.

It would have been impossible to design or build this machine without the development of computer modeling techniques.

Governments also have had to have a renewed care towards their sensitive information. The proliferation of Internet technologies has led to stories such as that highlighted below:

"The Web becomes the focal point of British politics as a list of MI6 agents is released on a UK Web site. Though forced to remove the list from the site, it was too late as the list had already been replicated across the net."

The governments data protection act Web Site gives the following eight rules regarding personal information:

* It must be fairly and lawfully processed;
* Processed for limited purposes;
* Adequate, relevant and not excessive;
* Accurate;
* Not kept longer than necessary;
* Processed in accordance with the data subject's rights;
* Secure;
* Not transferred to countries without adequate protection.

6.3.2. Commercial Businesses

The advances in information technology have heavily influenced commercial businesses in several ways. The most important role of information technology in a commercial business however is to provide a commercial advantage. Advances such as computer aided design, relational database technologies, spreadsheets, and word processing software all provide a commercial benefit to the business, as does automation of manufacturing processes (as Sara-Lee did in 1964). Advances in information technology over the last thirty years have lead to the television for example being more widely used today than thirty years ago (e.g. the introduction of transistor based televisions reduced costs while increasing reliability).

6.3.3. News & Media Organizations

Due to the nature of news and media organizations, the

information technologies have particular relevance to them. As noted earlier "Information technology is the technology used to store, manipulate, distribute or create information". News and media organizations are intimately acquainted with each of these elements of information technology. However this report will focus on the distribution and creation of information.

6.3.4. Educational Organizations

The developments that have occurred in information technology have also had other influences on educational establishments. The distribution of information is not the only concern of educational establishments. For example one of the aims of Universities is to create information. This "creation" is done by research. Information technologies have enabled researchers to access a wider source of information than previously available through such technologies as the Internet (the original Arpanet being set up primarily to assist research). The Internet and other related technologies such as electronic mail, also enable collaborative projects to be undertaken between geographically distant groups.

7 IMPACT OF INFORMATION TECHNOLOGY AND ELECTRONIC GOVERNANCE

E-governance is the effective way of governance utilizing IT to enhance efficiency of government offices. The Government of India is devising new policies to envisage a SMART – simple, moral, accountable, responsible, and transparent governance to bring nationwide reforms. The customs department plans to use electronic data interface (EDI) to handle all transactions relating to custom duties more efficiently for which initiatives have been taken by National Informatics Center (NIC). Other areas of computerization include railway and air reservation, allotment of permanent account numbers (PAN), processing of passport, results of examinations, vigilance information, etc. The income tax department has introduced an online tax accounting for collecting the income tax by RBI and 31 commercial banks throughout the country from 1 June 2004.[19]

7.1 IT Policy and Emphasis on E-governance

E-governance attempts in the country started with a bang. The initial impetus came from the Ministry of IT, which produced a concept paper, emphasizing the method by which the state has to deliver its services in the information age. The paper envisages a SMART government and promises to establish the required institutional mechanisms to facilitate initiatives towards synergic utilization of IT to enhance effectiveness of governance. NASSCOM conducted a survey of ten leading states (Andhra Pradesh, Tamil Nadu, Karnataka, Maharashtra, Madhya Pradesh, Kerala, Uttar Pradesh, Rajas than, Gujarat and West Bengal) and pointed out that all these states have an IT policy, expert group, e-governance cell, and some even have a separate IT department. Some of them have also included specific policy measures that not only aim to facilitate IT investments in the state but also focus on using IT for governance-related issues

7.2. IT Budget and E-governance Funding

Initially, IT budgets of Indian states have been very low, however, during the last half decade, the budgetary support for IT projects has shot up. NASSCOM survey of the ten states for 2002-2003 revealed a total allocation of about Rs. 3 billion. Kerala topped the list with an allocation of Rs. 964.2 million, followed by Andhra Pradesh and West Bengal with Rs. 548.3 million and 355.1, respectively; towards IT projects in the states.

7.3. Initiatives by states and union territories

Technology is playing an important role for the all-round development of the country. In 1988, the NIC set up NICNET, a satellite-based computer communication network connecting 439 cities and towns in India. Most of the states and union territories have taken initiatives in one way or the other, many of them have moved ahead of others. The efforts made by some of these states.[21]

CONCLUSION

Today, we are all in agreement that the world is becoming increasingly dependent upon technology as is evidenced the big role it is playing. The Internet has become a major shareholder. All developing nations can derive tremendous advantages from this technology for updating the knowledge of its researchers and scientists. The Indian software and services industry has significantly helped to boost the Indian economy. . Society expects to be able to store more than was previously conceived. Society expects to be able to manipulate the information they have for their benefit, to increase understanding and discover new relationships. Society expects to be able to distribute information quickly, efficiently and cheaply. However, the Government of India has been working gradually and successfully towards improving the IT policy climate in the country.

REFERENCES

1. Bell (Daniel). (1973). The Coming of Post-Industrial Society. Basic Books.
2. Kelly (Kevin). (1994) Out of Control: The Rise of Neo-Biological Civilization. Addison – Wesley
3. Ackoff (Russell). (1993) "From Mechanistic to Social Systematic Thinking" Systems Thinking in Action Conference, Pegasus Communications, Inc.
4. Lombardo (Tomas). (1997). The Impact of Information Technology: Learning, Living, and loving in the Future, vol.5; 2.
5. http://www.mcli.dist.maricopa.edu/labyforum/Spr97/spr97L8.html
6. Goel (Ritendra). (2005). Fundamentals of Information Technology. Paragon International pub. Lucknow.
7. http://www.mariosalexandrou.com/glossary/information_technology.asp
8. Kawatra (P S). (2000). Textbook of information sciences. A.P.H. pub.
9. http://www-rohan.sdsu.edu/glossary2.html#I
10. www.cs.princeton.edu/~kguinee/thesis.html
11. Callaghan (Martin). (2002). The Impact of ICT on Society
12. http://www.rdn.ac.uk/casestudies/eevl/ict/case3.html

11\. Kumar, (K.), Singh, (S.P). (2000), "From information society to knowledge society", Journal of Library and Information Science, Vol. 25 No.2, pp.104-11.

13. Abdul Kalam, A.P.J. (2001), "Knowledge society", Employment News, 3-9 February, pp.1.
14. http://www.linksfinding.com/directory.aspx?pr=Society/
15. www.m-w.com/cgi-bin/netdict?society
16. http://www.m-w.com/cgi-bin/netdict?tradition
17. http://info.isoc.org/guest/zakon/Internet/History/HIT.html
18. http://www.dataprotection.gov.uk/principl.htm
19. Meadowcroft. (Ben). The Impact of Information Technology on Work and Society. (Online)
20. http://www.benmeadowcroft.com/reports/impact/
19. Srinivasa (P.) (2004). "ISP float 'win-win' plan to slash costs", Hindustan Times, 1 June, pp.19.
20. NASSCOM (2003). "National Association of Software and Services Companies", The IT in India: Strategic Review, NASSCOM, and New Delhi.
21. India (2004). Ministry of Information and Broadcasting. India 2004: A Reference Annual, Ministry of Information and Broadcasting, New Delhi.

4

LIS Distance Education : A Snapshoot of Digital Resource Organization, Design of Information Services and Management in Networked Environment

Mahendra Kumar Rawat
Shaliendra Kumar Rawat

ABSTRACT

Now Internet has shown new paths to learning. The educational resources are accessible to students. Learner needs are increasingly seen to be continuous throughout the working life. Education is a means of empower their lives and future within workplace. In India e- learning systems and online courses are already started. The covers issues of developing e-learning system its requirement, and its implication in e learning. Digital learning in developed countries provides the learners with an interactive mode in a successful way, but in the case of developing countries such as India access to computer is limited to a few elite urban areas. Erratic power interruption, unaffordable investment cost for a normal citizen and obsolete software are some of the bottlenecks preventing for popularization of the e-Education. Although India tops the global list of software experts including teaching, their expertise could not be optimally utilized for the spread of e-Education due to the above-mentioned shortcomings. The important aspects and merits of e-Education through distance mode at an affordable cost for developing countries such as India. Through information technology is at its great speed still some steps and efforts needed at various levels for providing e-education. the global scenarios shows the invading role of information and communication technologies into education sector so it is necessary to adopt technologies for education. Faculty environment, creating and basic grounds for initiating e-education. Also mentions advantages of e-education. It is envisaged that the future will be better for e-education.

INTRODUCTION

Technology has dominated all spheres of life. The education is also one of the fields where we can see the impact of information technology. Education and library are twin sisters. Over several years the education process has seen drastic changes in imparting knowledge. During the last few years it ahs been seen, an almost exponential development and growth of the digitalization, automation and the Internet, with little sign of a slow down. No longer is Internet access restricted to a few select education establishments it is now available to anyone in their place of work, local libraries, the Internet cites and even in the home. It is the information that has becomes the key to the success in different walks of life.

1. WHAT THE 'E' IS ABOUT?

E- Education is electronic education, but the 'e' in E-education has a number of other implications as mentioned below:

Exploration

E- Learners sue the web as an exploratory tool to access a plethora of information and resources.

Experience

The web offers e-learners a total learning experience, from synchronous learning to threaded discussions to self-paced study.

Engagement

The web captivates learners by enabling creative approaches to learning that foster collaboration and a sense of community.

Ease of use

Not only is the web easy to sue for learner who are already familiar with the navigation capabilities of the medium, but to learning providers as well, as they can easily make content immediately available to learner across all technical platforms (Windows, N4AC, Unix, etc.)

Empowerment

The web puts learners in the driver's seal with a set of tools that enables personalization of content and allows learner to choose the way in which they best learn.

2. IN THE VIEW OF E-EDUCATION?

The term e-education means electronic education and it is basically the online delivery of information communication, training and learning, E-education seems to have a multiplicity of definitions to each of its users and the term seems to mean something different. A very comprehensive definitions has been given by the Cisco system, which defines E-education is internet - enabled learning, components can include content delivery in multiple format E-education provides faster learning at reduced costs, increased access to learning and clear accountability for all participants in the learning process in today's fast- paced culture, organizations that implement E-education provide their work force with the ability to turn change into an advantage.

3. WHY IS THE E LEARNING?

* Learning is self paced and gives students a chance to speed up or slow down as necessary
* Learning is self-directed, allowing students to choose content and tools appropriate to their differing interests, needs and skill levels
* Accommodates multiple learning styles using as variety of delivery methods geared to different learners, more effective for entrain learners
* Designed around the learner
* Geographical barriers are eliminated, opening up broader education options
* 24/7 accessibility makes scheduling easy and allows a greater number of people to attend classes on demand access means learning can happen precisely when needed travel –time is reduced or eliminated
* overall student costs are frequently less (tuition, residence, food)
* potentially lower costs for companies needing training and for the providers
* fosters greater student interaction and collaboration
* fosters greater student/instructor contact
* enhances computer and internet skills
* draws upon hundreds of years of established pedagogical principles
* has the attention of every major university in the work, most with their own online degrees, certificates and individual course

4. INSTRUMENT OF E- EDUCATION

To take the better opportunities of E-education we have to know the tools associated with E-education some of them are:

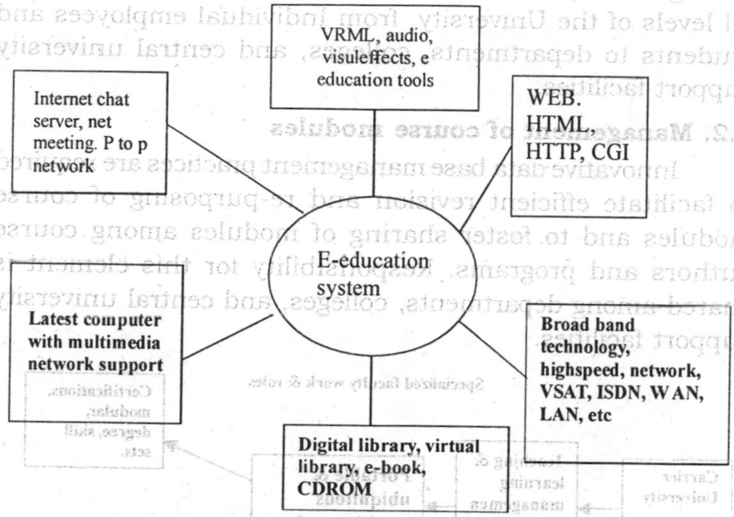

(E-education system)

5. DESIGNING ASPECTS OF E-LEARNING

Linking, analyzing and synthesizing at a conceptual level helps to facilitate learning, and to capture and manage the knowledge that results from learning. Relationships require interaction, including both intellectual and personal relationships. And strategy requires a synthesis of information about procedures and context, and the experience and knowledge against with to measure and evaluate them, Knowledge includes content, context, and relationships that learning required exploration , and links at the conceptual level, as well as personals an intellectual interaction, and the ability to manage information about procedures and contexts against the template of experience.

5.1. Creation of course modules

The quality of the e-learning experience follows from the quality of this of the course modules and of the interactions among students and instructors that make up on-line courses. The faculty members, students, and instructional staff who design and produce on-line courses modules need access to powerful, easy-to-use authoring tools and reliable pedagogical strategies. Responsibility for this element is distributed among all levels of the University, from Individual employees and students to departments, colleges, and central university support facilities.

5.2. Management of course modules

Innovative data base management practices are required to facilitate efficient revision and re-purposing of course modules and to foster sharing of modules among course authors and programs. Responsibility for this element is shared among departments, colleges, and central university support facilities.

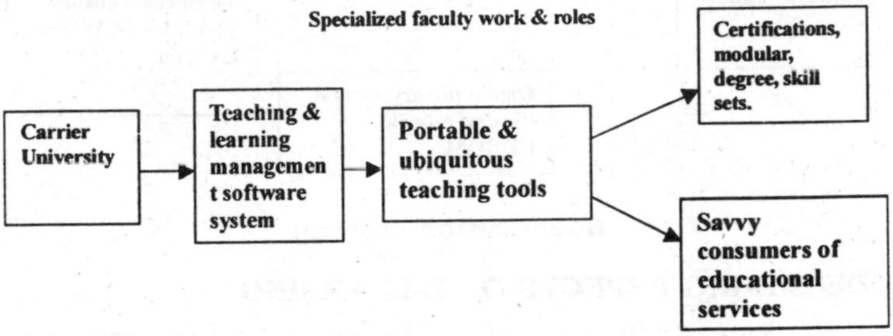

5.3. Delivery of courses

At the core of the common-learning environment is a delivery system that makes course modules available on-line, mediates interactions between instruction and students, and helps the university to efficiently manage student records. Primary responsibility for this element resides wi6th central university support facilities

5.4. Delivery of support services

All Penn State students – on campus or off –deserve access to technical support, library resources, advising services, and other key aspects of the university experience. A common e-learning environment will help facilitate this access. Primary responsibility for this element resides with central university support facilities

6. REQUIREMENTS FOR IMPLEMENTING E-EDUCATION

Taking on board May of the points raised above there are some requirements for a successful implementation of E-education, clearly most of these need addressing before attempting to implementation any electronically based education system.

* Provision of free or low cost access
* Collaboration to be encouraged between various organizations
* Mixture of different teaching models
* Closer monitoring of individual student progress
* Provision of greater support to motivate students where needed s
* Standards require monitoring
* Readily scalable service with high bandwidth an availability

7. CHARACTERISTICS OF A MODERN UNIVERSITY

In addition to the disaggregating of teaching, universities in the yeas ahead will do the following

* They will be challenged to remain intellectually free places seeking truth, defending those who tell , it and promoting the free flow of information and ideas
* a continuing distinction between them and competency-based vocational education institutions
* they will be institutions of both research and teaching
* they will be accessible 24 x 7 x 365
* greater diversity of student background, staff/student ratios in some disciplines
* relatively less government funding
* more internationalization, more entry pathway, ms morc credit transfer
* more flexibility of enrolment delivery and academic progress
* more technological opportunities to disaggregate teaching and learning
* continuing shifts in notions of curriculum ownership
* More local, national and global partnerships.

7.1. Tools for e-education

* Teaching and learning management software systems

can be linked to their back office administrative systems

* Web course management toll
* Student tracking and collaboration tools
* An entire suite of learning aids, personal bots will emerge
* Personal digital assistants
* Summarizers, finders, connectors, learners
* The wide gulf between students and practitioners will be narrowed by education coming to the desktop and practicing experts made available for testimonials, examples, actual observation of behavior through broadband methods

7.2. Faculty

* Highly more specialized researchers and content developers will complement each other
* Subsidy for reach through blind funding of faculty salaries will \become more difficult once legislators realize that much of the delivery will come form elsewhere

7.3. Environment

* Tools for teaching and learning will come as portable and ubiquitous as papers and books are today
* Teaching and learning anywhere any time
* A larger percentage of content will age rapidly
* Alternate models for paying for education will evolve with less of government subsidies and more on the desk training paid by employers
* Students will be savvy consumers with substantive amount of choice
* Increased level of student activism
* Degrees may be obtained with a much increased level of institutional mix (courses from multiple universities)
* Learning is moving off campus: to the home, the workplace, the files, or wherever the learner is
* Students will pick up and piece together certifications, skill sets, and knowledge sets

7.4. Creating a space for learning

* Designing strategies to introduce learners to each other
* Using effective teaching strategies
* Gaining agreement with the learners about rules, norms, and procedures for discussion.
* Using a free flowing and interactive content and structure.
* Encouraging students to evaluate information
* Encouraging students to analyze information
* Encouraging students to connect information

7.5. Basic grounds for initiating e-education

* Exploring the vital role of different information technologies (print, audio, visual and digital) in the development of human and knowledge capital.
* Sharing policies, strategies, experiences and tools in amusing technologies for knowledge dissemination, effective learning and efficient education services.
* Reviewing the latest systems and products of technologies of today, and peek into the would of tomorrow and
* Exchanging information about resources, knowledge networks and centers of expertise

8. CHANGING SCENARIO

The aim of learning is to explore and to accumulate useful knowledge over and above faster copying, searching and distribute. This might be called e-linking, e-relationships and networks and e-enhanced strategy. The trend in the market would show that the on- line education is fast catching up. As per a report by UNESCO, there are approximately 80 million students enrolled in higher education program world – wide in 1999, of which 6150,000 are on – line. Australia alone enrolled 690,000 students in higher education coursed. In the US, which is coming up as a big base for on – line education, 710,000 students were enrolled during 2001 and estimated to touch 2.2 million for 2002. According to IDC a whopping 90 percent of the on-line learning marked is still untapped.

9. SOME POINTS FOR CONSIDERATION

Though various efforts are being made to imitate and propagate e-education but some points are still to be faced:

* What are the possibilities for enhancing the quality of education using distance-learning methodologies?
* What is the cost effectiveness of suing ICT in education in the context of developing countries?
* What are the different approaches for funding e-education?
* What are the changes needed in pedagogy for preparing the next generation for the information age?

CONCLUSION

E-educations is not entirely new concepts but has grown as the WWW has dcveloped in each country E-Education is taking roots for Indian students as well. But first, it is important to understand exactly what we mean by e-education and quite simply it is education and training delivered and accessed via the internet. One of the major advantages of e-education is that one can access the best education in the world direct from the persons who wrote the courses for online study. In the 21st century, students may stay at home and taken distance education (synchronous and asynchronous) in their homes across the world. Geographic comparative advantage will shrink and shrink and shrink. More important, excellent students who could not be accepted as onsite students in pristine universities (due to lack of financing and considerations as to how many can fit into onsite classrooms) face new opportunities to get a prestige degree in their own homes. A picture that is as sharp, clear and well defined as that of the more classical library and information center, and that is applicable in most environments and organization, has not yet emerged. One standard solution or view is unlikely to fall from the sky today or in the future. Many different and interesting approaches can be observed. So this leaves room for constructive discussion among so- called " librarians" to learn from each other's ideas, efforts, opinions, and experiences.

It is expected that virtual environments will become wide spread by the year 2020. Such environments will greatly change the way we learn and do things.

REFERENCE

1. Hijazi, samer etal. Interactive technology impact on quality distance education. Electronic journal of e-learning 2003, V1 (1), P. 35-44.
2. E-education A class Act outlook India, April 9,2001 (www.tenet.res.in/press/094 2001.html)
3. When classrooms go hi-tech Hindustan times, HT line, 11june 2003, P3
4. Royal Dutch seeks to launch e-education venture in India March 6, Http://www. Hinduonnet.com/thehindu
5. Educomp's Learningonate to offer Blackboard e-education solutions in India www.itpeopleindia.com/carrers.html

5
Knowledge-Based Organisation: An Overview on the Existing Knowledge Management Models

Hafizi Muhamad Ali
Zawiyah Mohammad Yusof

ABSTRACT

In this knowledge economy environment, organisations particularly banks institutions are urged to know about their knowledge assets and thus draw a competitive plan and approach in order to manage and make use of these assets for maximum advantage. This paper provides an overview of various knowledge management models with particular emphasis on the varied definition accorded to knowledge management, the types and components of existing knowledge management models. As the result of the overview, an integrated business model to facilitate knowledge creation, knowledge sharing, and knowledge discovery is suggested to serve as a basis and generic guide particularly for adoption by banks and also for future research. This model is generated after taking into consideration the limitation that all the available models possess. The newly suggested model is believed capable in giving an insight to the type, form and availability of knowledge within a bank. This will in turn, enable bank institutions to develop new knowledge, trace, manage and preserve their knowledge and at the same time encouraging staff to use and share knowledge. Upon implementing the proposed Combined Knowledge Management Model, knowledge management will then be translated into effective and efficient resource management. This in turn will be able to provide a better customer support and service, eliminating redundancy or bottleneck, reduced cost and improves many other aspects in banks institutions.

INTRODUCTION

It is imperative to empower everyone in business to make decisions within their roles and capacity in this highly dynamic business environment. But, this can only be performed if they have all the required inputs, i.e the data and information. However, relying on data and information solely is far from sufficient for business to make decision. Decisions made purely based on data and information analysis simply would not be able to solve problem but instead will create another problem. It is therefore important to supplement data and information with knowledge. But providing knowledge is perhaps not easy. When converting data into information sound rather easy, but data conversion into knowledge is perhaps tricky. Many organizations fail to draw a distinctive line to separate between data, information and knowledge. Tapscott (1999) classifies them by 'raw data are indeed disorganized, empirical facts'. When organized and defined in some intelligible fashion, then data becomes information. Information that has been interpreted and synthesized, reflects certain implicit values and becomes knowledge, while knowledge that carries profound, transhistorical insights becomes wisdom.

Organizations have been actively automating manual processes since the past 25 years. This has led to the creation of many information systems. It has been proven that these information systems has helped organizations to better manage their processes and resources. However, they too have created a number of setbacks. One major setback of information system is the creation of huge volumes of data and information, resulting in phenomena such as information explosion or overload - a phenomenon whereby organisations are faced with over whelming amount of information. Nonetheless, it is a taxing job to go through the bulk of information and select the best one to use. When there is more information than a person could handle, the loads of information can result in less reactive responses and decline of capacity. With huge amount of information being created consistently, efficient and effective discovery of resource and knowledge has become an imminent research issue. Without proper management plans, procedures and tools, knowledge has become a very serious and annoying problem. Realizing the importance of knowledge, organizations give priority to capture and manage data and turn into organizational knowledge or business intelligence. But it is getting worse since there is as yet no process definition, classification, comprehensive knowledge management model, and a suitable knowledge based business model. In the process of implementing knowledge management, many questions and issues arise particularly how knowledge management could be used and where does it actually add value to organizations.

This paper attempts to give an overview on the varied definitions of knowledge management, types, and components of several knowledge management models. An integrated business model to facilitate knowledge creation, sharing, and discovery is then suggested to serve as a basis and generic guide for implementation by organizations and for further research.

This study is confined to three main knowledge management models those are suitable to organizations (Chase, 1997; Guthrie, 2000; Nonaka & Takeuchi, 1995; Audrey & Robert, 2001) and especially for banking sector

(Chin, 2001; Rodney & Sandra, 1999). Those are Knowledge Category Models (Nonaka's Knowledge Management Model and Boisot's Knowledge Category Model), Socially Constructed Model (Demerest's Knowledge Management Model) and Intellectual Capital Model. The proposed knowledge management model is based on the abstraction of all these three models. This study also provides a platform for an organization to establish, an enterprise wide framework that will identify, and, to reap the actual results of knowledge management. The application of these models will help to:

* prevent constant duplication of effort and poor decision-making, caused by lack of quality information.
* fully utilize the knowledge and skills of employees, to capture ideas and to contribute their initiatives.
* improve communication, reduce costs and develop competitive advantage.
* build strong customer relationships and enhance customer loyalty.
* unlock the potential of unique knowledge resources and harness their power – for everyone in the organization.

This paper is organised into three sections. First, the origin and domain of knowledge management. The authors study the varied definitions accorded to knowledge management, the types and the components that made up knowledge management models. The second section describes the existing knowledge management models. A few models will be evaluated with emphasis on their scope and applicability. In the final section, a business model or framework for the organizations to successfully identify, capture, and manage their knowledge will be proposed. In the process of drawing up a business model, organizational knowledge will be identified and classified, and the key concepts will be detailed. This will enable organizations to readily identify, organize and implement knowledge management.

KNOWLEDGE IN ORGANIZATIONS

Knowledge is a critical factor that affect an organization's ability to remain competitive in the new global marketplace. It is very much so that the sheer existence of any business now is partially attributed to the knowledge it possess. This is very much different from what has kept businesses running in those days. Badaracco (1991) asserts that in classical economies, the source of wealth are land, labour and capital but now, another engine of wealth is at work. It takes many forms such as technology, innovation, science, know-how, creativity, and information – the knowledge. In many organizations there is a strong reliance upon a small number of experts in accomplishing specific tasks. When the expert moves on either to an internal position or to a competitor they will perhaps take their knowledge along with them. This has make organization to realise the consequences of a sudden loss of knowledge. A new worker is then sent for training. As could have affected organizational knowledge if loss of expert is permitted repeatedly which in turn result in knowledge fluctuation. Knowledge fluctuation could presents problems internally, beside it may also be detrimental to the service that organizations can provide to their external customers, as the service provided to their customers may be defective until the replacement employee could rebuild the knowledge level as the previous expert. By retaining the knowledge of experts, organizations are actually protecting the investment made in the acquisition of knowledge via their experts and therefore lowering costs and maintaining customer satisfaction at the same time. To remain at the forefront and maintain a competitive edge organizations must have a good capacity to retain, develop, organize, and utilize their employee competencies (Gronhaug & Nordhaug 1992).

Effective knowledge management can also mean increased customer satisfaction by providing consistent information. Without it, many customers may be frustrated by inconsistency. For example, a customer may call a representative of an organization for advice. The same customer could call the very next day, talk to a different representative and receive a completely different answer. With a proper knowledge management solution in place any organization could ensure that all information received by their customer is consistent, and there are no two ways of doing or handling things. This, in a way could build customer trust and confidence, and help spread goodwill. With so much persistent problems surrounding them, organizations have started to recognize knowledge as a valuable resource and develop a mechanism for tapping into the collective intelligence and skills of employees in order to create a greater organizational knowledge base. Knowledge management accomplishes this goal. According to Audrey and Robert (2001) knowledge management has existed for many years, but only within the past few years it has gained noteworthy attention.

Knowledge management can be likened to both as a discipline and as an art. As a discipline it focuses on the process to capture and tend the knowledge; to make knowledge available to employee; to keep track of who is contributing to the knowledge bank; and identifying who is well applying knowledge management in an organisation (Chin Kwai Fatt 2001). On a broader perspective, the study of knowledge management evolved from the need for organizations to manage resources more effectively in a hyper-competitive, global economy. In an economy where the only certainty is uncertainty, the one sure source of lasting competitive advantage is knowledge. Successful companies are those that consistently create new knowledge, disseminate it widely throughout the organization, and quickly embody it in new technologies and products (Nonaka 1991).

KNOWLEDGE CATEGORIZATION

Knowledge is often regarded as the intellectual capital of a firm and is becoming very critical. A corporation gains knowledge from many years of experience in area such as manufacturing, engineering and sales. This cumulative experience, together from the outside sources, constitutes one of the firm's critical resources (Civi 2000). Basically, knowledge falls into two general categories, namely explicit and tacit knowledge. Explicit or articulated knowledge is specific as being in writing, drawings and computer programs, etc. (Hedlund 1994). This means, explicit knowledge could be found documented or in physical form. An example of this would be technical drawings and patents. Explicit knowledge can be expressed in words and numbers and is shared in the form of data, scientific formula, specifications and manuals. This kind of knowledge can migrate in the business community, and be accessible for most organizations regardless of their cooperative activities. It is codified and stored in databases where it can be accessed and used easily by anyone in the organization (Civi 2000).

Knowledge is primarily regarded as tacit. Tacit knowledge is non-verbalized, intuitive, and unarticulated (Polanyi 1962). It is the knowledge in a person's head which often difficult to describe and transfer. This includes lessons learned, know-how, judgements, rules of thumb, and intuition (Grayson & O'Dell 1998). Tacit knowledge is highly personal and hard to formalize, making it difficult to communicate or share with others (Polanyi 1962). There are two dimensions of tacit knowledge. Firstly, the technical dimensions encompasses the kind of informal personal skills or crafts often referred to as 'know-how'. Second, the cognitive dimension which consists of beliefs, ideals, values, schema and mental modes (Civi 2000). What is knowledge management?

ORIGINS OF KNOWLEDGE MANAGEMENT

Theoretical Origins

The field of knowledge management is seen as an essential part of a much broader concept known as intellectual capital (Roos et al. 1997). Knowledge management is about the management of the intellectual capital, controlled by the company. However, too often the delineation between the two terms is unclear and seldom adequately addressed (Guthrie 2000). The problem in managing knowledge is not new (Roos et al. 1997). The authors use the concept 'intellectual capital' as an umbrella term. 'Intellectual capital' is defined as 'the possession of knowledge, applied experience, organizational technology, customer relationship, and professional skills that provide organizations with a competitive edge in the market' (Edvinsson 1997).

A firm's tangible and intangible resources, which are under the control of the firm's administrative organization, may be grouped into two main categories, namely firm resources and firm capabilities (Grant 1991). The resources are the inputs into the production process whilst the capability of a firm is the capacity, what it can do, as a result of the teams of resources working together. While tangible resources could be identified and defined quite easily, intangible resource has many forms and concepts. Intangible resources usually consist of:

* Physical, human and monetary resources that are needed for business operations to operate; and
* Information-based resources, such as management skills, technology, consumer information, brand name, reputation and corporate culture.

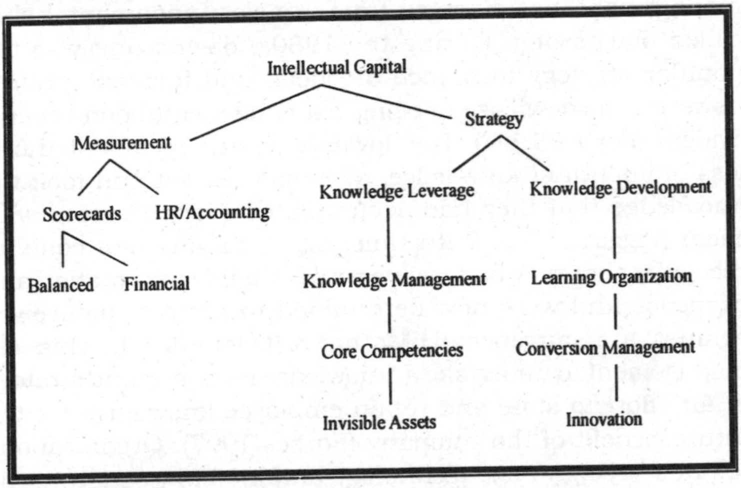

Fig. 1. Conceptual roots of intellectual capital (Roos et al. 1997)

A firm's distinctive competence is based on the specialized resources, assets, and skills it possesses, and focused attention on their optimum utilization to build competitive advantage and economic wealth (Ruthinda 1996). Knowledge-based theory of the firm postulates that knowledge is the only resource that provides sustainable competitive advantage, and therefore, the firm's attention and decision-making should focus primarily on knowledge and the competitive capabilities derived from it (Roberts 1998). This firm is considered being a knowledge integrating institute. Its role is neither the acquisition nor the creation of organizational knowledge; this is the role and prerequisite of the individual. Knowledge resides in and with individual people. The firm merely integrates the individually owned knowledge by providing structural arrangements of co-ordination and co-operation of specialized knowledge workers. That is, the firm focuses on the organizational process flowing through these structural arrangements, through which individuals engage in knowledge creation, storage and deployment (Roberts 1998).

EMPIRICAL ORIGIN

It is widely argued that the growth of 'knowledge management' has emerged from a major fundamental shift called downsizing. During the 1980s, downsizing was the popular strategy to reduce overhead and increase profits; however, the downsize to being 'lean and mean' soon became evident (Forbes 1997). The downsizing strategy resulted in a loss of important knowledge, as employees left and took the knowledge that they had accumulated over the years with them (Piggot 1997). With time, organizations had come to recognize that they had lost years of valuable information and expertise and were now determined to protect themselves against a recurrence (DiMattia & Oder 1997). This led management to undertake a 'knowledge management' strategy in an effort to store and retain employee knowledge for the future benefit of the company (Forbes 1997). Organizations are now trying to use technology and system to capture the knowledge residing in the minds of their employees, so it can be easily shared within the organization. When stored, it becomes a reusable resource that can provide a wealth of competitive advantage, including enhanced organizational capacities, facilitating output, and lowering costs (Forbes 1997).

TECHNOLOGICAL DEVELOPMENT

The technological development has heightened the interest in knowledge management. Phenomenon like the explosive growth of information resources, such as the Internet, and the accelerating pace of technological change have fueled this development (Hibbard 1997). The recent IT development has affected both the lives of people and organizations (Mayo 1998). The continuous flow of information overwhelms everyone in an organization, from the operations right up to the management level. Knowledge management is an attempt to cope with the explosion of information and to capitalize on increased knowledge in workplace (DiMattia & Oder 1997).

The emerging technological development enables global sharing of information across platforms and continents (DiMattia & Oder 1997) and can serve as a tool within an organization to use knowledge more effectively. Capturing a company's collective expertise in database can help organizations to 'know what they actually know', and then marshal and exploit this knowledge in a systematic way (Blake 1998).

KNOWLEDGE MANAGEMENT DEFINITION

Many people perceive knowledge in many forms. As such it is only logical that knowledge management has many definition according to the field it is being used in. A search of over 100 Web sites on knowledge management (Quintas et al. 1997) revealed a heterogeneous range of interests, perspectives and issues namely economics, intellectual capital, engineering approaches, organizational studies, computing and knowledge media, epistemology (learning, cognition and psychology), and other forms of definition informed by artificial intelligence, human resource issues and information system.

A review of current literatures reveals numerous definitions of knowledge management due to the wide range of interests, perspectives, and issues represented by various authors. According to these authors, there exist so many variations in what organizations refer to when they initiate knowledge management programs. Because so many different disciplines are interested in knowledge management, the resulting ambiguity in terminology leads to fragmented dialogue on the topic.

While deriving the accurate definition of knowledge is not easy, it is well agreed that knowledge is an organized combination of ideas, rules, procedures, and information. In a sense, knowledge is a 'meaning' made by the mind (Marakas 1999). Without meaning, knowledge is inert and static and a disorganized information. It is only through meaning, information acquire its life and becomes knowledge. Information and knowledge are distinct, based on their internal organization. Information is rather disorganized, but knowledge is well organized (Koniger & Janowitz 1995). Thus, information distinct from knowledge based on users' perspectives. Knowledge is context dependent, since 'meanings' are interpreted in reference to a particular paradigm (Marakas 1999).

During the industrial era, the foundation of knowledge was based on technical rationality and order. Knowledge was considered representative of a fixed reality, in which 'knowing' was considered isomorphic with the objective fact (Dervin 1994). However, at present 'knowledge' is believed to be based on interpretations and discourse between different members. Knowledge becomes public-goods which is continually examined and interpreted by different social members (Raelin 1997). As such, knowledge or knowledge management will have a continuously changing definition, based on the way it is interpreted by the society and will again change from one society to another. This is one reason why there is no one clear definition of knowledge management.

Knowledge management systems that are presently available or implemented, are just large electronic libraries of best practices, and needs to be rebuilt on more accurate understanding of what knowledge is. The following definitions are quoted from the works of a few experts in this field:

i. Knowledge management is a process of knowledge creation, which is followed by knowledge interpretation, knowledge dissemination and use, and knowledge retention and refinement (De Jarnet 1996).

ii. Powerful environmental forces are reshaping the world of the manager of the 21st century. These forces call for a fundamental shift in organization process and human resources strategy. This is knowledge management (Taylor et al. 1996).

iii. Knowledge management is the process of critically managing knowledge to meet existing needs, to identify and exploit existing and acquired knowledge assets and to develop new opportunities (Quintas et al. 1997).

iv. Knowledge management in the activity which is concerned with strategy and tactics to manage human centered assets (Brooking 1997).

If each and every definition of knowledge management is analysed, it can be summarize that knowledge involves thinking with information regardless of the environment or field from where the definition originate. Knowledge management models, which are converted into systems, must connect people to enable them to think, articulate and share information and insights that are useful to the others in the community.

There are currently three schools of thought on what knowledge management is (Poynder 1998). One school suggests that knowledge management is primarily an information technology issue, with networks of computers and group ware being keys. This school believes that if we build extensive computer networks and add communications tools that allow group collaboration, people will be more inclined to share information and knowledge. A second school suggests that knowledge management is more of a human resource issue with emphases on organizational culture and teamwork. A strong, positive organizational culture is critical to promoting learning, development and the sharing of skills, resources and knowledge. The third school promotes the development of processes to measure and capture the organization's know-how. Here, processes do not necessarily need to involve the use of information technology.

One of the best definition of knowledge management comes from two current researchers, whom are both very experienced researchers in the field are (Davenport & Prusak 1998) who defined knowledge management as "a fluid of framed experience, values contextual information and expert insight that provides framework for evaluating and incorporating new experiences and information'.

A simple definition of knowledge management as used as a base line in this paper is 'knowledge management is the identification and communication of explicit and tacit knowledge residing within processes, people, products and services'.

KNOWLEDGE MANAGEMENT MODELS

Knowledge Category Model

Nonaka and Takeuchi (1995) gave a high level conceptual representation of knowledge management and essentially considered knowledge management as a knowledge creation process. Their model is one of the simplest ways to represent knowledge management where knowledge is considered as consisting of tacit and explicit elements.

		to	
		Tacit	Explicit
From	Tacit	Socialization	Externalization
	Explicit	Internalization	Combination

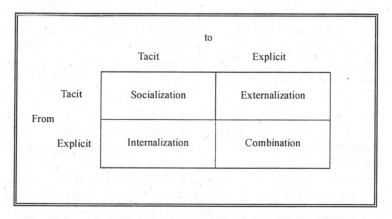

Fig. 2. Nonaka's knowledge management model

This model makes use of Polanyi's (1962) concept of explicit knowledge and tacit knowledge in defining knowledge dimensions. They also asserted that individual knowledge moves to group level and finally assimilates at the organizational level, through upward spiral of knowledge creation. Knowledge management in its simplest form is shown in Figure 2 (Nonaka & Takeuchi 1995). Another knowledge category model, which is widely used to represent knowledge, is that of Boisot (1987) as shown in Figure 3. This model considers knowledge as either codified of uncodified an as diffused or undiffused.

	Undiffused	Diffused
Codified	Proprietary Knowledge	Public Knowledge
Uncodified	Personal Knowledge	Common Sense

Fig. 3. Boisot's knowledge category model

Boisot used the term 'codified' to refer to knowledge that cannot be easily prepared for transmission purpose, e.g. financial data. The term 'uncodified' refers to knowledge that cannot be easily prepared for transmission purposes, e.g. experience. The term 'diffused' refers to knowledge that is readily shared while 'undiffused' refers to knowledge that is not readily shared.

SOCIALLY CONSTRUCTED MODEL

The Demerest's (1997) knowledge management model is adapted towards the learning organization and organizational learning, as shown in Figure 4. This model mainly emphasizes the construction of knowledge within the organization. This construction is not limited to scientific inputs but is seen as including the social construction of knowledge. This model assumes that constructed knowledge is then embodied within the organization, not just through explicit programmes but also through a process of social interchange. Ultimately through this model, knowledge is seen as being of economic use in regard to organizational outputs.

The solid arrows in Figure 4, represent primary flow direction while the lain arrows show the more recursive flows. This model does not assume any given definition of knowledge but rather invites a more holistic approach to knowledge construction.

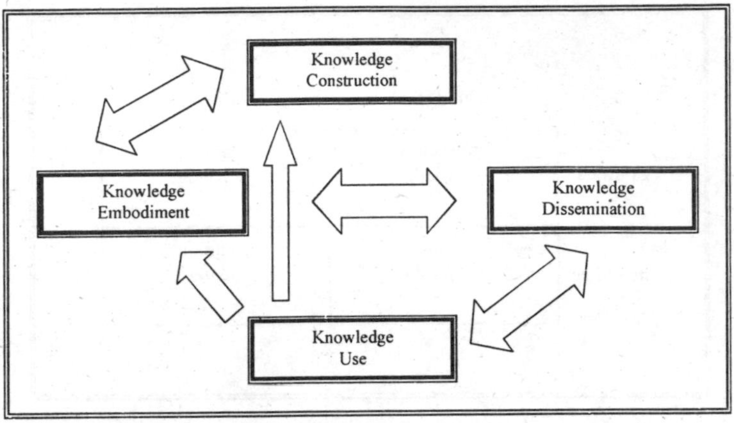

Fig. 4. Demerest's knowledge management model

INTELLECTUAL CAPITAL MODEL

Apart from the above models, a number of other models in the literature represent knowledge management as essentially intellectual capital. A typical intellectual capital model is the Skandia (Chase 1997) intellectual capital model. Skandia is a big insurance company. This model assumes knowledge management or intellectual capital can be segregated into human, customer, process and growth elements, which are contained in two main categories of human capital and structural/organizational capital. Skandia was the first company in the world to publish a supplement to its annual report on the company's intellectual capital philosophy and activities (Chase 1997).

However this intellectual capital view of knowledge management ignores the political and social aspect of knowledge management. This Skandia model (Rodney & Sandra 1999) assumes that knowledge management can be decomposed into objective elements rather than being a socio-political phenomenon. This approach results in simplistic mechanized approaches to complex social-related issues, e.g. reward and recognition, power relations and empowerment.

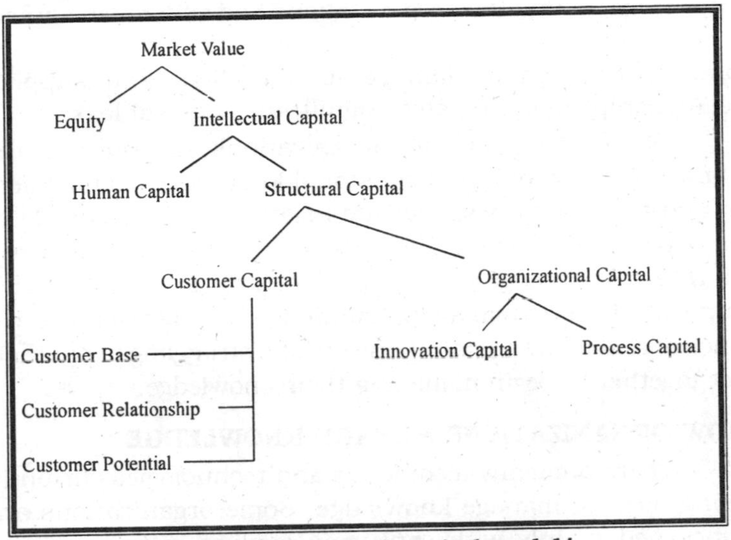

Fig. 5. Intellectual capital model/ knowledge management (Skandia)

STUDIES ON KNOWLEDGE MANAGEMENT

According to the knowledge management research report (1998), by failing to identify, capture and manage their knowledge, 43% of the respondents said the relationship with a key client or supplier had been damaged; 50% of the respondents said that they had lost knowledge of best practice in a specific area of operations; and 10% of them said that their organizations actually lost significant income.

This research was conducted to establish the extent to which organizations are aware of knowledge management, take it seriously and are pursuing initiatives to implement and benefit from it. The research was done among chief executives, financial directors, marketing directors and those with specific responsibility for knowledge management in their organizations at 100 leading UK companies with turnover exceeding $200 million a year. It has become clearer that much of an organization's knowledge is personal. It remains in employees' minds. According to this survey, there is little provision for capturing, sharing and disseminating it. When individuals leave, their knowledge is lost to the organization. Respondents confirmed they realize the value of this human knowledge, in that their organizations had suffered in various ways when individuals left from loss of knowledge of best practice through to damage to key client and supplier relationships and ultimately significant financial loss.

When some of the organizations do capture the knowledge, one third of them stored knowledge of customers in non-technology based formats such as people's heads or on paper. The commonality of the above studies is that they all regard knowledge as a critical factor for an organization's survival. However managing knowledge has always remained unclear and many organizations are still struggling to put their act together to begin managing their knowledge.

HOW ORGANIZATIONS MANAGE KNOWLEDGE

There are many techniques and technologies currently being used to manage knowledge. Some organizations are concerned mainly with capturing explicit knowledge and others are attempting to collect tacit knowledge through the use of expert systems and artificial intelligence. Knowledge-based systems (KBS) perform knowledge processing based on expert system or deductive databases to help users find acceptable solutions to problems (Hayes-Roth & Jaccobstein 1994). This approach allows firms to capture knowledge by capturing it from experts.

Intelligent tools can also be used to anticipate user needs and to create new knowledge from existing knowledge bases. Collaborative tools such as group ware are useful for facilitating team meetings, particularly when project teams are composed of participants from diverse locations.

At this stage we can say that knowledge management in most organizations is still at its infancy stage, if it exists at all. This is the result of organizations being unable to distinguish knowledge at its purest form and making use of it in the right way once it is captured.

KNOWLEDGE MANAGEMENT AND ENABLING TECHNOLOGIES

One key assumption underlying any discussion of knowledge management is that organizations use technology to capture, store, transform or process and disseminate information. In fact, effective knowledge management depends on people sharing their knowledge on computer networks, that users throughout an organization have access to. Davenport and Prusak (1998) commended 'technology' in recognition of the instrumental role certain technologies are playing in 'catalyzing the knowledge management movement'. These technologies continue to evolve rapidly, especially in areas of collaboration and search engines. This evolution combined with the advances in the web technologies, is enabling the knowledge management applications (Davenport & Prusak 1998).

There are a number of technologies that have fast become the best technology, which enable knowledge management to play its role efficiently and effectively in most organization. They include internet/intranet technologies, and generic web elements such as portals. Out of these and any other technologies, the web portal technology is regarded as the best technology to enable knowledge management implementation.

ISSUES IN KNOWLEDGE MANAGEMENT

The slow penetration of knowledge management in most organizations is attributed to a number of diverse factors and issues. But most of the barriers to effective knowledge management involve people. Humans are complex with diverse psychological needs. Most knowledge management systems require that data and documents be stored in knowledge bases. From an organizational perspectives, the process of building these knowledge repositories can be very time consuming, labor-intensive and costly. People are already busy and sharing knowledge may mean changing the way they work or adding extra steps to the process to extract the exact data and enter it into a repository (Cole-Gomolski 1999).

Another major set back is in the knowledge capturing stage. It is a very tough job to codify tacit knowledge. In addition to that, knowledge is constantly changing both at the individual and organizational levels. The gap between what people actually do in their job and what and how it is documented is difficult to bridge due to spontaneous actions people take in response to unexpected challenges and problems (Brown & Duguid 2000). Knowledge bases that require a great deal of upkeep may tend to fall into disuse and decay due to obsolete information. Also, information taken out of context can be misleading and misinterpreted (Shum 1997). Sometimes too much information is available and people are unable to assimilate it due to sheer volume and lack of appropriate tools. This results in information overload, frustration and demoralization. If workers do not see the benefits of the application, they will not use it (Cole-Gomolski 1997).

At the individual level, people are often reluctant to share information. Professional knowledge is perceived as a source of power (Quinn et al. 1996). There is a sense of worth and status to be gained because of expertise. There can also be fear that there will be diminishing personal value after giving up know-how (Hibbard & Carrilo 1998). In addition, competition among professionals have little respect for others outside their field. People are very mobile. Thus, knowledge is volatile and vulnerable to loss (Jordan & Jones 1997).

From a team perspectives, team members may be reluctant to share knowledge if they are fear of criticism from their peers, or recrimination from management. There may also be subversion of group efforts if there is a lack of respect, trust and common goals. Reward systems are sometimes based on what a person knows and individual effort, and may not be a source of advancement within an organization (Audrey & Robert 2001).

Organizations handle these issues in more than one way. Some organizations use a chief knowledge officer (CKO) to coordinate the knowledge management effort. However, this could send the wrong message (Cole-Gomolski 1999) since most knowledge sharing occurs within business units. Also knowledge management implies controlling people and if that is the employees' perception, it will be destined to fail (Manville & Foote 1996). Some believe that most of these problems could be averted if knowledge management is implemented within a business unit rather than organization-wide.

RESEARCH METHOD

Recently, knowledge management has started to emerge as an area of interest in both the academic and organizational practice. In order to get a better understanding and insight into knowledge management, more than one method is used. The findings made out of the following three methods to design the integrated knowledge management model.

(a) Document review. Literature review is used as the main method in the fact finding process and eventually writing of this paper. Available publication focusing on defining, classifying and comparing knowledge management models are being given preference and used extensively. World wide web is used as one of the main source to identify literatures in this field.

(b) Tools evaluation. Apart from literature review, knowledge management tools in the market will also be evaluated critically from the view point of knowledge architecture and management.

(c) Other knowledge management implementation. Current knowledge management initiatives in big organizations will also be investigated and the processes involved will be captured and compared. Consultation based organizations will be the prime focus for this study. Literature and surveys conducted at Ernst & Young, KPMG and Andersen Consulting are being scrutinized to gather information on the implementation of knowledge management in these organizations.

The specific tasks undertaken by this study are as follows:

i. Critical comparison : This initial investigation is to determine the definitions, kinds and components of knowledge management.

ii. Analysis : Knowledge gathered from the critical comparison will be analyzed and compared to practices in the organizations that have already implemented knowledge management. This is supported by findings from surveys conducted by professional consulting firms.

iii. Design and developing the framework : Upon the

completion of the analysis phase, a general business model for organizations to implement will be proposed before proceeding to the specific details of the model.

FINDINGS

Old and New Management Paradigms

Before discussing and defining the models of knowledge management, it is pertinent for us to identify the difference between the old management paradigm and the new management paradigm. Knowledge on the differences of both paradigms will give us better understanding on which type of paradigm a particular knowledge management model is driving at. The differences between both these paradigms will also act as a basis for us to compare between the models and critically review the models.

Clegg et al. (1996) defined the current emerging large paradigm of management in organizations, organization theory and practice in Table 1. This representation combines Kuhn's (1974) work on old management paradigms. In a current organizational context, the older paradigm on the right-hand side of the table is being continuously replaced by the paradigm on the left-hand side.

Table 1. Old and new management paradigms

New Paradigm	*Old Paradigm*
Organizational learning.	Organizational discipline.
Virtuous circles.	Vicious circles.
Flexible organizations.	Inflexible organizations.
Management leaders.	Management administrators.
Open communication.	Distorted communication.
Core competencies drive product . development	Strategic learning occurs at the apex of the organization.
Assumption that most organization members are trustworthy.	Assumption that most organization members are untrustworthy.
Most organization members are empowered.	Most organization members are disempowered.
Tacit and local knowledge of all members of the organization is the most important factor in success and creativity creates its own prerogative.	Tacit and local knowledge of all members of the organization must be disciplined by managerial prerogative.

Source: Clegg et al. 1996. Table 1.

Clegg et al. (1996) classification of old and new paradigm enabled Table 1 to be constructed, which will be helpful in examining knowledge management models and their associated assumptions. The assumptions can be compared with the details of each paradigm to determine which management paradigm the model falls into.

ANALYSIS ON KNOWLEDGE MANAGEMENT MODELS

It is essential for organizations to understand the types of knowledge and how they relate to each others in terms of conversion. An understanding of the knowledge transfer processes is essential for discerning organization's strengths and weaknesses (Dataware Technologies 1998). Many different kinds of knowledge management models, covering extensive range of viewpoints are available. When these models are critiqued, they must be always critiqued to understand the underlying assumptions in the representation, rather than accepting them as objective representations of reality (Rodney & Sandra 1999).

Acknowledging these deliberation and limitations, some typical and famous knowledge management models are selected and critiqued. The selected models originate from various views. Most literatures categorize knowledge management models into three main categories. They are knowledge category models, intellectual capital models and social constructed models (Rodney & Sandra 1999).

KNOWLEDGE CATEGORY MODEL

Nonaka and Takeuchi (1995) established a dynamic model of knowledge creation. They introduced an interesting assumption, through this model. This assumption explains that human knowledge is created and expanded through social interaction between tacit knowledge and explicit knowledge.

This model discussed the knowledge transfer within an organization from tacit to explicit and vice versa. They identified four different modes of knowledge conversion . They include:

1. Tacit knowledge to tacit knowledge, which is called as socialization. It is a process of sharing experiences,

which creates tacit knowledge such as shared mental models and technical skills.

2. Tacit knowledge to explicit knowledge or externalization. It is a knowledge creation process in that tacit knowledge becomes explicit, taking the shapes of metaphors, analogies, concepts, hypotheses or models.
3. Explicit knowledge to explicit knowledge or combination. It involves combining different bodies of explicit knowledge.
4. Explicit knowledge to tacit knowledge or internalization. It is a process of embodying explicit knowledge into tacit knowledge and is closely related to 'learning by doing'.

Socialization is the process of sharing experiences and is often done through observation, imitation and practice. It occurs in settings such as apprenticeships and at conferences. Externalization is concerned with articulating tacit knowledge and turning it into an explicit form. For example after attending a workshop or seminar, a report is prepared. Here, the report creation and distribution process is the actual process of converting knowledge from explicit form to tacit and a combination takes place.

Internalization is the process of experience knowledge through the explicated source. For example we read a report about something and we put ourselves in that situation and combine that experience with the previous involvements we have had in similar situations. By introducing this assumption that knowledge could be converted between tacit and explicit form, we can summarize that tacit and explicit knowledge are not totally different. They interact with and interchange into each other in the daily activities in an organization.

In their knowledge conversion model, Nonaka and Takeuchi (1995) gave emphasis on knowledge conversion methods, i.e. combination, internalization, socialization and externalization. But this model lacks the clarity on the flow of knowledge. This model could be redesigned to better illustrate the flow, as below, giving focus to both the knowledge and the conversion process between them.

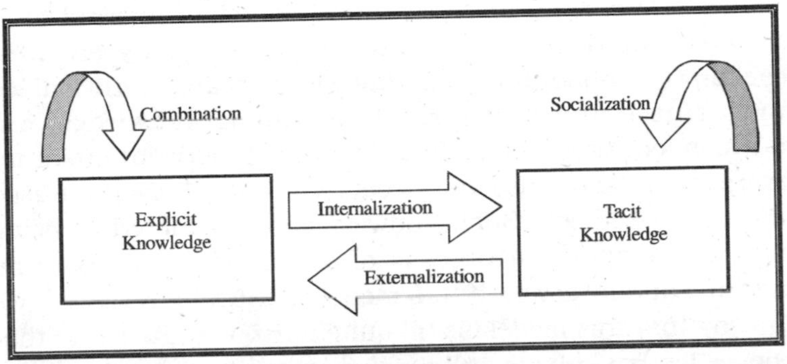

Fig. 6. Modified knowledge flow model based on Nonaka and Takeuchi (1995) model

In this modified model, it is very obvious that Nonaka and Takeuchi (1995) solely categorized knowledge into tacit and explicit only (this is not that clear in their original model). However Rodney and Sandra (1999) have pointed out that the model proposed by Nonaka and Takeuchi is perhaps limited or undimensional as it does not include the concept of P and Q knowledge, which was proposed by Mcloughlin and Thorpe (1993). Knowledge (McLoughlin & Thorpe 1993) can also be categorized to P, which is programmed knowledge, and Q, which is gained by questioning insight. Rodney and Sandra (1999) argued further that tacit knowledge does not exactly map onto Q and neither does explicit knowledge onto P. Thus P and Q represent a different categorization of knowledge. As such we can critically conclude that Nonaka's categorization of knowledge is rather limited or unidimensional (Rodney & Sandra 1999).

Unlike Nonaka's knowledge model, Boisot's model consider more categories of knowledge within organization, i.e. codified, uncodified, diffused and undiffused. If knowledge is categorized as both codified and undiffused then the knowledge is referred to as propriety knowledge. Proprietary knowledge here means that the knowledge is actually prepared for transmission purpose, but is deliberately restricted to a selective small group or population, on need to know basis, e.g. profits and loss, and share price issues.

The bottom left quadrant covers knowledge that is

relatively uncodified and undiffused, which is referred to as personal knowledge, e.g. perceptions, insights, experiences. The top right quadrant covers knowledge that is both codified and diffused and is referred to as public knowledge, e.g. journals, books, libraries. Finally, the bottom right quadrant refers to common sense knowledge, which is relatively diffused but also uncodified. Such knowledge is considered as being built up slowly by a process of socialization, harbouring customs and intuition. If this model is critically reviewed, we can say that this model is still quite narrow in the sense that knowledge basically is still divided into two, namely codified and uncodified only. When both knowledge is transformed from undiffused ti diffused the concerned knowledge still remains in its original form, within the codified or uncodified domain, but is just given a different name to reflect the domain which the knowledge is exposed to. As such, we can conclude that, propriety knowledge and public knowledge are subset of codified knowledge while personal knowledge and common sense are subset of uncodified knowledge.

Another limitation in this knowledge category model is that, there is no indication or representation on the flow of knowledge when the proprietary knowledge is diffused to public knowledge and when the personal knowledge is diffused to common sense. Apart from that, Boisot's model also fails to clarify if there exist any kind of link between codified and uncodified knowledge. There is no way for us to know if codified knowledge does interact or is converted to uncodified knowledge or vice versa at some point of time in an organization based on Boisot's (1987) model.

There are also several similarities between Nonaka's model and that of Boisot. Nonaka's categorization of knowledge into explicit and tacit knowledge is similar to Boisot's reference to knowledge in codified and uncodified form. Other than that both this models talk about spreading or diffusing knowledge across the organization. To get a clearer understanding, Boisot's model can be represented in a Venn diagram, by depicting knowledge as the universal set with the others as subsets.

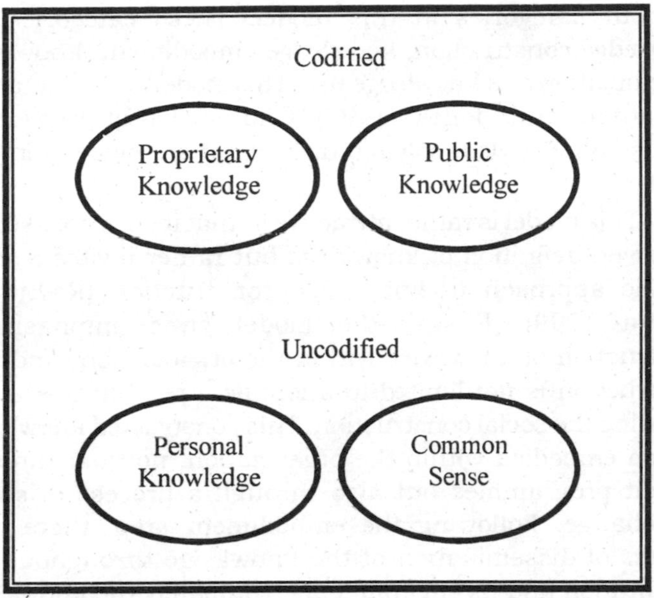

Fig. 7. Knowledge category model adapted from Boisot's knowledge category model

From this Venn diagram representation we can derive the below statements:

a. Knowledge = Codified Knowledge U Uncodified Knowledge
b. Codified Knowledge)•Uncodified Knowledge = Ø
c. Proprietary Knowledge ! Codified Knowledge
d. Public Knowledge ! Codified Knowlcdge
e. Proprietary Knowledge)•Public Knowledge = Ø
f. Personal Knowledge ! Uncodified Knowledge
g. Common Sense ! Uncodified Knowledge
h. Personal Knowledge)•Common Sense = Ø

Some of the suggestions and limitations of Boisot's knowledge category model as discussed earlier could be clearly reflected by these mathematical statements.

SOCIALLY CONSTRUCTED MODELS

Socially constructed models emphasize the construction

of knowledge in organizations. As with the other models there are four categories in this model. These categories are knowledge construction, knowledge embodiment, knowledge dissemination and knowledge use. This model is similar to that of Jordan and Jones (1997) who spoke of knowledge acquisition, problem solving, dissemination, ownership and storage.

This model is rather attractive in that it does not assume any given definition of knowledge but rather invites a more holistic approach to knowledge construction (Rodney & Sandra 1999). Firstly, the model gives emphasis to construction of knowledge within the organization. And this construction is not limited to scientific input but is seen as including the social construction. This constructed knowledge is then embodied within the organization, not just through explicit programmes but also through a process of social interchange. Following the embodiment step, there is a process of dissemination of the knowledge throughout the organization and its environments. Ultimately the knowledge is seen as being of economic use in regard to organizational outputs (Rodney & Sandra 1999). The solid arrows or main flow may be a limitation in that it implies that recursive flows are less important and it appears to be a simplistic process approach, while in reality, the flows of knowledge transfer may be extremely rapid and circulatory, as in the case for some form of action learning (Rodney & Sandra 1999).

INTELLECTUAL CAPITAL MODELS

Intellectual Capital models usually views knowledge management as a few elements within the intellectual capital umbrella. As with the Skandia approach, these knowledge management elements are contained in two main categories of human capital and structural or organizational capital. However this intellectual capital view of knowledge management ignores the political and social aspects of knowledge management. Also, like Nonaka's model, it assumes knowledge management can be decomposed into objective elements rather than being a socio-political phenomenon (Rodney & Sandra 1999). This mechanistic approach, more consistent with the right hand side of Table 1 can result in simplistic mechanized approaches to complex social-related issues like reward and recognition, power relations, empowerment and leadership (Rodney & Sandra 1999).

The Skandia example, gives a strong emphasis to measurement associated with each of these decomposed elements of knowledge management assuming it can be tightly controlled, as is the case for tangible assets (Lank 1997). Unfortunately this approach can result in attempts to fit objective measures of knowledge management to subjective elements in these intellectual capital models (Rodney & Sandra 1999). Based on this arguments on intellectual capital models, we can assume that intellectual capital models are mechanistic in nature and assume that knowledge can be treated as an assets. This kind of approach is more associated with the right hand side of Table 1.

COMBINED KNOWLEDGE MANAGEMENT MODEL

A single model, which could represent knowledge management as a whole, is hard to be found. If scrutinized further, we will notice that while Nonaka and Takeuchi's (1995) knowledge conversion model focuses more on the conversion of knowledge in many forms, Boisot's (1987) knowledge category model outlines what both types of knowledge is madc up of. On their own, both these models suffer serious lacking as discussed earlier. If both these models could be merged somehow, it could represent a knowledge category and conversion model and at thc same time compliment each other to reduce their lacking.

Both Nonaka and Takeuchi (1995) and Boisot (1987) have unconsciously made provisions in their models to enable us to merge both this models. Nonaka and Takeuchi group knowledge into tacit and explicit knowledge, while Boisot group knowledge into codified and uncodified knowledge. As mentioned earlier, Nonaka's tacit and explicit knowledge groups could be mapped onto Boisot's uncodified and codified knowledge. This similarity makes it possible to merge both this models together.

Other than that, both this models also unconsciously have provision or other enablers to make the merging process possible. Nonaka and Takeuchi (1995) has identified knowledge conversion within the same group in their knowledge conversion model where tacit knowledge could be converted to tacit by socialization and explicit knowledge could be converted to explicit by combination. On the Boisot's (1987) knowledge category model, both codified and uncodified knowledge is subdivided into diffused and undiffused categories.

As such, if both these models were to be combined, they would play an active role to compliment each other. At the same time it providing us a single model of reference for knowledge category and conversion.

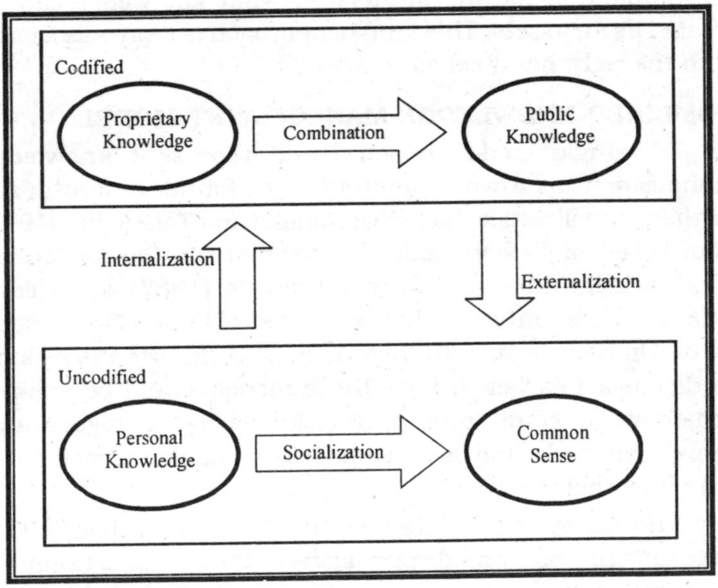

Fig. 8. Knowledge category and conversion model

This model inherits both the characteristics of Nonaka's model and Boisot's model. As such knowledge is still divided into codified (explicit) and uncodified (tacit), and it can exist in two forms, diffused or undiffused. Proprietary knowledge and public knowledge are grouped under codified knowledge, while personal knowledge and common sense are grouped under uncodified knowledge. In this scope, proprietary knowledge and personal knowledge are considered as undiffused while public knowledge and common sense are considered as diffused knowledge.

As such we can now identify four different models of knowledge conversion from this model as shown in Figure 8. They include:

1. Uncodified knowledge to uncodified knowledge (Personal knowledge to common sense), which is called as socialization. This means that, only through socialization can an uncodified knowledge be transferred or diffused to a whole group of people. Socialization in this context means sharing experiences.
2. Uncodified knowledge to codified knowledge (Personal knowledge to proprietary knowledge), or externalization. It is a knowledge creation process in that uncodified knowledge becomes codified, taking the shapes of metaphors, analogies, concepts, hypotheses or models.
3. Codified knowledge to codified knowledge (Proprietary knowledge to public knowledge), or combination. This conversion is very straight forward as knowledge is only diffused to more number of people.
4. Codified knowledge to uncodified knowledge (Public knowledge to common sense), or internalization. It is a process of learning the codified knowledge and converted into uncodified knowledge within a person, by repetitively doing it.

Using this combined model, discussion about the knowledge transfer within an organization from tacit to explicit and vice versa goes one step deeper to include the subgroups of tacit and explicit knowledge.

DISCUSSION AND CONCLUSION

The examination of existing models, definitions and classifications of knowledge management shows a wide scale of perspectives. These perspectives range from the more mechanistic to more socially orientated. The mechanistic type of definitions and classifications assume an intellectual capital approach while the social type assumes a socially constructed approach where knowledge is constructed in social relationships within organizations.

Three broad classifications of models were identified and critiqued in the course of this paper. Firstly, knowledge category models made reference to social processes for transforming knowledge from one category to another. Secondly, the intellectual capital models were found to be more mechanistic, where asset is assumed and treated similar to other assets, and finally the socially constructed models were seen as taking into consideration on a more balanced approached between the scientific and social approaches to knowledge management. And finally after evaluating the advantages and the disadvantages if these models, a combined model to reflect knowledge management is proposed.

A concise knowledge management model such as the proposed knowledge category and conversion model facilitates for the easier adaptation of knowledge management concept into organizations. This in turn modifies the organization into a knowledge intensive enterprise. In organizations such as this, knowledge is more readily available, and easily transferred and made accessible to workers throughout the organization. When people have access to organizational knowledge, they can then understand their environment and give it meaning. They can find new and better ways to perform, work together, break down barriers, share a vision, fill gaps of knowledge, increase productivity, satisfy customers and ultimately make the organization more competitive in the market.

Furthermore, analyzing the knowledge category and conversion model, we can make a few deductions. Firstly, knowledge is seen as originally taking the form of uncodified and undiffused in any organization. From this point forward, it can be diffused to become common sense throughout and organization. Or it could be externalized to become a proprietary knowledge, which is codified but still remains undiffused. This proprietary knowledge could be diffused throughout the organization by combining it with other knowledge the organization already has to become public knowledge. Finally the public knowledge becomes common sense when it is internalized or used repeatedly to perform tasks. This deduction on the flow of knowledge proves the fact that knowledge is not created by the organization but only exists within the organization's staff. This view is also consistent with Nonaka and Takeuchi's (1995) assertion that individual knowledge moves to group level and finally assimilates at the group level, through upward spiral of knowledge creation.

It is in line with Argyris and Schen's (1978) argument that organizational knowledge is individually shared knowledge that individuals come to understand and interpret in a particular organizational context. Huber (1991) took a similar view arguing that organizations learn through their people by developing and sharing ideas and meanings. Knowledge capturing process happens in the externalization process. Here then uncodified knowledge is codified and stored in the knowledge base. After capturing the knowledge, it adopts and uses a numbers of metaphors and analogies based on the existing knowledge and modifies it to make it suitable and practical for it to be distributed. The distribution and sharing could happen either before or after knowledge is reviewed or revised. Once the organization has distributed the codified knowledge throughout the organization, the knowledge then becomes a public knowledge. And with prolonged usage, it then becomes a rule of thumb in the daily activity of the staff in the organization.

This paper is limited to the conceptual representation of knowledge and knowledge management. It does not include any knowledge representation or knowledge acquiring techniques. In the suggested knowledge category and conversion model, there are a few limitations. As the title suggests, this model only focuses on knowledge category and conversion only. This model has a limited scope in that it does not shed any light on the knowledge creation and any knowledge review or refinement process. It focuses mainly on knowledge categories, knowledge adoption and knowledge distribution.

By enhancing the suggested knowledge category and conversion model, future research on knowledge management models could be employed. This model could be enhanced in more than one way. It is suggested that this model is used as a useful guide for future research and literature evaluation in the area of knowledge management.

REFERENCE

Argyris, C. and Schen, D.A. 1978. *Organizational learning: A theory of Action Perspective.* Reading: Addison Wesley Publishing.

Audrey, S.B. and Robert, D.S. 2001. Managing organizational knowledge as a strategic asset. *Journal of Knowledge Management* 5(1): 8-18.

Badaracco, J.L. 1991. *The knowledge link: How firms compete through strategic alliance.* Boston: Harvard Business School Press.

Boisot, M. 1987. *Information and organizations: The Manager as anthropologist.* London: Fontana Collins.

Brooking, A. 1997. The management of intellectual capital. *Journal of Long Range Planning* 30(3): 364-365.

Brown, J. and Duguid, P. 2000. Balancing act: How to capture knowledge without killing it. *Harvard Business Review* 78(3): 73-80.

Chase, R. 1997. The knowledge based organization: an international survey. *Journal of Knowledge Management* 1(1).

Chin Kwai Fatt. 2001. Knowledge management in borderless world. Malaysian Business August: 3.

Clegg, S., Barret, M., Clarke, T., Dwyer, L., Gray, J., Kemp, S. and Marceau, J. 1996. Management knowledge for the future: innovation, embryos and new paradigms. In Clegg, S. & Palmer, G. (Eds.), *The politic of management knowledge.* London: Sage.

Cole-Gomolski, B. 1997. Users loathe to share their know-how. *Computerworld* 31(46): 6.

Cole-Gomolski, B. 1999. Knowledge 'czars' fall from grace. *Computerworld* 33(1): 1-13.

Dataware Technologies. 1998. Knowledge management linking people to knowledge for bottom line result. *Corporate Executive Briefing*: 16.

Davenport, T. and Prusak, L. 1998. *Working knowledge: How organizations manage what they know.* Boston: Harvard University Press.

De Jarnett, L. 1996. Knowledge the latest thing. *Information Strategy, The Executives Journal* 12(2): 3-5.

Demerest, M. 1997. Understanding knowledge management. *Journal of Long Range Planning* 30(3): 374-84.

Dervin, B. 1994. Information democracy: an examination of underlying assumptions. *Journal of the American Society for Information Science* 45(6): 365-385.

DiMattia, S. and Oder, N. 1997. Knowledge management: hope, hype or harbinger? *Library Journal* 122(15): 33-35.

Edvinsson, L. 1997. Developing intellectual capital at Skandia. *Long range Planning* 30(3): 366-373.

Emin Civi. 2000. Knowledge management as a competitive asset: a review. *Marketing Intelligence & Planning* 18(4): 166-174.

Forbes. 1997. Knowledge management: the era of shared ideas. *Forbes* 160(6): 28.

Grant, R.M. 1991. The resource-based theory of competitive advantage: implications for strategy formulation. *California Management Review* 30(3): 114-135.

Grayson, C.J. and O'Dell, C.S. 1998. Mining your hidden resources. *Across the Board* April: 23-28.

Gronhaug, K. and Nordhaug, O. 1992. Strategy and competence in firms. *European Management Journal* 10(4): 438-444.

Guthrie, J. 2000. Intellectual capital review: measurement, reporting and management. *Journal of Intellectual Capital* 1(1).

Hayes-Roth, F. and Jacobstein, N. 1994. The state of knowledge-based systems. *Communications of the ACM* 37(3): 27-39.

Hedlund, G. 1994. A model of knowledge management and the N-Form Corporation. *Strategic Management Journal* 15: 73-90.

Hibbard, J. 1997. Knowing what we know. *Information week* 653(20): 46-64.

Hibbard, J. and Carillo, K.M. 1998. Knowledge revolution getting employees to share what they know is no longer technology challenge. *Informationweek* 5(January): 663.

Jordan, J. and Jones, P. 1997. Assessing your company's knowledge management style. *Long Range Planning* 30: 392-398.

Koniger, P. and Janowitz, K. 1995. Drowing in information, but thirst for knowledge. *International Journal of Information Management* 15(1): 111-125.

Kuhn, T. 1974. Second thoughts on paradigms. In Suppe, F. (Ed.),

The search for philosophical scientific theories. Chicago: University of Illinois.

Lank, E. 1997. Leveraging invisible asset: the human factor. *Journal of Long Range Planning* 30(3): 406-412.

Mayo, A. 1998. Memory bankers. *People Management* 4(2): 34-38.

McLoughlin, H. and Thorpe, R. 1993. Action learning – a paradigm in emergence: the problems facing a challenge to traditional management education and development. *British Journal of Management* 4:19-27.

Manville, B. and Foote, N. 1996. Harvest your workers' knowledge. *Datamation,* July.

Marakas, G.M. 1999. *Decision support systems in the twenty-first century.* Engelwood Cliffs: Prentice Hall.

Nonaka, I. 1991. The knowledge-creating company. *Harvard Business Review* 6(8): 96-104.

Nonaka, I. and Takeuchi, K. 1995. *The knowledge creating company: How Japanese companies create the dynamics of innovation.* Oxford: Oxford University Press.

Piggot, S.E.A. 1997. Internet commerce and knowledge management – the next megatrends. *Business Information Review* 14(4): 169-172.

Polanyi, M. 1962. *Personal knowledge: Towards a post critical philosophy.* New York: Harper Torchbooks.

Poynder, R. 1998. Getting to the nuts and bolts of knowledge management. *Information World Review* April: 20.

Quinn, J.B., Anderson, P. and Finkelstein, S. 1996. Managing professional intellect: making the most of the best. *Harvard Business Review* March-April: 71-80.

Quintas, P., Lefree, P. and Jones, G. 1997. Knowledge management: a strategic agenda. *Journal of Long Range Planning* 30(3): 385-391.

Realin, J.A. 1997. A model of work-based learning. *Organization Science* 8(6): 563-578.

Roberts, II. 1998. The bottom line of competence-based management: management accounting, control and performance measurement. *Journal of Knowledge Management* 4(3): 204-216.

Rodney, M. and Sandra, M. 1999. A critical review of knowledge management methods. *The Learning Organization* 6(3): 91-100.

Roos, J., Roos, G., Edvinsson, L. and Dragonetti, N.C. 1997.

Intellectual capital navigating in the new business landscape. New York: Prentice Hall.

Rutihinda, C. 1996. *Resource-based internalization.* Stockholm: AB.

Shum, S.B. 1997. Negotiating the construction and reconstruction of organizational memories. *Journal of Universal Computer Science* 3(8): 899-928.

Tapscott, D. 1999. *Growing up digital.* New York: McGraw Hill.

Taylor, F., John, K., Marcell, Y. and Parker, J. 1997. The knowledge in the organization. *International Journal of Technology Management* 11(3): 385-391.

6

Knowledge Sharing and Digital Libraries in Indonesia: Facing Lot of Constraints and Challenges to Disseminate The S&T Information for the Society

Bambang Setiarso

ABSTRACT

The purpose of this an article is to gain a better understanding of how some factors are critical for the successful application of knowledge sharing and digital libraries. Knowledge sharing and digital libraries with a new paradigm covers a wide range of functionalities and support different sets of activities. Therefore, to achieve knowledge sharing, this work limits the field of investigation to that knowledge sharing models, devoted to the formalization and sharing of best practices and experiences within the organization.

Usability issues should be considered during the model of knowledge sharing in order to build systems which people with limited technological skills and readily use, we discuss two key forms of knowledge sharing usability, interface usability and the human-computer-interaction has helped model knowledge sharing principles to improve interface usability.

We cover the following phases with a new paradigm:

(1) The dimension shift is quite obvious with respect to knowledge sharing from an organizational perspective,

(2) The communicative dimension of knowledge sharing is also increasingly relevant as a means of organizing learning processes as collaborative, cooperative, exchange knowledge processe,

(3) Knowledge sharing in the communicative paradigm which at least with respect to the topic, self-organizing paradigm will have major consequences for librarians work and the structure and information transfer institutions.

Also the development of digital libraries among academic and research institutions libraries in Indonesia is relatively new. What ever their progress, usually the digitalization encountered three constraints that are administrative, technical and cultural ones.

INTRODUCTION

There are many definitions about digital library, however, this paper used the definition taken from Digital Library Federation which stated that digital library as organizations that provide the science and technology resources, including the specialized staff, to select, structure, offer intellectual access to interpret, distribute, preserve the integrity of, end ensure the persistence over time of collections of digital works so that they are readily and economically available for use by defined community or set of communities.

The elements that have been identified as common to those definitions are:

1. a digital library is a managed S& T collection of digital objects
2. the digital objects are created or collected according to principles of S&T collection development
3. the digital objects are made available in a cohesive manner, supported by services necessary to allow users to retrieve and exploit the resources just as they would any other library materials
4. the digital objects are treated as long-term stable S&T resources and appropriate process are applied to them to ensure their quality and survivability (Deegan and Tanner 2002).

HISTORICAL BACKGROUND

The establishment of digital library in Indonesia began in 1999 (Fahmi 2001) when the team of Computer Network Research Group (CNRG) of Bandung Institute of Technology (hereafter called ITB), Knowledge Management Research Group (KRMG) ITB and the ITB Library are working together in developing a system called ganesha (the name of wisdom God in Hindu belief) Digital Library (GDL) which explored the possibility of research document digitalization. In 1999 the GDL vesion 1 and 2 was tested at the ITB Library conducted by librarians, students and lecturers attached to the KMRG.

In June 2000 International Development Research Centre (IDRC) of Canada provided a grant of US $ 60,000 for the development of the system, ordering software, training, the installment of hardware and software, seminar, workshops and the dissemination of the result. As the first step, the KRMG set up as Internet site called *Indonesian Digital Library Network* with its sites http://www.itb.ac.id. The website launching was conducted in August 2000 covering the project's mission, method, framework,development, a mailing list and others. GDL version 3 was launched in October 2002, covering undergraduate final works, master's theses, dissertation produced by ITB through its websites http://digital.lib.ac.id.

In October 2000 in a workshop in Bandung, the

participants agreed to change the name form IDLN to IndonesiaDLN which destined to be the first digital library network in Indonesia (http://ideln.itb.ac.id) Indonesia DLN's mission is to unlock knowledge of Indonesian people, especially the local content, and share it nationally (Fahmi 2002). It means to provide information about Indonesia such as students' final project, theses, dissertations, research reports, heritage, regional potency, etc. Aftermath the librarians which participated in the seminar established a form called the Indonesian Cyberlibrary Society (ICS) with its forum i_c_s@yahoogroups.com. Making it as the first virtual discussion forum for Indonesian librarians.

Meanwhile State Ministry of Research and Technology, here after called KMNRT, issued a software for digital library called *Docushare.* KMNRT awarded the software to the higher education institutions. This software pushed the development of academic digital library faster because the awardees can utilized the software. By early 2003 there are 3 institutions which got the docushare and there is a programme to widen its by the year 2003.

Pendit (2002) classified the initiatives toward the development of digital libraries in Indonesia into 4 groups. The first group is in the university, pioneered by research group in ITB with its software Ganesha Digital Library and latter on with Indonesia Digital Library Network, commonly shortened into IndonesiaDLN. The second group located in the government offices like *Warung Informasi Teknologi* or Warintek which as a goal to reach the greater part of the community.

From digital point of view the mission content education and appropriate technology. The third group also located at the government offices however it has bigger mission and wider than the second group. This digitalization activities conducted as a part of e-government. This group include the department offices in Jakarta as well as at regencies and towns which provide information through Internet. The fourth group focused on arts, more on preservation of national and local heritage such as conducted by Universitas Kristen Petra (Petra Christian University) in Surabaya with its project called

Surabaya heritage and the national Library which digitized Johannes Krachts Drawings.

SCIENCE AND TECHNOLOGY INFORMATION

Indonesia Institute of Sciences (LIPI) has been a referered centre for science and technology in Indonesia. This institute has a scientific capability to produce numerous scientific discovery and services. Some of products have been utilized by stakeholders, namely industries, and government institutes for the benefit of the people. However this system should be strengthened and improved by efficient and effective science communication programmes : such as science briefing, industry relation, public advocacy, press release, etc. Knowledge based resource management plays important role in this endeavour. The Centre for Scientific Documentation and Information, The Centre for Innovation, Bereau for Cooperation and Popularising Science and technology work together to bring science to the people for their better life.

The Indonesia Institute of Sciences which is in Indonesian is called as Lembaga Ilmu Pengetahuan Indonesia, abbreviated by LIPI as a research institution which is owned by the Government of the Republic of Indonesia. It carries a main task to assist the President of the Republic of Indonesia in developing science policy in Indonesia. The coverage of LIPI task are organizing research and development, providing guidance and services to scientific and technological enterprises and conducting strategic and fundamental research in science and technology.

LIPI has 19 research centers ranging from hard scaiences to social sciences, 3 supported centers, 4 Bureaus which are responsible for any administrative matters, 20 technical implementation units and a number of research stations. The location of those units are scattered in the Indonesia archipelago, from Sumatra island until Irian Jaya island.

LITERALLY MEANS CAFÉ FOR SCIENCE AND TECHNOLOGY

In the field of library and information sector, LIPI conducts Warintek Programme in Iptekda scheme during the fiscal years of 1998-1999. The pilot project is located at Palembang, South Sumatra. Later, the first Warintek was established in Palembang and it was derived from the phenomena of that improving intense remote communication amongst society in the field of production, trade, research, education and cultural aspects. The aim of establishing Warintek are to support society understanding on the importance of information, to encourage Warintek users having ability to seek information when they need and to locate, evaluate information and to use information effectively. Warintek Pilot Project in Palembang provides catalogue on selected databases and internet lines.

The existence of Warintek is critically important in the situation where technology changes very fast and the availability of information in different formats exists. If people have no information access point, their condition probably could be worsen.

Warintek tries to facilitate its users such as teachers, local research, and development unit and units SME's to access information with affordable price. Futhermore, LIPI can share its knowledge more effective because warintek will able to support its local stakeholders. So far, Warintek programme which is a kind of cyber café, is considered successful.

Because this programme is considered successful, the Ministry of Coordinating Science and Technology is offering small Warintek program to be a national scaled programme. The argument is the program is inline with the National Strategic Policy on Science and Technology Information accessibility and utilizing the advance of global information infrastructure. Then, Warintek is launched by the Ministry of Coordination Science and Technology.

In the development of Warintek, there is a need to launch Warintek 9000. The 9000 indicates the amount of Warintek will be in the year of 2008. This ambitious programme is aimed at supporting the better quality of bereucrats, administration services, improving local government integrated management information systems, improving human resources development, etc.

Through the above examples, it is indicated that information access in Indonesia leans on the availability of infrastructure supported by information (content), information resources, policy and legal aspects.

KNOWLEDGE SHARING PROCESESS

Drucker (1993) described knowledge, rather than capital or labour as the only meaningful resource in the knowledge society, and Senge (1990) has warned that many organizations are unable to function as knowledge based organizations, because they suffer from learning disabilities. Strategies to investigate knowledge management would be to increase the level of social interaction that occurs in the organization, as only some of which may be technologically assisted, Earl and Scott (1999), Bontis (2001).

To some extent, every human process issues is a key success factor. Every one has been important since people first formed organizations to accomplish tasks too big to be performed by individuals working alone and every one will continue to be a challenge as long as people work together.

DEFINITION

Although Knowledge Management concepts have been around for a long time, the term " *Knowledge Management*" seems to have arisen in the mid-70s. Nicholas Henry (1974) uses "*knowledge management*" in a manner that resembles our current understanding of the expression.

Defined broadly " *KM is the process through which organizations extract value from their intellectual assets*" (Kaplan, 2002).

"*Knowledge Management*" caters to the critical issues of organizational adaptation, survival and competence in face of increasingly discountinuous environmental change. Essentially, it embodies organizational processes that seek synergistic combination of data and information processing capacity of information technologies and the creative and innovative capacity of human beings" (Malhotra, 1997).

THE TERM OF KNOWLEDGE SHARING

Knowledge sharing aims to do something useful with knowledge and enhance knowledge sharing is made in two paradigm: one paradigm is to manage existing knowledge, which includes developing of knowledge repositories (memos, reports, articles, reports), knowledge compilation, etc. Another paradigm is to manage knowledge-specific activities, that is, knowledge acquisitions, creation, distribution, communication, sharing and application (Stenmark, 2001).

Knowledge management consists of the administration of knowledge assets of an organization and sharing and enlargement of those assets.

KNOWLEDGE SHARING PROCESESS

For the next phases: best practices should be shared within the company's network, though it is understood that in current, networked. Companies today live in knowledge ecologies where one company feeds knowledge into another. Therefore, the firm's openness to external experts and the sharing of ideas.

A very important area of knowledge management is *how to encourage people to share what they know.* Usually knowledge is considered to be a source of power, and by not sharing, a person is increasing his or her personal value to the organization thus making him/herself less likely to be replaced, for this reason, it is important to encourage people to share instead of hoarding knowledge. To solve this, it is vital to make sure that knowledge sharing is encouraged and that the people in possession of the knowledge understand the benefits of sharing it. Coleman suggests that" *a clearer lingkage between knowledge sharing and business benefits may motivate workers to take the time to share what they know*" .

Hence, the quest for each organization is to value constributions from its individual. By doing so, more constributions will be encouraged since it will become clear that *sharing knowledge does not imply losing it.* Sharing knowledge will only generate new knowledge and increase the value of the organization as well as its individuals. On this matter, Agren Olofsson and Persson point out that "*real competitiveness stems from being willing to share, and not the other way around, and that it is crucial to get this point across to the people who are supposed to do the sharing".*

Agren, Olofsson and Persson also identify the prerequisites for knowledge sharing. These prerequisites are an encouraging environment, motivation, and forums in which to share providing relevant information and making it accessible and giving the employees sufficient time to share their knowledge.

As a means to motivate people to share their knowledge, many organizations use incentives. However, as another side of the coin. Fitzek referring to Kleiner and Roth, brings forward another important aspect in relation to the incentive system. They state, that people becoming aware of being judged and measured seek to satisfy the evaluation criteria instead of improving their capabilities. The intrinsic motivation, which drives learning and knowledge transfer, is then supplanted by the desire to look successful. Yet evaluation is vital to learning as a feedback process that provide guidance and support, from explicit to combination and then get explicit to internalization, and then tacit need socialization to get tacit also externalization to explicit.

KNOWLEDGE SHARING PHASES

Knowledge Sharing Phases, that model an integrated approach to identifying, capturing, evaluating, retrieving, and sharing all of an enterprise's information assets. These assets may include databases, documents, policies, procedures, and previously uncaptured expertise and experience in individual workers.

In this kind of projects, major emphasis is put into trying to *capture knowledge* and to *treat knowledge* from the researchers LIPI (Indonesian Institute of Sciences) who create and use the knowledge. According to Davenport et al, " *there are three types of knowledge repositories : external knowledge, structured internal knowledge and informal internal knowledge".* For capturing external knowledge , competitive intelligence systems are used. These systems can filter, synthesize and add context to information from the external environment in order to make it more valuable, including this kind of knowledge, referred to as tacit, is not structured as a document and is therefore not easily converted.

Improving knowledge access and transfer, this kind put emphasis on activities providing access to knowledge or facilitating its transfer between researchers and users, one aspect of this is difficulty in finding the person with the desired knowledge and then effectively transferring it from that person to another. One activity of this kind is a community of practice, which can be either online-communities or face-to-face communities. A community of researchers LIPI is a group of people sharing knowledge, learning together and creating. Community researchers LIPI members frequently help each other to solve problems and develop new approaches for their field. Other examples of activities to improve knowledge access and transfer are workshops, seminars and different kinds of networks. Desktop video conferencing system, document scanning and other sharing tools are examples, which supports the communication of knowledge between researchers who would not otherwise work together, and hence, improve knowledge transfer.

SHARING KNOWLEDGE EFFECTIVELY

Many input that LIPI got from working in partnership with CSIRO. A lesson that is learned from CSIRO is no matter how good the researches LIPI does, it becomes less meaningful if it is not share. An important advice from CSIRO is that LIPI needs to strengthen its science communications activities. An effective marketing communications strategy in every year must be developed and evaluated at the end of the year. LIPI has to address its work to various audiences through the appropriate means or channels. Among the audiences are stake holder, personnel, government, industry, media and public.

To respond to the advise, LIPI have to look at its strengths, weaknesses and what it had been done in the past. This institute has a scientific capability to produce numerous scientific discovery and services. Some of its products have been utilized by stakeholders, namely industries, and government institutes for the benefit of the people. Good work of the public relation office contributed to its success. However that work of the public relation office contributed to its success. However that work is not enough. Therefore this system should be strengthened and improved by efficient and effective science communications programmes, such as science briefing, industry relation, press release, etc. to respond to the development of every aspects in the world as a whole.

Beside providing assistance for small and medium scale industry, LIPI also builds relations to large scale industries. Working with industry means using industry to be the mediator between research and the people who get the benefits from the research. Industry will facilitate to change the research to become a product used by the people. Communications to the industries is maintained through informal personal approach between LIPI's executives and top executives of industries, industry briefing, regular meetings between LIPI and industries, meeting with industry associations, industry visit, forum industry and information to industry. So far, LIPI starts to develop co-operation in the filed of research and development activities with engineering industry for preparing a pilot plan for oleo chemical industry and national food industries, pharmaceutical industries, cosmetics industries, herbal medicine industries in the filed of product development. LIPI also provides services for industries which services on measurement, standard, and testing quality.

LIPI realize that sharing its knowledge using media means sharing the knowledge to people as a whole as media can reach people even in a remote distance.

Sharing knowledge from research institution to the outside world is a must and important in order that outside world know what the institutions does and the fact that they are one entity, that is the unity between the supplier (producer) and the user. In a simple way, it can indirectly be transmitted in the form of marketing communications of the institution.

There is always an excellent co-operation inside as organization to perform a great task, that is the contribution of the related units responsible to perform the task. Within LIPI, the Centre for Scientific Documentation and Information (PDII) is responsible for providing S&T information.

ORGANIZATIONAL LEARNING

Organizational Learning, specialists point out the heavy investment in ICT by institutions to transfer information and knowledge and make them available at the institutional level. QL specialist point out that technology approach is a purely mechanistic solution to information issues. They should consider these solutions as naively promoting software and hardware packages to resolve KM problems. QL experts claim that information technology has never addressed the tacit knowledge, which includes not only the actions, expertise, and ideas of staff, but also the values and emotions of staff. QL emphasizes that the efficiency and effectiveness of knowledge workers depends mostly on how workers communicate and collaborate in their efforts and expose themselves to communities of practice within the institution as well as outside the institution.

In terms of a general model for KS and QL, a descriptive model is proposed integrating explicit knowledge, tacit knowledge, and the infrastructure. Explicit knowledge and tacit knowledge have a symbiotic relationship whereby tacit knowledge contributes to explicit knowledge. Some examples of explicit knowledge are found in the following: commercial publications, organizational business records: web, groupware: intranets, databases, and self-study material. Similarly, some examples of tacit knowledge are reflected in: face to face conversation, both formal and informal: telephone conservations, both formal and informal, the knowledge that individuals possess in their heads as well as in their desk drawers and file cabinets.

Enhancing knowledge environment, unlike data or information, knowledge is created invisibly in the human brain and only the accurate organizational climate can influence researchers to create, reveal, share and use this knowledge. This kind of activities to establish an environment constributing to a more effective knowledge creation, sharing and use. Activities involved are trying to build awareness and cultural attention to knowledge sharing, a culture supporting knowledge environment eliminates researchers possible reluctance for sharing knowledge.

This activities are trying to change behaviour and attitude within the organization researchers need to fell part of the knowledge network and in some cases this may imply having to learn to trust colleagues in a new way. Knowledge, which previously has been kept individually, is to be shared. Therefore, part of enhancing the knowledge environment is making clear that a win-win situation will be the result, both for the organization and for the individual. Other activities make efforts to change the organizational norms and values related to knowledge and to support and promote the re-use of different kinds of knowledge, so that the new culture needs to be developed to become a natural way of working.

Many of the features in enhancing the knowledge environment of an organization, such as behavioural changes, are not developed rapidly. Researchers may need to learn how to work a bit differently than what they are used to, since sharing not always comes naturally.

To ensure an overall organizational performance, the organization needs to manage and measure their technological, human and financial resources. One knowledge learning consists of a communication system on the organization's both intranet or internet, which is linked to a database. In this database researchers may share for instance repair tips, which they all may access from their laptops. When many researchers are traveling on the job, this means they will not have to miss out on any information that normally may have been shared among them, as a learning process.

To encourage knowledge sharing the organizations observe and encourage active involvement. Some organizations use incentive systems, others post lessons learned and success stories to motivate knowledge sharing among researchers.

ORGANIZATIONAL KNOWLEDGE MANAGEMENT AND KNOWLEDGE SHARING SYSTEMS

Organizational Knowledge Management/ Sharing System, most of the concrete applications of knowledge management described to date consist of creating and supporting communities of shared interest and information need. Current knowledge management thinking is almost entirely about establishing the structure and the climate to enable and encourage those who have knowledge to share it.

Knowledge management is in essence an organizing principle, which lays foundation for capturing the potential of the possessed knowledge within an organization. The knowledge content of products and services is increasing and their is a need to add competence and the knowledge surrounding the product in order to become more competitive. To make the most of the organization's and enhance knowledge sharing it is important to acknowledge that it is about managing both technology and researchers in order to provide a beneficial knowledge-sharing environment.

At IIS, there are several ways of motivating researchers to exchange their knowledge. Top management involvement and commitment are of huge important and a prerequisite for a successful knowledge management project. Management can promote knowledge sharing by repeadtedly emphasize its importance for the whole IIS. There are also workshops and training to introduce users to the advantages of knowledge sharing. It is of vital importance for the researchers to understand that knowledge sharing is important. One needs to understand this, not only for efficiency's sake, but also to increase the essential humanization of social environtment. One way of encourage knowledge sharing is, when working in different systems, letting a researcher accumulate points, which can be exchanged for a variety of knowledge-related events.

Researchers are awarded with conference facilities through website, telecommunication equipment, depending on the number of shared accumulated during a year. The number of shares given to the contributor depends on the re-use feedback of the taker of knowledge, thus rewarding the usefulness of the transferred knowledge. Based on this feedback, knowledge of lesser quality can be removed from share-net, whereas high-quality knowledge can be highlighted and further developed. This process leads to a constantly improving quality of the available knowledge. The purpose of implementing knowledge sharing among research center as the research organizations is to take advantage of the available research results and improve its transfer between individuals. The majority of the participating research organizations have established some kind of technological platform to facilitate knowledge sharing. The structured document storage appears on a majority of organizations, and is usually databases with document where documents may be shared. Another common activity among research center at IIS is that have implemented systems to facilitate the communication between researchers in various locations of the IIS organization. communities of researchers, or discussion databases, in which researchers may contact other researchers and share their experiences appear frequently. To be able to locate the right person at the right time is a paramount issue when trying to take advantage of the knowledge embedded in the IIS organization. There are also face-to-face communities, workshops and seminar held in order for researchers from various parts of the IIS organization, as well as externally, to get together and share their experiences on various topics.

SUSTAINABLE COMPETITIVE ADVANTAGE

Knowledge Management is generally understood as a means of having better control over the production and usage of explicit and tacit knowledge in organizations of any kind, preferably business, but also public administration or research center. Using and applying tacit and explicit knowledge to solve the problem, also the result of communication processes, this can be called the network or communications approach to knowledge sharing.

Knowledge sharing in the communicative paradigm which at least with respect to the topic, self-organizing paradigm will have major consequences for librarians work and the structure and information transfer institutions, so that the paradigm shift is quite obvious with respect to knowledge sharing from an organizational perspective. The paradigm shift towards communicative knowledge sharing has also consequence from an Indonesian culture perspective, the communicative paradigm of knowledge sharing is also increasingly relevant as a means of organizing learning processes as collaborative, cooperative, exchange knowledge processes, KS also dramatically changes the way how the production and the exchange knowledge is and will be organized in scientific environment.

The majority of the organizations states the purpose is to increase knowledge sharing and to make the most of the collective knowledge they possess in order to meet users needs more efficiently. As of today, the projects are about connecting researchers in communities and networks to establish new relationships and gain experience. Databases, which store documentation to enable re-use at later points, are common, as well as researcher-directories to help locating the right person at the right time. The KS studied, are in line with Davenport's categorization. Projects that fall in the first category are projects focused on storing documents with knowledge embedded. These are stored in a repository where can easily be accessed. This type of activities stands out among the participating organizations. This involves community-based electronic discussion and lessons learned, which also appear among the studied organizations. By posting lessons learned, the researchers may see what has been generated from taking part of the stored knowledge.

In Davenport's second category are projects, which provide access to knowledge as well as facilitate its transfer. Earlier, a problematic area has been to locate the researcher who has the desired knowledge and then being able to transfer this knowledge to the researcher in need of it. By implementing system similar to directory this problem is solved. Even though the PDII organization directories of researchers take slightly different form, for instance handling complete researcher profiles, they all aim to keep track of who knows what within the PDII organization in order to provide the competence of a specific researcher at the right time and place.

Davenport's third category are activity focusing on changing behaviour and attitudes as well as organizational norms and values. In order to fully be able to take advantage of the knowledge embedded in the organization there is the implication that individuals must feel comfortable sharing what they know. Also, apart from being willing to share what they know themselves, it is also important that they feel comfortable using somebody else's solution to a problem. When studying the participating organizations from this perspective there are a few differences that stand out. The PDII organizations mention a lack of focus on sharing knowledge in the organizational culture, even though it is about to change. This reluctance may stem from the idea of researcher feeling that they may easier be replaced if the do not have some kind of unique knowledge which makes them irreplaceable. There is also general encouragement to knowledge sharing, as well as efforts to introduce the benefits of knowledge sharing to researchers by having workshops and seminars. These activities are vital in order for researches to begin, and then continue, sharing what they know.

From the foregoing discussion above of this paper, it is clear that a knowledge networked society will have profound impacts in different walks of life and their is a distinct possibility of the life style changing completely. The promise made to the common man by the knowledge networked society can be stated as "*A*" raised to the power of five: *anyone, anytime, anywhere, any knowledge, and any format.*

A full-fledged the knowledge networked society implies that every researchers have an access to the network. Network connectivity to home would become an essential infrastructural facility. Anywhere has implication for researchers who are accessing knowledge as well as for the knowledge resources being accessed. A knowledge networked society should pose no transborder barriers and be able to communicate knowledge in any format.

Network personal computers or simply NetPCs are based on advanced microprocessors and are specially architectured using hardware and software techniques to provide maximum efficiency under knowledge networked environment, NetPCs would support a variety of sophisticated network access protocols and navigation mechanisms in attempt to make network access as user-friendly as possible. Network computing implies powerful server machines on the network instead of powerful client or end-users systems. Multimedia PCs will have specially designed architecture and configuration to handle multimedia applications. The emphasis on multimedia PCs is to provide adequate local computing power to run multimedia applications.

Communication infrastructure and powerful personal computers tell only one half of the story of the knowledge networked society. Other important components include data, information and knowledge bases and the associated knowledge management techniques and the navigation mechanisms required for accessing these bases. In order to substantiate the view point of knowledge explosion, one tends to quote the annual publication figures such as one million journal issues, hundred thousands monographs, one million patents and tens of thousand of reports and dissertations. Apart from the current knowledge, the world has been accumulating knowledge over millions of years which are stored in different forms in different parts of the world. This knowledge, when digitized would perhaps run into several million terabytes. Perhaps, a large knowledge of the researchers would spend its time in evolving effective and efficient knowledge management techniques.

CONSTRAINTS

Knowledge sharing and digital libraries encountered various constraints when they digitized the documents or shareds. Those constratints are as follow:

a. Manpower : Digitizing documents need computer-literate-library staff while some of the library staffs belong to techno-phobia category.

b. From cultural point of view : Access to Internet is still very low, less than 10% of the population. The users still use the printed matters because it is more convenient than the electronic ones. However, behind this resistance also the technology awkwardness among users to sharing their knowledge including the researchers.

c. Policy for publishing point of view : The constraints originated from those who are afraid of plagiarism owing to the accessibility of the digitized documents and the heavy burden of digitizing activities. The pros argued thay by digitizing the documents, the result increased the institutions research's prestigate as well as has social value for the society.

d. Copyright infringement : Many research centers especially head of research center still afraid of copyright infringement caused by the easy character of the digital library.

SUMMARY

Knowledge Management/knowledge sharing is in essence an organizing principle, which lays foundation for capturing the potentials of the possessed knowledge within an organization. To make the most of the organizations resources and enhance knowledge sharing it is important to acknowledge that it is about managing both technology and people in order to provide a beneficial knowledge sharing environment. Knowledge Sharing and digital libraries projects aims to do something useful by structuring people, information technology and knowledge content. Some of the projects are based on IT-systems. While others put emphasis on relationships and communications based on networks. However, a majority of the **KS** projects emphasize activities for managing, sharing, creating and distributing knowledge within an organization.

I understand that the researchers participating organizations in this **KS** are storing the knowledge locally and are also sending them to the Central Servers. What we need at this time is also concurrent measures to make very useful and highly user-friendly interfaces. This will make the **KS** a friend of every one and its utility would enhance many folds. It is important that we take on this **KS** of integrating all forms of knowledge sharing into our digital form.

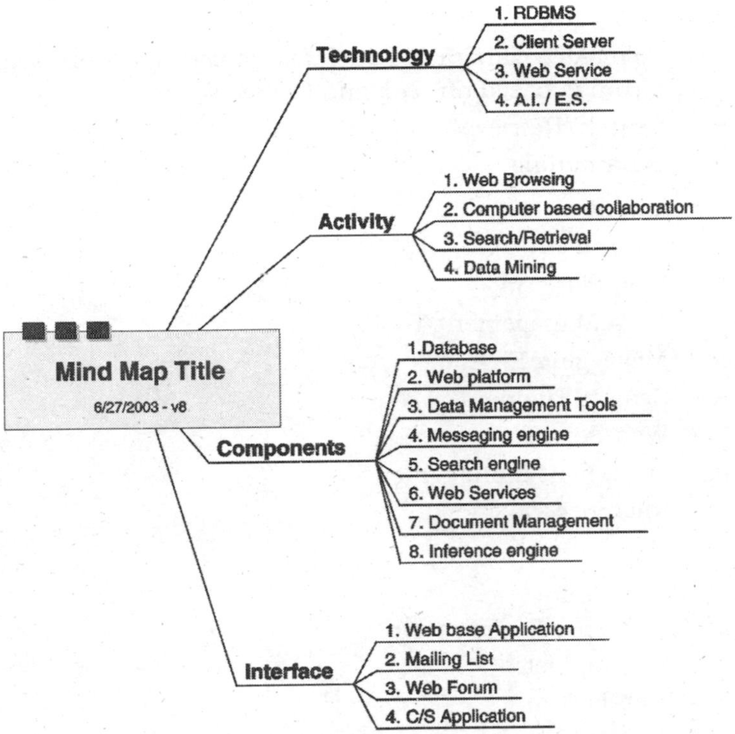

Fig. 1. A Conceptual form Digital Library and Knowledge Sharing Systems

Technology

a. Technology *Database Relational* (RDMBS)

RDBMS systems should be *portability* and *scalability*

b. *Client Server.*

Client server approach which used to *web based client server (PHP)* and *conventional client server (Delphi, VB,* etc)

c. Web Service

Client server technology is used by team.

Artificial Intelligence / Expert Systems as a tools for building the systems.

Activities

a. Web Browsing

To make an *interface web*.

b. Computer based collaboration

To make collaboration such as : *mailing list*, discussion forum is based on *web* and GDSS

c. Search/Retrieval

d. Data mining

Components

a. Database
b. Web Platform
c. Data Management Tools
d. Mesagging Engine
e. Search Engine
f. Web Service
g. Document Management
h. Inference Engine
i. etc

Interface

a. Web based application
b. Mailing List
c. Web Forum
d. C/S Application

etc

REFERENCES

Blacker, F. (1993). Knowledge and the Theory of Organizations : Organizations as Activity Systems and the Reframing of Management. *Journal of Management Studies 30, no.6: 863-84.*

Boston, J .(2000). The Challenge of evaluating systemic change: the case of public management reform. *International Public Management Journal.* no.3: 23-46.

Choo, C.W. (1995).*Information Management for the Intelligent Organizations: The Art of canning the Environment.* Medford, NJ: Information Today.

Cohen, W.M., and D.A. Levinthal. (1990). Absorptive Capacity : A New Perspective on Learning and Innovation. *Administrative Science Quaterly 35. No.1 (March)* : 128-52.

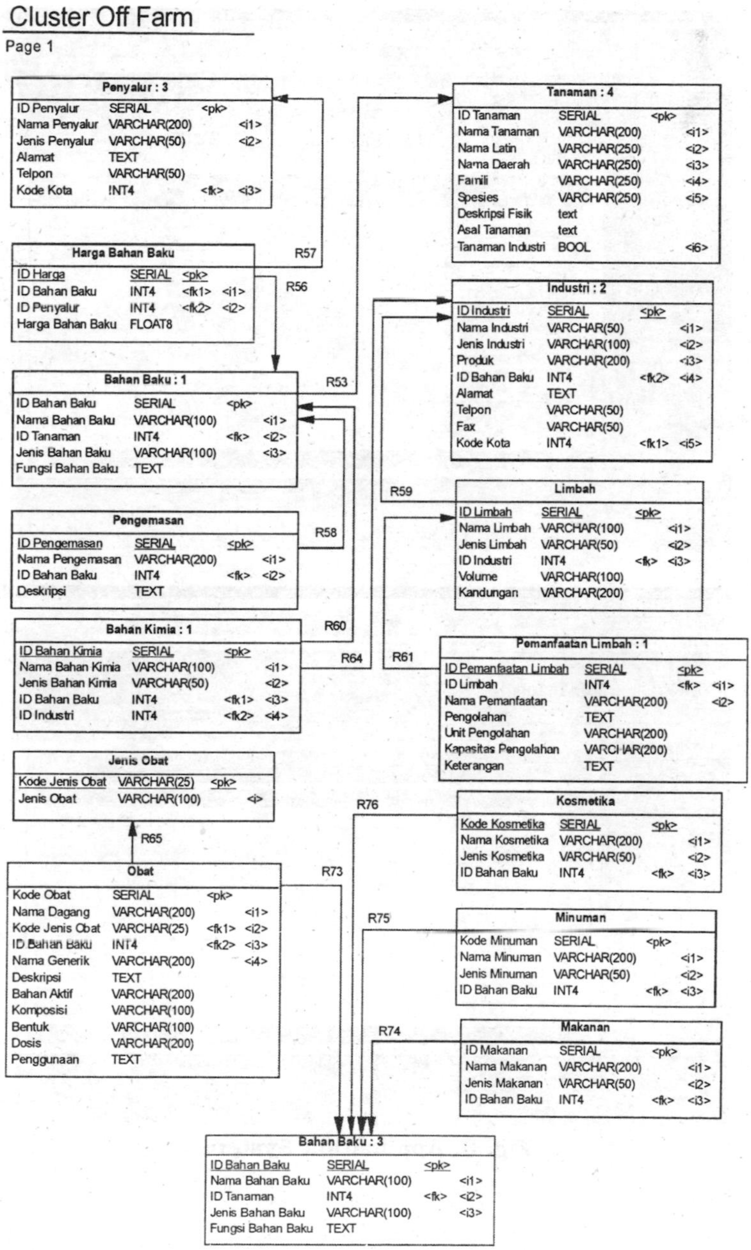

Fig. 2. Example about Cluster off-farm

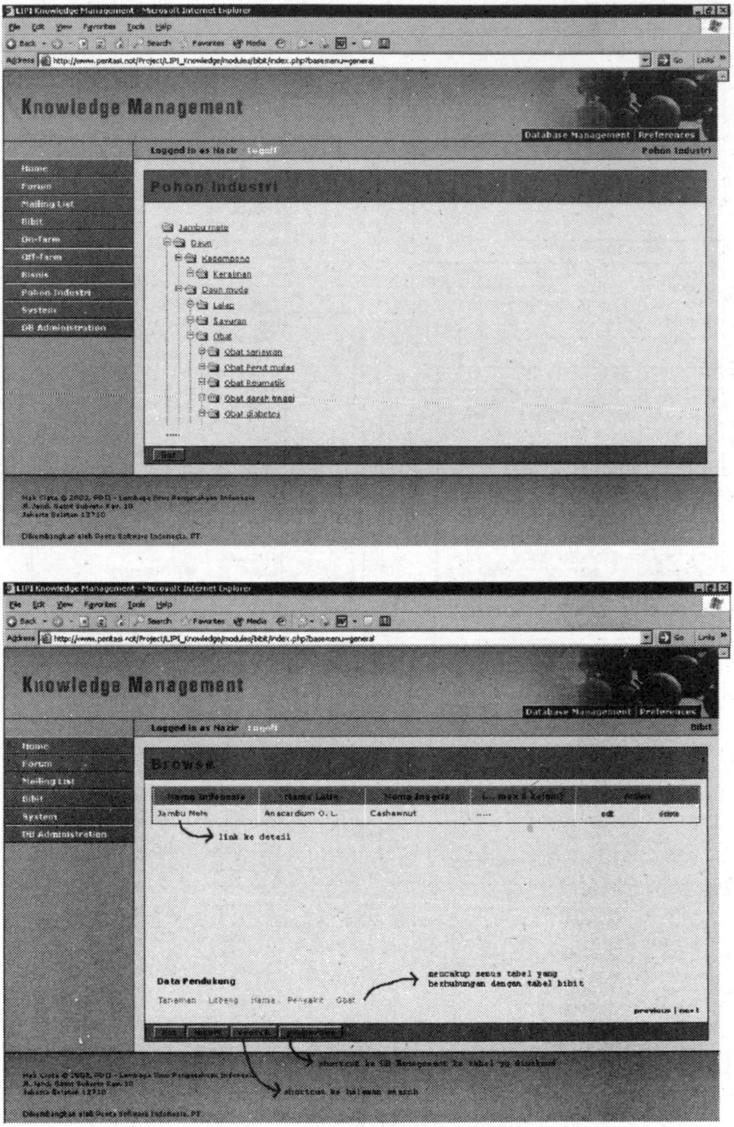

Fig. 3. Application System

Coleman, D. (1999). Groupware Collaboration and Knowledge Sharing . *Knowledge Management Handbook*, New York : CRC Press.

Cribb, Julian and Hartomo, Tjempaka Sari (2002). *Sharing Knowledge : a Guide to effective science communications.* Melbourne , Australia : CSIRO Publishing.

Daft,R.L., and K.E. Weick. (1984). Toward a Model of Organizations as Interpretation Systems. *Academy of Management Review* 9. no.2: 284-95.

Davenport, T.H. (1993). *Process Innovation : Reengineering Work Through Information Technology.* Boston, MA: Harvard Business School Press.

Davenport, T.H.., de Long, D.W. & Beers, M.C. (1998). *Successful Knowledge Management Projects.* Sloan Management Review: 43-57.

Deegan, marilyn and Tanner, Simon (2002). *Digital futures : strategies for the information age.* London : Library Association Publishing.

Ellis. D. (1989). A Behavioural Approach to Information Retrieval System Design. *Journal of Documentation* 45, no3: 171-212.

Emma Orr and Marie Persson. (2003). Performance Indicators for Measuring Performance of Activities in Knowledge Management. Thesis. School of Economics and Commercial Law, University of Gothenburg- Department of Informatics.

International Seminar on Digital Library Network, (2002). Bandung : Proceedings.

INASP Newsletter. (2003). "*Information partnerships and networking*" , no 24. November: 2-15.

Kogut, B., and U.Zander. (1992) . Knowledge of the Firm, Combinative Capabilities and the Replication of technology. *Organization Science* 3, no. 3: 383-97.

Leonard-Barton, D. (1995). *Wellsprings of Knowledge: Building and Sustaining the Sources of Innovation.* Boston, MA: Harvard Business School Press.

Nonaka, I., and H. Takeuchi. (1995). *The Knowledge-Creating Company: How Japanese Companies Create the Dynamics of Innovation.* New York, NY: Oxford University Press.

Setiarso, Bambang (2000). *Science and Technology Information Services in Indonesia : a Case PDII-LIPI.*

Setiarso, Bambang (2004). *Indonesia Traditional Knowledge Management : a case study Cashew Nut Shell Liquit (CNSL).*

New Delhi, India : International Conference on Digital Libraries, 24-27 February 2004: pp.611-620.

Sulistyo-Basuki. (2002). " Digital Libraries as stepping stone toward a wider and better library co-operation and information network among academic libraries in the Asia Pasific region". Paper for 8th Association of Universities in Asia pacific, Forum of learning and sharing. Denpasar-Bali : May 14-17, 2002.

Skyrme, D.J. (2000). *Knowledge Networking. Creating the Collaborative Enterprise.* Read Educational and Professional Publishing Ltd.

Stein, E.W. (1995). Organizational Memory: Review of Concepts and Recommendations for Management. *International Journal of Information Management* 15,no. 2 : 17-32.

7
Levels of Knowledge

Purushothama Gowda M

ABSTRACT

21st century is the Knowledge century . Knowledge production , knowledge use and knowledge dissemination, is an integral activity of the knowledge society. Information and knowledge are not mutually exclusive and contradictory to each other and they rather enrich each other. Mainly there are two types of knowledge viz. Materialistic knowledge and spiritualistic knowledge. The Information in Relation to Knowledge can be classified into three category: Transparent knowledge, Relative knowledge and Independent knowledge. These three principles of knowledge can be applied to any thing under the sun, such as life of Buddha to laws of Newton who formulated the concepts of Kaivalya and theory of gravity, respectively.

INTRODUCTION

Knowledge production, knowledge use and knowledge dissemination, is an inevitable initiative in the current context of Liberalization, Privatization and Globalization (LPG). More importantly in a country with such large population, shifting targets of mere literacy to qualitative education, growing numbers of uneducated youth due to lack of employment opportunities and socio-cultural transformation due to urbanization have brought about a need for providing a direction to the country in terms of what to achieve in the 21st Century which is being termed as Knowledge Century.

WHAT IS KNOWLEDGE

Knowledge is a term, which is used widely and indiscriminately. It ranges from simple information to absolute mastery over any field of knowledge. For a common man if one does not have information of a thing he/she says that he/she has no knowledge of it. Here it is lack of information, which is viewed as synonymous with knowledge. One speaks of oneself as 'I am not a knowledgeable person in this field', it means one who has not reached a level of being 'Very high in regard 'so as to be considered oneself as an authority in that field

For most of philosophical history "Knowledge" was taken to mean a belief that was justified as true to an absolute certainty. Any less justified beliefs were called mere " probable opinion ". Philosophers often define knowledge as a justified , true belief. "In Plato's view knowledge is merely an awareness of absolute, universal Ideas or Forms, existing independent of any subject trying to apprehend them. Though, Aristotle puts more emphasis on logical and empirical methods for gathering knowledge , he still accepts the view that such knowledge is apprehension of necessary and universal principles. Following the renaissance, two main epistemological postions dominated philosophy: *empiricism,* which sees knowledge as the product of sensory perception, and *rationalism,* which sees it as the product of rational reflection".

However, knowledge may in fact be defined as a unique imprint left by an individual for the advancement of the living beings either materialistic or spiritualistic.

INFORMATION VERSUS KNOWLEDGE

Information and knowledge are not mutually exclusive and contradictory to each other. They rather enrich each other and lead to the perfect development of human potential.

Information is the basis for knowledge and knowledge grows as one become informed.

However, while layman's terminology of knowledge is confined to information, intellectual usage goes much beyond this embrace knowledge developed by the self creativity and innovation etc.. Though this kind of division of the functioning of human mind is nothing but simplifying of the complex process, it is quite relevant in the current context where we observe the increasing influence of information over knowledge.

Information according to some educationists is considered as mere acquisition of facts or rote memory and knowledge as a mental process that take shape in the mind or an intellectual process. Which has very little or nothing to do with outside elements. Emphatically speaking the society is slowly drifting from knowledge based society to information –based society and human being have become transponders of information rather then the repository of knowledge. This is mainly because of the revolutionary development of Information Communication Technology (ICT).

TYPES OF KNOWLEDGE

Knowledge can be two types:

(i) Materialistic Knowledge (Excellent Attainment) The western concept of Knowledge, which is related to development, and takes place to further the cause of materialistic achievement, is one kind of Knowledge.

(ii) Spiritualistic Knowledge (development of Soul) The development of soul in which the things beyond materialistic life and existence are given importance.

CLASSIFICATION OF INFORMATION IN RELATION TO KNOWLEDGE

Knowledge philosophically is distinct from simple information. Both knowledge and information consist of true statements, but knowledge is information that has a purpose of use. Philosophers would describe this as information associated with intentionality.

Knowledge = Information + Intention

On the basis of the above the following classification can be made based on different types of intention, levels of comprehension and ingenuity.

(i) Transparent knowledge (Information devoid of knowledge)

i.e. Information + Deviant Intention (unorganized collection of information in bits and pieces, ignorance, lack of interest, different goals etc.)

(ii) Relative knowledge (Information intertwined with knowledge).

i.e. Information +Intention +Comprehension.

(iii) Independent knowledge (knowledge beyond the realm of Information).

i.e. Information +Intention +Comprehension +Ingenuity

However, the above classification cannot be considered as independent entities. They are on a continuum and if all the three are to be placed on a scale of attainment of Knowledge of 0-100% then it can be shown as below.

0% 100%

Transparent Relative Independent

Though absolute Zero and absolute 100 do not exist, as any information will not be absolutely transparent, there will be a certain amount of retention. While Independent knowledge can never be 100%, as it will also have the impact of previously accumulated information and information related understanding.

TRANSPARENT KNOWLEDGE (INFORMATION DEVOID OF KNOWLEDGE)

Under this knowledge is considered as transparent because it comes in and goes out with hardly any retention. Acquiring information i.e. acquisition of facts is considered as a reflex action, which does not require any thinking process. "Knowledge is an appreciation of the possession of interconnected details, which in isolation, are of lesser value". But in Transparent knowledge things are often learnt in isolation or in disconnected fashion. For example things, which are learnt in rote memory, would remain in memory in separate blocks and unless they are linked together they cannot be comprehended. As long as repeated recollection or memorizing of the things take place, they are retained and once when it stops automatically they are removed from the memory. In simple terms, the processing of information that takes place as follows:

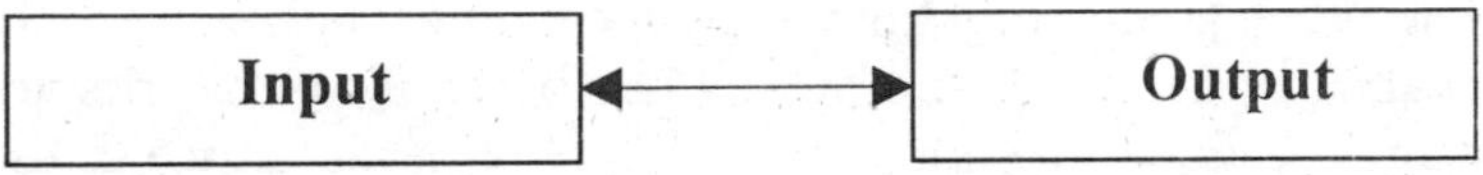

Here one can see that there is a two way direction of arrow between input and output which means, things are received and reflected like rays without any kind of processing involved in it. The best example for this is rote memory through which things are recollected. This is what is leading to transparent Knowledge, in the world of information revolution. Because the things are not taught in relation to each other but presented to the student in abstract terms. Transparent knowledge does not involve in looking at the things with body, mind and soul put together. In the modern educational system there is an enormous predominance of this information loaded teaching-learning-evaluation pattern. It makes the student breathless in acquisition of facts and leaves no room for their comprehension. In this process the students are treated as audio or videotapes, which are used for recording and replay.

The transparent knowledge is not to be confused with memory because in memory only biological process is involved whereas under knowledge, it is intention, which is a social act that plays a dominant role in addition to the biological activity. In case of transparent knowledge the purpose of acquiring the information is not with the intention of fulfillment of the objective, but something else. For example if a student collects a piece of information, not with the intention of developing an interest in that or further processing of it but to satisfy the teacher by reproducing it so that he gets a good impression of the teacher, he is acquiring transparent knowledge.

The purpose of acquiring such knowledge is mainly to serve the immediate purpose rather than the ultimate aim of attaining still higher levels of knowledge. Another example is if a student intends to score good marks in a subject of study, and strives to pursue that with more emphasis on obtaining marks then acquiring competence, he/she is not interested in acquiring the real knowledge. His ultimate aim is a goal, which is different from that of the real goal, set by the society i.e. developing an understanding about a particular subject, Here goal (acquiring knowledge) becomes subservient to means (good marks), and means has become goal. Marks are means because they indicate the level of performance of the students.

Though it is true that mere acquisition of information would always not solve any purpose either in education or real life, but that should not undermine the abilities that can be acquired by the students through information. From times immemorial verbal recital has been ingrained in our Culture. There are occasions, when one even does not understand the meaning of a verse still one may enjoy it. That does not mean that one should not attempt to try to understand the meaning of it. That also means that one should not simply stop reciting a verse because he does not understand the meaning of it, as one can do it at a later date. This is possible only when one can receive the information and store it. (This may be compared to the cow eating stalk and later when it is free, chewing it so that it could be digested fully.) Otherwise also further processing of the information can be done later by others also. The inquisition comes only when one has information and otherwise not.

Western philosophers have distinguished between two kinds of knowledge a priori and a posteriori knowledge. A priori knowledge is knowledge gained or justified by reason alone, without the direct or indirect influence of experience (here, experience usually means observation of the world through sense perception). Most of the a Priori knowledge is nothing but Transparent knowledge because this is not experienced by the people, but at the same time it can also lead to the higher levels of knowledge.

RELATIVE KNOWLEDGE (INFORMATION INTERTWINED WITH KNOWLEDGE)

Unlike in the first category here Knowledge and Intention go together and that's why it leads to the development of relative knowledge. Also, under this knowledge revolves around information and it is relative to the information acquired. There may be instances where it becomes highly difficult to differentiate between what is information and what is knowledge, and that falls under this category. It is a situation of synthesis of the two or it may be an instance where it is not possible to see them as independent entities. There is no complete detachment between Information and knowledge, as we find in the above mentioned first category and at the same time Information is not absolutely independent of its existence of the domain of knowledge as it is observed in the third category.

"The posteriori knowledge that is, knowledge the attainment or justification of which requires reference to experience" (called as empirical knowledge) can also be termed as relative knowledge. This can however lead to Independent knowledge, but not in itself is independent knowledge. The processing of information may be explained as follows:

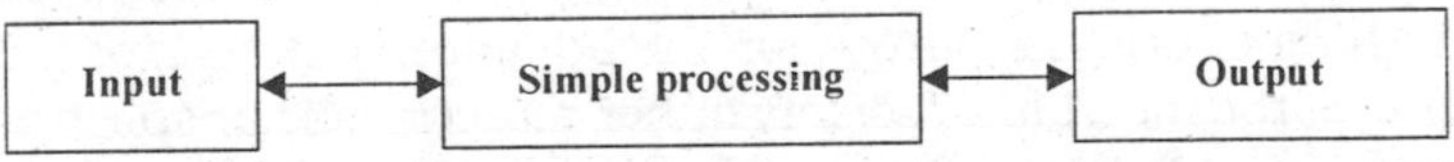

Between input and output there is simple processing involved which leads to the comprehension of facts and that's how it is different from transparent knowledge. But this processing does not go beyond the level of comprehending what is present and that's why it cannot reach the level of independent knowledge. But it is a step in right direction for the attainment of independent knowledge.

INDEPENDENT KNOWLEDGE (KNOWLEDGE BEYOND THE REALM OF INFORMATION)

All knowledge received by an Individual cannot become Independent knowledge. It can either become transparent knowledge (if the student to whom it is transmitted does not bother to understand that or fails to understand due to the reasons mentioned above) or relative knowledge if the student concerned can have a foil understanding of the process, and/ or even when it is practiced. It cannot go above and beyond these two levels. The development of Independent knowledge is where human ingenuity comes into play, which can have any number of its expressions. It is independent from the information and does not have close relation with the information. Though under this category, information too has some influence but it is highly negligible and remote. The ultimate goal of any educational system should be the pursuit of this objective i.e. to bring about the excellence out of each individual. As each individual is a unique creation, there is always scope to extract the best out of every one. The system of Education should not stifle the individual's growth but become a conduit for the expression of oneself. The information processing under this category may be explained as follows:

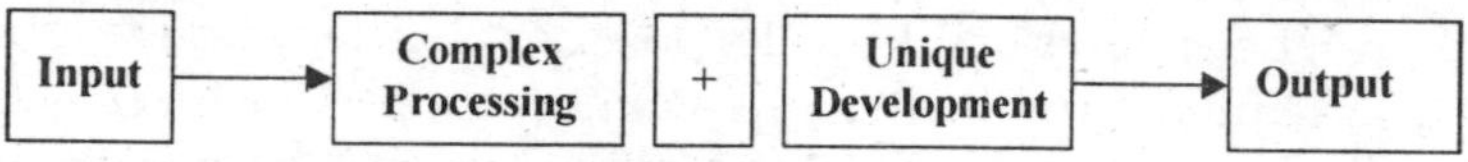

Under this the processing is not very simple to understand the things but a complex one to find solutions for what is not present. This complex processing may also lead to the development of unique ideas/innovations/discoveries/ anything of original nature for the advancement and/or well being of the individual/society either materialistic or spiritual. This should be the ultimate goal of the system of education.

The development of Independent knowledge among students is also necessary from the point of view of well being of the individual, Society and Nation because otherwise knowledge becomes a monopoly of few. The monopoly of knowledge through patents can be very disturbing and it questions the very survival of common man and puts his life at stake, unless the generation of knowledge and consequent distribution of it is not taken care of. The issue of whether innovation justifies a certain amount of monopoly was a point raised most strikingly by the Microsoft case. In October 1998, America's Department of Justice launched an anti-trust case against the World's largest Software Company which resulted, in April 2000, in a ruling that the Company was an "abusive monopolist" that should be broken up. (Cairncross, frances-2001).

CONCLUSION

These principles of knowledge (transparent, relative and independent) can be applied to any thing under the sun, such as life of Buddha to laws of Newton who formulated the concepts of Kaivalya and theory of gravity, respectively. To illustrate how the above three levels work on an individual, the life of Buddha can be cited. Siddhartha (Gautama Buddha) who led a life of comfort and luxury when went with a charioteer for an excursion from his palace he saw an old man, a sick man and a dead body in succession. When he asked his charioteer the meaning of the sight he had witnessed for the first time in his life, the charioteer said This happens to all men. Here comes the transparent knowledge of the charioteer, and to great extent most of the people who witness such events. They are simply brushed aside (ignored) as part of life, which need no importance. The events enter mind and disappear.

However the conversation with the charioteer had a tremendous effect on the mind of the young man, and brought about a sea change in his outlook on life. This can be defined as relative knowledge, as for Buddha the information did not disappear, but the thinking process went on around those very events. Many people reach this stage also, but Buddha underwent the third stage. i.e. Independent Knowledge stage, as he renounced everything and after undergoing different kinds of self-torture attained *Enlightenment or Bodh.* He discovered the 'Law of Dependent Origination' a cycle of twelve causes and effects that conditioned the world. This law is the special contribution of the Buddha, never expounded by any other sage or philosopher hitherto.

The above story describes how the information of the suffering did not become a mere transparent knowledge, but revolved in the mind (Relative knowledge) of Buddha and ultimately led to the development of Independent knowledge. To put it alternatively, the thinking of Buddha was different, rational and unique.

REFERENCES

1. Cairncross. Frances (2001). The death of Distance 2.0. How the communications revolution will change our lives. London: Texere Publishing Limited, Leadenhall Street, ECS A 3DE, pp.71-77.
2. Creath, Richard. (1992). Induction and the Gettier Problem, Philosophy and Phenomenological Research, Vol.II, No.2, June.
3. Feldman,Richard. (1974). Anb Alleged Defect in Gettier Counterexamples, Australasian Journal of Philosophy, 52 (1974):68-69.
4. Sreekjanth Y.(2005). Information Vs Knowledge: Third Concept, An International Journal of Ideas (ISSN 0970-7247), Vol.19 No.222, LB-14, Prakash Deep Building 7, Tolstoy Marg, New Delhi – 110 001.
5. Whitehead N, Alfred (1949). The aims of Education and other Essays, New York: New American Library, pp.13-26.

8

Knowledge Management: The New Challenges for Libraries in Digital Era

Sunil Kumar Satpathy

ABSTRACT

Knowledge management (KM) is about enhancing the use of organizational knowledge through sound practices of information management and organizational learning. It has emerged as a new area in the field of Library & information science. This paper attempts to define the concept of KM. It critically analyses the concept of KM in libraries. Also describes about the contents of KM in libraries and issues related to it. Concludes with the remark that KM has already emerged as a new challenging area for libraries and a rational design of the organizational structure and business procedures of libraries is required for proper Knowledge Management.

1. INTRODUCTION

The rapid development of Information communication Technology (ICT) has changed the Information Society into a Knowledge Society. Accordingly, keeping pace with the changes, the emphasis of libraries has been shifted from documents to information and then to knowledge. Knowledge

Management (KM) in libraries does not mean to management of existing knowledge of the library, rather it refers to effective identification, acquisition, organization, and development, using, storing and sharing of both existing and new knowledge. The aim of such effort is to create an approach to transforming and sharing of tacit and explicit knowledge and to raise innovation capability by utilizing the wisdom of the people of an organization. Since knowledge has become the driving force for educational development, the attention of library users to information and knowledge is rising and users' demands for information and knowledge are more rapidly increasing in digital library environment step by step. This has provided new challenging cnvironment for many libraries. Further, information and knowledge has become an important productive factor for the modern economic system, hence the academic community and society will inevitably require better management og information and knowledge. In this changing context, the main challenge for libraries is to manage knowledge properly.. Knowledge management in libraries normally focuses on effective research and development of knowledge, creation of knowledge bases, exchange and sharing of knowledge between library staffs and its users, training of library staff, quick processing of knowledge and realizing of its sharing.

2. CONCEPT OF KNOWLEDGE MANAGEMENT

Knowledge management is about enhancing the use of organizational knowledge through sound practices of information management and organizational learning. The purpose is to deliver value to the business. It rests on two foundations i.e. first utilizing and exploiting the organization's information (which needs to be managed for this to occur) and second, the application of peoples' competencies, skills, talents, thoughts, ideas, intuitions, commitments, motivations, and imaginations.

In the context of Business organization, KM refers to make explicit the knowledge of the mangers, executives, product developer, marketers, and field staff and captured and then factored into decision-making processes with the help of electronic databases to increase its business or sales. Similarly, in the library context the Librarian knows something about why products or services are not utilized by the users the way the organization desires. The main reason is that the products and services are not of organizational knowledge. But it becomes organizational knowledge when there are management processes in place, which capture that often personal, tacit, front-line information from which others in the organization learn and make decisions. This is the meaning of knowledge management—purposeful management processes that capture often personal and contextual information that can be used for the organization's benefit.

Knowledge management represents a quantum shift for most organizations. It is a form of expertise-centered management focusing on using human expertise for business advantage.

Knowledge management practices aim to draw out the tacit knowledge people have, what they carry around with them, what they observe and learn from experience, rather than what is usually explicitly stated. In firms that appreciate the importance of knowledge management, the organizational responsibilities of staff are not focused on the narrow confines of traditional job descriptions. Managing knowledge goes much further than capturing data and manipulating it to obtain information. The aim of knowledge management is for businesses to become more competitive through the capacities of their people to be more flexible and innovative. These characteristics are organization-specific, the context is critical, and they are hard to imitate—attributes, which deepen the sustainability of knowledge management as a competitive advantage.

Tacit and Explicit Knowledge

The distinction between tacit and explicit knowledge is critical in appreciating the scope of knowledge management and how it differs from information and data management. A new knowledge always begins with the personal which is tacit knowledge, but when it becomes public it becomes the explicit knowledge. For example, a researcher has insights that lead to a new patent, which is the tacit knowledge. A manager's informed and intuitive sense of market trends becomes the catalyst for utilizing the patent of the researcher in a new type of product. The marketing executive draws on both experience and rethinking processes to develop a new process, which brings the product to the market more quickly. In each case the tacit knowledge of an individual becomes explicit as part of the organizations' management processes.

The basic steps of getting started in knowledge management are:

* Making knowledge visible
* Building knowledge intensity
* Creation of a knowledge base
* Building knowledge infrastructure
* Developing a knowledge culture
* Sustain the values of library

3. KNOWLEDGE MANAGEMENT IN LIBRARIES

Libraries deal with the document, information and knowledge. Knowledge can be divided in two categories, tacit knowledge and explicit knowledge. Tacit knowledge is the 'know-how' acquired by persons. It is usually intuitive and generally demonstrated in how an individual makes accomplishment in his work, even though this knowledge is not recorded anywhere. But one of the goals of the knowledge management is to make tacit knowledge more widely available. Explicit knowledge is systematically documented records in any kind of format, which guide the users to gain the knowledge, as the individuals need and to expand the knowledge base further.

Libraries, the institutions for knowledge management deal with both categories of knowledge, tacit knowledge for the library personnel and the explicit knowledge for the end-users. Library personnel must know the 'know-how' of information sources, management, retrieval and dissemination, as well as global access to information. This tacit knowledge helps the end-users to gain explicit knowledge, as any individual requires. They must be guided to the gateway of knowledge. If these two categories of knowledge do not match, then an 'Information-rich' organizations can be 'knowledge-poor' organizations Therefore libraries should deal with both information management as well as knowledge management.

Knowledge management in libraries is about the acquisition, creation, packaging or application or reuse of knowledge.

(a) **Acquisition** : Finding existing knowledge, understanding requirements, searching among multiple sources and conveying it in an appropriate form to a user, such as competitor intelligence
(b) **Creating :** Research activities, training
(c) **Packaging :** Publishing, editing, design work
(d) Applying or using existing knowledge
(e) Creation of a knowledge base
(f) Building Knowledge Infrastructure
(g) Developing a knowledge culture
(h) Reuse of knowledge for new purposes: leveraging knowledge in product development processes, software development.
(i) Motivate users for its proper use

The Knowledge Management in Libraries can be diagrammatically represented as follows.(Fig.1)

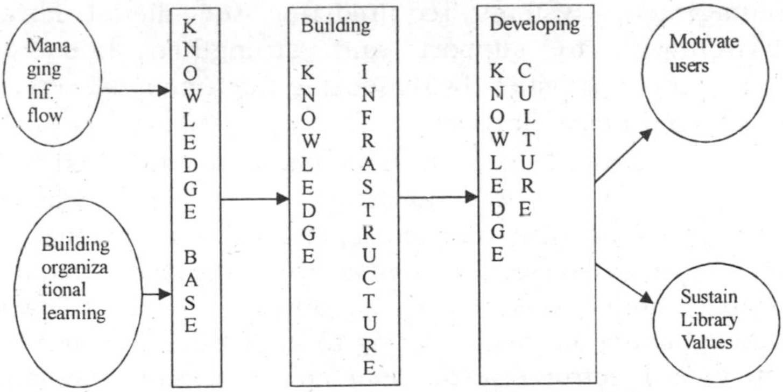

Fig. 1. Knowledge Management in Libraries

4. CONTENTS OF KNOWLEDGE MANAGEMENT IN LIBRARIES

Knowledge management in libraries leaves much to be desired in its theoretical system as a completely new method of management. Knowledge management in libraries should includes various management processes

4.1. Knowledge Innovation Management

In libraries, the Knowledge innovation management refers to the management of the production, diffusion and transfer of knowledge as well as of the network systems constructed by related institutions and organizations. Thus it includes three aspects, namely, theoretical innovation management of knowledge, technical innovation management and organizational innovation management.

Theoretical innovation management is to enrich and enlarge the theoretical and practical research fields of library and information science through pursuing the latest development trends in the field.. Technical innovation management is to manage the network systems constructed by institutions and organizations. The evolution of libraries from conventional libraries to electronic libraries or digital libraries, Libraries has made technical breakthroughs and progress to build up technical facilities to support knowledge management. The purpose of organizational innovation management is to create a set of effective organizational management systems required for the digital library environment to support and strengthen knowledge management activities, by optimizing the functional services and procedures of libraries.

In the knowledge management systems, the head of the library responsible for knowledge management in library should formulate the management plans and coordinate all knowledge management related activities. Further, t requires establishment of special leading groups of knowledge flow for accomplishing all tasks relating to knowledge management activities. Electronic resources committees are established composed of various types of specialists to take charge of evaluating, procuring and creating the electronic resources on the one hand, and coordinating activities of libraries such as procurement and organization of the electronic information resources as well as providing services on the other hand.

4.2. Knowledge Dissemination Management

Knowledge creators do not have much time and energy to look for knowledge users and knowledge dissemination. Since the attitude and interests of knowledge users differs tremendously, it is very difficult to acquire knowledge that already exists in the minds of knowledge creators as restricted by various objective and subjective conditions. Therefore, libraries may use diverse media and channels to disseminate various new knowledge. In the 21st century, the Internet, with its mass information and extensive contents, will provide people with the main approach to searching knowledge and acquiring information. But now a large numbers of absurd, salacious; false and uncivil information is resulting from Internet search due to commercial profits and political objectives on the Net. Therefore, it is necessary to strengthen knowledge dissemination management in libraries as follows:

1. Strengthening the creation of libraries' own document resources and deepening the development of document information resources (knowledge);
2. Raising the quality of library professionals continuously
3. Full attention should be given to the special role of the expert system in knowledge dissemination;
4. Making a comprehensive utilization of all media to ensure security of operation of networks, and prevent online criminal activities and online dissemination of inappropriate information.

4.3. Knowledge Application Management

In digital era, libraries should not only acquire and disseminate the available knowledge but also motivate users to apply the knowledge for the generation of new knowledge and achieve maximum functions and efficiency of knowledge information. Therefore, knowledge services based on high-speed information networks such as setting up virtual libraries, digitized knowledge services, digitization of library resources should be carried out

4.4. Human Resources Management

An essential theme in managing knowledge effectively is the understanding the importance of people as organizational assets. Human resources management takes it as the basic starting point of Knowledge Management to train high quality specialized talents and to revitalize the library undertaking. In practice, full attention should be given to diversity and variation of library staffs' requirements, strengthened management of different library staffs by applying contingency management approach etc.

5. ISSUES OF KNOWLEDGE MANAGEMENT

Knowledge management is emerging as a key concern of organizations, particularly those who have already redesigned their business processes and embedded a total quality approach into their practices. Major consulting firms are now gearing up to add knowledge management to their lines of business.

The main issues of KM in libraries are

(a) Knowledge work is inherently hard to manage
(b) Variety and uncertainty in inputs and outputs
(c) Unstructured and individualized work rules and routines
(d) Lack of separation among process, outputs and inputs
(e) Lack of measures
(f) Worker autonomy
(g) High variability in performance across individuals and time
(h) Lack of information technology support

These challenges underlay the difficulty in managing knowledge itself. As work becomes more knowledge intensive, richer forms of communication become more important. Hence there is need to know more about the people in organizations, their expertise and the nature of their work.

CONCLUSION

Knowledge management requires a holistic and multidisciplinary approach to management processes and an understanding of the dimensions of knowledge work. Knowledge management should be the evolution of good management practices sensibly and purposively applied. One of the aims of knowledge management in libraries is to promote the knowledge exchange among library staffs, strengthen innovation consciousness and abilities, arise the library staffs' enthusiasm and abilities for learning, making the knowledge most efficiently applied to academic activities of the library, and rebuilding the library into a learning organization. Therefore, the main train of thought in realizing knowledge management of libraries is a rational design of the organizational structure and business procedures of libraries, and cultural fostering, as well as modernized information support, thus creating an environment and incentive mechanism for innovation, exchange, study and application of the knowledge.

The knowledge management programme should provide a sound foundation for knowledge evolution. The programme should not only focusing debugging, refining, structuring and modularizing the knowledge but should also address critical issues like controlling formal or structured knowledge generation process, quickly interpreting feedback and integration with the knowledge policy and considers how the knowledge depreciates and explores techniques to fill up the gap.

REFERENCES

1. Andrzej (P W). Modelling as a way of organizing knowledge, European Journal of Operation Research.176, 1, 200; 610.
2. Bellinger (G). *The Knowledge Centered Organization*
3. Chung-Hung(T) and Hwang-Yeh(C).Assessing Knowledge Management system success: An empirical study of Tawians High Tech Industry. Journal of American Academy of Business.10, 2, 2007; 257-63.
4. Harari, (O). The Brain Based Organization. *Management Review.* 83, 6, 1994; 57-60.
5. Lucy (M). Facilitating Knowledge Management and Knowledge Sharing: New Opportunities for Information Professionals. *Online.* 21,5, 1997; 92-98

9
Information Management

Prativa Acharya
Amitava Pani

ABSTRACT

Information management can be viewed as the keystone of information science and technology. Every activity in the field of information science and technology is related to the complex process of information management. The backgrounds, characteristics of information management are mentioned here. It is a process which involves converting the internal and external information of the institution into actionable knowledge. The three basic facts of information management are: management of change, management of information systems and services and the planning process. Information management is concerned with economy, efficiency and effectiveness of organizations information resources. Numerous tools and techniques both conventional and non-conventional have been developed to find the ways of satisfying demands for relevant up-to-date and accurate information at an economic cost. It enumerates the process of information management cycle.

INTRODUCTION

The information management combines skills and

resources from librarianship and information science, information technology, record management and general management. Information management focus on information as a resource and it has physical form. The scopes of the information management are books, periodicals, electronic database, microforms, audio-visual media and the information which are in the people's head.

Information management is a process and it has been the issue of concern to library and information professionals all over the world. Information management system accomplishes the data and information in a systematic manner. It includes the methods and procedure for collecting and processing information on a particular resource and formatting that data useful for users.

Now the libraries are more serious towards the management of resources. Information management includes the management of information in any form, particularly the written form. Today major parts of the information are on paper, electronic or image form. Information management is the efficient and effective co-ordination of information from internal and external sources. It is concerned with obtaining the best possible value for money from an organization's information resources. Information resources cover both data and information and to include all information irrespective of the media on which it was recorded.

The aim of information management is to promote organization effectiveness by enhancing the capabilities of the organization's cope with the demands of the internal and external environments in dynamic as well as stable conditions. It includes organization, development and maintenance of integrated, systems and services, optimization of information flow, functional requirements of end users.

DEFINITION AND SCOPE OF INFORMATION MANAGEMENT

According to Blaise Cronin, there is nothing to stop librarians or information scientists from retitling themselves as information Managers. But the change of label does not necessarily imply a change of activity or attitude. He argues that information management is more than value added librarianship. In addition to the usual functions of library administration, information management involves data processing, automation activities, systems analysis, management services, the new skills and techniques needed by the information managers to deal with the IT and strategies for delivering corporate information plan. According to Peter Vickers Management of Information is not concerned simply with documents, message and data, but the entire apparatus of information handling. He identifies the characteristics of information management as follows:

* Information has to be treated as a resource requiring proper management, like money, manpower and materials.
* At the simplest level, information management involves planning and co-ordination of the following:
  — information handling skills
  — information technology
  — information sources and services
* Information management requires a careful watch on new developments that can contribute to the better management of information resources.
* Information management requires an understanding of the patterns of information flow within the organization and thus it demands a systematic means of mapping and monitoring such flows.

Definitions of Information Management on the web

* Information is an asset to an organization and the management of this information is a means to manage a document during its entire life cycle. The ability to know what documents exist regarding a particular subject, where they are located what media they are stored on, who owns them and when they should be destroyed. Information management encompasses document management, imaging and knowledge management systems.
* Information management is the handling of knowledge acquired by one or many disparate sources in a way that

optimizes access by all who have a share in that knowledge or a right to that knowledge.

* The function of managing the organizations information resources includes creating, capturing, registering, classifying, indexing, storing, retrieving and disposing of records and developing strategies to manage records. Also includes the acquisition, control and disposal of library and other information products, items kept for reference purposes and the provision of services to internal and external customers, based on information resources...............
* The art of collecting and/or managing data in a manner that affects program operations, the use of technology to improve use of data.
* The provision of relevant information to the right person at the right time in a usable form to facilitate situational understanding and decision making. It uses procedures and information systems to collect, process, store, display and dissemination information.
* The entire process of defining, evaluation, protecting and distributing data within an organization.
* The administration of information, its uses and transmission and the application of theories and techniques of information science to create, modify or improve information handling systems.
* The planning, budgeting, manipulating and controlling of information throughout its life cycle.

The three basic facts of information management are:

* Management of change
* Management of information systems and services
* The management process

Management of change

In the present day scenario, management of change is a very crucial process. The enormous changes are taking place our professional work and these are mostly due to the following-

* Technical changes

* Social-political, educational and demographic changes
* Change in the Government politics
* Change in user needs and requirements
* Change in structure and dimension of Information industry

Information technology is developing and forcing a change in the structure and dynamics of information society. The management of change need to develop and improved strategies for coping with changes and for introducing innovations into organizations.

Introduction of technology in work environment will create new relationships and altering the existing ones within an organizational framework. This is known as the dynamic leadership in quality with other managerial skills. Users change their requirements very frequently for many reasons. An information manager has tackled these changes very carefully. Changes in the structure and dimensions of information industry have direct effect on information sources and its impact on information management. Today information resources are available in different format and media like paper form, microform, CD-ROM's, online and on the internet. Now the question is will we prefer

* Printed materials?
* Online databases?
* CD-ROM databases?
* Web sources?

It is believe that the printed materials are likely to use less then the electronic media. Online services require unlimited budget. Now most of the online journals are available on the web and for use these journals the library must have the infrastructure to access them. These changes have the impact on information management.

MANAGEMENT OF INFORMATION SYSTEMS AND SERVICES

The application of information technology in libraries and information centres increases the effectiveness of information system and services. IT management requires systematic approach and an integral part of corporate planning process. It is very important to take into consideration the availability and efficiency of computer based information services. In the computer based information services the role of information scientists as intermediaries between the users and their sources.

Information scientists have an important role in development of system and software. It is the responsibility of information manager to provide adequate training program to the information professionals. It is an obligation of information manager to design and develop information systems such that the end user can access them directly.

The Management Process

The management processes are directly related to planning process and manpower management. There is another process which is known as the decision making process.

Planning Process

For an information manager systematic planning is necessary for effectiveness of library operations. Planning is not a one time activity, it is cyclic in nature. It helps to carry out the priority actions in achieving specified goals of a library and information centre. This is because of the addition of information technology including the internet in libraries and information centres. The effective use of information technology depends upon the provision of appropriate technical and supervisory training to the users.

MANPOWER PLANNING AND MANAGEMENT

In organization manpower planning has been defined as a strategy for the acquisition, utilization, improvement and retention of an enterprise's human resources. There are two categories of staffs are required in the library and information centres are professional and support staff. Appropriate training programmes should be conducted from time to time for existing staff to make use of information technology as and when required.

DECISION MAKING PROCESS

The information managers take certain decisions under certain circumstances. The situation may be

* Decisions under strict uncertainty
* Decision under certainty
* Decisions with risks

There are certain steps in decision making process-

1. Identify the problem
2. Collect facts related to that problem
3. Generate and specify alternative solutions.
4. Choose the best alternative
5. Gain explaining the basis of the decision to other members of the decision making groups
6. Communicated the decision to affected persons
7. Put the decision into action
8. Supervise the effect of the decision
9. Evaluation the result

In this process one can use different tools and techniques. Depending upon the situation, one can adopt different approaches in getting the solutions. In an IT environment everyday managers are involved in decision making processes.

TOOLS AND TECHNIQUES FOR INFORMATION MANAGEMENT

When the question arise How Information Management? The answer lies that various tools and techniques available to the library and information profession. Some of them are:

Standards

Standards may be considered as important tools in information management. ISI (Indian Standard Institution) have developed and published a number of Indian Standards for documentation pertaining to bibliographical reference, book binding, cataloguing, classification, lighting, furniture, microfilms etc. A number of Institutions and individuals have formulated standards both official and non official, for management of libraries and information centers.

System Analysis

System analysis is a tool for information management has invaluable in analyzing complex organizations. System analysis has limited use in library and information centers.

Information Technology

The field of librarianship and information science has a great change during the past three decades due to the impact of information technology on the storage, retrieval and dissemination of information.

Components of information technology:

* Invention of Mainframe Computer
* Invention of Microcomputer
* Personnel computer
* Development of computer network and linking of PC's
* Development of LAN to linking individual group of PC's
* Development of WAN via satellite to linking users in one network
* Creation of Optical Storage Device for mass storage of text and document
* Preparation of microfilm
* Invention of CD-ROM
* Invention of Optical Juke Box for storing vast image and document
* Emergence of relational database making separation of data and program
* Evaluation of Massive Parallel Processing
* Crcation of clcctronic mail systcms for providing much more than message between people and for moving information around efficiency
* Creation of electronic document
* Emergence of Microsoft and Windows as a generic PC-based user interface
* Speech Recognition Technology to make data input just a matter of speaking into a machine and end of the keyboard eventually

From the above process, one can know that the role of Information Technology as a tool for Information Management.

WORK ANALYSIS TECHNIQUES

This technique is essential to analyze operations step-by-step. Some of the techniques of work analysis are useful for information management situations are:

* Block diagram,
* Flow diagram
* Flow process chart,
* Decision flow chart,
* Operations analysis
* Form analysis
* Man-machine chart
* Other techniques of work analysis
* Multiple activity or Gantt chart
* Micro motion

These techniques facilitate efficiency and effectiveness of a library by studying its operations in detail.

MONITORING TECHNIQUES

A monitoring technique is a time negotiated procedure which resources will be committed to achieving objectives. It is known as a tool or a guideline. The best techniques are those which are not rigid and have provision for adjustments of future events. These includes operations research (OR), management information system (MIS), management by objectives (MBO), PERT/CPM etc.

EVALUATION TECHNIQUES

Evaluation of any process or activity in management, usually refer as assessment valuation, appraisal, criticism, review, measurement etc. Some of the basic techniques which are applicable for evaluation process are performance measurement, cost effectiveness and cost benefit studies etc.

CONVENTIONAL TECHNIQUES

Librarians were the first people to bring some discipline to information management with their classification and cataloguing schemes. Classification has such an important place in online systems that we take interest in both theory and practice. Walker Liu, Svenaxius, Nohr and Watanabe have used classification techniques in the context of OPAC searching.

INFORMATION MANAGEMENT PROCESS

The information manager will have a central role in:

* Managing and coordinating the mechanism for keeping a business term aware of market developments.
* Designing, implementing, monitoring and updating information systems.

Information management is a discipline must be concerned with the management of some processes. Some processes are performed by individuals and some are performed by organizations. In figure 1, the left hand side of the model is the processes which are performed by the individual in information management. On the right hand side of the model the processes are performed by the organization. In figure 1 the relationships between the processes of left-hand side and those on the right-hand side is many-to-many. It means that, an individual may interact with the information management process with many organizations, on the other side any one organization will draw on the contribution of many individuals in the management of its knowledge base. This is the nature of the many-to-may relationship which is the most significant challenges to information management. This figure shows that information and knowledge management involves a series of stages in a cycle.

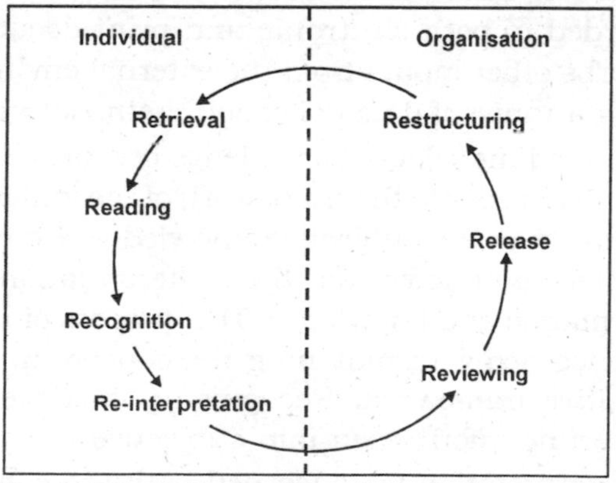

Fig. 1. The Information Management Cycle

This model uses the term and concept of information as subjective and objective knowledge. This model proposes definitions for these terms. The definitions of information are complex and include contributions from a range of different disciplinary perspectives. The figure 2 explains the process that comprise the information management cycle in details to examine the inputs and outputs from each of the process.

Relevant Knowledge	→Reading	→ Information
Information	→Recognition	→ Subjective Knowledge
Subjective Knowledge	→Re-interpretation	→ Public Knowledge
Public Knowledge	→Reviewing	→ Validated Knowledge
Validated Knowledge	→Release	→ Knowledge Domain
Knowledge Domain	→Re-structuring	→ Resource Bank
Resource Bank	→Retrieval	→ Relevant Knowledge

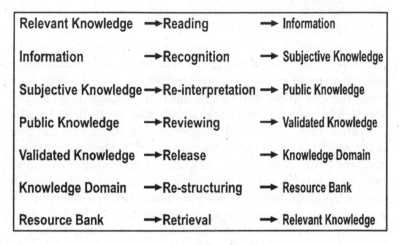

Fig. 2. Input and Output for Each Process in the Information Management Cycle

The information management cycle can be described like:

1. A person reads a collection of relevant knowledge recorded in both electronic and print documents. He absorbs other inputs from the external environment or using a range of data collection methodologies.
2. Once read the relevant knowledge becomes information and absorbed into the framework of the individual. This is known as the subjective knowledge. Here the word adopted is known as the differentiation between information and knowledge. This process of recognition is concerned with matching the concept in the user's cognitive framework. Recognizing is concerned with converting information into subjective knowledge.
3. Re-interpretation is concerned with the conversion of

knowledge into a form such as in a document. Documents are the primary concern of information managers and it is important that public utterances can also be in verbal or graphical form. This is known as the public knowledge.

4. Review is concerned with the conversion of public knowledge into validated knowledge. This process is conducted through the various channels for filter communications from individuals. Typical activities that are concerned with validation include reviewing, refereeing, listing and other processes for evaluation public knowledge.
5. Release or distribution concerned with the making of public knowledge which widely available within the community, marketplace or organization find it to be of value. Release for documents is typically in the form of publication but other public announcements can also be made through television, cinema and other information media.
6. Organizations will interact with this knowledge domain, select and collect item from it and access to a subject of the knowledge domain that they judge to be of specific interest in meeting their objectives. This is happen in the libraries, document collections and document management systems. This is known as the re-structuring of knowledge to meet a specific purpose.
7. This collection of knowledge will be used by the user for relevant knowledge. Relevant knowledge, once retrieved must be read before the knowledge recorded in documents of various types can be converted into information.

CONCLUSION

The basic elements of information management include accessing, evaluating, managing, organizing, filtering and distributing of information in such a manner that the information should useful for end users. Information management involves the combination of internal and external information of the institution and converts it into actionable knowledge through a technology platform. So information management is a logical extension of the information society.

Whatever information management is, it perhaps is concerned with obtaining the best possible value for money from an organization's information resources. the field of Information Management has never been more exciting than it is today.

REFERENCE

1. Seetharama, S. Guidelines for planning of libraries and information centre. Calcutta; IASLIC; 1993.
2. Taylor, A and Farrell, S. Information management in context. Aslib Proceedings, 44(9), September 1992, pp.319-322.
3. Vishwanathan, T. Application of information technology in libraries. Ann.Lib.Sc.Doc. 1991; 38;1-7p.
4. Choudhury, N B.: Seminar on co-operative in Information Manner Management. Jamshedpur;14-15 Feb.1988;35pp.
5. Choudhury, N B.: Impact of information system on academic libraries.CALIBER-98;24-26pp.
6. Seetharama, S.DRTC Workshop on information management, 6-8 January,1999.

10

Perceptions of Service Quality in Academic Library: A Case Study

Ashok Kumar Sahu

ABSTRACT

This article determines the perception of the users of the Jawaharlal Nehru University (JNU) Library, New Delhi, India, with regard to the quality service provided by JNU Library. A questionnaire was used as data gathering instrument. The SERVQUAL is a diagnostic tool to measure service quality, defined as the difference between customer perceptions and expectations of service. Service quality is essential to change the work culture among the employees for their involvement in the services of the library to provide quality service and customer satisfaction. It focuses on continuous improvement in products and services, with greater employee involvement and an increased emphasis on customer needs.

INTRODUCTION

With the great competition for resources, rising expectations of users, increasing complexity of information provision from a variety of new providers, ever increasing cost of information carriers have enhanced the operational transparency and accountability of libraries. The rapid development of information technology, tremendous speed of 'socio-technical development, changed needs of users have all added to the expectations from a service organization. It is evident that management skills must match these demand on and threats to library and information services. The application of quality management in libraries is to establish a culture of never ending improvement of quality of products and services. Its implementation in libraries improves the image of the library staff and helps in public relations and marketing. (Rajan and Ravi, 2001).

Traditionally, the quality of an academic library has been described in terms of its collection and measured by the size of the library holdings and different count of its use. This traditional method no longer fulfills the goals for successfully the user's demands for information. This time has now come to evaluate the quality and significance of library service through SERVQUAL. The SERVQUAL has evolved as a new instrument to measure the service quality (Thapisa, A.P.N. and Gamini, 1999).

Quality is the basic philosophy and requirement of library profession and all libraries strive to deliver the highest quality of service. A quality service is one that fully meets expectations and requirements of the users. If a library provides right information to right user at right time and in required form, then it is maintaining quality. Quality library services mean satisfying the query of each and every user pin pointedly, exhaustively, and expeditiously (Sharma, 2001).

SERVICE QULAITY CONCEPT IN LIBRARIES

The concept of service quality defined as the difference between a library user's expectations and perceptions of service performance to the mid 1970 (Oldman & Wills, 1977). Quality become a big issue when libraries try to expand the scope and improve their service. Quality can be defined as to how good a service is, and not necessarily how large or extensive (Orr, 1973). In the library, quality may be recognized by the customers in terms of prompt delivery or lack of error in services.

Quality can also be seen as relating to the fitness of a

service or product to its intended purpose or use, subject to the expectations of the customer or user. Quality, therefore, must be in conformity with the customer's requirements or needs. This means that the quality of a service can be a definition of the customer's perception of what is good or bad, acceptable or not acceptable service (Barnad, 1993). Therefore, quality is an ongoing process where the user is a key determinant.

Quality assurance is a continuous process of examination and re-examination of needs of the user, providing the means by which expectation can be met or satisfied. So, quality service is helping a user to define his/her needs, clarifying user benefits, building confidence and monitoring and assessing the organization and the impact of its services (Thapisa, A.P.N & Gamini, V., 1999).

Within the library literature, the concept of quality has not yet been well developed, depending on the context in which a library organization seeks to assess its service quality. Recently, some librarians are shifting their perspective of library services to represent a user driven view. The assessment of how well a library succeeds depends on the user as judge of quality. The primary goal of any library therefore should be to maximize user satisfaction and to exceed expectations. Parasuraman, Berry and Zeithaml's (1998) customer based approach to conceptualize and measure service quality suggest intriguing alternative to view and measure the quality of library services. They identified five dimensions with which consumers judge services (Fitzsimmons, and Fitzsimmons, 2000).

* **Reliability:** The ability to perform the promised service both dependably and accurately.
* **Responsiveness:** The willingness to help customers and to provide prompt service.
* **Assurance:** The knowledge and courtesy of employees as well as their ability to convey trust and confidence.
* **Empathy:** The provision of caring, individualized attention to customers.
* **Tangibles:** The appearance of physical facilities, equipment, personnel, and communication materials.

Zeithamn, Parasuraman, and Berry identify the five service quality dimensions and also use them to develop a model of service quality which commonly known as the Gaps Models (Fitzsimmons, and Fitzsimmons, 2000).

1. Not Knowing What Customers Expect
2. The Wrong Service Quality Standards
3. The Service Performance Gap
4. When Promises Do Not Match Delivery
5. Expected Service—Perceived Service Gap

SERVQUAL

The SERVQUAL instrument easily identifies service quality from the customer perspective. To measure those gapes, Zeithamn, Parasuraman, and Berry (1998) developed 22 item questionnaire called SERVQUAL. The Gapes Model and its SERVQUAL instrument is probably the most frequently used approach to discuss and measure service quality. The Gaps Model provides valuable insight into under standing challenges of delivering quality service. The first four gaps are the major contributors to the service quality gap that customers may perceive. The fifth gap is the basis of a customer oriented definition of service quality, it is discrepancy between customer's expectations for excellence and their perceptions of actual service delivered. This discrepancy is the conceptual basis for the SERVQUAL instrument (Nitecki, and Hernon, 2000).

LITERATURE REVIEW

SERVQUAL is a New approach to measuring service quality, one that produces finding useful for local planning and decision-making. It also differentiates between service quality and satisfaction and points the direction for further research (Nitecki, D.A and Hernon, 2000).

Thapisa and Gamini studied Determine the perceptions of the clients of the University of Botswana Library as they relate to quality service, and how far the university library has succeeded in delivering quality services.

A study by Dadzie (2004) indicated the important role of top management in an organization and examined the possibilities, challenges and constraints posed to librarians in the provision of quality service to the university community in Ghana.

In another study the SERVQUAL's importance as a diagnostic tool to measure service quality, defined as the difference between customer perceptions and expectations of service is discussed. This study draws implications for library management and future explorations of a tool applicable to academic libraries (Nitecki, 1996).

Rajan and Ravi (2001) discuss some of the limitations and possibilities of the service quality model for academic libraries. The model was originally developed in a commercial environment and may require some adaptation to the non-commercial environment of the academic library. Various ways in which the model might be adapted are suggested.

Walmiki (2001) demonstrates how to take effective steps towards the larger goal or total readers satisfaction. It defines the meaning of quality control and its evolution, and depicts the relation between quality and user's. It describes and the implementation of TQM in library and information services. It also examines the benefits of quality management such as efficiency, continual and systematic improvement in the activities of the library as a whole. Finally, it elaborates on the modern concept of TQM.

Fitzsimmons & Haksever,c. both are discussed about the importance of service quality, five dimensions, gape model in their chapters. There are also explained about the SERVQAL. A survey instrument that measures service quality called SERVQAL.

OBJECTIVE OF THE STUDY

At a glance the provision of facilities and staffing at the JNU Library appear to be adequate, and staffs also very efficient to provide the relevant information, there seems to be less emphasis on quality service delivery. (Sahu, 2004) So get a better understanding of the subject matter the aim of this study is to examine the perceptions of the JNU Library users as they relate to quality service and to determine how far the JNU Library has succeeded in delivering such service to its users.

The objectives of this study are:

* Determine how the students and staff of the Jawaharlal Nehru University perceive quality service at the JNU Library
* Establish whether the library is meeting the quality expectations of the users.
* Find out if there are any differences in the perception of quality library service between student & faculty
* Make recommendations on how to improve the level of quality service.

JAWAHARLAL NEHRU UNIVERSITY LIBRARY - CASE STUDY

In the early 1970s, JNU opened its doors to teachers and students, frontier disciplines and new perspectives on old disciplines were brought to the Indian university system. The JNU campus is a microcosm of the Indian nation, drawing students from every nook and corner of the country and from every group and stratum of society (Gopal, Krishan, 2001, http://www.jnu.ac.in/)

The Library is located at the heart of Academic complex and is accessible easily from all schools on foot. The library opens from 9 A.M. to Midnight on all days of the week throughout the year. The JNU Library has a variety of customers/users such as full-time and part-time students, faculty, and staff. It has a carpet area of about one lakh sq. ft. JNU library is housed in a nine-story building. The library follows the open access system.The library has a collection of Books, serials, and Non book material at the tune of 5 lakhs approximately, 1000 serials and 27 online databases & e-journals. The JNU Library is also providing the following services to users like Reference services, Interlibrary Loan , Photocopying service, Audio-Visual aids, use of CD-ROMs, micro-print, dissertations, Newspaper clippings. Online Public Access Catalogue (OPAC) for records available in Delhi Libraries, through DELNET. Access to Online Journals through JSTOR and UGC-INFONET Consortium and the URLs listed under Online journals in the library page of the JNU Library website. The library provides Tape Recorders and Audio

Cassettes for Blind students. Readers are also provided typewriters on request within the premises of the library. It has also proposed to build a digital library section (http://www.jnu.ac.in/).

METHODOLOGY

The research has been carried out using Jawaharlal Nehru University (JNU) Library as a case study. The research has carried out among the students and faculty members of the Jawaharlal Nehru University. This research study is to determine the perception of the JNU users as they relate to quality service provided by the JNU Library.

The study has been taken total 100 samples, among of them 70 students and 30 faculty members. The samples were randomly selected among the students & faculty members of JNU. Since the user segment comparison of two segments, faculty and student, so a survey method was used to carry out the study. The advantage of a random sampling method is that the result can be analyzed faculty-wise and student-wise, drawing certain conclusions from each category of respondents.

RESEARCH INSTRUMENTS

Both qualitative and quantitative data were collected. The instruments for data collection consisted of structured (open/closed-ended) questions. The questionnaire was administered to a sample of students & faculty members to collect data on their perceptions of quality service at JNU Library. Open-ended questions were used to generate free response from the respondents. The questionnaire has covered three main section of the library i.e the aspects relating to the 1) physical facilities, 2) technical facilities such as computer appreciation and 3) the attitude and competence of staff.

QUESTIONNAIRE DESIGN

The framework was developed using the variables which suggested by Parasuraman et al (1998).

The questionnaire was designed for the investigation of quality service perceptions of JNU Library among students and faculty members of JNU. It consisted of 47 structured, open-ended and closed ended questions. The questionnaire reflected seven determinants of the quality services. Each section is summed up by an open-ended question, which allowed the respondents to assess the overall impression of a given criteria of quality service. All the closed ended questions were designed to responses on a five point Likert scale to measure both respondent satisfaction and perception of service quality. Respondent and replying to these items indicated 1 representing "strongly agree", 2 "agree", 3 "disagree", 4 "strongly disagree", and 5 "not sure". Except those seven variables, two independent questions (Q.9 & 10) were given in questionnaire which helped the respondent to give their view on overall impression on services & physical facility of JNU Library.

Reliability

This refers to the delivery service as it relates to dependability and accuracy. It includes:

* giving correct answers to reference questions;
* making relevant information available;
* keeping records consistent with actual holdings/status;
* keeping computer databases up and running;
* making sure that overdue notices and fine notices are accurate.

Responsiveness

Responsiveness measures the readiness of library staff in providing service. It includes:

* Timeliness in delivering needed information;
* Making new information available;
* Checking in new journals and newspapers promptly;
* Calling back a patron who has telephoned with a reference question immediately;
* Minimizing computer response time;
* Re-shelving books quickly;
* Minimizing turnaround time for interlibrary loans.

Assurance

Assurance measures the knowledge and courtesy of the

library staff and their ability to convey confidence. This includes:

* valuing all requests for information equally and conveying the importance of an inquiry to the client;
* clean and neat appearance of staff;
* thorough understanding of the collection;
* familiarity with the workings of equipment and technology;
* learning the customer's specific requirements;
* providing individual attention; and
* recognizing the regular customer.

Access

Access measures the ability to reach out for something and finding or getting it as and when it is needed. It includes:

* waiting time at circulation desk;
* availability of computer terminals, Online Public Access Catalogue (OPAC), etc.without waiting too long;
* library hours meeting expectations;
* location and centrality of the library and convenience.

Communications

Communications measures the ability to keep clients informed in a language they understand and the ability to listen to them:

* avoiding library jargon;
* determining the needs of the client through gentle follow-up questions;
* developing precise, clear instructions at the point of use;
* teaching the customer library skills;
* assuring the customer that her/his problem will be handled.

Empathy

Empathy measures the behaviour, attitude and approach of the library staffs towards users. It includes:

* Determine the attitude of the staff
* Giving equal importance to all user's request

(*Source*: Thapisa, A.P.N and Gamini, 1999)

DATA COLLECTION, DATA ANALYSIS AND FINDINGS

Total 130 questionnaires were distributed among the students and faculty members of Jawaharalal Nehru University (JNU). The questionnaire consisted of 47 structured close-ended and open-ended questions. From 130 questionnaires, 100 responses were received . This represents an effective response rate of around 77% of the total sample.

Out of 130 questionnaires, 90 questionnaires were distributed among the students and 40 questionnaires distributed among faculty members. We received 70 responses from the students (the rate of around 77%) out of the total 90 questionnaires. 30 responses from the faculty members were received (the rate around 75%) out of the total 40 questionnaires.

STATA-7 has used to analyze the responses of this study. Statistical methods are used to give a general picture about the result of this study. Chi-Square is used to test the level of significance of variables of this study. The null hypothesis is tested using the chi-square test. The hypotheses are accepted at level of significance 0.05 or greater and rejected at less than 0.05. Some responses are presented diagrammatically.

GENERATION OF HYPOTHESESES

The study of quality service perceptions amongst students and faculty members of Jawaharlal Nehru University serves as the basis for the development of the following hypotheses which are tested in the sample under study. (Sahu, A., 2004)

H1 : The reliable information search (REL.2.1) relates with the level of efficiency of library staff (ASS.4.2)

H2 : The reliability of available Information in the OPAC (REL.2.5) relates with level of User-friendliness of OPAC (RES.3.6)

H3 : The user-friendliness of electronic databases (ASS.4.3) relates with level of use of Electronic database manuals (COM.6.4)

In this study, the following variables are analyzed on the basis of response percentage and presented in diagrammatically/graphically which helps to develop the quality services in the library:

* Analysis of the user's perception on Tangible (Q.7)
* Analysis of the rcsponses of faculty & students perceptions on JNU Library services (Q.9)

HYPOTHESES TESTS

The null hypotheses are tested using the Chi-Square test. The hypotheses are accepted at level of significance 0.05 or greater and rejected at less than 0.05. Questionnaire for the investigation of Quality Service Perceptions amongst students and faculty members of the Jawaharlal Nehru University is used to testing the following hypothesis. (Sahu, A., 2004)

H1: The reliable information search (REL.2.1) relates with the level of efficiency of library staff (ASS.4.2)

Null Hypothesis (H_0): There is no significance relationship between two variables

Alternative Hypothesis (H_a): There is a strong relationship with two variables

Table 1. Reliable Information Search (REL.2.1) and Efficiency of Library Staff (ASS.4.2)

	Efficiency of Lib. Staff (ASS. 4.2)			
Reliable Info Search (REL.2.1)	*Positive*	*Negative*	*Not Sure*	*Total*
Positive	33	4	1	38
Negative	45	11	5	61
Not Sure	1	0	0	1
Total	79	15	6	100

Note : The Value of Chi-Square: 2.863064,
Degree of Freedom : 4
The Tabulated Value at 95% (0.05)
confidence interval : **9.488**

The test of statistic shows that Null Hypothesis is accepted. There is no significant relationship between the efficiency of staff and the availability of reliable information.

The JNU library has adequate stock of the reference collection and most respondents have a positive perspective on it. However, when they have to locate a particular reference material, the efficiency of the Library staff may become important. But as per the hypothesis indicates Table-1 (Positive: 38% and Negative: 61%), there are differences in reliable information search for different user groups. (See Table-1)

H2: The reliability of available Information in the OPAC (REL.2.5) relates with level of User-friendliness of OPAC (RES.3.6)

Null Hypothesis (H_0): There is no significance relationship between the reliability of available Information in the OPAC (REL.2.5) and User-friendliness of OPAC (RES.3.6)

Alternative Hypothesis (H_a): There is a strong relationship with the reliability of available Information in the OPAC (REL.2.5) and User-friendliness of OPAC (RES.3.6)

Table 2. Reliability of OPAC (REL.2.5) and User-friendliness of OPAC (RES.3.6)

	User-friendliness of OPAC (RES.3.6)			
Reliability of OPAC (REL.2.5)	*Positive*	*Negative*	*Not Sure*	*Total*
Positive	64	15	3	82
Negative	0	3	1	4
Not Sure	4	3	7	14
Total	68	21	11	100

Note: The Value of Chi-Square: 37.06875,
Degree of Freedom : 4
The Tabulated Value at 95% (0.05)
confidence interval : **9.488**

The test of statistic shows that Null Hypothesis is rejected. There is strong significant relationship between the reliability of the OPAC and User-friendliness of OPAC. The JNU library has used LIBSYS software for library automation. OPAC system of the JNU Library is very reliable to search the information. As per the statistic table-5.2 shows that 82% responses positive for the reliability of OPAC and 68% responses positive for the user-friendliness of OPAC. However, when the search of any reliable information, the OPAC must be user friendliness. As per the result of statistic & questionnaire 11% of responses of student not sure about the user-friendliness of the OPAC. That means lack of user awareness programme, users don't know to the use of OPAC. (see Table-2)

H3: The user-friendliness of electronic databases (ASS.4.3) relates with level of use of electronic database manuals (COM.6.4)

Null Hypothesis (H_0): There is no significance relationship between the user-friendliness of electronic databases (ASS.4.3) and use of Electronic database manuals (COM.6.4)

Alternative Hypothesis (H_a): There is a strong relationship with the user-friendliness of electronic databases (ASS.4.3) and use of Electronic database manuals (COM.6.4)

Table 3. User-friendliness of Electronic Databases (ASS.4.3) and Use of Electronic Database Manuals (COM.6.4)

User-friendliness of Electronic Databases (RES.3.6)	*Use of Electronic Databases Manual (COM.6.4)*			
	Positive	*Negative*	*Not Sure*	*Total*
Positive	50	14	11	75
Negative	5	7	1	13
Not Sure	2	2	8	12
Total	57	23	20	100

Note: The Value of Chi-Square: 26.75565,
Degree of Freedom : 4
The Tabulated Value at 95% (0.05) confidence interval : 9.488

The test of statistic shows that Null Hypothesis is

rejected . There is strong significant relationship between the User-friendliness of Electronic Databases and use of the Electronic databases manuals. The JNU library has very good collection of electronic databases and Digitalize statistical databases. Electronic databases are very reliable source for search the latest information on any specific subject. As per the statistic table-5.3 shows that 75% responses (student & faculty) positive for the user friendliness of electronic databases and 57% responses positive for the use of electronic database manuals. But as per result, compared to the responses of use of electronic databases manuals with user friendliness of electronic databases, generated little positive responses. As per the questionnaire maximum positive responses received were from the faculty members on use of manual & user-friendliness of electronic databases. Due to difficult use of the manual of electronic databases, maximum students still don't know how to use the electronic databases. (see Table-3).

In this study the following variables are analyzed on the basis of responses percentage and presented in diagrammatically:

1. Analysis of the user's perception on Tangible (Q.7)

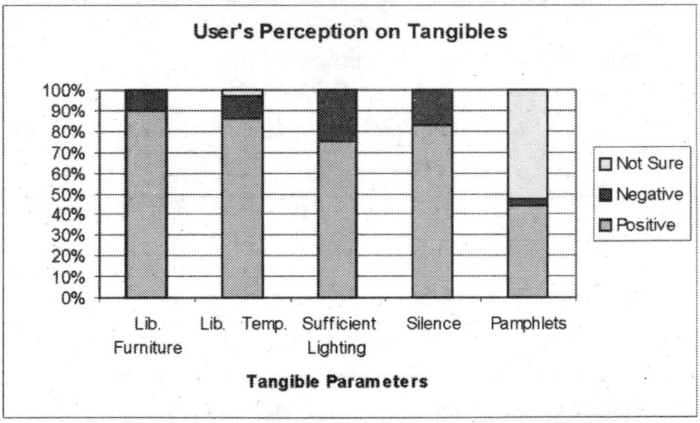

Fig. 1. Analysis of User's perception on Tangible

It can be seen from Figure-1 that most of the users are impressively satisfied with the services provided by the Library. Considering the furniture of the Library, it can be analyzed that 90% of the users responded positively in the survey. 85% of the users replied positively in respect to the temperature of the Library. In order to concentrate, lighting plays a very crucial role and 75% of the users have satisfactorily responded in the survey. One of the most important requirements of any excellent library is to preserve and maintain silence and in the survey 82% of the users retorted that the library retains adequate silence.

It the primary duty of any library to provide sufficient pamphlets and notes to guide the users and provide them maximum knowledge. In the survey just 45% of the users were satisfied with the leaflets provided by the library and majority of the users were either dissatisfied or were not sure regarding the service. So, it would be important for the library to improve the service and generate the awareness to their users.

2. Analysis of the Student and faculty's perception on Library Services (Q.9)

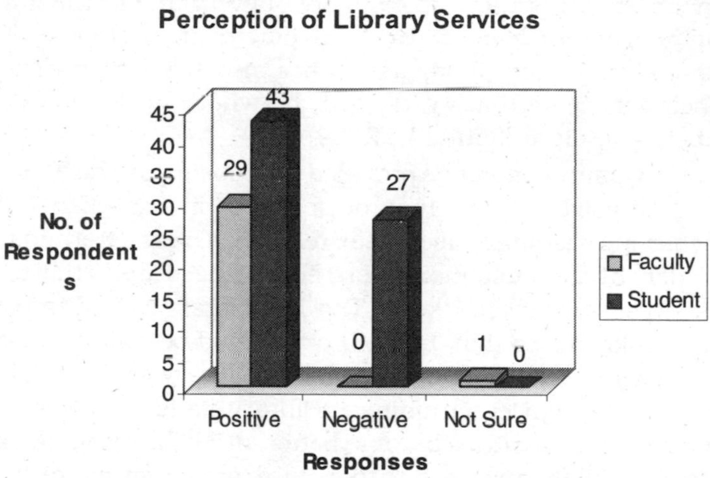

Fig. 2. Analysis of the Student's and faculty's perception on Library

It can be seen from Fig. 2 that the 63% students has given positive responses and 97% faculty members has given positive responses on perception of all library services which are provided in JNU Library. From Figure-2 we concluded that the library staffs has given to much importance to faculty members and less importance to students. Students are mainly frequent users of the academic library. So the staff library should also give equal importance to student needs.

RESULT & DISCUSSIONS

The hypotheses tests would appear to show that the user's information seeking behavior might be determined not only by their needs for information but also by their status. This has been clearly demonstrated by the significant differences in the perception of students and faculty. Information seeking behaviour therefore is relative to the situation and contingent upon the problem or decision at hand. So, the library staffs should not differentiate between the request of student and faculty for search of information always try to give equal importance on both request and provide them right information in a right time.Total quality management is the responsibility of every one in the library or information center. Every department, section or unit should introduce quality assurance measures in provision of their service so that in the end the whose library is quality abiding or alert. (Sahu, A., 2004)

Quality can not be provided by focusing on the "System" and "Procedure". It must be focused on the client/user. Achieving customer/user focus requires a clear determination to delight the customer/user there is need nevertheless to "take care of the care takers". The JNU Library should empower its employees, so that JNU Library should be conduct quality management training programme for library staffs. And also provide the high level trainings to library staffs to improve their work environment. To become better, JNU library should also evaluate all its approaches to service, set performance goals, solve and prevent problems and communicate fed base to both its internal and external customers/users. The JNU Library should create constancy of purpose for improving service, constantly improving the system of providing service, conducting training for all workers and remaining barriers.

This study would appear to suggest that the users of

JNU Library were largely satisfied with various aspects of services quality except responsiveness and communication. Communication is brought in here because some students suggested that they did not know about the existence of some of the available services. Adequate publicity should be given to the services that are available in JNU Library and assistance provided in accessing and using them. Proper and effective communication system should be made available to the users, so that they can be informed about the availability of the things they requires. Information seeking there fore is a function not only of awareness of the possible existence of documents but also their availability are accessibility.

For responsiveness, some students has given negative responses. The maximum students told that they considered important that the library should provide the latest publications to the users difference subjects as per their demand. Another point is that books should be re-shelved every day. As per the survey, maximum users suggested that the books could not be found at proper place. So the re-shelving of the books properly and timely is a important job for library staffs.

CONCLUSION

The results would appear to indicate that the JNU Library is not lacking quality service. However we need to note that quality information service (QIS) is about helping users to define and satisfy their information needs, building their confidence in using information retrieval systems, and making the whole activity of working with library staffs a pleasurable experience. To achieve total quality in information service (TQIS) the JNU Library should provide a comprehensive information programme that in predicated on the needs and activities of the users.

Service providers, no matter what their profession, need to know that the definition of quality is a subjective matter. It is a fact that the users will always dictate what he/she wants, when and how. The service provider, though certainly not a bystander in this transactional relationship, is always influenced to a large extent by the demands of the users. The user can always change the direction, form and character of any service depending on his/her needs. The provider's responsibility to the user is to adapt to such needs. The service therefore should always be tailor-made to accommodate the needs and wants of the customer. Quality means conforming first to customer requirements, and then to standards or specifications. Users have a tendency of voting with their feet if things do not work out their way. Quality service therefore is a two way and symbiotic relationship where the user prescribes the needs and the service provider capitulates to them within available capabilities and resources. The user is always boss.

The JNU Library may wish to evaluate their each service for improving and successfully implementing the service quality.

REFERENCES

1. Barnard, S.B. (1993) 'Implementing total quality management: a model for research libraries', *Journal of Library Administration*, 18:1-2, 57-70.
2. Broady P.J., and Preston, H. (1999) 'Demonstrating quality in academic libraries', New Library World, 100:1148, p. 124.
3. Butterwick, N.B. (1993) 'Total quality management in the university library', *Library Management*, 14:3, 28-31.
4. Clausen, H. (1995) 'The Nordic information quality project: Final report', *New Library World*, 96:1121, 4-10.
5. Dadzie, P.S. (2004) 'Quality management initiatives in blame library: possibilities, challenges and constraints for top management commitment', *Library Management*, 25:1/2, 56-61.
6. Fitzsimmons, J.A., and Fitzsimmons. M.J. (2000) *Service Management: Operations, Strategy, and Information Technology*, (3rd ed.) Boston, McGraw-Hill, 43-67.
7. Gopal, K. (2004) 'JNU Library: A profile', *JNU News*, Jan-Feb, 2001.
8. Gopal, K. (2004) 'Total Quality Management (TQM) in Libraries and Information, In the Dhawan, S.N. (ed.), *Library in Cyber Age*, New Delhi, 2004.
9. Haksever, C., Render, B., Russell, R.S., and Murdick, R.G.

(2000) *Service Management and Operations*, 2nd ed., Prentice Hall, New Jersey, p. 328-344.

10. Jawaharlal Nehru University *http://www.jnu.ac.in/*
11. Nitecki, D.A. and Hernon, P. (2000) 'Measuring service quality at Yale University's Libraries', *Journal of Academic Librarianship*, 26:4, 259-273.
12. Nitecki, D.A. (1996) 'Changing the concept and measure of service quality in academic libraries', *Journal of Academic Librarianship*, 22:3., 181-190.
13. Oldman, C. and Wills, G. (1977) The Beneficial Library, MCB Book, Bradford, UK, MCD Book .
14. Orr, R.H. (1973) 'Measuring the goodness of library services: a general framework for considering quantitative measures', *Journal of Documentation*, 29:3, 315-32.
15. Osman, S., Goon, C. A., and Aris, W.H.W. (1998) 'Quality services: policies & practices in Malaysia', *Library Management*, 19:7, 426-433.
16. Parasuraman, A., Berry, L.L., and Zeithaml, V.A. (1988) 'SERVQUAL: a multiple item scale for measuring consumer perceptions of service quality', *Journal of Retailing*, 64:1, 12-40.
17. Pritchard, S.M. (1995) Library benchmarking: old wine in new bottles?', *Journal of Academic Librarianship*, 21:6, 491-495.
18. Quinn, B. (1997) 'Adapting service quality concepts to academic libraries', *Journal of Academic Librarianship*, 23:5, 359-369.
19. Rajan N.V., Ravi B. (2001) 'Total Quality in Libraries: The Reality'. In Quest for Quality, edited by S.M. Dhawan. New Delhi: Indian Library Association, 149-154.
20. Sahu, A. (2004) 'TQM for organizational excellence: a case study of Jawaharlal Nehru University library', M. Phil thesis, Alagappa University, Karaikudi.
21. Seay, T.S. and Cohen (1996) 'Measuring and improving the quality of public services: hybrid approach', *Library Trends*, 44:3, 464-90.
22. Sharma J.C. (2001) 'Total Quality Management in Library and Information Services'. *In Quest for Quality*, edited by S.M. Dhawan, New Delhi, Indian Library Association, 166-171.
23. Thapisa, A. P. N., and Gamini. V. (1999), 'Perceptions of quality

service at the university of Botswana library: what nova says', *Library Management*, 20:7, 373-383.

24. Walmiki R.H. (2001) 'Total Quality Management in Librarianship' In Quest for Quality, edited by S.M. Dhawan. New Delhi, Indian Library Association, 155-160.
25. Whitehall, T. (1992) 'Quality in Library and Information Services: A review', *Library Management*, 13:5, 23-35.

11

Total Quality Management: Implication on Library Services

Neha Joshi

ABSTRACT

The libraries in future are going to play important role. The factors for success will definitely be determined by maintaining quality in all respects including resources, services, use of management skills, creation of local content etc. With the continued trend of emerging high power technologies, it has become increasingly necessary that libraries at all levels need to understand how to plan, evaluate, procure, install and use new technologies successfully. The article gives an overall view of how TQM principles can be applied in library services and how it can improve the functionality of any library.

INTRODUCTION

The concept of quality of a product or service has been existing since the very existence of mankind. However expectations have been changing over the change in time due to availability of better technology. Today no organization can progress, grow and be competitive unless it pays attention to quality of its product or service. Though the word quality is very familiar to us, it is different for different people.

Whenever we talk of any good product or service we look upon it s quality. To define quality of the product becomes easier because of the physical presence or easy methods of comparing with others. But when we come to service it's not so easy to decide about its quality. Quality of the service is based upon speed of response, dependability, control, facilities.

Thus whether it is service or product quality matters "Quality is the degree to which a set of inherent characteristics fulfills a need or expectation that is stated general implied or obligatory".

The word quality has many meanings:

* A degree of excellence
* Conformance with requirements
* The totality of characteristics of an entity that bear on its ability to satisfy stated or implied needs
* Fitness for use
* Freedom from defects imperfections or contamination
* Delighting customers

Garvin, 1988, identified the following types of quality:

* Transcendent quality (quality always exists)
* Product based quality (product meeting high quality standard)
* User based quality (quality to meet users' requirements)
* Output based quality (manufacturing based quality)
* Value based quality (cost-benefit relation)

In the context of library and information centers quality relates to performance of the system, quantity and quality of the collection, quality of services and finally users satisfaction. In a world that is forever changing, the only certainty is change. Therefore strategies for building up library of 21st century librarians should not just adapt to change but to prepare for it, facilitate it and shape it. Libraries are confronting challenging dynamic technological environment demanding the exhaustive and effective utilization of information and communication technologies in order to survive and meet the information needs of user community.

WHAT IS TQM? AND ITS IM PLICATION ON LIBRARY

Total quality management is enhancement to the traditional way of doing business.

Analyzing the word

Total: made up of the whole

Quality: degree of excellence a product or service provides

Management: act, art or manner of handling, controlling, directing etc.

Therefore TQM is the art of managing the whole to achieve excellence.

TQM requires six basic concepts:

* a committed and involved management to provide long term top to bottom organizational support
* an unwavering focus on the customer, both internally and externally
* effective involvement and utilization of the entire work force
* continuous improvement of the business and production process
* treating suppliers as partners
* Establish performance measures for the processes.

Some of the components of TQM which are related to library for its successful management are as follows:

* Library as an organization becomes important for providing good services to its users. As an organization librarian becomes manager for library. As being the head of the library, librarian should plan out for providing better services. The library manager has to determine the different aspects of the plan and fix the parameters for making services more effective. Librarian should involve top management for financial decisions as well as subordinate to work well.
* The readers or users are the customer for library. All the readers rely on the working of the library to get their information needs satisfied. To satisfy users library should anticipate the needs of readers and should

acquire the necessary techniques and respond well to them. Here the customers are different than the industry customers. Users will satisfy if only they will get ongoing good service and good collection. So each library should be user centered.

* Effective involvement and utilization of the entire work force emphasizes on the importance of ensuring the services that are to be rendered in the library, which add value and importance to the final output. The whole staff should serve the purpose of users satisfaction by lending the various services with appropriate training if required.
* To have quality in the library output and services the librarian should adopt the approach of continuous improvement in the library management. The 5th law of Dr. Ranganathan stays the same philosophy as library is a growing organism. It should be continuous process to improve its quality of services and facilities to make library a grown ....
* Any organization can achieve the TQ if only it sets some measurable objectives to achieve. This is true with library also. If librarian sets some objective for betterment or improvement of the library services, the library will automatically serve the purpose of satisfying its users. The 4th law of Dr. Ranganathan states that save the time of the reader means provide services to users by which they can use the facilities without spending much time. For e.g. a library can set an objective as users should not stand on circulation counter for more than 2 minutes.

PRINCIPLES OF QULITY MANAGEMENT

* Customer focus
* Leadership
* Involvement of people
* Process approach
* System approach to management
* Continual improvement
* Factual approach of decision making
* Mutually beneficial supplier relationships

Customer Focus

This principle expects as "organizations depend on their customers and therefore should understand current and future customer needs, meet customer requirements and strive to exceed customer expectations"

In library also the users or the members are the customers. Librarian should see the requirements or the needs of the users. For libraries, customer focus applies in three areas:

* Resources: information content
* Organization: service environment and resource delivery
* Service delivered by staff

The quality management can serve the purpose of satisfying customers by :

* Proper guidance
* Reduction in waiting time
* Trained Library staff with friendly, courteous behaviour
* Materials as per requirements
* Materials in their correct place
* Equipment is kept in good working order
* Latest services like electronic services
* Material arriving within a set time
* The good environment
* Library furniture in good condition and facilities and so on.

Leadership

Leaders establish unity of purpose and direction for the organization. They should create and maintain the internal environment in which people can become fully involved in achieving the organization's objectives.

In the library librarian is the leader. It is always say that if the leader is not good the workforce is unhappy, de-motivated, dissatisfied. Good leadership strives to bring about a set of shared values- a shared vision so that everyone knows what the organization is trying to do. The culture, vision, values, beliefs and motivation in an organization arise from leadership. In the library the librarian has to play the duel role of motivating staff as well as users.

In today's world librarian has become technology application leader. Librarian as a leader should acquire all skills like

Communication skills to maintain sound environment among staff and users.

Record keeping skills: to keep a record of all aspects including materials as well as staff member's strength and weaknesses.

Teaching skills: many a time librarian should be able to teach his or her subordinates to improve upon some required skills for e.g. learning about new technology

Information search skills: librarian should be trained enough to search for any kind of information whenever required. And he or she should encourage all staff to do some this kind of exercises.

Management skills: A manager is someone who works with and through other people by coordinating their work activities in order to accomplish organizational goals. That may mean coordinating the work of a departmental group, or it might mean supervising a single person.

Paper published by Luther Gulick has mentioned seven basic functions of a manager as "POSDCORB" means Planning, Organizing, Staffing, Directing, Coordinating, Reporting and Budgeting which the librarian should also have for becoming the good leader.

Involvement of people

People at all levels are the essence of an organization and their full involvement enables their abilities to be used for the organization's benefit.

Librarian should tap the source of knowledge, encourage personnel to make a contribution and utilize their personal experience. Librarian should encourage teamwork by maintaining good relations with others, sharing and delegating responsibilities and encouraging members to make a variety of contributions in joint ventures. The dictionary meaning of empowerment is to invest people with authority. Its purpose is to tap the enormous reservoir of creativity and potential contribution that lies within every worker at all levels.

Librarian can involve others in deciding the objectives of the library, implementing new upcoming technology, reducing cost factor, for providing good services etc.

Process approach and continual improvement

A desired result is achieved more efficiently when related resources and activities are managed as a process.

Continual improvement of the organization's overall performance should be a permanent objective of the organization.

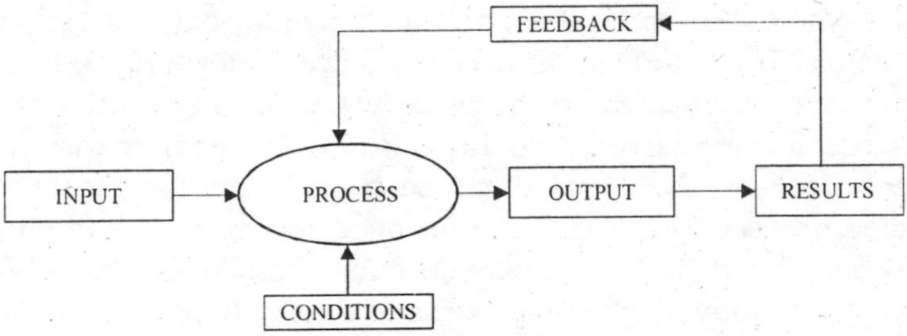

Input may be materials, money, information, data etc. output may be information, data, service etc. the output of the one process can be input of the other process. Output requires performance measures. The results can be user's satisfaction. Feedback is the method to measure the performance level of the organization. Continuous process improvement is designed to utilize the resources of the organization to achieve a quality driven culture.

In the library the process is purchasing of the material, processing of the material, acquisition, stamping and labeling, data entry if required on computer, stacking, circulation, preservation and weeding out outdated or material in bad condition. In library inputs are the resources available to the system ranging from financial, staffing and material in any form. Outputs are activities the system exports like transactions, working hours, availability of the staff and facilities, use and usability of the materials. The results may be like whether users are satisfied or dissatisfied. The methods can be used to review the results by taking feedback or by questionnaire which will help library to improve in its services provided to users. The process should be on the basis of continual improvement and not for one time.

System approach to management

Identifying, understanding and managing interrelated processes as a system contributes to the organization's effectiveness and efficiency in achieving its objectives.

A system is an ordered set of ideas, principles and theories or a chain of operations that produce specific results. The system approach recognizes that the behaviour of any part of a system has some effect on the behaviour of the system as a whole. If the individual processes are performing well, the system as a whole is not necessarily performing equally well. In the library also we do have different departments like technical section, periodical section, circulation section, reference section. Each section or a department has given specific work. If any one section fails it may affect the whole system or may affect the process of that section only.

Factual approach of decision making

Effective decisions are based on the analysis of data and information.

Facts are obtained from observations performed by qualified personnel using devices, the integrity of which is known. The factual approach to decision making leads to take certain actions.

In library the different sections or departments are dependent on each other. Library should have a goal or an aim which will serve its purpose. While deciding its goal and objectives librarian should look upon the facts. The facts may be like total area, collection capacity, financial support etc. Thus librarian should take reviews on the functioning and requirements of the library. Librarian should also put some measurements for checking the level of the performance. Librarian should be able to analyze the obtain fact from the collected information. Record keeping of all the data is always helpful to come over the drawbacks. Thus librarian should be able to accept facts for taking good decisions.

Mutually beneficial supplier relationship

An organization and its suppliers are interdependent and a mutually beneficial relationship the ability of both to create value.

Customers and suppliers have the same goal- to satisfy the end user. The better the supplier's quality the better the relation. The key elements for partnering relationship are long term commitment, trust and shared vision.

For the library the suppliers may include publishers, vendors, distributors etc. who provides various kinds of material to the library.

Dr. Kaoru Ishikawa has suggested ten principles to ensure quality products and services and eliminate unsatisfactory conditions between the customer and the supplier:

1. Both the customer and the fully responsible for the control of quality.
2. Both the customer and the supplier should be independent of each other and respect each other's independence.
3. The customer is responsible for providing the supplier with clear and sufficient requirement so that the supplier can know precisely what to produce.
4. Both the customer and the supplier should enter into a nonadversarial contract with respect to quality, quantity, price, delivery method, and terms of payments.
5. The supplier is responsible for providing the quality that will satisfy the customer and submitting necessary data upon the customer's request.
6. Both the customer and the supplier should decide the method to evaluate the quality of the product or service to the satisfaction of both parties.
7. Both the customer and the supplier should establish in the contract the method by which then can reach an amicable settlement of any disputes that may arise.
8. Both the customer and the supplier should continually

exchange information, sometimes by multifunction teams, that will improve the product or service quality.

9. Both the customer and the supplier should perform business actives such as procurement, production and inventory planning, clerical work, and systems so that an amicable and satisfactory relationship is maintained.
10. Both the customer and the supplier, when dealing with business transactions, should always have the best interest of the end user in mind.

BENEFITS OF TQM

Savell and Williams outlines quality management implementation process for improving the internal quality of service functions as:

* Select area of quality management emphasis
* Define the service process or operation
* Analyse current system/ process
* Develop excellence model
* Identify key performance areas
* Develop process control system
* Integrate process control into management control
* Establish ongoing improvement process

By implementing the above steps any organization can lead towards becoming best.

Tangible Gains of TQM	*Intangible Gains of TQM*
Better product quality	Effective team work
Productivity improvement	Enhancement of job interest
Reduced quality costs	Improvement in human relations and work area Morale
Increased market	Participative culture
Increased profitability	Customer satisfaction
Reduced employee grievances	Improved communication.
	Enhanced problem – solving capacity. Better organization image

CONCLUSION

The libraries in future are going to play important role. The factors for success will definitely be determined by maintaining quality in all respects including resources, services, use of management skills, creation of local content etc. With the continued trend of emerging high power technologies, it has become increasingly necessary that libraries at all levels need to understand how to plan, evaluate, procure, install and use new technologies successfully. The user friendly infrastructure will lead users towards more usage of all kinds of resources. Quality service focuses on the interaction between users and service providers, and the gap or difference between expectations about service provision and perception about how the service is provided.

REFERENCES

Besterfield, Dale (1999), Total Quality Management-2e, Pearson Education, Delhi

Hoyle, David (2000), ISO 9000: Quality Systems Handbook, Butterworth Heinemann, Oxford

Kaul, H. K.(2004), "Quality Library Management: the key principles", In Library and Information Networking, NACLIN, Pune.

Koganuramath, Muttayya, Angadi, Mallikarjun, "Interpersonal Skills for Effective Library Management", http://eprints.rclis.org

Krishan, Gopal (2004), "Information Qulaity Service and User's Satisfaction in the Digital Era", In Library and Information Networking, NACLIN, Pune.

Kumar, P.S.G. (2002), A Student's Manual of Library and Information Science, B.R. Publishing Corporation, Delhi

Livingstone, David (2005) "Total Quality Management for Library and Information Centre", SRELS: Journal of Information Management, Vol.42 No1, pp. 75-80

Mohanty, R. P., Lakhe, R.R (2004), Handbook of Total Quality Management, Jaico Publishing House, Mumbai

Mohanty, R. P., Lakhe, R.R (2002), Total Quality Management in the Service Sector, Jaico Publishing House, Mumbai

Mounissamy, P, Swaroop Rani, B. S.(2004) "Application of Total Quality Management in Library and Information Services", SRELS: Journal of Information Management, Vol.41 No3, pp 267-274

Patil, S. K. and Others (2004), "Nature and Quality of Digital Information Hunting: a case study of the University of Pune", In Library and Information Networking, NACLIN, Pune.

Talukder, Tridibesh, Ghosh, Saptarshi (2004) "Total Quality Management and its Implication On Library Laws", SRELS: Journal of Information Management, Vol.41 No3, pp. 255-266

12
Marketing of Information Products and Services

Sujata Santosh

ABSTRACT

Significant changes have taken place all over the world and these changes in various arenas have had a significant effect/impact on information requirements and its use. Libraries and information centres, therefore, have to generate revenue for self-sustenance. Public sponsorship and subsidy arc drying up giving rise to the need to find alternate sources of revenue. Then there is complexity involved in identifying clients and their requirements, and servicing them. There is a strong need to leverage the technology and find new levels of economics of scale to serve the increasing potential clientele. It is extremely essential for libraries and information centres to be marketing orientated to guarantee their future. This article discusses the various issues related to marketing of information products and services at the same time highlighting its importance. Various factors like prerequisites for marketing, barriers to marketing, factors inhibiting marketing orientation and marketing plan and guidelines for preparation of marketing plan are discussed in detail.

INTRODUCTION

The concept of marketing has emerged as the underlying philosophy of library and information services in this information age. Over the years, factors like information explosion, rising costs of information sources, declining support and funds, under use of information sources, budget cuts, increased costs involved in the application of technology, etc, have forced libraries and information centres to focus on the area of information marketing. In view of the fast changing information scenario, mainly due to multifaceted developments in information technology, the realization is now dawning that a coherent marketing programme needs to be integrated into a library's organizational structure.

Before 1970, the concept of marketing was confined to organizations supplying products rather than services. It was after Second World War, that American marketing expert Philips Kotler first suggested extending the application of marketing to services and non-profit making organizations. It was in 1970 that the public libraries in North America first applied the marketing concept to library profession (28).

In the last decade, significant changes have taken place all over the world and these changes in various arenas have had a significant effect/impact on information requirements and its use. First, developments in computer and networking have brought about a kind of information revolution. The boundaries and utility of information, and the speed and quantity of handling it are expanding (10). Second, the winds of globalization and privatization have been radically changing the long-held political and economic beliefs. Governments have been propagating that social institutions — be they hospitals, schools, colleges and libraries — become self - sufficient if they are to purposefully work and demonstrate their relevance and competence to their clients. Competition has now become the criteria for achieving excellence. Because of the change in political outlook and the economic compulsions, the generous attitude for the social institutions is changing. Libraries and information centres, therefore, have to generate revenue for self-sustenance. Third, the ever-rising social and economic expectations and demands have made information all the more important for the overall development of a country. Developing countries are no longer interested in information for the sake of information, knowledge for the sake of knowledge, or education for the sake of education (10).

Till now, librarians and information scientists have been happy in catering to the limited clientele of the school, college, university, research organization, government department, or public organization that has sponsored them. But now information has become an essential requirement for everyone. The value of information varies from clientele to clientele as well as from circumstance to circumstance; right information to the right user at the right time is very valuable. The role of information provider has, therefore, to be more aggressive. Today, computer and information technology has made possible, not only networking among information centres but also made possible availability of information to a larger clientele than the existing one. With the mushrooming of new information providers such as cyber cafes, mega-bookstores, online book dealers, the Internet community, consultants and individual customers, libraries, for example, cannot continue to assume that they are the only sources of information that people will consult (11). The new technology has made possible the creation of newer information products and services, and has facilitated their quick availability.

As a result, librarians are facing a four-pronged challenge (10).There is an increase in clientele, their variety, their demands, and their expectations coupled with an increase in the initial or capital cost of information and information technology. There is a strong need to leverage the technology and find new levels of economics of scale to serve the increasing potential clientele. Public sponsorship and subsidy are drying up giving rise to the need to find alternate sources of revenue. Then there is complexity involved in identifying clients and their requirements, and servicing them.

The traditional concept of a library or information centre as a social service for the sake of knowledge, and library, for the sake of library, has outlived its need. Preparing information products and services only when asked for, has to give in to a more systematic anticipation and research of the future requirements of different clients, leading to the preparation of appropriate products and services, and making these available to the clients.

RELEVANCE OF MARKETING FOR LIBRARIANS AND INFORMATION MANAGERS

Dr. S. R. Ranganathan described library as".... public institution or establishment charged with the care of a collection of books, the duty of making them accessible to those who require the use of them and task of converting every person in its neighborhood into a habitual library goer and reader of books" (15). In the early conceptualization of library and information centre's business, Dr. S.R. Ranganathan had the concept of customer orientation embedded into it. A focus on customer needs (Second Law) and wants through saving of time (Fourth Law) is clearly emphasized in his laws, as far back as 1931.

Brown (1) in his paper mentioned that marketing activities are a prominent part of life today. Many people work in marketing jobs or hold position with marketing departments. Most people think of marketing solely as advertising or selling. In reality, marketing is much more than selling the product or services. It is one to one interaction and an exchange of value in which both parties gain something.

With the acceleration of the process of liberalization and globalization coupled with unprecedented technological developments in vast information flow, the need for timely, correct and reliable information is more realized then ever before for scientific and industrial research. Availability of right information for the right user at right time and at right cost has become most vital. This scenario has posed major challenges to the information sector where prime function is to satisfy the complex and increasing demand for information products and services. Library and Information Centre should change their old practices to cope with the changes in social, technological, economical environment. Pressure for accountability and the emergence of enterprise culture has led the library and information professionals to take aggressive actions for financial self-sufficiency. So efficient marketing is very necessary for revenue generation.

INFORMATION MARKETING: AN OVERVIEW

Marketing is a comprehensive term and it includes all resources and a set of activities necessary to direct and facilitate the flow of goods and services from producers to consumers in the process of distribution. There is a common misconception that promotional activities alone constitute marketing (12). Marketing must include ascertaining, creating and satisfying the customer's wants and doing it at a profit. This is the proper concept of marketing function.

WHAT IS MARKETING?

Encyclopedia Britannica (5) defines marketing as directing of the flow of goods and services from producers to consumers or users. It is not confined to any particular type of economy, since goods must be marketed in all economies, societies except perhaps the most primitive'.

According to Smith (26), marketing is a stance and an attitude that focuses on meeting the needs of users. Marketing is a means of ensuring that libraries, librarians, and librarianship are integrated into both today's and tomorrow's emerging global culture. Marketing is not separate from good practice. It is good practice.

Peter Drucker, the management guru, defines marketing as follows:

It (marketing) is the whole business seen from the point of view of its final result, that is, from the customer's point of view...

Philip Kotler (14), the marketing guru, calls marketing 'a social and managerial process by which individuals and groups obtain what they need and want through creating, offering, and exchanging products of value with others'. Kotler further defines marketing concept as, the key to achieving organizational goals consists in determining the needs and wants of target market and delivering the desired satisfactions more effectively and efficiently than competitors.... The marketing concept rests on four pillars, namely target market, customer needs, coordinated marketing and profitability (17). Most organizations involved in information and development areas do not have profit as their sole objective. The fourth pillar of the marketing concept may then be changed to 'achievement of organizational objective(s).

Dragon (4) neatly defines that the concept of marketing and outlines its major aspects when he observed "marketing is a systematic approach to planning and achieving desired exchange relations with other groups. Marketing is concerned with developing, maintaining, and/or regulating exchange relations involving products, services, organizations, persons, places or causes".

In the opinion of Gopinath (7) marketing is a three tier process:

1. Marketing is an economic activity wherein productivity of information access and usage in studied.
2. Marketing is a social process wherein information is activised to serve a set of social activities.
3. Marketing is a managerial process as it helps in controlling information flow.

Bushing (2) explains "marketing offers both a theory and a process by which libraries can link products, results, and roles. Marketing can assist libraries in determining their future and in identifying quality products — services, programs, and materials. A marketing audit and the resulting plan can contribute to a library's ability to find a niche in the present as well as in the future and to fill that niche by an optimal allocation of resources. A marketing orientation can assist libraries in defining their role and in guaranteeing their future".

From the above definitions one can make out that Marketing is a managerial process of discovering and translating consumer's needs and desires into products and services (through planning) and producing the planned products, creating demand for these products and services (through promotion and pricing), serving the consumer demand (through planned physical distribution) with the help of marketing channels. Marketing, therefore, is the on-going or continuous process of defining, anticipating and creating customer's needs and wants, and of organizing all the resources of the enterprise to satisfy customer's demand by offering right good, in right quality, at right prices, at right places, at right time, to right consumers.

WHY INFORMATION MARKETING?

Information marketing is essential for the following reasons:

1. The information centres spend/invest huge funds on collection, processing and storage of information resources, and these resources are put to very meager use, which implies wastage of funds. For the promotion of the use of information resource, there is need for marketing. Kassel (13) talks about transforming libraries into recognized corporate assets.
2. The needy has casual or almost nil need perception because of which he does not use and demand information. Therefore, information marketing is essential to facilitate need perception on the part of the needy and thereby create demand. In other words, it is supply/ marketing, which creates demand.
3. Information is a very essential product, "Information may be considered to be the life blood of planning, directing and controlling any enterprise". But still as it is freely and widely available in certain cases and to certain extent it can be dispensed with, these factors play a key role in affecting the demand for information but every demand for information is very intensive one. Lack of realization of this aspect puts one to disadvantage and thereby loss of fruits reaped by proper information use. Marketing of information eliminates these lacunas and renders every information needy information rich.
4. Information marketing is required because information is inevitable for solving day-to-day problems yet there is no information needs perception on the part of the information needy. Thereby lack of demand for information. In certain cases marketing is essential to create awareness and thereby demand for a product. Further, in certain other cases though there will be need but the needs are unperceived, unmet and suppressed.
5. To ensure the optimum use of information, information providers should try to publicize their products or resources.

6. For elevation of the image and status of the information centres and the profession, marketing is essential. The image of the information centres and status of information providers would improve as marketing creates and increases demand for information.

ECONOMIC FEATURES OF INFORMATION

Research in the field of information economics has proved beyond doubt that information is an economic resource. An information resource represents a complex web of institutional relationships that cut across traditional economic, socio-legal boundaries. The market in information has pretty much the same nature and the same motivation as any other sort of market (22). But information products and services can be economic commodities to only a limited extent, as these possess certain other features, which are not always shared by other economic goods (9). These features are:

1. Information is a collective commodity. That is, if one person in a group purchases it, then the rest get it, either free or at a much lower cost, which brings about failure of markets. Thus it is not easily divisible or appropriate (8).
2. The end users of information are not always the purchasers of information because the information centres buy it for them.
3. The information requirements of end users are not totally reflected by the demands of the library and hence difficulties arise in studying the demand pattern of end users (8).
4. One of the unique and salient characteristics of information as a commodity is that it is inherently not scarce and that its value-in-use often increases with use.
5. Unlike other commodities, which are non-renewable, and with few exceptions depletable, information is self-regenerative and often feeds on itself so that the identification of new piece of knowledge immediately creates both the demand and production of subsequent pieces.

INEFFICIENT USE OF INFORMATION

Inefficient use of information wastes money. Many examples of inefficiency can be found including (6):

* Information which is collected but not needed.
* Information stored long after it is needed.
* Useful information, which is inaccessible to the potential users.
* Information disseminated widely than is necessary.
* Inefficient methods used to collect, analyze, store and retrieve information.
* Collection of the same basic information by more than one group of people in the same department.
* Duplication in storage of the same basic information.

THE MARKETING APPROACH

The marketing approach in managing a library or an information centre, therefore, involves the process of asking questions and seeking information on the following four-fold dimensions to evolve an organizational strategy (10):

MARKET

* What is the target public or audience and what are their needs, wants and demands? What adds value to whatever they are trying to achieve or perform?
* What is the competition? How should the product/ library centre be viewed by the target public in relation to competition?

EXTERNAL MARKETING

* What is the product/service and what should it be? Should there be an introduction of a new product / service? And what kind of support could be provided to the client in using the information effectively?
* How should it be priced so that the client can pay his/ her fair share and it can still generate the required revenues?
* How should it be promoted to selected customers to communicate the desired position?

* How should it be delivered to the place where the user needs it, when he/she needs it, and the way he/she needs it?

INTERACTIVE MARKETING

* How should the requirements of the target audience be assessed and value delivered to the customers?
* What kind of customer contact personnel and systems should be employed to assess the requirements?
* What should be the mechanism to constantly update systems and recruit, train, and motivate customer contact personnel so as to assess and deliver the requirements of target customers?

INTERNAL MARKETING

* How the internal organization should be oriented to serve the external target segments and how should customer contact personnel assess, produce and deliver the required products and services?
* What kind of planning, control and organizational mechanism should be set up to achieve all the above steps?

The marketing approach can be used to make the existing planning process of a library or an information centre more rigorous. The annual reports or libraries and information centres would then look like that of any 1business organization indicating the targets set at the beginning of the year and the performance achieved. Moreover, organizational planning and performance evaluation would lead to the much needed vitality in the information profession and management (10).

PREREQUISITES FOR MARKETING

For marketing any commodity including the information commodity certain prerequisites are needed. In case of information commodity the following conditions may be taken into consideration (21):

* A well-developed store or collection of data or information
* Repackaging of the data of information into a marketable commodity.

* A target community, which would need the commodity.
* Creation of awareness about the commodity.
* Creation of demand for the said community.
* Marketing of the commodity
* Satisfaction of the consumer with the commodity.
* Continuous supply of the commodity without break or delay.
* Obtaining the feedback from the customers on the commodity.
* Conducting of research with regard to the changing needs of the customers with a view to improve the quality of the commodity.

WHAT INHIBITS FROM BEING MARKETING ORIENTED

The same factors, which inhibit, any other social organization or profession, are responsible for inhibiting the librarians and information managers, from adopting the marketing approach. Lafond (16) indicated "because most librarians and documentalists have not been trained with the concept of marketing, the introduction of marketing to information services has not always been easy. There is also some reluctance to market because many documentalists and librarians still feel information should be free. In most cases, because of lack of expertise in marketing, documentation and information centres have difficulty in introducing the marketing concept, which starts by the identification of the potential user to fulfill the mandate of the service, the identification of their needs, etc".

According to Seetharama (24) confusion at the conceptual level among librarians and information scientists that marketing is nothing but promotion and sales is a major factor responsible for lack of use of marketing concepts and tools in libraries and information centres. There is a lack of a definite marketing policy. Users themselves are reluctant to pay for information services resulting in the adoption of economy measures. Moreover, user needs assessment studies are inadequate due to methodological deficiencies and due to the fact that they are not carried out on a continuing basis.

THE FOUR BARRIERS TO MARKETING

The four barriers to the adoption of the marketing approach are Attitudinal, Structural, Systemic and Environmental.

1. Attitude : Library and information professionals have been content by providing the required information to the client as per his/her specific request/need. And in case the library professionals intend to bring market orientation in their library and information centres they need to attempt something beyond that. This means a major shift in approach of the library and information professional is required for the purpose.

2. Structure : Libraries and information centres are part of a large organization, thus they are just as a sub-system of the main system. And if main system follows a marketing approach then only it (marketing) can be integral to the sub-system. Moreover, only the counter clerks for circulation and reference and less frequently, the librarian, is the only staff which comes in contact with the public or clients. As a result, there is no staff to reach out, understand, and capture the needs and requirements of the client. Also, traditional security of job, and lack of involvement of professionals in the management of the library or information centre hinders marketing approach.

3. System : Libraries and information centres have been more concerned with storage and security aspects of the information rather than its use, because of various well known reasons like physical verification, audit, etc. Guarding or protecting the information is therefore given more importance than the proper utilization of information for the satisfaction of the client. Therefore, system needs to be changed to make it more client and service oriented i.e. it should lay more emphasis on the use and user of information.

4. Environment : In developing countries, like ours, it is still believed that information should be free and should be sought by clients themselves. There is no attempt at seeking out clients or creating a market for itself, as they do receive grants and funds from the government or private organizations so Marketing and payment are never given any attention.

NEEDS FOR MARKETING

The reasons for this marketing approach are several and include the following:

1. Information for development : The present age is rightly characterized as the age of information. The fact that information is a key resource for the economic, socio-cultural and political development of a nation is gaining increasing acceptance. Therefore, availability of right information at right time and at right cost is very important. This means library and information professionals will have to play a more pro-active role, they need to put the information to effective use rather than just having and storing it. And for this they should work towards bringing the user and information closer (20).

2. Information Technology : Information Technology (IT) has ushered in a variety of media that can help in efficient and effective acquisition, organization and dissemination of information. Computers and CD-ROMs have found increasing acceptance in library and information centres; multimedia has shown much potential for library and information centres; and information networks have broken down time and space barriers (20). Thus these IT tools and techniques have enabled generation of various kinds of information products and services. But library and information professionals need to generate awareness among the clientele and thereby market their products and services.

3. Increasing Resource Constraints : On one side library and information centres need to acquire and organize learning resources and satisfy the complex and ever increasing information needs of their users and on other side they are facing resource constraints. Therefore, they need to develop into out-reaching centres and revenue generating ones also.

4. Inadequate Resource Utilization : The rich learning resource materials built-up by library and information centres remain largely underutilized as they are accessible only to the clientele of it's parent organization. Therefore, library and information centres will have to look out for ways and means to increase their client base in the external sectors and open up their resources, facilities and services to meet the information needs of this external sectors and open up their resources, facilities and services to meet the information needs of this external clientele without jeopardizing the interests of the internal clientele (20).

5. Increasing cost of Information and IT : Information is becoming increasingly expensive as it costs quite a bit to acquire, organize and retrieve it. Cost is further escalated when IT (acquisition and up gradation) is to play its role in designing and delivering information services and products.

6. Decreasing Public Sponsorship : The traditional concept of certain social services like health, education, justice, etc. being made available free of cost, is now becoming irrelevant. Same is true for library and information centres also. They are being asked to become self-sufficient to survive in cost conscious and competition oriented social and environmental set ups.

SERVICES MARKETING: SOME CONSTRAINTS

Marketing experts acknowledge that marketing service is more difficult than marketing a tangible product. The following unique characteristics of services make them so different from products:

1. Intangibility : A service cannot be touched or smelled or viewed. This makes it difficult for the clients to specifically anticipate what they will be finally getting. It is also very difficult to judge quality and value in advance.

2. Inseparability : Inseparability of production and consumption process (i.e. a service is produced at the same time as it is to be consumed) requires the presence of a producer and involves direct sale, limited sale of operations and geographically limited market.

3. Consistency : Rendering of service involves the human element and this makes standardization a very difficult task to achieve. In the absence of standardization, the user cannot make a comparable judgment of the services before making a final choice (28).

4. Heterogeneity : As services involve people, there may be a lot of difference between rendering of the same service by different people.

5. Perishability : Most services have a short shelf life; they are offered and used at the same time. Also the unused capacity cannot be stored for future use (28).

Basic Marketing Concepts

There are five basic concepts of marketing, viz. Market segmentation, Market Positioning, Consumer Analysis, Marketing Programme and Marketing Audit.

Market Segmentation

Market segmentation aims at evaluating the total heterogeneous market into homogeneous segments and deciding which segments require great priority. This involves the identification of the users (target groups), actual and potential and their needs assessment. Thus market segmentation gives formal recognition to the fact that wants and desires of consumers are diverse and we can formulate a specific market catering to specific category or segment of the users so that the supply will have the best correlation with demand. Public libraries segment their clients on the basis of demographic characteristic and use 'Community Survey' to know about the actual and potential users of the library and quantify them. A public library may segment its users in different groups such as children, adults, senior citizens, visually impaired etc (17).

Market Positioning

It is a process of prioritizing among different groups of clients that provides the best opportunity for the company (17). Market positioning thus involves prioritizing clients, groups and information services; and also policy making. Having the market segmentation of the library, the librarian decides the major target group according to the objectives of the library and available resources.

Consumer Analysis

Consumer analysis refers to the process of determining the needs and preferences of the target group (17). It also involves information collection. It helps in answering questions about the needs of the individual clients, homogeneous sub-groups and their preferences for delivery of information products or services, and their perceptions about the services, their requirements etc. In libraries user surveys are done to know the needs and preferences of the users and call them 'Information Gathering Habits', 'Information seeking Behavior', 'Information Needs' etc.

Marketing Programme

The concept of marketing programme underlines the "coordinated effort which utilizes information gained and policies established in the interests of the parent company" (29). This step is also known as 'marketing mix'. This entails the design and promotion of products and services for each of target audiences. Thus, once the market segments are established and needs of users are known, the marketing strategy can be developed by the library using the marketing tool known as 'marketing mix'. The 'marketing mix' or "Four Ps" of marketing can be summarized as follows:

Product (or service) : working from a precise knowledge of customer needs, a product or service should be designed to meet their needs.

Place : The second factor in marketing mix is the place decision on the channels of distribution system that will be used. Thus once a product or service is developed, a distribution system must be designed to make the product conveniently available to the customers (17).

Price : The product must be made at a cost that allows the company to market it at a price the customer can afford and that is competitive with alternate products.

Promotion: Promotion is also an important factor in marketing mix which implies communicating with current and potential clientele to make them aware of the services that are currently available. Promotion should tie into the needs, preferences, and decision-making practices of your users (19). The product's availability, advantages and price must be made known to be purchasing public.

MARKETING AUDIT

It is the performance evaluation of the marketing programme in the light of the data gathered from market segmentation, consumer analysis and the objectives of the organization (17). Measurement of the 'Effectiveness of Library Service', evaluation of 'User Satisfaction', etc. are the similar concepts available with us as techniques of marketing audit. This is evaluation of plan and implementation, information gathering, quantification, making judgments and reporting.

MARKETING ACTIVITIES OF THE LIBRARY AND INFORMATION CENTRES FOR REVENUE GENERATION

Professional marketing approach will help in achieving maximum utilization of information products and services, and thus generate more and more revenue. It is thus very important for library and information centres to develop a marketing programme which includes the following group of activities:

1. Awareness of Information for Development

The library and information centres should develop information that can be given to potential end users and make them aware of the same. This should include visit or talks of or demonstration to potential end users, communities, preparation of attractive well presented brochures describing objectives, services, etc., of the library and information centres, publication of information articles about its services and products in various journals (25).

2. Promotion of Services

The library and information centres should engage in activities that help to promote the services to the specific individuals who can get benefit from them. This should include identification of user's groups, finding their information needs, sending them the promotional material/information, publication of newsletter, periodical survey of end users, sending of specimen copies of information products/ pamphlets etc., to prospective users, users group meets, provision of evaluation card along with library and information centres services/products, identification of market opportunities (25).

3. Marketing in Day-to-Day Operation

Marketing needs to be added to the day-to-day

operations of the library and information centres. So that activities are established and maintained. This will improve their credibility and service level. This should include help desk activities like walk-in counseling, quick response, regular sending of pamphlets to new prospective clients, etc (25).

4. Prioritization

Priorities the market segments to be served first according to the strength in areas. This will help in initial acceptance as well as getting financial support (25).

5. Innovation and Creativity

For better marketing activities, information producers should concentrate on new avenues of products or services, which will attract more and more potential users. New innovative ideas need to be generated in the context of information types, quality, economics, etc (6).

6. SWOT (Strength, Weakness, Opportunities and Threats) Analysis

Before devising any marketing strategies, the library and information centres should do a detailed SWOT analysis of their products and services. This will not only help the library and information centres to market the products easily and confidently but also explore the possibility of market segments and create niche for themselves (6).

MARKETING PLAN

A marketing plan is a policy document, taking as its starting points, the mission, aims and objectives of the organization of institution. It is also a strategic planning document, which needs to address priorities and consequent allocation of resources in the light of external and internal variables. It should be management blueprint too, in that it is also a document about implementation: setting out targets, how to search them, who is responsible, the timetable involved and the budget devolved. It may include alternative methodologies with reasons for the decisions made.

The plan would act as a tool to guide the staff in its approach towards marketing. It would also ensure good communications between all those involved by laying down the exact specifications as to what is to be done in each sector of the organization and in the process, also highlight the direction in which the organization is moving. A marketing plan would thus help in answering broad questions like What is the current situation regarding the library/information centre, the product or the service? Where should the information centre/product/service be in the next year? How does the information centre/product/service get there to realize specific targets? It would also help in assessing whether the information centre, product or service realized the set goals and targets. In order to obtain answers to all these questions, several steps and processes need to be gone through. These steps require current information about the information centre, objectivity in approach and a vision for the future. The planning process should focus on analysis of the organization, analysis of the marketing place, setting of objectives, deciding on strategies and formulation of tactics.

BENEFITS OF MARKETING PLAN

The development and implementation of a marketing plan can be beneficial in several ways. It would help in:

* Identification of objectives in line with parent organization's goals and information centre's requirements.
* Identification and selection of target client groups to be served by the centre.
* Increasing the demand for existing products and services.
* Developing of new and viable products and services, which have a sound client base.
* Collection and analysis of relevant data and the monitoring of marketing targets enabling the information centre to become more objective in decision making.
* Execution of preparatory analysis assists staff in developing a customer oriented outlook.
* Preparation of the plan and the implementation of activities encourage and motivate information staff to develop a proactive stance in the target market.

* Development of the marketing plan brings the information centre into focus within the organization-through its contribution to the marketing objectives of the parent organization (10).

DEVELOPING A MARKETING PLAN

While developing a marketing plan for a product or service at a library and information centre, various steps need to be followed. The first step in developing a marketing plan would be the analysis of the current performance. Then, the next step would be to conduct a marketing audit. The third step, would be to decide the strategic direction for the information unit. Development of a marketing strategy would be the fourth step. A detailed marketing plan can be then prepared followed by the last step of implementation and control. Evaluation and performance measures must be built in and reporting lines clearly identified. A strategic plan provides a structure for analyzing the current and future opportunities and challenges an organization faces (27).

1. Measure the performance

To measure the performance of a library and information centre, and to deploy the available resources in the best possible manner it is important to develop specific targets or goals. The performance of the center would ultimately depend on the performance of its products and services in specific targeted markets and segments. Specific parameters need to be identified for measuring the performance of the center and its products and services in the specific markets and segments. These parameters could be number/ proportion of total clients served, number of units of product/ service sold, total revenue generated and image of the center and its products in target segments.

2. Conduct marketing audit

Marketing audit involving critical assessment of the external and the internal environment of the library and information centre will have to be undertaken. It would provide significant insights into the opportunities and the threats facing the center. Moreover, marketing audit must be carried out within the context of contributing to the parent organization's goal.

(a) Identify Organizational goals : It should be assessed whether library and information centre's programmes conform to the overall policy and directives of the organization. The targeted sectors for the institution and the information unit should be assessed. The measures required for building up that image e.g. promotional mechanisms, pricing strategies etc, should be identified. Finally, the set time frame for realization of the goals should be analyzed.

(b) Analyze Market and Users : A market and customer analysis should be taken for final decision regarding the set of markets/segments to focus on and the set of products and services to offer to them. This will enable the library and information centre to identify specific groups of products and services that are required in the market to satisfy the requirements of the customer.

(c) Assessment of Market size and characteristics : A thorough assessment should be made about the market size, each of the segment, and for each of the products and services.

2. Select Strategic Direction

Strategic direction should be selected for an information center and the required steps are:

(a) Development of Marketing Objectives : Marketing objectives must be set for the information center keeping a realistic approach. These marketing objectives will give direction for the formulation of various marketing strategies and the final marketing plan. Besides specific objectives, the Critical Success Factors (CSFs) for achieving the objectives must also be specified. And the marketing objectives must be set in context of the marketing objectives of the parent organization, the SWOT analysis and the opportunities assessed.

(b) Positioning : Another objective that needs to be clearly defined and decided upon is about the kind of image the library and information wants to have for itself and, its products and services in the minds of the target customers. And this decision should be based on a thorough assessment of various available resources and the requirements of customers.

(c) Selection of marketing strategies : A marketing strategy should be aimed at achieving the marketing objectives. The marketing strategy can be devised for both, the information unit as a whole and for each product or service. Moreover, a marketing strategy must be within the broad strategic direction determined, while ensuring that the CSF's are taken care of by the organization. Basic idea should be to try to target specific customer groups, called segments. Market should first be segmented and then a choice of specific segments should be made.

(d) Identification of Critical Success Factors : Identification of Critical Success Factors would enable in defining inputs which are critical to the achievement of marketing objectives within the context of the marketing plan. CSFs can therefore be defined as resources which have a direct influence on the successful implementation of the plan. The CSF's could be in the areas of base resources, technology resources, human resources, systems and processes of generating products and services, delivery as well as specific elements of marketing plan(like product, price, promotion and distribution) (10).

KEY ELEMENTS OF STRATEGY

The strategy document should summarize the following:

* Product market to be focused, target customers, and position top be achieved in the targeted segments.
* Products and services, pricing, promotion and distribution strategies to be deployed (for achieving the position in the target segment of the market).
* Various resources like information resource and human resources, hardware and software needed.
* Market research and feedback systems to be deployed for planning and controlling all elements of the strategy.

The marketing plan should include the following:

1. **Executive Summary** providing a brief summary of various goals and objectives, and recommendations providing a quick grasp of the plan.

2. **Current Marketing Situation** providing information on the current market situation; product, price, distribution, and promotion situation; competitive situation; external environmental situation, etc.
3. **SWOT Analysis** describing the output of the analysis of strengths and weaknesses of the organization.
4. **Marketing Objectives** stating the objectives in terms of both financial and marketing objectives to be achieved in a set time span.
5. **Description of Market, Product and Promotional options :** This should incorporate a proper description of specific products and services, their features, price, promotion tools, dissemination channels and market research to be conducted, target customers and support needed from parent organization.
6. **Action Plan :** A brief description of organizational arrangements for implementing the plan with specific and time bound activities.
7. **Revenue and Expensive Statement**: Describing the resources and costs with their relevant elements along with a cash flow statement.
8. **Controls**: Describing the means of monitoring the progress of the plan and setting out time bound goals and budgets for important elements.

GUIDELINES FOR PREPARATION OF THE PLAN

1. **Prepare an executive summary :** Prepare a table of contents which should include the following headings- Situational Analysis and SWOT, Objectives, Target Segment, Position, Service/Product, Pricing, Promotion, Distribution, Partners, Criteria for Evaluation, Projected Income
2. Include forms and charts which will be used in the implementation and monitoring of the plan.
3. Prepare a cover, using the layout which clearly identifies with the library and information centre or its product or service.

MARKETING OF DIGITAL RESOURCES

Digital libraries, institutional repositories, electronic journals, and open access publishing are some of the new digital resources and services that are influencing the library and information centres of today's digital age. Libraries offer a variety of electronic resources in addition to collections of print documents, photographs, video, recordings, and other artifacts. It is equally important to market these new resources and services effectively. A well-focussed marketing strategy is required to connect the users with these digital resources and services. Some of the marketing solutions which can be adopted are Site search optimization, e-mail marketing, and Web content management. The Web site of a library and information centre can be used as a powerful advertising and promotional tool. It can be used to convey huge amount of information cost-effectively at the same time enhancing visibility and communicating the brand image. Steps should be taken for tracking usage of the digital library or institutional repository. This can be done with the help of a counter to check usage or use of data to help evaluate the site traffic and various resources being accessed. Digital collections are aimed at much wider audience. It is critical to identify the core group at which the collection is actually targeted. Proper target audience must be identified and analyzed. Web Blog, wiki and RSS feeds are some other technologies that provide means to encourage active user participation thus adding value to the library websites. Web Blogs provide simple means of putting content on the web. Web blogs could be used to disseminate information about the library and information centre and its activities. It also enables active user participation. Wiki provides a platform to the users to create content collaboratively. RSS enables aggregating (gathering RSS from others), and feeding (making your RSS content available for other websites). RSS can be used for disseminating information about latest products, services and activities to the users. Library's OPAC, E-newsletters, targeted email alerts sent to academics by the information specialists are some other means that can be used to enhance visibility and accessibility of a library and information centre. Federated database searching is another way to increase the functionality and use of electronic resources. The information handlers should be able to understand the new technologies and use them to reap maximum benefits.

CONCLUSION

Marketing is very important for the library and information centres of today. It is extremely important to understand what the users want and how they think and then to design and market the products accordingly. Google and Yahoo are increasingly being used by scientists and students as reliable online sources. In today's digital age Internet has provided better means of communication and interaction. The Internet environment has an interactive nature facilitating many-way communications between information providers and users. The Internet is host to interactive environments like online communities and chat rooms, carrying informal information as well as formal sources like organization Web sites. The information-based, technological and continuous communication technologies offered by the Web make it a versatile environment for advertising and marketing. The marketing programme of any library and information centre should be aimed at understanding how to position it in the information environment of targeted user community.

REFERENCES

1. Brown, S.A. (1997). Marketing the corporate information centre for success. *Online,* 74-79.
2. Bushing, Mary C. (1995). The Library's Product and Excellence. *Library Trends,* January, 1995, 43(3), Pg. 384.
3. Cronin, B., ed. (1981). The marketing of library and information services 2. London: Aslib.
4. Dragon, Andrea C. (1979). Marketing the Library. *Wilson Library Bulletin,* 53(7), 498-502.
5. Encylopedia Britannica. (1974). Chicago: Encylopedia of Britannica Inc., 2, 505-6.
6. Ganguly, S. and Kar, Debal C. (2002). Marketing - A critical policy for Today's Information Centre. *DESIDOC Bulletin of Information Technology,* 22(3), 15-25.
7. Gopinath, M.A. (1988). Curriculum of Library and Information

Service courses and Marketing of Information Services. In Marketing of Library and Information services in India, Calcutta, *IASLIC*, 125-129.

8. Inder Mohan, R. (1996). Economics of Information Marketing. In Chopra, H.S., ed. Information Marketing.. Jaipur : Rawat publications.
9. Inder Mohan, R. (1987). Information Marketing : Implications for Information Professionals, DRTC Silver Jubilee Seminar, Paper BG.
10. Jain, Abhinandan K et. al. (1995). Marketing of Information Products and Services, Indian Institute of Management, Ahmedabad.
11. Kaane, Sophia (2006). Marketing reference and information services in libraries: a staff competencies framework. 72ND IFLA General Conference And Council, Seoul, Korea Available at: *www.ifla.org/IV/ifla72/papers/118-Kaane-en.pdf*
12. K.J., Joseph Jestin and Parameswari, B..(2002). Marketing of Information Products and Services for Libraries in India. Library Philosophy and Practice,5(1) . Available at: *www.uidaho.edu/~mbolin/lppv5n1.htm*
13. Kassel, A. (2002). "Practical Tips to Help You Prove Your Value." Marketing Library Services, 16(4), 1-4.
14. Kotler, P. (1994). Marketing Management : Analysis, Planning, Implementation, and control.. New Delhi: Prentice-Hall of India.
15. Kumar, Krishna. (1985). Library Manual.. New Delhi: Vikas Publishing House.
16. Lafond, Renald. (1995). Information Products and Services: Marketing- The New Thrust Area. In Abhinandan K. Jain et al., Marketing of Information Products and Services, Indian Institute of Management, Ahmedabad,.
17. Mishra, Sanjaya. Marketing of Library and Information services and Products : Old wine in new bottle. *Library herald*, Oct 1994-March 1995, 32(3-4).
18. Natarajan, M. E-mail as a marketing tool for information Products and Services. *DESIDOC Bulletin of Information Technology*, May 2002, 22(3), 27-34.
19. Ohio Library Corporation (2005) Promoting the Library: Introduction to Marketing the Library Module 4. Available at: *http://www.olc.org/marketing/index.html*
20. Raina, Roshan.(1998). Marketing in the Library and Information Context. *DESIDOC Bulletin of Information Techology*, 18(3), 7-10.

21. Ramaiah, L.S. (1996). Resource Sharing and Marketing of the Information In English Language and Literature in India. In Chopra, H.S., ed. Information Marketing. Jaipur: Rawat publications,.

22. Rescher, Nicholas. (1989). Cognitive Economy : The Economic Dimensions of the Theory of Knowledge, Pittsburg: Pittsburg University Press, 46.

23. Saez, Eileen Elliott De. (1993) Marketing concepts for libraries and information services. London: Library Association Publishing.

24. Seetharama, S. (1990). Guidelines for Planning of Libraries and Information Centres. IASLIC, Calcutta.

25. Shah, PC. (1998). Marketing Vis-à-vis Revenue Generation in Libraries and Information Centres: An Indian Experience. *DESIDOC Bulletin of Information Technology*, , 18(3), 21-28.

26. Smith, Duncan. (1995) Practice as a Marketing Tool: Four case studies. Marketing of Library and Information Services, *Library Trends*, January, 1995, 43(3), Pg. 450.

27. Spalding , Helen H., & Wang, Jian. (2006). "Marketing Academic Libraries in USA: Challenges. Available at: *http://www.openj-gate.com/include/redirect.asp*

28. Vij, Rajeev and Bedi, D S. (1999) Information Marketing: Preparing University Libraries for Next Millennium. In Sardna J L, ed. Challenges before the University Libraries in India in the 21st century. Seminar papers of the ILA National Seminar, Vadodara, 9-12 Aug, 1999. New Delhi: ILA.

29. Zachert, Marta Jane and Willims, Robert V. (1986) Marketing measures for information services. *Special Libraries*, 77(2), 63.

13

Application of 4Ps to Marketing the Information Product & services in Academic Libraries

Ashok Kumar Sahu

Rabindra Kumar Mahapatra

Sujata Padhy

ABSTRACT

This study discusses the marketing of library and information services in 21st century on the basis of traditional concept of marketing. The aim of this study to attempt to correlate marketing as a concept to the provision of library services. In view of the social, economic and technological changes, Library and Information centers have begun to realize that marketing of information products and services is an integral part of administration. Mainly, the information explosion, the technological revolution and escalating library costs are responsible for encouraging the library profession to develop a marketing approach in its operations and services. This paper discusses from the traditional marketing system into more vibrant and dynamic, strategic marketing of library services. It helps to provide right service at right time and the right price to right users in the right place with support of quality staffs. This paper provides useful information on the marketing of library and information services.

INTRODUCTION

Marketing a service-base business is different from marketing a product-base business. Services marketing is marketing based on relationship and value. Marketing services and other intangibles is considered as valid as the marketing of products and commodities, as the key future of the marketing model is its emphasis not on maximising profits, but on sensitively and satisfying human need (Kapoor, 1988). Services marketing concepts and strategies have developed in response to the tremendous growth of service industries resulting in their increased importance to the U.S and world economics (Zeithaml, 2000). Services marketing is a comprehensive term that describes all the processes and interactions that result in satisfaction for customers and revenue for the organisation. According to Kotler (1995) points out, organizations such as museums, universities, libraries, and charities need to market their causes and their products to gain political and social support as well as economic support.

Mainly the information explosion, technology revolution and escalating library costs are responsible for encouraging the library profession to develop a marketing approach in its products and services. Present society is moving towards a knowledge-based society for which information is primary importance. Due to improving the user satisfaction and promoting the use of services, marketing of information product and services is an integral part of libraries and information centers (Joseph and Parameswari, 2004).

WHAT IS MARKETING?

Marketing is not only for publicity or promotion; publicity and promotion are just one aspect of the marketing process. Marketing also includes product creation, pricing, and distribution. Marketing deals with identifying and meeting human and social needs.

According Kotler "Marketing as a social and managerial process where by individuals and groups obtain what they need and want through creating and exchange products and value with others" (Kotler and Armstrong, 2001).

Marketing is the study of exchange processes especially those associated with the provision of goods and services (Adcock, 2001).

According the British Chartered Institute of Marketing "Marketing is the management process responsible for identifying, anticipating and satisfying customer's requirements profitability. (Adcock, 2001)

Marketing people are mainly involved in marketing of goods, services, events, experiences, persons, places, properties, organizations, information, and ideas.

INFORMATION AS A PRODUCT

Information can be produced and marketed as a product. This is essentially what schools and universities produce and distribute at a price to parents, students, and communities. The production, packaging and distribution of information is one of our society's major industries.(Kotler, 2006).

As the world's economy enters the Information Age, all types of information become more important to many aspects of business, to say nothing of daily life (Drucker, 1994; Naisbitt, 1982).

Information is the primary importance of the present society. Information production needs human efforts, investment of time, energy, cost etc. Information and decision making clearly has a cost, time personnel, money and other related factors. The fact of understanding the time spent for making lists, thinking, organizing and other related activities leads to conclude that information produced is available against money. The following factors information economy, industrial economy, service economy, and rising costs of information are strengthening to view information as commodity.

WHY MARKETING OF INFORMATION PRODUCT & SERVICES REQUIRED?

Many library professional are feeling that library is a non-profit organization. Marketing concept is not required for libraries and information centers. But in modern world, marketing of information product/services is very essential for library to survive. According to Kotler (1995) points out, organizations such as museums, universities, libraries, and charities need to market their causes and their products to gain political and social support as well as economic support. The following factors are responsible for encouraging the library profession to develop a marketing approach in its operations and services.

i. Each institution wishes to achieve high levels of customer satisfaction

ii. Each wants to enhance the perceived value of their services

iii. Each institution wants to insure the survival

Morgan & Noble (1992) advise that library survival is dependent on the acceptance of marketing as a fundamental management philosophy. Weingand (1995) points to the social & technological changes of our age as reasons for the need to focus on the customer and argues that marketing and planning are a natural partnership.

Due to information explosion, technology revolution and escalating library costs, library professionals have begun to realize that marketing is the integral part of administration, especially as a means for improving user satisfaction and promoting the use of services by current and potential users. (Joseph, 2004)

WHAT IS MARKETING CONCEPTS IN RELATION TO LIBRARY?

Marketing is principally necessary in libraries of all kinds due to the sophisticated nature of the market, i.e. the users, services, and the competition posed by other alternative source of information service. The public—that is the consumers and sponsors of the library service—must be satisfied that they are getting the value for the money spent on the service.

Librarey users seek the service because they derive benefit and satisfaction from using it.

According kotler, marketing concept states that the societal marketing concept is customer oriented backed by integrated marketing aimed at generating customer satisfaction and long term consumer welfare as the key to organizational goal. (Ojiambo, 1994). As per the above definition, we could derive that concept of marketing revolves on three pillars namely.

i. *Customer orientation*: Offering a product or a service which people's real needs

ii. *Integrated marketing*: Coordinating within every function or organization, also known as market process

iii. Customer Satisfaction and long run consumer welfare: Working towards the interests of consumer, not only in the short run but in the long run too.

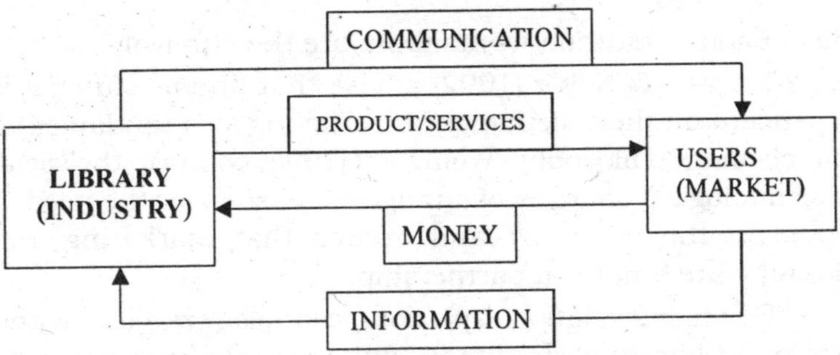

Sellers (Library) and buyers (Users) are connected by four flows. The sellers (Library) send goods/services and communications (ads, direct mails, pamphlets) to the market; in return they receive money and information (User attitude, Use of data etc.). The inner loop shows an exchange of money for good/services and the outer loop shows an exchange of information. (Kotler, 2006).

Marketing research in library service may help to identify strategies and concomitant course of action to take in order to satisfy the needs of the consumers and sponsors. On the whole, the application of the marketing concept to libraries does provide a wholesome view without exception of the entire range of library marketing mix. Marketing enables library professionals to look critically at the strength and weaknesses of the library service as an enterprise.

Library staff must be educated in the purpose and effectiveness of marketing. To give it meaning and momentum, a full-time professional to deal with marketing in the library is recommended. Marketing ideas should also be made clear to the higher authority of organization. The support of the powerful higher authority must be sought if meaningful progress is expected. In academic library, the academicians have also a key role to play in library policy formulation. Their views are important in determining key policies, which are crucial for library development and survival.

It will be seen that marketing concept is only worthwhile if the product and service match the users' needs and goals. The product and service must be convincing to both the marketer and the user. Reasonable investment must be made in the service (product) in order to make it attractive and beneficial to the user. The objectives of developing and financing library services need to be justified.

APPLICATION OF MARKETING APPROACH TO LIBRARY SERVICES/PRODUCT

Marketing approach has mainly consisted of market segmentation, marketing position, marketing mix and marketing audit.

MARKET SEGMENTATION, TARGETING AND POSITION

The purpose of segmentation is to identify customer/user groups that have as much similarity as possible within group, but dissimilarity with other groups with respect to the relevant characteristics. And deciding which group or groups of customers/users the organization is equipped to serve and can do so profitably. (Haksever, 2000)

The selection of market segmentation strategy is very important for marketing any product and services. Marketing segmentation helps planning of other elements of marketing mix more meaning fully and effectively. Identifying the customers and groups are on the basis of demographic, socio economic, geographic, and psycho-graphic. Library as a non-business organization serves many diverse groups. This is particularly determined by the type and objective of library. A target market is broadly defined as a collective of individuals who have an interest in or concern about an organization, a product or a social cause. (Adeyoyin, 2005).

The organization/institution should decide how to position its services in the minds of its current and potential customer/users. It should be recalled that an organization develops a service strategy to differentiate itself and its services from the competition. Positioning is a very important step in service/product design and development. Positioning can be used for reemphasizing the position of an old product or to move it to new position as well as new products.

MARKETING MIX

The marketing mix is the planned package of elements that makes up the product or service offered to the market. It is aimed at supporting the library and information service to reach target markets and specified objectives. The marketing mix helps to position the library or information service very firmly in the perceptions of their communities served. The marketing mix consists of four elements Product, Price, Place, Promotion, (Kotler, 2006)

I. Product

A product is anything that can be offered to a market to satisfy a want or need. Products that are marketed include physical goods, services, experiences, events, persons, places, properties, organizations, information, and ideas. (Kotler, 2006)

Services and products offered must present value to the user, over and above actual cost. The design and quality of services are manifest in tangible factorssuch as timely, up-to-date, appropriate formats, and implicit in intangibles such as staff motivation and training, effective use of resources, and knowledge of user and client needs. The product line can be offered differently from different market segments.

The library and information centers should be considered following parameters for planning, designing and development of product/services: (Seetharama,1990)

* The target user groups and the appropriate product mix to be developed should be decided
* The existing infrastructure facilities available for the creation of the products has to be examined
* Planning individual information services/products taking into consideration the various parameters, including packaging/repackaging and naming of the product

Product refers to the services, which the library generally offers to its clienteles and prospective users. In the general sense, library services encompasses the following:

* Loan : Charging and discharging of library materials
* Referral services: Offering reference services to the library patrons.
* Organization of library materials: Cataloguing, Classification of materials.
* Inter Library Loan: Through this method , unavailable materials needed by the patrons are sourced and borrowed in another library.

II. Place

Place is usually translated into 'Distribution' in a commercial marketing mix, but for libraries and information services, it refers to dissemination means where and how a service is made available to the users and clients. Saracevic and Wood (1981) have identified the following major channels for dissemination:

* Interpersonal delivery – Products specially delivered either on request or in anticipation of a need.
* Group Personal delivery- products delivered to a whole group of users as at meetings, conferences, seminars, demonstration etc.
* Strategic location- Product placed at strategic location
* In-House dissemination- Reference and referral services
* Dissemination through news papers, professional journal, magazines
* Broadcasting through Radio and television
* Telecommunication and Computer Network

III. Promotion

Promotion involves mechanisms by which the target groups are informed about the resources available, services and products offered by library and information center. In the information technology era, increased the level of competition. So library and information center needs to be improve their promotional activities. Generally the library and information centers are using traditional systems such as display book jacket, windows display, book exhibition, posters, and advertisement to promote their products/services. The traditional approach is no longer tenable in this present era. Aggressive marketing of library services is required if the significance of the library's contribution to the development of the intellectual world in particular and economic in general is ever to be acknowledges, appreciated and reciprocated.

IV. Pricing

Price is the element of the marketing mix which for many in the library profession will be the most difficult to consider. Pricing of information services and products is relatively a new concept. Mostly library and information centers are providing services on free of cost to their users. Pricing has not considered seriously for library products/services. But due to increased emphasis on accountability and self-sufficiency in relation to resources it has become necessary to cost the various activities and to recover costs as much as possible. Pricing of products should be based on costs incurred in the generation of a product or a service.

MARKETING AUDIT

The final element in any marketing plan should be the marketing audit. This is basically an evaluation of the success or failure of a specific marketing campaign, especially promotions. It is therefore essential that identifiable, and preferably quantifiable, objectives are set for a promotional campaign. It is difficult to measure the success of any promotion, but the intangible nature of most library services complicates matters still further. However, by targeting promotion campaigns towards a specific audience it should be easier to measure any increase in the use of the service by members of that particular group—perhaps by carrying out a post-implementation customer survey.

MARKETING AND LIBRARIANSHIP

All to often the concept of marketing leaves a bad taste in the mouths of librarians. In profit institutions, the process of making money for making money's sake, and the efforts to convince people to use unneeded services or products. This is the "hard sell" concept of marketing. The more "soft sell" approach puts the emphasis on customer satisfaction and meeting the expectations of customers. We are often seen from reference desk that the patron does not always know what they want nor can articulate their information need. These are direct contractions to idea of "the customer is always right." As librarians of the future we must learn to balance our professional ethics and teachings with the cultural environment in which we work — an environment of consumerism — or the environment in which we work will work against us. (Morgan, 1998)

CONCLUSION

Library and information professionals are grasping a marketing approach, as it is an essential weapon in the competition age. With the entry of business organizations in the information market, libraries are facing serious competition from the profit-making information industry, which has seen the potential of an ever-increasing information service. Libraries can improve their situation by promoting themselves with the same marketing and advertising techniques used by successful business organization. Marketing of information is not just disseminating information, it includes the optimum use of resources of the library. The library can be called information market and the library user is a consumer of information. Information is a vital resource for national development. Increasing realization of the role of information has resulted in the establishment of information systems to provide a variety of information services and products. It is an essential stcp in the planning, designing, and use of such services and products for optimal use of information. Library acquisition, organization and dissemination must be based on the modern concept of marketing to achieve reader satisfaction. It must endeavor to nurture culture of customer service to enhance its image in the eyes of the users. Adoption of marketing approach that will help libraries not only in their own sustenance, but also in the sustenance and self and self sufficiency of their information products/services.

REFERENCES

1. Adcock, D., Halborg, A., and Ross, C.(2001) Marketing: Principles and Practice. London, Prentice Hall
2. Booth, J.(1993) "Marketing public library services: the gap between theory and reality in Britain". *Library Management*, 14:1, 9-24.
3. de Sáez, E.E.(2002) Marketing Concepts for Libraries and Information Services. London, Facet Publishing
4. Drucker, P.F. (1994) "The age of social transformation". *The Atlantic*, 247. 53-80.
5. Haksever, C...[et al] (2000)Service Management and operations. New York, Pearson Education.
6. Kapoor, S.K.(1988) "Marketing approach to library and information services" in Kapoor, S.K.and Chatterjee, A.(eds.) Marketing of library andinformation services in India, Calcutta, IASLIC, pp.21-28
7. Kotler, P. and Armstrong, G (2001) Principles of Marketing. New Delhi, Prentice Hall of India.

8. Kotler, P. and Keller, K.L (2006) Marketing Management. New York, Pearson Education.
9. Lovelock, C. and Wright, L. (1999) Principles of Service Marketing and Management. New Jersey, Prentice Hall.
10. Morgan, Eric Lease (1998) "Marketing library services". *Computers in Libraries,* 18:8. 50-51.
11. Morgan, P. & Noble, S.(1992) "Marketing library and information services in the '90s". *Australian Library Journal,* 41 : 4. 283-293.
12. Naisbitt, J. (1982) *Megatrends: Ten New Directions Transforming Our Lives.* New York, Warner Books.
13. Saracevic, T. and Wood, J.B. (1981) Consolidation of Information: A Handbook on Evaluation, Restructuring and Repackaging of Scientific and Technical Information. Paris, UNESCO
14. Seetharama, S.(1990) Guidelines for Planning of Libraries and Information Centres. Calcutta, IASLIC
15. Tanui, T.A. and Kitoi, A.S.(1993) "Why marketing? The experience of Moi University Library Kenya". Library Management, 14:4. 43-48.
16. Weingand, D.E. (1995) "Preparing for the new millennium: the case for using marketing strategies". *Library Trends,* 43 : 3. 295-317
17. Zeithaml, V.A and Bitner, M.J (2000) Services Marketing. Boston: McGraw Hill.

14

Getting Out to Help Students where they Learn: Marketing Library Services to Distance Learners

Sunil Karve
Vrushali Rane

ABSTRACT

Marketing of Information Products and Services has been a popular topic in the library profession in recent years. Therefore each librarian today needs to introspect and has to look for needs, wants and demands of various clients, innovative products and services and to reach out to the clients rather than wait for them to come. Distance learners are a unique target population for marketing of library services and resources. These students do not visit the libraries often, therefore marketing strategies for distance learners library services need to take a multifaceted approach to reach distance learners in as many ways as possible and may take advantage of high tech option. Collaborations with various other academic libraries at different location are important. The prime objective of this paper is to understand the distance learner's needs and how a library can fulfil them & create marketing awareness among librarians than to report any exhaustive findings.

PROLOGUE

Distance learning has become a buzzword for educational programming in many institutions of higher learning in recent years. The library can be even catalyst in improving the quality of distance education programs. The higher education sector is undergoing rapid changes and universities are already becoming more flexible in the types of courses and modes of attendance that they offer. Many academic libraries are recognising that these services and policies need to change order to take account of emerging groups of students who do not conform to the traditional student stereotype.

The challenge of distance-learning comes from the fact that until very recently most library collections (books, journals and media) were selected for on-campus use, and most library services (instructional classes, print reserve services, research indexes or databases and physical library tours) were designed for on-campus programs. These collections and services are often not well suited to the needs of distance-learning students.

Distance-learning students require access to the full range of library services; from reference assistance and bibliographic instruction to interlibrary loan, course reserves, circulation, and information network connections. Distance education for training and education is gaining popularity due to the desire for flexibility and control by the learners over learning, the mobility of today's workforce, the needed skills upgrades by the workforce, a generation raised on the interactive media and various technologies, and an increasing fear of travel, especially to specific parts of the globe.

Therefore Distance learners are a unique target population for marketing of library services and resources. These students do not visit the libraries often, therefore marketing strategies for distance learners library services need to take a multifaceted approach to reach distance learners in as many ways as possible and may take advantage of high tech option.

THE MARKETING CONCEPT

Marketing is basically the wide range of activities involved in making sure that you're continuing to meet the needs of your customers and are getting value in return. Marketing analysis includes finding out what groups of potential customers (or markets) exist, what groups of customers you prefer to serve (target markets), what their needs are, what products or services you might develop to meet their needs, how the customers might prefer to use the products and services, what your competitors are doing, what pricing you should use and how you should distribute products and services to your target markets. Because each one of us is a consumer, marketing can have a direct impact on us. Marketing can help us make better consumption decisions, deal more effectively with sellers and communicate more effectively with others in our everyday activities. Thus a marketing approach helps the organization to focus its limited resources for better management and determines what the user wants and needs and then produces a product or services to meet those needs.

With changing scenario, everybody talks about resource generation programs and practices for the library. Therefore marketing in libraries is a challenging task. The basic objective of marketing is to maximize the use of libraries. Padmashri Dr. S. R. Ranganathan's five laws explain the marketing concept.

The marketing of library and information services and products is a relatively new concept. The level of awareness is very high but implementation is still in infant stage.

Today libraries have well defined target customers, which include ambitious students, academicians, professionals, policy and decision makers. The performance of library is measured by number of members and their profile, the services rendered etc.

Exibit 1

Sr. No.	*Laws of Library Science*	*Marketing opportunities*
1	Books are for use	Marketing Potential
2	Every Reader his/her book	Need, interest of the customer
3	Every book its reader	Reaching out to the customer
4	Save the time of the reader	Quick/ready reference available
5	A library is a growing organism	Long term relationship with customer

Marketing of library strongly emphasis on the following:

1. Relationship marketing: Building relationship between customer and library providing quality services, user friendly systems, customer relations etc.
2. Societal Marketing: Determining needs and interest of target markets and enhancing customer's well being.

Marketing information products and services is not the same as marketing customer products like soap, refrigerator, motor cars etc. However principles and most activities of both are same. The imperative to market library emanate from the following rationale:

1. Growing importance of information
2. Emergence of new technology
3. Changing customer behaviour
4. Increasing market opportunities
5. Increasing competition

OBJECTIVES

1. To understand the information seeking behaviour of distance learning students.
2. To gauge their awareness and level of their library use.
3. To determine their needs for information resources and library use instructions.
4. To identify how the library can improve its services to distance learning students.

METHODOLOGY

Data was collected from 100 distance learners enrolled in NMIMS University under distance learning programme. These students are enrolled for Post Graduate Management Programmes at different study centres all over India. The programmes are in the area of Marketing, HR, Systems and Finance for one to two years of duration. Researcher has used random sampling method so that each study centre and each programme has an equal chance of being selected for research study. Random samples were selected from homogenous categories or strata from the list of study centres all over India. Utmost care was taken so that each sample will represent different parts of India, programs, area etc. Primary data was collected mainly through questionnaire and interviews.

LITERATURE REVIEW

Much of the literature on distance education does not address the issues of library services to distance learners. As Carty outlines, it was not until the 1980's and 1990's that library services for distance education students began to take on a higher profile, leading to an increase of literature addressing surrounding issues. Earlier literature on library services to distance education students focussed on issues of quality and accreditation of distance education programs in higher education (Simmons. 1991; Council for Adult and Experimental Learning, 1993; Kaina, 1991).

In more recent years, with the proliferation of distance education programs resulting from employment of new and more advanced technologies that facilitate virtual delivery of course content globally, the focus of the literature is now increasingly on resources and services to support the emerging virtual academic communities. The ACRL *Guidelines for Distance Learning Library Services* (ACRL, 2000) has become a yardstick for developing or assessing library services for remote users. The guidelines stress the importance of equal library services to both remote students and traditional campus students. They also advise librarians to regularly survey distance learning library users to monitor and assess both the appropriateness of their use of services and resources and the degree to which needs are being met.

Other professionals have expressed the need for the library to be visible and active within the virtual academic milieu. Lebowitz laments that:

> ..... there seems to be little or no correlation between how innovatively an institution delivers distance courses and the way in which it provides library services to distance students... Although many consider the library to be the heart of the University, the use of the library is often not incorporated into courses being prepared for distance delivery.

She recommends that librarians convince fellow educators and administrators that as they are expanding their institutions educational offerings beyond the campus boundaries, they need to provide their students with access to library services, which include among others, instruction in use of resources, document delivery, and communication facility between the students and librarian. Lebowitz also outlines three models of providing library service to off-campus students.

1. a department or unit dedicated to providing services staffed by a librarian co-ordinator to ensure that student have access to library resources and services;
2. integrated or decentralised services where there is no dedicated unit or co-ordinator and students direct their requests to the same service units as on-campus students;
3. a branch campus structure where a branch library provides resources to students who are away from the main campus.

Of the three models presented, Lebowitz suggests that the most effective of the models is that of a dedicated unit.

Cooper and Dempsey discuss issues surrounding remote users in an academic environment. This approach is that of focusing on who is using electronic information resources, how they do so, and what are their needs and expectations. They suggest that there should be a differentiation between the remote user who is a few buildings away, and the remote user participating in a distance-learning curriculum involving a distance of hundreds or thousands of miles. Cooper and Dempsey suggest that a paramount factor of remote access is the quality of the services associated with a particular electronic resource or service. Remote users are likely to require point of need assistance.

Wolpert explores a number of issues in academic librarianship and distance education. She equates the novelty of library services at a distance to the novelty of teaching at a distance. "Just as teaching at a distance is a new 'product line' for faculty, so too is library service at a distance a new 'product line' for libraries."

Dew reports a survey conducted at the University of lowa, on their off campus students. He emphasises the need for librarians to understand their students and what they want in order to have successful programs for off-campus students. Dew states that:

> ..... librarians tend to focus on disseminating the information that we think our students need. We talk at length to students about library services; we give presentations to them about all kinds of information resources, and we develop web pages full of information just for them...occasionally we need to reverse roles, listen instead of talk, and let the students tell us a few things.

This survey was one way in which librarians at the University of lowa "listened" to what their off-campus students are saying. The students were asked to rank various library services on basis of importance. The following services were ranked highest: Web and /or e-mail references 71.3 percent, remote access to full text databases 65.1 percent, home delivery of books and articles 60.7 percent. Guides to doing library research were ranked tenth with only 30.9 percent. The survey revealed that reference services, electronic services and document delivery were ranked high, while user education services were ranked lowest.

One of the key issues raised by Carty that academic libraries positioning themselves to serve remote students should work in collaboration with the teaching departments and institutional administrators to ensure that as key players in the distance education environment, they share a common vision regarding academic support to remote learners.

DATA ANALYSIS

Exhibit 2 : Profile of distance learners

I: Enrolment to the course

Course	*Responses %*
DBM	11
DFM	6
PGDBA	10
PGDBM	4
PGDFM	22
PGDHRM	25
PGDMM	4
PGDSM	8
SGDHRM	10
Total	100

It is found that more number of students are enrolled for Human resources and financial management courses.

II: Sex

Sex	*Responses %*
MALE	44
FEMALE	56
Total	100

% of female students enrolling for distance learning is more than the % of male students.

III: Classification on Age

Age	*Responses %*
20-25 YRS.	68
25-30 YRS.	16
30 YRS. & ABOVE	16
Total	100

From the above it is found that students at a young age enrol for distance learning programmes.

IV: Study habits

Period	*Responses %*
REGULARLY	18
6 MONTHS BEFORE EXAM	06
3 MONTH BEFORE EXAM	25
1 MONTH BEFORE EXAM	51
Total	100

Maximum number of students studies just a month before their exams.

Exhibit 3: Information Seeking Behaviour

I: Methods of getting required information

Methods of Information Seeking	*Responses %*
Internet	31
Reading material provided to DL students	39
Through Online Databases	16
From Notes	12
Other	02
Total	100

II: Preference for contacting Librarian

Method	*Responses %*
E-MAIL	37
TELEPHONE	34
FACE TO FACE	14
ONLINE	13
Other	02
Total	100

III: Level of interest for library facility through website

Website	*Responses %*
YES	97
NO	03
Total	100

Information seeking behaviour is a concept which includes Information needs, information seeking and formation behaviour. These are intertwined concepts. A general view of information seeking helps in understanding the various ways in which students seek information. Hence, if it were accepted that there is more than one type of information process, it would stimulate a deeper understanding of the information-seeking process in general within the field.

What we see from the data is that students are more prone to Internet. They pick up information form the Internet more than the notes and the online databases. However students do make use of the Distance Learning material that is provided to them. It is also found that they would prefer having a library facility through websites. The awareness level seems to be at a lower level especially in terms of the online databases that the library subscribes to. This can be one of the assets that any student can have. Students also prefer contacting Librarian through e-mail or telephone to get the information they are looking for.

Exhibit 4: Awareness, level of use & Need for Information

I: Registration

Registration	*Responses %*
YES	10
NO	90
Total	100

II: Reasons for not joining library

Reasons	*Responses %*
You have sufficient reading material for study	02
Library does not have resources like books, journals etc pertaining to your needs	01
Library is at a far off distance	44
Your Tight Schedule	51
Any other	02
Total	100

The students were of the view that the Library being a societal serving part of any institution or University, there should be no fee. The services and the resources should be made available free of charge to the clientele. The library membership was not taken especially because of the high fee factor.

III : Usefulness of resources

Resources / Ranking	*Responses %*
Text Books	17
Reference Books	05
Course Notes	12
Distance Learning Material	23
Website	10
Lectures	12
Past Papers	21
Total	100

Every institution does not employ a full time distance education librarian, but most institutions have a librarian who works with distance learners and is available to address their needs. University libraries are traditionally set up for on campus use, therefore libraries must necessarily do restructuring and re-orienting their services to accommodate off-campus users as well. Working closely with the distance learning office, other librarians, course instructors and users is crucial to the development and delivery of library services.

It is found that only 10% of the students have library membership. The rest 90% fall into the category wherein they are not aware of the library membership, they are at a far off distance or their schedule is so tight that they are not able to come down to access the library.

Students find Textbooks, Distance Learning material and past papers as the most useful resource, which is available to them form the Library. Faculty lectures and Websites are also seen as the useful resources.

Online orientation programmes for distance learners should be delivered at the beginning of the year and may be every three months.

Exhibit 5: Scope for marketing library services
I: Kind of library services required

Areas	*Responses %*
Document Delivery	8.93
Inter Library Loan	1.98
Online databases	14.96
Reading Room	6.20
Book Exhibition	3.47
Current Awareness Service	4.53
Photocopy facility	7.21
Renewals	2.23
Claims	00
Suggestions	3.11
Feedback	3.23
Audio Video Room	3.47
Internet	11.41
Digital library services	0.74
Online CD viewing	9.43
User Orientation	2.23
Information notification / display	1.49
Book bank	10.67
Computers	4.71
Total	100

The library should identify key library services, which must be offered to distance learning. e.g., instruction, reference, document delivery, reserve, circulation, etc. The library should work with the computing offices to assess student computer needs and site accessibility. Ideally, computer labs with sufficient numbers of computers should be made available to distance learners at the outset of any program.

The library should begin to migrate toward electronic formats for many of its resources; that is, increase online databases and full-text resources, develop electronic reserves, and design web pages for academic courses (e.g., course syllabi, readings, etc.). It is also useful to place large posters in the centre detailing what services students can get and how to do it.

Document Services played an important role. Quick access to material and subsidized library services were the most popular aspects of the library delivery system. Students were impressed by the quick response and delivery time of material and were pleased with having access to library resources via the catalogue and databases on the campus network.

Exhibit 6 : Need for amalgamation with other libraries / information resources

Use of library facility if made available near residence/ workplace	*Responses %*
Yes	77
No	10
Total	87

Visit to local Public Library	*Responses %*
Yes	41
No	59
Total	100

Visit to College Library	*Responses %*
Yes	22
No	78
Total	100

The most important element, which will impact the future of off-campus library services, involves the increasing number of cooperative ventures with other academic institutions. This cooperation will be driven politically and financially as educational organizations becoming more cost-conscious. Libraries of all kinds will be making agreements among themselves to underwrite the high cost of technology-oriented services such as networked journal indexes, full-text resources, and even their own library catalogues. Such "split the cost and share" plans may result in less restrictive limits on services for off campus users.

The distance librarian may also promote distance library services by establishing communication with other libraries that are more local to the distance students. For example, a group of distance students is based in a known location, it may be helpful to communicate with that area's local public library in order to effectively refer students to the remote resources provided to them by their local library. In this sense, public libraries can assist, redirect, and market the university's library services and resources to distance students.

THE WAY FORWARD – Innovative Marketing Strategies

A master plan for distance learning must be developed and in place early on and should include cost breakdown, identification of essential support services, numerical projections of distance learning programs, classes and student enrolees, configuration of library units and delivery services, etc. The plan should also determine whether the programs and services should be centralized or decentralized, what kind of reporting structure should be set up, and the protocols for service delivery.

1. The library must have a clear sense of the extent and nature of its involvement in any distance learning program. This means addressing the following

questions: what type of distance learning program is being offered, what is the library's mandate for delivering services and what types of services, and what kinds of support should the library expect?

2. Establish toll free number to facilitate library contact.
3. Making distant students aware of services is essential for the success of marketing. KEY: Library Information Packet: Students found the information packet to be extremely useful. The packet, which was distribute early in the course, detailed library instructions, procedures, and forms; provided valuable information on available library resources, services, and service referrals; and contained resource listings and important program contacts.
4. Electronic Library is the best tool that can be seen in marketing to distance learners. The electronic databases like full text electronic journals, the indexing and abstracting services would help students to pick up information they need from their own desktop from anywhere across the globe. Besides journals the information is also available in e-books from. The library catalogues are available online. The news papers, government information, statistical information is also available in electronic from. The resources like the exam papers, CDs or VCDs are also available electronically. If library can provide its clienteles with the above type of electronic library, it will be a boon for them.
5. Librarian can market library with a weblog. Blogs are a natural evolution in marketing and public relations for any library and an effective means of extending the reach of library instruction. Marketing and public relations are the two main reasons a library should have a blog. A blog is a great way to provide up to the minute news about library & its activities. Librarian can create a blog for library and tailor it to do exactly what librarian wants. Think of a blog as an inexpensive newsletter and a versatile information management tool

CONCLUSION

Many academic libraries are now offering their traditional students the kinds of services that were previously limited to off-campus students if available at all. Marketing is a comprehensive term that describes all the processes and interactions that result in satisfaction for users and revenue for the information firm. As Kotler points out, Organizations such as museums, universities, libraries, and charities need to market their causes and their products to gain political and social support as well as economic support.

Academic libraries venturing into distance learning must seriously consider the enormous cost and manpower involved in setting up a distance delivery system. For academic libraries caught between serving students on-campus and off, the need to meet the demands of all users equally, efficiently and cost-effectively requires a general mapping of library resources to fit curriculum needs, the establishment of new guidelines and cost-saving strategies for delivering services, and the restructuring of the delivery system to include full-text access via computer networks.

Off-campus services will become technology-driven. The problem is that this is all very expensive—microcomputers and servers, Internet connectivity, technical up-grades and software—plus staff to develop, maintain and train users of Web-based resources, etc.

There is still a need for off-campus students to have access to a local library to complement the resources and services available to them online. This is reflective to the fact that the library has not lost its value as a physical space. i.e. as a place for quiet study, or a place to go and photocopy material, or even as a place for group discussion of an assignment or project.

One of the major barriers to operating a profitable information business is the lack of business expertise among librarians and information scientists. Modern business libraries should be run like a business within the organization. The study recommends that currently efforts for increasing user-awareness and separate financial support are requisite for efficient marketing. For this purpose business librarians should deal more with information rather than a document in traditional library & must know the techniques of "information marketing."

In short marketing library services to distance students can present unique challenges to distance library service planners. When the audience is remotely located, has more demographic differences than similarities, and yet, still has the need for library services, a different marketing perspective must be taken.

BIBLIOGRAPHY

1. The ACRL (Association of College and Research Libraries) Guidelines for Distance Learning Library Services. June 2000. http://www.ala.org/ala/acrlstandards guidelinesdistancelearning.htm as on 10/09/2006.
2. Adams, Chris. The future of Library Services for Distance Education: What are we doing, where are we heading, what should we be doing? The journal of Library Services for Distance Education. Vol 1, No. 1 August 1997. P. 44-45.
3. Dermody, Melinda. We Cannot See Them, but They Are There: Marketing Library Services for Distance Learners. *Journal of Library and Information Services in Distance Learning* Vol 2, no. 1. 2005: 41-50.
4. Dooley, Kim E; Linder, James R; Dooley, Larry. Advanced methods in distance education: applications and practices for educators, trainers and learners. Information Management; Spring 2005, Vol 18, No.1/2. P. 9-10.
5. Heller-Ross, Holly. Library support for distance learning programs: a distributed model. The journal of Library Services for Distance Education. Vol II, No. 1 July 1999.
6. Lee, Angela. Delivering Library services at a Distance: A case study at the university of Washington. The journal of Library Services for Distance Education. Vol II, No. 1 July 1999. P. 3-10.
7. Moyo, Lesley Mutinta; Cahoy, ellysa Stern. Meeting the needs of remote library users. Library Management. Vol.24. No. 6/7, 2003. P. 281-290.
8. Karve, Sunil; Rane, Vrushali. "Marketing of information products and services: a study of marketing potentials of management libraries in Mumbai". 8th Annual Manlibnet National Convention, Institute of Management, Nirma University, Ahmedabad.2006.

9. Sambrook, Jessica. Information and library needs of part-time distance learning and variable attendance students at Southampton Institute. Southampton Institute. www.solent.ac.uk/library/dilvapas on 10/09/2006. November 2000.

10. Thórsteinsdóttir, Gudrún.Information-seeking behaviour of distance learning students. Information Research, **6**(2). 2001. http://InformationR.net/ir/6-2/ws7.html as on 15/10/2006.

15

Implications for Library and Information Services: A Study of India's it Revolution and Public Policies

Tariq Ashraf

ABSTRACT

The paper describes the role of Information, Information Technology (IT) and discusses the infrastructure, human resources, tele-communication, research and development in IT in Indian context. It Highlights the features of liberalization policy of the Indian government; software policy of 1986; development in networking and growth of IT industry in the country, and documents the proliferation and focuses on the relationship among policies and outcome in terms of its impact on various fields of life specially library and information services . It describes the limitation of Indian digital revolution in reaching out to the general masses and the various factors responsible for the lopsided character of information revolution.

1. INTRODUCTION

Information is a basic resource for all human beings, and it is as important to us as food, air and rest. It is the basis for all our decisions as all public policies are made on the basis of information only. Information policy, thus provides the basis, or the support, for all other public policies. Therefore, policies concerning information, both public and private, profoundly affect the society.

Information technology has emerged as the most potent tool to collect, organise and disseminate information to the people at large scale through communication networks. It is one of the fastest spreading technologies in the world in terms of use and production. It is diffusing rapidly into all industrial and service sectors and is seen as one of the most crucial technologies affecting economic growth in developing countries. Its use is ubiquitous in the industrialized countries to the extent that in United States investment in IT accounts for about 50% of total new capital investment by corporations. The production of IT products and services is a major industry in the US, Japan and Europe. Several newly industrialized countries, such as China, Korea, Taiwan, Singapore and Brazil have become significant producers and users of IT.

This evolution of IT has been marked by hcavy government involvement in virtually all countries. Of all the newly industrializing countries, India stands out for the degree to which its governments has intervened in the IT sector and the complexity and nuance of that intervention.

2. INFORMATION TECHNOLOGY: INFRASTRUCTURE

The assimilation of any new technology requires the presence of an infrastructure with which to acquire, learn and successfully apply the technology. This includes sufficiently available human resources, well developed telecommunication networks, research and development capabilities and capital for investments.

2.1. Human Resources

India, a country of more than 1 billion people, turns out an estimated 400, 000 graduates with technical and engineering degrees per year constituting the third largest pool of engineering and scientific manpower in the world and second largest pool of English speaking manpower with IT qualifications. According to a recent survey of National Association of Software and Services Companies (NASSCOM) from a base of 6,800 IT software and services professionals knowledge workers in 1985-86, the number is projected to increase to 522, 000 shortly. But the NASSCOM projections also reveal a shortage of nearly 530,000 of IT professionals over the next 3 years, assuming optimistic growth in industry.

2. 2. Telecommunications

A good telecommunications network is another vital element of IT infrastructure. Since 1985 the government has initiated a new telecommunication policy to strengthen the telecommunications sector and from 7th five year plan onwards, the sector is identified as one of the top development priorities. The telecommunication sector has now been widely opened to private players and is attracting massive investment. The government is progressively moving from a structure where the incumbent operator was a part of the government to a structure where the incumbent operator is corporatized and subsequently privatized.

2.3. Research and Development

India's R&D expenditures are well ahead of other developing countries in the Asia-Pacific region but the business R & D accounts for only 13% of the total and R&D is largely conducted by public sector and universities where it is not that relevant to economic application. In an effort to remove this anomaly, the government is establishing "science cities" around research institutions to serve as centers for high tech industrial development.

2.4. Capital

Initially capital for investment in information technology was scarce thus making the broad environment for IT diffusion very poor. However situation began to change drastically under the policy of economic restructuring and reforms initiated in the year 1991 to the extent that 70 percent FDI is now allowed in telecom sector as per decision taken in year 2006.

3. IT POLICY: HISTORICAL OVERVIEW

The history of IT Policy in Indian can be divided into two distinct periods. From the mid-1960s through the early 1980s policies aimed at achieving technological self-sufficiency through state production, regulation of private production. The second period, from 1984 to early 1990s, saw a shift in focus to moderate liberalization of the industry and promotion of domestic IT production.

Another era is now in the making as the government moves towards more extensive liberalization of the economy.

3.1. 1960s and 1970s: Indigenization and self sufficiency

India was motivated to try to develop self sufficiency in computers and electronics largely by national security concerns related to border conflicts with China and Pakistan. The government created an Electronics Committee to devise a strategy for achieving self sufficiency in electronics. The main vehicle chosen to gain access to advanced computer technology was negotiation with multinationals, primarily IBM, which accounted for 70% of all computers installed in India from 1960-1972.

In an attempt of satisfy the government's interest in developing domestic production, both IBM and British owned ICL (International Computers Limited) began to refurbish the used computes in Indian plants and sell them to Indian customers. IBM felt that Indian should evolve technologically from one level of sophistication to the next.

A 1966 report by the Electronics Committee objected to step-by-step technological evolution and recommended that India should leap ahead to the latest technologies. Government however failed to impose its will on IBM due to its strong position with users and export earnings. The government's early attempts to regulate the IT sector worsened the degree of technological backwardness.

In 1966 the responsibility for implementing the Electronics Committee report strategies was given to Department of Defense Supplies, with monitoring by a new agency, the Electric Committee of India. In 1971 the government announced the formation of Department of

Electronics (DoE) and a new Electronics Commission, responsible for policy formulation and oversight for day-to-day implementation of policies. In 1975 the DoE was given power over the licensing of computer imports and the first step taken by it was the establishment of Santa Cruz Electronics Export Processing Zone (SEEPZ) near Bombay followed by the creation of state-owned ECIL (Electronics Corporation of India Ltd.) as a national champion in mini computer production.

In 1975, in a landmark development, the US computer maker. Burroughs, entered into a joint venture with Tata Consultancy Services to export software and printers from SEEPZ. In the same year governments established Computer Maintenance Corporation (CMC) with a legal monopoly on the maintenance of all foreign computer systems in the country, reducing the advantage which IBM had with the users.

In 1978, due to increasing political pressure IBM quit India which was a seminal event. Illustrating the extent of government's ability to exert its power over Multinational Corporations and direct the IT development in India. One effect of IBM's departure was to open the market to a number of competitors, including ECIL, ICL and Tata Borroughs.

3.2. 1980s: Partial Liberalization and Industry Promotion

India's IT policies in 1980s were aimed at modernizing a industry that was estimated to be about 15 years behind the current frontiers of research and production. In a departure from the import substitution approach of the past, exports software and peripherals were now promoted and the import of mainframes and supercomputers were encouraged under certain conditions.

3 3. The New Computer Policy of 1984

The new computer policy of 1984 announced by DoE *(India, Department of Electronics, 1984)* aimed at promoting the manufacturing of computers based on latest technology, at prices comparable to international levels and with progressively increased indegenization. An Important policy change was the liberalization of imports to foster domestic hardware. Duty levels were lowered on components needed by computer manufacturers and companies producing CPUs, peripherals and subsystems were permitted liberal imports of "Know-how" with a low excise duty.

3.4. 1986: Software Policy

Following up on the 1984 hardware policy, the Department of Electronics (DoE) announced the 1986 policy on Computer Software Export, Software Development and Training. *(India, Department of Electronics, 1986)* The main objectives of the policy were to promote the integrated development of software in the country for domestic as well as export markets and to promote the use of computes as a tool to decision making and to promote appropriate applications that will catalyze economic development software imports and the duty was reduced to 60% which was further reduced in 1992 to 25% for computes and software used software producers.

In 1990, a 100% income tax exemption was extended to profits from software exports and the double taxation of software imports was eliminated. It was also decided to develop twelve additional software technology parks.

Though India's IT Policies have focussed heavily on regulations of foreign as well domestic producers and on protection of domestic market and the 1984 and 1986 policies consisted mostly of loosening of existing regulations, still a number of programmers, initiatives and institutions have been established to implement policy and promote various aspects of IT.

The DoE invests in IT and R&D through large multiyear programs involving various research units. The Knowledge-Based Computer Systems (KBCS) programme involves the five IITs, The Indian Institute of Science in Bangalore and the National Centre for Software Technology (NCST) in Bombay. The Education and Research in Computer Networking (ERNET) experiments with new concepts in computer networking and promotes Integrated Services Digital Network (ISDN).

In 1988, the National Informatics Center set up NICNET, a satellite-based computer communication network connecting 439 cities and towns to support computerization of governments at the central, state and districts level. A

Computer Aided Design project was set up with links to five centers, and a Computer Aided Management Infrastructure has been established with feeder centers in four cities. A number of projects have been under taken to promote IT use in public and private sectors and to mobilize a favorable bias towards its use.

Government's attempts to spur the development of an indigenous IT industry have been quite successful and after the 1984 Computer Policy announcement production shot up by 100% while prices declined by 50%. A boom in minicomputer sales began when HCL dropped its prices dramatically, starting in price war that greatly increased the affordability of PCs.

3.5. 1991 to 1996: Impact of Economic Liberalization

During this period, the IT policy was affected by general changes in industrial policy. Early in 1991 its import became more difficult thanks to the devaluation of the rupee, raising the software import duty to 112 percent, Simultaneously there was an effort to encourage exports by streamlining the process for exports incentive payments and for creation of export-only units. There were several software related promotional measures during this period, including reduction in telecommunication charges for satellite links, duty-free import of telecommunication equipment into EPS, excise duty exemptions.

At the end of 1992, the DoE was reorganized to emphasize its promotional rather than regulatory role.It amended and updated interventions in areas such as training and research and development.The copyright Act was also amended, confirming that raids, fines and prison sentence could be used against software pirates. Import rules were also changed and liberalization gathered pace for software.

Duty for software import was reduced to 110 percent in 1992, 85 percent in 1993, split in 1994 to 20 percent for applications software and 65 per cent for system software and then reduced to 10 percent for both categories 1995. *(Export & Import Policy, 1995)* In April 1993, duplication of software in India was permitted for the first time.

The beginning of 1990s also witnessed emergence of Software Technology Parks of India (STPI) under the state initiative. STPI was created as autonomous organization under the Department of Electronics, to provide facilities such as duty-free import of capital goods, income tax holiday for 10 years, high-speed data communication links etc.

The year 1996 can be described as landmark year in the history of information technology as Internet service was started in India by Videsh Sanchar Nigam Limited, a public sector company with a great promise. The policy makers recognized the potential of the Net for a quantum group in the knowledge-based economy. The subsequent ISP policies of the Department of Telecommunications (DOT) were very pragmatic with free licensing to ISPs. Setting up of gateways for Internet, laying of fibers & cables was freely permitted to the ISPs. Tax incentives were showered on the industry, infrastructure status given & mergers and acquisitions facilitated.

4. NEW MILLENNIUM-NEW CENTURY: NEW IDEAS

The dawn of new century brought tremendous improvement in India's regulatory environment. India was one of the few countries to enact the Information Technology Act in year 2000 to enable digital signatures. It aims to provide the legal infrastructure for e-commerce in India. *(India, Ministry of Communication and Information Technology, 2002)*

4.1. Cyber Laws

In May 2000, both the houses of the Indian Parliament passed the Information Technology Bill. The Bill received the assent of the President in August 2000 and came to be known as the Information Technology Act, 2000. Cyber laws are contained in the IT Act, 2000. Passed in August 2000 as a part of the information technology bill, cyber laws aim, to provide the legal infrastructure for e-commerce in India.

Additionally, the Information Technology Act, 2000 aims to provide legal framework so that legal sanctity is accorded to all electronic records and other activities carried out by electronic means. The Act states that unless otherwise agreed, an acceptance of contract may be expressed by electronic means of communication and the same shall have legal validity and enforceability. Some highlights of the Act are listed below:

1. Recognition of e-mail as a valid and legal form of communication in the country that can be duly produced and approved in a court of law.
2. Companies can carry out electronic commerce using the legal infrastructure provided by the Act.
3. Digital signatures have been given legal validity and sanction in the Act.
4. The Act throws open the doors for the entry of corporate companies in the business of being Certifying Authorities for issuing Digital Signatures Certificates.
5. The Act now allows Government to issue notification on the web thus heralding e governance.
6. The Act enables companies to electronically file form, applications and other documents with any office, authority, body or agency owned or controlled by the appropriate Government
7. That act addresses important issues of security, which are critical to the success of
8. electronic transactions. The Act has also given a legal definition to the concept of secure digital signatures.

4.2. IPR Laws

In India, the Intellectual Property Rights (IPR) of computer software is covered under the Copyright Law. Accordingly, the copyright of computer software is protected under the provisions of Indian Copyright Act 1957. Major changes to Indian Copyright Law were introduced in 1994 and came into effect from 10 May 1995. These changes or amendments made the

Indian Copyright law, one of the toughest in the world. The amendments to the Copyright Act introduced in June 1994 were in themselves, a landmark in the India's copyright arena. For the first time in India, the Copyright Law clearly explained:

1. The rights of a copyright holder
2. Position on rentals of software
3. The rights of the user to make backup copies

4. The imposition of heavy punishment and fines for infringement of copyright of software.

   NASSCOM: Strategic Review 2003

4.3. Broadband Policy 2004

Recognising the potential of ubiquitous Broadband service in growth of GDP and enhancement in quality of life through societal applications including tele-education, tele-medicine, e-governance, entertainment as well as employment generation by way of high speed access to information and web-based communication, Government have finalised a policy to accelerate the growth of Broadband services.

Demand for Broadband is primarily conditioned and driven by Internet and PC penetration. It is recognised that the current level of Internet and Broadband access in the country is low as compared to many Asian countries. Penetration of Broadband, Internet and Personal Computer (PC) in the country was 0.02%, 0.4% and 0.8% respectively at the end of December, 2003. Currently, high speed Internet access is available at various speeds from 64 kilobits per second (kbps) onwards and presently an always-on high speed Internet access at 128 kbps is considered as 'Broadband'. There are no uniform standards for Broadband connectivity and various countries follow various standards.

Government envision an accelerated growth in Internet penetration and PC as the success of Broadband would largely be dependent on their spread. It has been decided that following shall be the framework of the policy.

The Broadband Policy Framework visualises creation of infrastructure through various access technologies like Optical Fibre Technologies, Digital subscriber Line on Copper Loop, Cable TV Network, satellite media like VSAT, DTH, AND Terrestrial wireless WI-FI system. which can contribute to growth and can mutually coexist. Spread of infrastructure is a must for healthy competition and therefore it would be the endeavour of the Government that the telecommunication infrastructure growth in the country is not compromised in any manner

5. IT: PROLIFERATION AND APPLICATION

5.1. Economics

In a very short time, India has risen to considerable eminence in the world of information technology, enlarging from $ 1.73 billion in 1994-95 to a $13.5 billion industry in 2001-02 In terms of share of GDP, the IT industry figures have risen from 0.59 percent to 2.87 percent in 2001-02. According to the NASSCOM report revenues from hardware, peripherals and networking are estimated to touch $ 2,983 millions during 2001-02, India's software and services exports are expected to account for $ 7,678 millions of revenues. Revenue from IT enabled services sector grew from US$ 554 million in 1999-2000 to US$ 897 million in 2000-2001 Customer Interaction Services, which included call centers and customer support centers were the prime areas of growth. In 1999-2000, the volume of e-commerce transactions in India was only US$ 104 million whereas this is a growing segment in the international market. *(NASSCOM, 2002)*

The Indian domestic IT market has been spurred by various developments including a growth in PC penetration, increased usage of networking and peripheral equipment and proliferation of software application. The Internet revolution is sweeping across the country, coupled with lowering hardware prices and cheaper bandwidth availability. Within eight years, predicts a recent study by McKinsey & Co. and the NASSCOM, India's annual IT exports could hit $50 billion — about 33 per cent of global software exports. Such a surge is expected to generate 2.2 million jobs — and push our growth rate near the double digits that many East Asian Tigers enjoyed before the 1997 crash.

The policy framework governing the ICT sector has catalyzed the growth of the industry, boosting its prospects for exports. Policy liberalization initiatives in key areas such as taxation and infrastructure (particularly telecom) have had a direct fallout on the IT software and services industry. A series of initiatives including the IT Act 2000, special tax sops for the ICT industry and a new Copyright Law, among others have enabled the IT industry in India to globalize. Today, India ranks among handful of nations across the world that boast cyber laws. These policies have also helped the country position itself as a key destination for investment, especially in segments such as IT services, IT-enabled services, BPO, and R&D. Owing to the continuous policy changes, it is now easy for potential players to enter the ICT Market. 1 Special Economic Zones (SEZs): SEZ is a new scheme announced by the Government of India. SEZs are areas where export production can take place free from the plethora of rules and regulations governing imports and exports. Units operating in these zones have full flexibility of operations and can import duty free capital goods and raw material. The movement of goods to and fro between ports and SEZ are unrestricted. The units in SEZ have to export the entire production..

5.2. Governance

In a recent policy initiative the government has recommended each ministry to allocate 2-3 per cent of its budget on IT promotion. Central Government has taken various steps, legislative, regulatory and promotional measures to facilitate IT use in corporate, financing and taxation matters. Different projects have been initiated to come up with IT based solutions for development purposes. Different ministries and departments have come out with their web sites. Major areas of computerization include railway reservation, allocation of Permanent Account Number (PAN) for Income Tax payers, processing of passport, results of public examination, Regional Transport Offices, custom clearance, schemes under implementation by the NGOs, vigilance information, single counter services and VSAT based money order under the Department of Post, computerization of Supreme Court cases, land records, Parliament questions, debates and deliberations.

Central and State government and their field organizations, financial institutions, insurance companies, educational institutions are proceeding ahead with introduction of computerization and use of IT in the sphere of work. It is reported that 12,000 out of 45, 000 bank branches have implemented major computerization.

Many state governments have declared IT policies. State effort to promote IT is through development of IT infrastructure, e-governance, IT education and providing enabling environment for IT proliferation. Substantial growth in demand for Internet and PCs has been experienced in the recent past. There are 1.6 million estimated Internet connections in India in August 2000 as against 0.14 million in March 1998. The number of Internet subscribers in the year 2004-05 are likely to reach 7.7 million, with the user base increasing to 50 millions. The PC base in India, according to a survey of the NASSCOM, numbered 5 million, i.e., 5 per 1000 people in August 2001 as against 3 per 1000 in 1999. The NASSCOM forecasts PC prices to decline to by nearly 40 percent and PC penetration to reach 13 per 1000 persons. *(NASSCOM, 2005)*.

In the area of job creation, according to a survey conducted by the NASSCOM, software industry including user organizations have employed 340,000 professionals as on 31 March 2000 as against 160,000 professionals in 1996. It has been reported that cyber kiosks in India have generated 600,000 jobs under private initiative.

6. ICTS: IMPACT ON LIBRARIES

Libraries, Museums and archives are digitizing their resources and services on large scales. Libraries with computerized catalogues are now becoming part of networks. Scores of premier institutions like Indian Institute of Technology (s), (IIT) Indian Institute of Management (s) (IIM) and laboratories under Council for Scientific and Industrial Research (CSIR) are spending huge amounts on digital collections. In national library, Calcutta nearly 750,000 pages have been scanned and stored in CDs under the ongoing schemes for digitizing selected books and old documents. In Central Secretariat Library, New Delhi, the bibliography of rare books in CD-ROM format linking images of the title and content pages is in progress.

Recently, the government has decided to create a Traditional Knowledge Digital Library (TKDL). The purpose is to integrate the widely scattered knowledge in Indian system of medicine. TKDL will comprise of 35, 000 formulations collected from 35 texts available in public domain.

University Grants Commission, the apex regulating body for Indian Universities has launched its UGC-INFONET programme under which all central universities are being provided access to scores of electronic databases covering all areas of higher education and research. The University Grants Commission has set up an autonomous Inter-University Centre in 1991 called INFLIBNET. It is involved in modernizing university libraries in India and connects them through a nation-wide high-speed data network. It promotes automation of libraries, develops standards, creates union catalogues of serials, theses, books, monographs and non-book materials; provides access to bibliographic information sources; creates database of projects, institutions, specialists; provides training, etc. Almost all academic libraries, especially university libraries, are members of INFLIBNET.

Digital Library of India, part of the online services of the *Indian Institute of Science, Bangalore* and partner in the *Million Book Project*, provides free access to many books in English and Indian languages. The scanning of Indian language books has created an opportunity for developing Indian language *optical character recognition* (OCR) software. The publications are mainly in *PDF* or *QuickTime* format. As of November 10, 2006, DLI had scanned 84,895 titles.

Vidyanidhi (Meaning 'Treasure of Knowledge' in Sanskrit) is India's yet another premier Digital library initiative to facilitate the creation, archiving and accessing of doctoral theses. Vidyanidhi is an information infrastructure, a digital library, a portal of resources, tools and facilities for doctoral research in India. Vidyanidhi is envisioned to evolve as a national repository and a consortium for e-theses through participation and partnership with universities, academic institutions and other stake holders. Vidyanidhi enhances access to Indian theses and enlarges the reach and audience for Indian doctoral research works.

IT is being harnessed extensively to digitize rare and fragile material al over the country. Similarly research out put by faculty is now being made available through open source solutions like Dspace and Greenstone.

Prime minister launched the National Mission for Manuscripts (NMM) on February 7, 2003, in New Delhi. This Mission with an initial outlay of Rs.35 crore aims at surveying, identifying, collecting, copying, cataloguing and publishing of manuscripts that are lying scattered all over the country in the custody of various sources.

6. INFORMATION FOR ALL: EQUITABLE INFORMATION ORDER VS. DIGITAL DEPRIVATION

The big question is, will IT do an encore for India as a nation, and not just for a wafer thin percentage of IT-literate Indians, mostly the poster boys of the IITs?. Asks Dipankar Das. *(Das, 2001)*

The answer is that economic life in rural India, for that matter of the poor in particular, is yet to evolve around IT. IT has not yet touched the lives of the average citizen and India is nowhere close to being much hyped up "knowledge economy or society". The above cited initiatives and projects , if not selective, can largely be described as peripheral in nature. A large section of Indian society is still living in a state of digital deprivation. Despite the urban wealth of hi-tech cities like Bangalore, three quarters of the population still live in villages and deeply entrenched poverty makes the daily struggle to survive a more immediate priority than computer literacy.

As per the International Data Corporation (IDC), survey of 55 countries, India ranks 54th on its Information Society Index. The 2000 World Times/IDC index measures the global impact of IT and Internet adoption and establishes a standard by which all nations are measured according to their ability to assess and absorb information and IT. *(IDC, 2002)*

India's growing digital divide separates a narrow upper crust of "bandwidth-hungry urbanites" from the vast majority of their malnourished, illiterate countrymen, who may have to walk days just to get to the nearest working telephone. The major metropolises are at par with some of the developed countries, but rural areas in states like eastern Bihar and Orissa are worse off than several of the least developed countries. Online banking, online transactions and e-commerce and many other IT related applications are still alien to rural economy.

Groaning under basic problems such as illiteracy, malnutrition and sheer poverty, India's rural populace may as well be living on a planet different from, say, Bangalore, which, according to the United Nations Development Program **(UNDP)** human development report for 2001, is better off than many cities in the United States, Europe and Japan when it comes to technological innovation. The report clearly brought out India's digital divide between a few urban centers and the vast rural hinterland. Among India's 1.4 million Internet connections, more than 1.3 million are cornered by the states of Delhi, southern Karnataka (of which Bangalore is capital), Tamil Nadu and western Maharashtra.

The situation is worse in India's vast rural hinterland. Barely 25 km from New Delhi is India's most populous state Uttar Pradesh which according to U.N. Development Programme estimates will take all of this century to make all its 170 million people literate. **(UNDP, 2001)**

7. DIGITAL DIVIDE: CAUSES, CONSTRAINTS AND SOLUTIONS

India being one of the poorest countries in the world with extremely low literacy rates in rural areas, 25 percent without health services, 71 percent without access to sanitation, nearly 30 percent living below the poverty line has extremely powerful inbuilt constraints towards establishing an equitable information order. Huge linguistic diversity, deeply ingrained ideologies of caste-hierarchy, gender inequality and communal divisions further hinder the developmental efforts

Access to technology is further constrained by infrastructure parameters like electricity, the number of personal computers (PCs) and telephone lines. Per capita electricity consumption in India remains around 363 kW, far below the 4,959 kW in Hong Kong, one of the region's technology powerhouses, the 5,421 kW in Britain and the 11,822 kW in the U.S. India has 22 telephone lines per 1,000 people compared with 70 in neighboring China and three PCs per 1,000 compared with nine in China. The installed base of PCs in the country is five million, which means only five out of every 1,000 people have a PC.

When it comes to bringing computers to the masses, it's hard to make progress without government systems. There's limited use for example in giving free computers to village schools if there's no electricity. Internet programs aren't much use without phone connections

Despite government initiative in promoting rural telephony, tele-density in the rural area is low. By the end of December 2001, there were 7.6 million Direct Exchange Line (DEL) in rural areas meaning thereby availability of 7 phones per 1000 people. The cost of access network is still very high and is not affordable for the population in the low-income group. **(ICTs' 2001).**

7.1. Public Policy: Constraints and Limitations

Privatization of telecommunications pursued since 1994 had brought in investments. But these were concentrated in the profitable urban centers because private players were unwilling to invest in the non-profitable rural areas, where 70 percent of India's 1 billion people lived. This was a pity because investment in the rural areas could transform the lives of millions of farmers - not only in terms of freeing them from the stranglehold of middleman traders with reliable, real-time market information, but also by getting to them and their families virtually non-existent health care and educational facilities.

This could largely be attributed to India's slow telecommunications expansion to a number of factors, including tight bureaucratic control, poor policies and inadequate investment by private companies and lack of funds of the government, which until recently held monopoly control. Cost in installing backbone communication lines throughout the country is an awesome task. Even if they can somehow manage to buy PCs, maintenance, supplying parts, and training people how to use them are more difficult.

Unfortunately nowhere is the digital divide more glaring then in IT education. India's 'obsession' with the software industry and its export orientation is leading to the churning out of unemployable students on one hand and bright whiz kids on the other. While the latter are lured away by overseas employers, the former remain unemployable. Experts ask for cautions against the 'hype' associated with the phenomenal growth of India's software industry — defying rational explanations and built up into a 'mystique of sort' which breeds false hopes.

This situation itself is a product of the skewed priorities: spending 60 per cent of the education budget to subsidize the IITs and IIMs, while spending the rest on secondary and primary education. "The revolution in information technology (IT), far from helping India to leapfrog to a post-industrial society, threatens to rupture the social fabric by enriching a few at the cost of many". *(Das, 2002)*

7.2. New Possibilities

For bridging digital divide with effective practical applications of technology, three elements are crucial, entreprenuership, government policy encouraging and supporting equity and ground level programs with local community participation. A significant proportion of India's population belongs to the traditionally backward communities and a process of computer education, particularly focussed on these groups is required. By developing of relevant software for interaction in regional languages and through pictures and icons to enable illiterates acquire information.

There is a need for establishing rural information networks which will allow knowledge, services, money, and certain kinds of information products to flow easily across long distances, from one public access information center to another. Each village node might have multiple institutional identities, serving as a virtual community center, bank, medical resource, government counter, matrimonial bureau, public library and educational resource center all at once.

An urgent requirement in this direction is to break the barrier of language so as to provide content in local languages. In a country where nearly 70 percent of the population is working in agriculture sector it is very important that contents are relevant to the agricultural economy. By enhancing access to education and health care through distance learning and tele-medicine, IT can improve the quality of life for poor rural communities who do not have access to these facilities. The Indian fishing village of Veerampatinam in Tamil Nadu is a case in point, where weather forecasts downloaded from the Internet and broadcast by loud speakers at the beach enabled the poor fishermen to know better when to venture into the sea in their boats for fishing.

Similarly the public call booths dotting the countryside in Bangladesh only go to show how the poor rural communities in developing countries can access the state-of-the-art telecommunications without owning any equipment, per se.

8. CONCLUSION

Tremendous gains have been made by the computerization of the government functioning, not only in strengthening the delivery of existing services but also by improving policy planning and implementation through more effective provision of information to policy makers. The direct and immediate benefits of use of IT in Government are improvements in service quality, efficiency and government-people relationships by providing quick, easy and transparent access to information.

There is an urgent need to target basic needs such as primary education, basic health services, water and sanitation requirements particularly in rural and backward areas. The new ICT applications and content relevant to the demand in rural areas, can drastically improve the delivery of information related services to people in general and agriculture extension services and provision of health and social services in rural areas in particular.

The policymakers must take into consideration the broader picture when designing IT policy and treat it as a part of an overall economic strategy in which sound economic policies will benefit IT sector and diffusion of IT will have positive effects on economic development and social welfare. Formation of partnerships between local bodies, the local administration and NGOs appears to hold the key.

Development of applications, such as an online system for community banking, will contribute to the economic sustainability of the operations. It will also go a long way to humanize and sensitize Indian information revolution.

REFERENCES

Das (Dipankar) Great Indian digital divide. at *http://www.hindustantimes.com/nonfram/290600/detOPI03.htm http://www.uncrd*

ICTs' (2001). ICTs in rural poverty alleviation. Economic and Political Weekly. 36(11), 917-920.

India, Department of Electronics(1988) Policy on computer software exports, software Development and training, New Delhi.

India, Department of Electronics, Government of India. 'New Computer Policy', Electronics Information and Planning , 12.(2).89 - 94

India, Ministry of Commerce and Industry. Export & Import Policy. 2000

India, Planning Commission(2002) Approach paper to tenth five year plan.

India, Science & Technology (Department of) A draft paper for a new technology policy. New Delhi. 1993.

India, Ministry of Information & Broadcasting. IT Act 2000. at *www.mit.gov.in/it-bill.htm*

NASSCOM (2002) The IT in India: Strategic Review . New Delhi;. p21-22.

NASSCOM (2002) The IT in India: Strategic Review . New Delhi. p54

NASSCOM (2002) The IT in India: Strategic Review . New Delhi. p67

UNICEF Newsletter .Children in India. November 2002.

United Nations Development Program Human Development Report for year 2001.

www.apnic.net/mailing-lists/s-asia-it/ archive/2000/08/msg00007.html

www.mssrf.org

www.trahatt.com

http://www.ugc.ac.in

16

Concepts and Architecture of Digital Library with Special Reference to the Creation of Digital Library through Institutional Repository by Using Dspace

Sibsankar Jana

ABSTRACT

This paper provides an overview of digital library, institutional repository, open source software and Dspace software. Enumerates differents steps and prerequisites to create digital library through institutional repository by using the open source software "Dspace". Different types of architectural approaches and components of digital library are described.

INTRODUCTION

Creation of digital library involves many prerequisite and technical issues. Before the creation of digital library by using

DSpace we have to know – what is digital library? What are the components of digital library? What are the technical issues for the development of digital library? How institutional repository or simply repository is related to digital library? How DSpace is working in digital library? It will be very much relevant to enumerate all the elements and components of digital library, institutional repository and finally the DSpace the digital library software. In introduction it is meaningful to sketch all about digital library.

1. DIGITAL LIBRARY

1.1. Definitions and capabilities of digital library

Digital libraries are organizations that provide the resources, including the specialized staff, to select, structure, offer intellectual access to, interpret, distribute, preserve the integrity of, and ensure the persistence over time of collections of digital works so that they are readily and economically available for use by a defined community or set of communities. Digital library was viewed as system providing a community of users with coherent access to a large, organized repository of information and knowledge. The ability of the user to access, recognize, and utilize this repository is enriched by the capabilities of digital technology. The scope and definition of the field of digital libraries has been the subject of intensive debate, which is well summarized in (Borgman, 1999). Here we simply remind the reader of the integrative nature of the field through three definitions that show such combinations:

* Library++ = library + archive + museum + ?
* Distributed information system + organization + effective interfaces
* User community + collection (content) + services

According to 5S framework of Fox, in 1999 digital libraries are complex systems that:

* Help satisfy information needs of users (societies),
* Provide information services (scenarios),
* Locate and present information in usable ways (spaces),
* Organize information in usable ways (structures), and

* Communicate information with users and computers (streams).

Digital library systems compose a family of automated systems that together provide a comprehensive capability to manage the digital content of an enterprise. It is useful to divide the capabilities of digital library systems into the following areas:

* capture or creation of content
* indexing and cataloging (metadata)
* storage
* search and query
* asset and property rights protection
* retrieval and distribution

1.2. Components of digital library

To build digital libraries we must ensure that each of the "S" constructs is addressed, and so can use 5S as a checklist or guideline. In operational terms, however, many digital libraries are built out of components that are integrated into a production quality system. Figure 2 highlights some of the most important such components.

1.2.1. Digital objects

The actual content of digital libraries is made up of a number of digital objects. In some cases these may be thought of as data sets (e.g., a table of results, the genomic information for an individual). In others they may be multimedia information, such as an image, graphic, animation, sound, musical performance, or video. Digital Object has the following components (Figure-1).

1. Handle : The handle is a unique identifier. The following are desirable properties of identifiers in the digital library:

* Location independent name
* Globally accessible unique names
* Names that are persistent across time
* Choice of automatic generation or use of assigned names
* Fast resolution of identifiers
* Replication and caching of objects and resolvers

- Decentralized administration
- Change control
- Support from standard user interfaces

2. Content : The content is a sequence of bits or a set of sequences of bits. The content of digital objects is defined as sequences of bits, but in most practical uses those bits have structure and semantics. Data models (schemas) are used to give semantics to digital objects. Current thinking is that digital objects should be typed and that schemas can be built up from three base types: *sequence-of-bits, digital-object* and *set-of.* Sets of objects can be represented in the digital library in two ways, composite objects, in which the content contains a set of objects (Figure-2), and meta-objects, in which the content includes handles for a set of objects(Figure-3). Combinations are also possible.

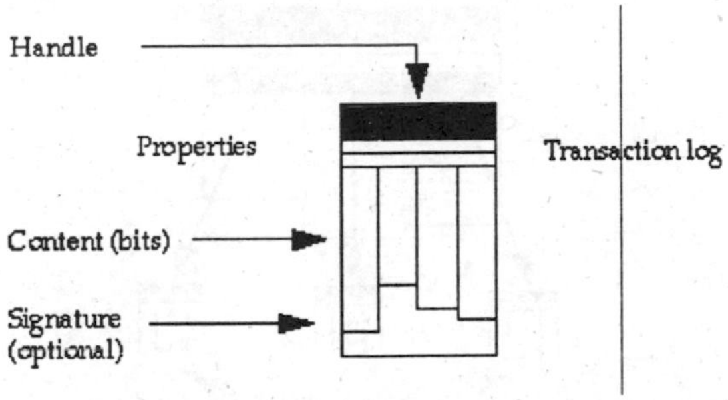

Fig. 1. Components of digital object

3. Properties: The associated properties information is used to record properties, such as rights, formats etc. Information associated with a digital object is called properties. This information can be considered from various viewpoints, including the type of information, who creates it and where it is stored.

Types : There are many types of properties including: bibliographic information (content), technical (formats, schemas, protocols), rights (ownership, terms and conditions), administrative, etc.

Creation : Properties can be created by the originator

of the object, an administrator, third party, etc.

Storage : Properties are stored in many places, including: properties records, meta-objects, separate digital objects, information retrieval servers, external indexes, etc.

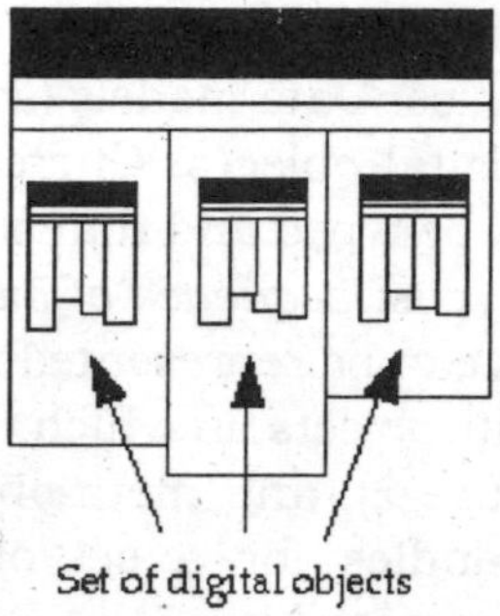

Fig. 2. The following diagram shows a composite object.

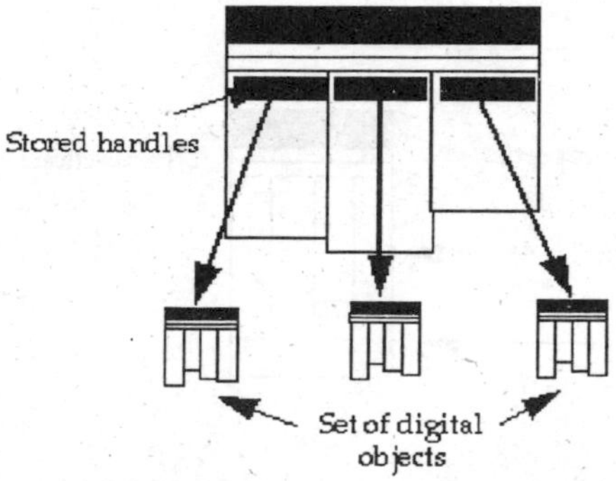

Fig. 3. The following diagram shows a meta-object.

4. Transaction log : The associated transaction information is used to keep a log of uses made of the object.

5. Signature : The optional digital signature guarantees that the object has not been altered.

1.2.2. Metadata

Digital objects are described, structured, summarized, managed, and otherwise manipulated in surrogate form through the use of "metadata", which literally means data about data. Three types of metadata are often distinguished: descriptive, structural, and administrative. Metadata is usually produced through a process called "cataloging" that is often carried out by trained librarians. Collections of such information are commonly stored in "catalogs". In computerized environments, metadata may be automatically or semi-automatically extracted or derived from the original content, or the "full-text" may simply be indexed and searched without involving metadata.

1.2.3. Repositories and Harvesting

Digital library contains a collection of digital objects (DOs), each of which has one or more sets of metadata objects (MDOs) associated stored in the repository. This "repository" part of a digital library may, as is the case in the Open Archives Initiative, follow certain. In particular, according to the latest specifications, an "Open Archive" (OA) is a computer system with a WWW server that behaves according to an OA protocol to allow other computers to harvest metadata from it. That protocol supports requests to, for example:

* list what types of metadata format are present,
* list what structure of sets and subsets are used to organize or partition the content,
* disseminate or return a particular MDO, or
* list URIs (unique identifiers) for all MDOs added during a particular date range.

1.2.4. Rights Management

In repository there is the "rights manager" which must protect intellectual property rights. In the trivial case, which fortunately is common, content is freely available so nothing is needed here. In some cases too, where content is encrypted, content management is outside the scope of the digital library, since secure objects are stored and retrieved and the steps of encryption and decryption occur remotely. Similarly, some content may have "watermarks" added in a way that makes removal difficult, so that subsequent access outside the digital library can be monitored or controlled.

1.2.5. Indexing, Resource Discovery, Searching, and Retrieving

Finding DOs, directly or through MDOs, so that they can

be identified, retrieved, and used. Often, DOs and/or MDOs are automatically indexed so that some index structure is built to speed up search. Such indexing may build upon any manual indexing carried out by authors, other creators, or indexers. Automatic indexing also may involve first classifying Dos.

1.2.6. Linking, Annotating, and Browsing

Once a DO is found, it often is appropriate to follow links from it to cited works (or vice versa). Further, notes can be recorded as annotations and linked back to the works, so they can be recalled later or shared with colleagues as part of collaborative activities. If suitable clustering is in place, other DOs that are "near" a given work may be examined. Or, using a classification system appropriate for the content domain, users may browse around in "concept space" and link at any point between concepts and related DOs. Browsing also can proceed based on any of the elements in the MDO. Thus, dates, locations, publishers, contributing artists, language, and other aspects may be considered to explore the collection or refine a search.

1.2.7. Interfaces and Interaction

Ultimately, users will connect through a human-computer interface and interact with the digital library, though in some cases the digital library may be an embedded system that is seen only indirectly (e.g., through a word processor that allows one to search for a quotation). Most commonly, a digital library has an interface for users to search, browse, follow links, retrieve, and read documents. The interface may be specialized according to what roles the user will play.

1.2.8. Architectures and Interconnecting

Since the field of digital libraries is young, there still is active investigation regarding architecture, interconnection, and interoperability (Paepcke, Chang, Garcia-Molina, & Winograd, 1998). Figure 2 shows one, rather high-level, decomposition of a digital library into components. Given the range of legacy systems that are used today as parts of digital libraries, the actual situation often is more complex.

1. Operational Architecture : Operational architecture is an information management system represented in terms of the business/library processes it supports, and how information related to conduct of the business/library processes passes through the system's components. Although the information is generated in several different libraries/ enterprise domains, effective utilization of information often depends on cross-domain searches and retrievals. Therefore, digital library services must provide information interoperability in middleware.

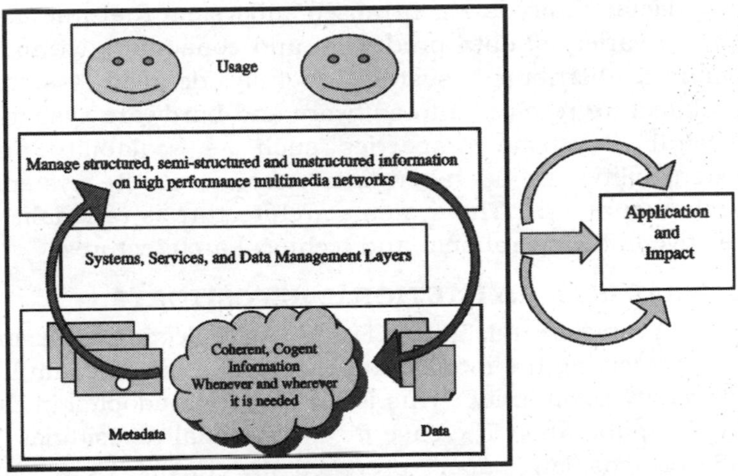

Fig. 4. Operational Architecture

2. Technical Architecture : A technical architecture breaks down operational processes into functional components and capabilities (Figure 5). Hardware and software implementations are still not resolved. The utilization of digital library materials depends on the existence of metadata to give an efficient and accurate view of content. Metadata must be created as content is added to the digital library. Metadata and data must be bound together logically, and there must be a robust underlying technology to manage the logical connection through time, across platforms, and over geographical separations, all on a networked, distributed system.

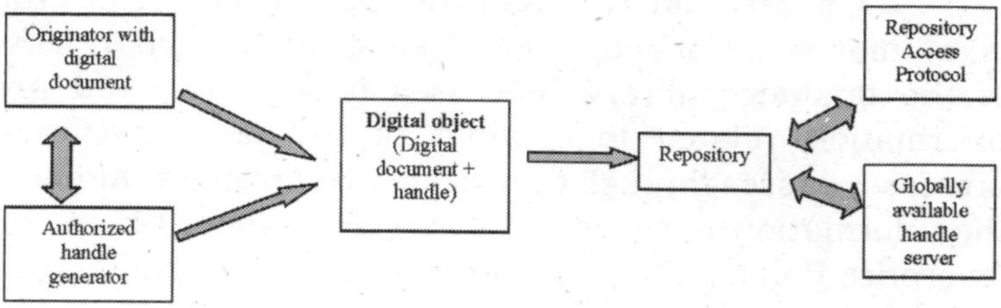

Fig. 5. Technical Architecture

3. Systems Architecture : A systems architecture shows the technology enablers and their inter-relationships. The digital library is a centralized subsystem that interacts with a variety of data producers and consumers within a complex distributed system. A fully detailed systems architecture resolves into software and hardware systems. Desirable systems properties such as scalability and extensibility can be taken into account at the systems architecture level. The systems architecture is rationalized relative to the operational and technical architectures.

3. WHAT IS AN INSTITUTIONAL REPOSITORY?

A convenient definition is a "digital collection capturing and preserving the intellectual output of a single or multi-university community". This is the definition adopted in the SPARC publication The case for institutional repositories: a SPARC position paper prepared by Raym Crow. An **Institutional Repository** is an online locus for collecting and preserving — in digital form — the intellectual output of an institution, particularly a research institution. For a university, this would include materials such as research journal articles (before (preprints) and after (postprints) undergoing peer review, and digital versions of theses and dissertations, but it might also include other digital assets generated by normal academic life, such as administrative documents, course notes, or learning objects (Figure-6).

The two main objectives for having an institutional repository are:

* to provide open access to institutional research output by self-archiving it;

* to store and preserve other institutional digital assets, including unpublished or otherwise easily lost ("grey") literature (e.g., theses or technical reports).

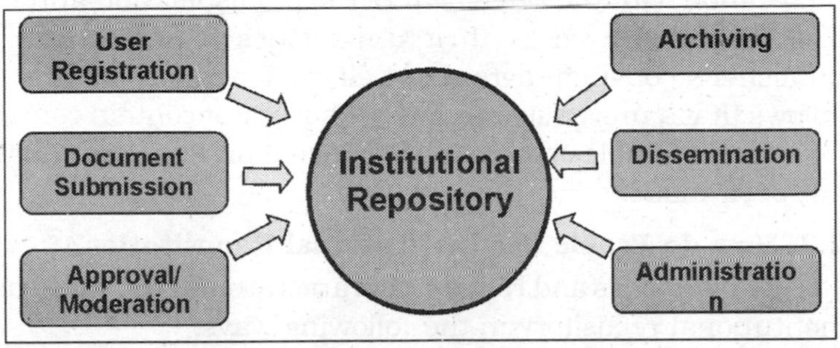

Fig. 6. Repository functionality

2.1. What might an institutional repository contain?

The intellectual output of a university is very diverse and may include the following:

* pre-prints of articles or research reports submitted for publication
* the text of journal articles accepted for publication
* revised texts of published work with comments from academic readers
* conference papers
* teaching materials
* student projects
* doctoral theses and dissertations
* datasets resulting from research projects
* committee papers
* computer software
* works of art
* photographs and video recordings

2.2. What might an institutional repository not contain?

The answer to this question is linked to the ownership of copyright or licensing terms. An institutional repository may contain work of which copyright is owned by the author or university, or for which permission has been obtained to include a copy of the work in the repository. Thus - for example

- a repository might contain the text of a journal article with the agreement of the author or as a condition of an employment contract. A repository may also contain a copy of the formatted publication with the agreement of the publisher, and authors may be encouraged by their universities to ensure that a publisher's copyright agreement allows for this possibility. It follows that a university repository should not contain content for which suitable copyright or licensing arrangements have not been made.

2.3. How do People Use Institutional Repositories?

Universities and research libraries around the world use institutional repository in the following ways:

* Scholarly communication
* Storing learning materials and courseware
* Electronic publishing
* Managing collections of research documents
* Preserving digital materials for the long term
* Adding to the university's prestige by showcasing its academic research
* Institutional leadership role for the Library
* Knowledge management
* Research assessment
* Encouraging open access to scholarly research
* Housing digitized collections

Each university has a unique culture and assets that require a customized approach. The information model that best suits your university would not fit another campus.

2.4. How much does it cost a university to set up an institutional repository?

The cost of setting up an institutional repository contains too many variables to give a simple answer to this question, but the evidence from those universities which have set up repositories is that the set-up costs are not high given an existing information-service infrastructure. Most academic information is already produced in digital format and can be added relatively easily to a web-site. Establishing the copyright position on some content can be labour-intensive but this problem can be eased in time as universities establish clear copyright policies. Maintenance costs for an institutional archive are still problematic, as all stakeholders in scholarly communication are exploring the long-term preservation of digital content, but the cost to a university of preservation in an institutional repository should be no greater than the payments to a publisher or other third party to undertake long-term preservation.

2.5. Essential elements of an institutional repository

The essential elements of an institutional repository are:

* Institutionally defined;
* Scholarly;
* Cumulative and perpetual; and
* Open and interoperable.

2.5.1. Institutionally Defined

In contrast to discipline-specific repositories and subject-oriented or thematic digital libraries, institutional repositories capture the original research and other intellectual property generated by an institution's constituent population active in many fields. Defined in this way, institutional repositories represent an historical and tangible embodiment of the intellectual life and output of an institution. And, to the extent that institutional affiliation itself serves as the primary qualitative filter, this repository becomes a significant indicator of the institution's academic quality.

2.5.2. Scholarly Content

Depending on the goals established by each institution, an institutional repository could contain any work product generated by the institution's students, faculty, non-faculty researchers, and staff. This material might include student electronic portfolios, classroom teaching materials, the institution's annual reports, video recordings, computer programs, data sets, photographs, and art works-virtually any digital material that the institution wishes to preserve.

2.5.3. Cumulative and Perpetual

Essential to the institutional repository's role both within the university and within the larger structure of scholarly communication is that the content collected is both cumulative and maintained in perpetuity.

2.5.4. Interoperability and Open Access

Providing no- or low-barrier access to the intellectual product generated by the institution increases awareness of research contributions. The goals motivating an institution to create and maintain a digital repository-whether pan-institutional, as a component in the changing structure of scholarly communication, or institution-centric-require that users beyond the institution's community gain access to the content. For the repository to provide access to the broader research community, users outside the university must be able to find and retrieve information from the repository. Therefore, institutional repository systems must be able to support interoperability in order to provide access via multiple search engines and other discovery tools.

2.6. In simple terms, success in building a repository involves eight "C" words:

1. Comprehension : Comprehension means that all members of the team must share a common vision and understanding of the purposes and scope of the repository.

2. Collaboration : Collaboration involves thinking and working together, with different people contributing their different talents, working with others to solve problems, and making important decisions.

3. Context : Context is each person's world view and working environment. Each person has a unique mind-set based on background, education, and experience. Thinking and working together in a non-threatening atmosphere helps people integrate other contexts into their own.

4. Change : Repositories involve change in the way research is disseminated, preserved, and published. This change requires faculty to deposit their research results, data sets, and other materials in the repository — a new step in the research process. In corporations, management may require staff to deposit items, such as strategic plans, marketing plans, and working papers.

5. Caring : Caring motivates the desire to share research results and joint scholarly endeavors, preserve history, and provide knowledge and information needed for future generations to learn.

6. Commitment : Caring leads to the commitment to deposit one's scholarly work in the repository, encouraging others to do likewise by contributing ideas and energy. Managers show their commitment by understanding that repositories will grow and require support and funding in perpetuity

7. Creativity : Creativity involves imagination and the ability to visualize a new way of doing things. New ideas can come from anywhere — from individuals or groups of individuals.

8. Competence : Competency means knowing how to make the repository work for all its constituents. Librarians and archivists need to carry their collection development skills and operational know-how to the repository project. Information technology staff demonstrates their competencies by knowing about the software, hardware, networking, and standards needed to make the repository serve everyone.

2.7. Most Common Challenges

The problems and hurdles which implementation teams face in building a repository include the following:

* Adoption rate by academics
* Providing for sustainability
* Developing policies
* Managing intellectual property rights
* University support
* Cost management
* Digital preservation
* Identifying key stakeholders

This workbook addresses these key challenges and points you to examples and references for further investigation. Also, see the Case Studies to learn how other implementation teams meet these challenges.

2.8. Key Issues to Consider when Developing Repositories

* the institutional culture
* the scope of the repository
* content
* access levels
* legal aspects
* standards
* sustainability
* funding

2.9. Major Steps in Building an Institutional Repository

Broadly speaking, the following steps are the major milestoncs you will encounter in building an institutional repository. We present them here in logical order but realise that many of you will experience them differently.

* Learning about the process by reading about and examining other institutional repositories.
* Developing a Service Definition and Service Plan:
    * Conduct a needs assessment of your university.
    * Develop a cost model based on this plan.
    * Create a schedule and timeline.
    * Develop policies that govern content acquisition, distribution, and maintenance.
* Assembling a team
* Technology – Choose and install software platform
* Marketing
* Launching a Service
* Running a Service

3. OPEN SOURCE SOFTWARE

Open source software is software that has source code that is open, viewable, unrestricted and redistributed, and is available by downloading it from the Internet. It may be system software or application software. Examples of proprietary operating systems are windows and windows NT, and open source operating systems are LINUX and FreeBSD. OSS is both a philosophy and a process. As a philosophy it describes the intended use of software and methods for its distribution.

Depending on your perspective, the concept of OSS is a relatively new idea being only four or five years old. On the other hand, the GNU Software Project (a project advocating the distribution of "free" software) has been operational since the mid '80's. Consequently, the ideas behind OSS have been around longer than we may think. Here 'free' refers to freedom in some aspects: Free to-

* study the functions of the program
* run the software for any purpose
* access the software source code
* modify the source code in accordance with specific tasks
* modify the software to suit their needs
* redistribute of the software gratis or for a fee
* redistribute copies of the software to others
* distribute modified versions of the software
* run the software for any purpose by any users

3.1. Terms and Conditions of Distribution of Open Source Software

Open source doesn't just mean access to the source code. The distribution terms of open-source software must comply with the following criteria:

Free redistribution : No license can restrict anyone from selling or giving away the software as a component of an aggregate software distribution having software parts from several different sources.

Inclusion of source code : The distributed program must include source code. The software with source code must be the preferred form in which there is a provision for a programmer to modify the program. Intermediate forms and deliberate obscure of source code are not allowed.

Modified and derived works : The licensing of software must allow modifications and derived works, and must allow to be distributed under the same terms as the license of the original software.

Integrity of the author's source code : The license may restrict source-code from being distributed in modified form only if the license allows the distribution of "patch files" with the source code for the purpose of modifying the program at build time.

Irrespective of persons or groups : The license should be given irrespective of individuals and groups.

Irrespective of fields of endeavor : The license must not restrict anyone from making use of the program in a specific field of endeavor. For example, it may not restrict the program from being used in a business, or from being used for genetic research.

Distribution of license : The rights attached to the program must apply to all to whom the program is redistributed without the need for execution of an additional license by those parties.

Not product specific : The rights attached to the program must not depend on the program's being part of a particular software distribution. If the program is extracted from that distribution and used or distributed within the terms of the program's license, all parties to whom the program is redistributed should have the same rights as those that are granted in conjunction with the original software distribution.

No restrictions to other software : The license must not place restrictions on other software that is distributed along with the licensed software. For example, the license must not insist that all other programs distributed on the same medium must be open-source software.

Not technology dependant : No provision of the license may be predicated on any individual technology or style of interface.

3.2. Major Facets of Open Source Software

Open source software are comprised of major two facets namely mutual development and license (Figure-7).

Fig. 7. Two major facets of open source software

3.2.1. Mutual Development

The idea of mutual development of open source software

is an act of collaborative works between programmers and technicians. They mutually can create, read, modify and redistribute the source code of that software. After creation/ development of software people improved the software; adopt it and people fix it bugs in it. For example Fujitsu, Hitachi, IBM, and NEC have contributed to the development of better tools for analysis LINUX performance and troubleshooting LINUX kernels.

3.2.2. Licenses

Licenses of open source software provide an unconditional right to modify and redistribute any part of the software for free. In case of the software downloaded from Internet the users must need to license agreements. The copyright of open source software belongs to the author rather than vendor. There are verities of open source licenses (like the GNU General public license (GPL), the GNU library or "lesser" public license, the mozilla public license) but they are all premised on the author giving some fundamental freedoms to the user inside a license agreement.

3.3. Dspace

DSpace is is open source software, originally developed for setting up a digital repository to capture, store, index, preserve, and redistribute the intellectual output of a university's research faculty in digital formats. MIT Libraries and Hewlett-Packard (HP) have developed Dspace jointly. It is now freely available to research institutions worldwide as an open source system. In terms of metadata, DSpace is currently using a qualified version of the Dublin Core schema based on the Dublin Core Libraries Working Group Application Profile (LAP). The LAP is used as a starting point for the DSpace application of Dublin Core, borrowing most of the qualifiers from it and adapting others to fit. Some further qualifiers were added to suit DSpace needs. The DSpace software platform serves a variety of digital archiving needs. Research institutions worldwide use DSpace to meet a variety of digital archiving needs:

* Institutional Repositories (IRs)
* Learning Object Repositories (LORs)

* eTheses
* Electronic Records Management (ERM)
* Digital Preservation
* Publishing

Dspace is for user, contributor and institution

For the user : DSpace enables easy remote access and the ability to read and search DSpace items from one location: the World Wide Web.

For the contributor : DSpace offers the advantages of digital distribution and long-term preservation for a variety of formats including text, audio, video, images, datasets and more. Authors can store their digital works in collections that are maintained by MIT communities.

For the institution : DSpace offers the opportunity to provide access to all the research of the institution through one interface. The repository is organized to accommodate the varying policy and workflow issues inherent in a multi-disciplinary environment. Submission workflow and access policies can be customized to adhere closely to each community's needs.

3.3.1. Features and Functionality of Dspace

In March 2000, Hewlett-Packard Company (HP) awarded $1.8 million to the MIT Libraries for an 18-month collaboration to build DSpace™, a dynamic repository for the intellectual output in digital formats of multi-disciplinary research organizations. HP Labs and MIT Libraries released the system worldwide on November 4, 2002, under the terms of the BSD open source license, one month after its introduction as a new service of the MIT Libraries. As an open source system, DSpace is now freely available to other institutions to run as-is, or to modify and extend as they require to meet local needs. From the outset, HP and MIT designed the system to be run by institutions other than MIT, and to support federation among its adopters, in both the technical and the social sense. The DSpace Federation will be explored in a later section.

DSpace is designed to make participation by depositors easy. The system's information model (Figure- 8) is built around the idea of organizational "Communities"—natural sub-units of an institution that have distinctive information management needs. In the case of MIT (a large research university) "Communities" are defined to be the schools, departments, labs, and centers of the Institute. Each Community can adapt the system to meet its particular needs and manage the submission process itself.

Metadata : DSpace uses a qualified Dublin Core metadata standard for describing items intellectually (specifically, the Libraries Working Group Application Profile). Only three fields are required: title, language, and submission date, all other fields are optional. There are additional fields for document abstracts, keywords, technical metadata and rights metadata, among others. This metadata is displayed in the item record in DSpace, and is indexed for browsing and searching the system (within a collection, across collections, or across Communities). For the Dissemination Information Packages (DIPs) of the OAIS framework, the system currently exports metadata and digital material in a custom XML schema while we work with the METS community to develop the necessary extension schemas for the technical and rights metadata about arbitrary digital formats.

User Interface : DSpace's current user interface is web-based. There are several interfaces: one for submitters and others involved in the submission process, one for end-users looking for information, and one for system administrators. The end-user or public interface supports search and retrieval of items by browsing or searching the metadata (all fields for now, and specific fields in the near future). Once an item is located in the system, retrieval is accomplished by clicking a link that causes the archived material to be downloaded to the user's web browser. "Web-native" formats (those which will display directly in a web browser or with a plug-in) can be viewed immediately; others must be saved to the user's local computer and viewed with a separate program that can interpret the file (e.g., a Microsoft Excel spreadsheet, an SAS dataset, or a CAD/CAM file).

Workflow : DSpace is the first open source digital repository system to tackle the complex problem of how to accommodate the differing submission workflows needed for a multidisciplinary system. In other words, different DSpace Communities, representing different schools, departments, research labs and centers, have very different ideas of how material should be submitted to DSpace, by whom, and with what restrictions.

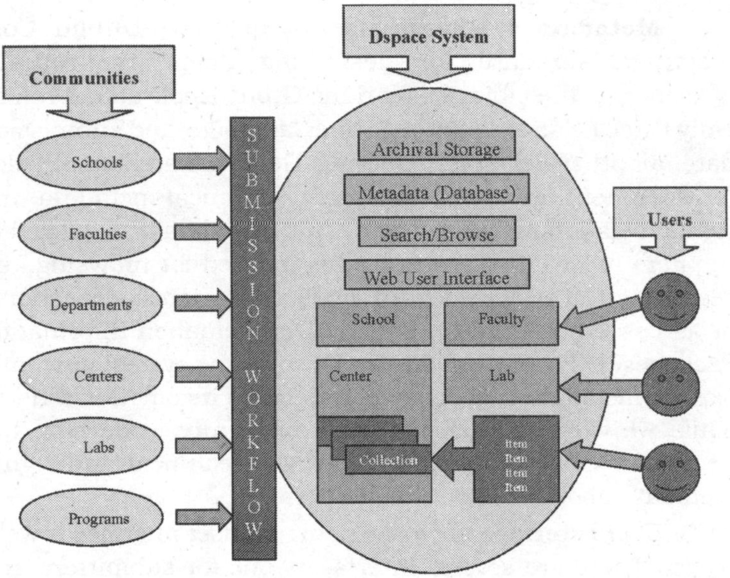

Fig. 8. DSpace information model

The DSpace architecture : The DSpace architecture is a straightforward three-layer architecture **(Figure-9)**, including storage, business, and application layers, each with a documented API to allow for future customization and enhancement. The storage layer is implemented using the file system, as managed by PostgreSQL database tables. The business layer is where the DSpace-specific functionality resides, including the workflow, content management, administration, and search and browse modules. Each module has an API to allow DSpace adopters to replace or enhance that function as desired. Finally, the application layer covers the interfaces to the system: the web UI and batch loader, in particular, but also the OAI support and Handle server for resolving persistent identifiers to DSpace items. This is the layer that will get much of the attention in future releases, as we add web services for new features (e.g., to support interoperation with other systems) and define Federation services across the range of institutions adopting DSpace.

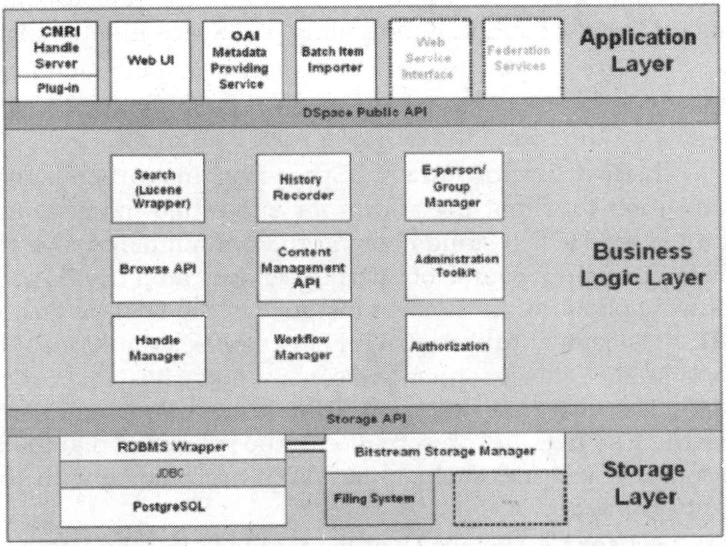

Fig. 9. DSpace technical architecture

Open Archives Initiative (OAI) : To further its goal of supporting interoperability with other DSpace adopters, and with other digital repositories, preprint, and e-print servers, the system has implemented the Open Archives Initiative Protocol for Metadata Harvesting (OAI-PMH).

Persistent Identifiers (Handles) : One goal of persistent digital repositories is that it be possible to find and retrieve deposited items far into the future. In particular, it is considered crucial that citations to archived material, whether found in printed articles or online, remain valid for long periods. Handle resolution can be done using a special client, or handles can be packaged in the form of URLs and a proxy server used to resolve these into the handle form, which is, in turn, resolved to the local system location for the item. This second approach is the one we have taken in DSpace. The main alternative to using handles is to use persistent URLs with HTTP redirection to allow items to move around over time. The long-term viability of these alternatives is not yet sufficiently understood.

3.3.2. Core Concepts and Relationships

Familiarity with these concepts and the relationships among them will aid understanding of DSpace functionality.

1. Site : A DSpace Site is a specific installation of the DSpace software, upon which services are offered that are backed by the committement of a host institution.

2. Host Institution : A DSpace Host Institution is that institution to whom use rights for submitted material are granted, and which stands behind the commitments that are made during the course of offering services atop the DSpace software platform. In the first instance of the DSpace Site at MIT, the host institution is MIT. For example, submitters offer distribution rights for submitted content to the host institution (MIT); The host institution (MIT) makes some commitment regarding storage and preservation of the submitted materials, and that it will use such materials in accordance with the rights granted.

3. User : A DSpace User is an individual who uses the DSpace system, by visiting a DSpace site with their web browser. DSpace users can be at any given time either unknown, or credentialed to the system to some degree, for example via username/password or IP-address-based network presence. DSpace keeps some basic information for registered users (email address, name, credential information), so that they can take advantage of all of the systems functionality (For example: Submission, My DSpace).

4. Group of Users : DSpace administrators can organize DSpace users into groups, which may be used to define participants in a role within a collection's submission process (e.g. "approver"). Policy statements can also refer to groups of users (for example, allow users in group "thesis-administrators" to edit the collection metadata for the thesis collection). While it is true that there may be some organizational or sociopolitical group of people that correspond to an overall social "community", DSpace functionality is concerned with defined groups for specific roles within the community. For example:

* Who can edit the community's home page?
* Who can add collections to the community?
* Who can submit items to a collection's submission process?

5. Community : A DSpace Community is a convenient entry point or "portal" into the corpus of material in the repository. A Community consists of a configurable home page for the community, a set of collections referred to by the community, and a group of users with management and administrative responsibility for the community. Because communities must be administered, DSpace communities typically correspond – at least initially – to an organizational entity, for example, a school, department, laboratory, or research center.

6. Collection : A DSpace Collection groups together a set of DSpace items that are related in some way. A DSpace Collection consists of a configurable home page for the collection, a set of items referred to by the collection, a configurable submission process for content entry into the collection, and a group of users with management and administrative responsibility for the collection. Users who submit items to DSpace can choose a collection to submit to. Further, DSpace administrators can re-organize items into another collection – or even multiple collections – after their initial submission. Collections typically contain items that are similar in some dimension (for example: source, purpose, existing serics or audience, subject matter, research topic). Administrators can also use collections to organize a submission process for consistency of submitted content (for example, with respect to scope of content, metadata requirements, required bitstream formats, etc.)

7. Approval Process : In institutional settings, decisions about what enters the archive often must be distributed, with decisions made close to communities. In DSpace, each collection can have its own approval process, and specify individuals who will participate in it. Such approval processes can range from very simple, to multistage review with multiple individuals participating at each stage.

8. Item : A DSpace Item is a logical grouping of a useful set of content and metadata that are related in some way. Items correspond to DSpace Internal Reference Specification – Functionality Version 2002-03-01 2 "Archival Atoms" in DSpace. Examples of DSpace items include: a working paper, a conference presentation, a monograph (book), an annotated series of images, a video clip, materials for a course lecture, a research paper with auxiliary material (e.g. dataset, extended bibliography, rich media images).

9. Bitstream : In DSpace, a bitstream is simply a reproducible sequence of bits, with a corresponding bitstream format. Bitstreams typically correspond to content or metadata files that are submitted to DSpace.

10. Bitstream Format : Because preservation services are an important aspect of the DSpace service offering for Libraries, it is important to capture the specific formats of files that users submit. In DSpace, a bitstream format is a unique and consistent way to refer to a particular file format. An integral part of a bitstream format is an either implicit or explicit notion of how material in that format can be interpreted. For example, the interpretation for bitstreams encoded in the JPEG standard for still image compression is defined explicitly in the Standard ISO/IEC 10918-1. The interpretation of bitstreams in Microsoft Word 2000 format is defined implicitly, through reference to the Microsoft Word 2000 application. Bitstream formats can be more specific than mime-types or file suffixes. For example, "application/ms-word" and ".doc" span multiple versions of the Microsoft Word application, each of which produces bitstreams with presumably different semantics.

4. TOOLS REQUIRED AND STEPS INVOLVED FOR DSPACE INSTALLATION

DSpace was developed to be open source, and in such a way that institutions and organizations with minimal resources could run it. The system is designed to run on the

UNIX platform, and comprises other open source middleware and tools, and programs written by the DSpace team. All original code is in the Java programming language. Other pieces of the technology stack include a relational database management system (PostgreSQL), a Web server and Java servlet engine (Apache and Tomcat, both from the Apache Foundation), Jena (an RDF toolkit from HP Labs), OAICat from OCLC, and several other useful libraries. All leveraged components and libraries are also open source software.

While DSpace is open source and freely available, neither MIT Libraries nor HP offer formal support for DSpace adopters. It is our assumption that institutions that use DSpace will have resources to use the system, including adequate hardware that runs the UNIX operating system, and a UNIX systems administrator to install and configure the system. Most institutions using DSpace will also want the services of a Java programmer who can localize and customize for them, or enhance it, although this is not absolutely necessary to run the system.

4.1. Tools required for Dspace installation

Different tools for Dspace installation are listed below:

* Operating System: UNIX-like OS (Linux, HP/UX etc)
* Programming language: Java 1.4 or later (standard SDK is fine, no need J2EE)
* Java make-like tool: Apache Ant 1.5 or later
* Database: PostgreSQL 7.3 or later, an open source relational database, or Oracle 9 or higher
* Language for interface between database and users: PostgreSQL is database plus interface language
* Web server: Jakarta Tomcat 4.x/5.x or equivalent, such as Jetty or Caucho Resin
* Browser: for searching and browsing
* Storage device: SAN, Disk array etc
* Language software: Unicode compatible

4.2. Steps involved for Dspace installation

Dspace installation can be done mainly in two ways namely Quick Installation Steps and Advanced Installation.

4.2.1. Quick Installation

The steps are listed below.

1. Creation of the DSpace user. This needs to be the same user that Tomcat (or Jetty etc) will run as. e.g. as root run: useradd -m dspace
2. Downloading of the latest DSpace source code release and unpack it: gunzip -c dspace-source-1.x.tar.gz | tar -xf -
3. Copying of the PostgreSQL JDBC driver (.jar file) into [dspace-source]/lib. PostgreSQL may be compiled. Alternatively it can be downloaded directly from the PostgreSQL JDBC site. Make sure of getting the driver for the version of PostgreSQL which are running and for JDBC2.
4. Creattion of a dspace database, owned by the dspace PostgreSQL user: createuser -U postgres -d -A -P dspace ; createdb -U dspace -E UNICODE dspace. Enter a password for the DSpace database. (This isn't the same as the dspace user's UNIX password.)
5. Editing *[dspace-source]*/config/dspace.cfg, in particular it will be needed to set these properties:
   * dspace.url
   * dspace.hostname
   * dspace.name
   * db.password (the password you entered in the previous step)
   * mail.server
   * mail.from.address
   * feedback.recipient
   * mail.admin
   * alert.recipient (not essential but very useful!)
6. Creation of the directory for the DSpace installation. As root, run:

   mkdir *[dspace]* ; chown dspace *[dspace]*

   (Assuming the dspace UNIX username.)
7. As the dspace UNIX user, Dspace will be compiled and installed:

cd *[dspace-source]* ; ant fresh_install The most likely thing to go wrong here is the database connection. See the common problems section.

8. Copying of the DSpace Web application archives (.war files) to the appropriate directory in the Tomcat/Jetty/ Resin installation. For example:

   cp *[dspace-source]*/build/*.war *[tomcat]*/webapps

9. Creation of an initial administrator account:

   [dspace]/bin/create-administrator

10. Tomcat will be started up (or restarted). DSpace home page will be seen at the base URL of the server.

4.2.2. Advanced Installation

The above installation steps are sufficient to set up a test server to play around with, but there are a few other steps and options one should probably consider before deploying a DSpace production site.

A. 'corn' Jobs : The command is used for automatic execution of service in 24x7. A couple of DSpace features require that a script is run regularly — the e-mail subscription feature that alerts users of new items being deposited, and the new 'media filter' tool, that generates thumbnails of images and extracts the full-text of documents for indexing.

B. DSpace over HTTPS : Plain old HTTP is totally insecure, and if the DSpace uses username/password authentication or stores some restricted content, running it over HTTPS (HTTP over a Secure Socket Layer (SSL)) is advisable. There are two options for this: Using Apache HTTPD, or Tomcat/Jetty's in-built HTTPS support.

(a) *To use Apache HTTPD* : The DSpace source bundle includes a partial Apache configuration apache13.conf, which contains most of the DSpace-specific configuration required. To use it directly, in the main Apache httpd.conf, one should:

* Making sure mod_ssl and mod_webapp are configured and loaded
* Removing/commenting out etc. any existing or default SSL virtual host
* Ensuring Apache will run with the UNIX user and group DSpace will run as

* Including the DSpace part, e.g. with: Include *[dspace]*/config/httpd.conf. One can decide where the DSpace part will go in the file system

(b) ***To use Tomcat or Jetty's HTTPS support*** consultation should be required to the documentation for the relevant tool.

C. The Handle Server : First a few facts to clear up some common misconceptions:

* One does not **have** to use CNRI's Handle system. At the moment, one need to change the code a little to use something else (e.g PURLs) but that should change soon.
* One should notice that while playing around with a test server, DSpace has apparently been creating handles looking like hdl:123456789/24 and so forth. These aren't really Handles, since the global Handle system doesn't actually know about them, and lots of other DSpace test installs will have created the same IDs.
* They're only really Handles once one has registered a prefix with CNRI and have correctly set up the Handle server included in the DSpace distribution. This Handle server communicates with the rest of the global Handle infrastructure so that anyone that understands Handles can find the Handles the DSpace has created.

5. SUBMISSION STEPS OF DIGITAL DOCUMENTS

5.1. Submission criteria

Before submission of the digital documents in the repository through DSpace, we have to fulfill the submission criteria.

5.1.1. Anonymous vs. Credentialed Access

Any user can use DSpace to search and browse items and collections that are globally accessible. Only users who are registered with DSpace can submit items, administer items, collections, or communities, or view items that are not globally accessible. DSpace will ask that the user authenticate themselves to the system whenever the system's current policy configuration indicates that some credential is required to perform the action.

5.1.2. Register with DSpace

Users that have been "bulk identified" into the system may register with DSpace, by providing a valid email address to uniquely identify them, and a corresponding password. (X.509 certificates will be supported shortly). The user registration process:

* Gathers the user's email address
* Verifies that individuals are registering using an email address that they can access.
* Allows the user to initially set their user profile: password and basic personal information (name, etc.).
* Stores the password securely within the system

5.1.3. Forgotten Passwords

DSpace provides a secure process for users who have forgotten their password to select a new password without human administrative intervention. Users provide their email address, and the system mails them a special hyperlink which, when clicked, allows them to update their password.

5.1.4. Edit User Profile

Registered DSpace users can edit the basic personal information that the system keeps for them:

* Lastname, Firstname
* Contact Telephone (optional)
* Password

The system tracks users by the single email address with which they initially registered. A user's mail address cannot currently be changed via the end-user interface, but can be changed using the administrative user interface. Thus, end users can update their email address through a call to the help desk.

5.2. Submit to Collection

DSpace provides an easy way for materials to enter the archive in a distributed fashion across the host institution. The Dspace submission process gates entry of submitted material into the DSpace archive (Figure-10). Materials within DSpace are always in one of three stages:

* **Items Being Assembled** – the submitting user is still in the process of entering the Item's Metadata, or uploading the file(s) to be included with the item.
* **Submissions Pending Archive** – the submitting user has submitted the item to the initial Collection's submission approval process. But this approval process is not yet complete, and the item is not yet archived.
* **Archived Items** – the item is archived, having been approved for entry into the collection to which it was submitted.

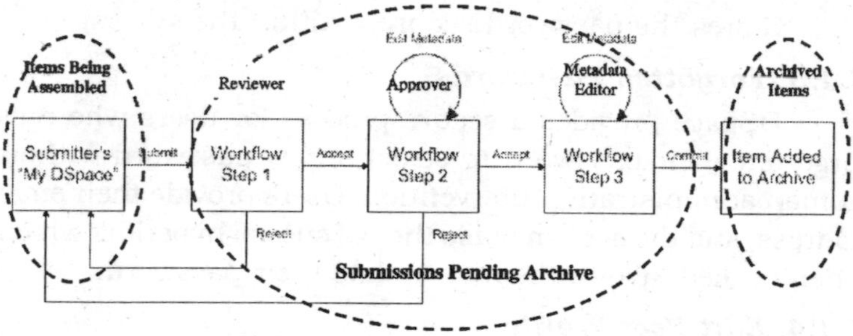

Fig. 10. Submission workflow

Authorized users can initiate submissions to a DSpace collection that they have chosen. Users can choose the collection to submit to in one of two ways:

(a) Explicitly, from a list of all collections in Dspace (accessible from DSpace home)

(b) Contextually, by first navigating to the collection of interest (accessible from each collection's home page)

5.3. Submit Baseline Metadata

With their submission, users can specify baseline metadata. Users fill in the same form for all submitted items. This baseline metadata will enable users to search across all of DSpace, and to easily find submitted items in the future. The baseline metadata requested for each submitted item is based upon the qualified Dublin Core Metadata Schema, adapted to DSpace requirements by MIT Libraries. The elements captured through the end-user interface are:

(a) Author(s) : Zero or more supported. Currently no authority control for authors (i.e. DSpace does not currently know that "Samuel Clemens" and "Mark Twain" are the same author, nor does it distinguish well between two authors that share the same name).

(b) Title(s) : Including alternative titles, if applicable.

(c) Date of Issue

(d) Series Name and Report Number;

For example "Sloan School of Management Working Papers, Number 2002-128". If applicable. Zero or more supported.

(e) Identifiers : Including ISBN, ISSN, ISMN, URI, and other. Zero or more supported.

(f) Language (in which submitted material is written).

(g) Subject Keywords;

Zero or more supported. Currently no thesauri or authority control for subject keywords.

(h) Abstract

(i) Sponsors / Funding Codes

(j) Other Description

Additional elements are modeled and stored internally. Some of these are generated automatically by the system. Others may be managed by DSpace administrators using the admin user interface.

5.4. Submit Domain-Specific Metadata

In addition to DSpace baseline metadata, Users can submit domain-specific metadata that is specific to their item, or that is required by the curators of the collection to which they are submitting, by uploading a file that contains the relevant metadata. For example, a collection of images might require that each image be submitted with GIS metadata indicating the location of the corresponding image. Users may annotate their item using as many metadata formats as desired.

5.5. Upload File(s) to Item

Submitted DSpace Items are destined to become "archival atoms", that is some amount or boundary of material that make sense together. As such, each item can include multiple pieces of content. Each piece of content might comprise several files. Users must submit one or more files to be included with their item.

5.6. Grant Distribution License

To enable the host institution to administer, preserve, and distribute the submitted material, DSpace asks the user to grant to the institution a non-exclusive license to distribute the material, and to translate it for the purposes of preservation. License agreements can vary by Collection, and are specified by the collection administrator(s) for the Collection. Because license terms are likely to change over time based on the needs of submitters and the host institution, DSpace stores a copy of the license that was granted at the time of submittal as a bitstream within the item, so that the specific terms agreed upon are always available.

5.7. Augment & Approve Submissions

When the user submits an item to a DSpace collection, the system routes the submission through the approval process previously configured for that collection. The system routes the submission to individuals (if any) who have been chosen to assume each of the following roles for the target collection:

1. **Reviewers :** review the content of the submission for appropriateness to the collection. Reviewers act as the gatekeepers for the collection. Reviewers are empowered to return a submission back to the submitter because it is deemed inappropriate for the collection. Reviewers do not edit submission metadata.
2. **Approvers :** check the submission for completeness and/or obvious errors (e.g. wrong file uploaded). Approvers can edit the submission's metadata to fix obvious errors, and are empowered to return a submission back to the submitter because it is incomplete or in error.
3. **Metadata Editors :** check and/or augment the submission's metadata. For example, a metadata editor may be assigned to add the appropriate series name and

number to each submission in a collection. Metadata Editors can only edit the submission's metadata.

5.8. My DSpace

DSpace offers each user personalized access to information within the system through their *My DSpace* page. As appropriate given their role(s) in the system, users can view their:

* Items being assembled
* submissions pending archive
* archived Items that they submitted
* review tasks for Items pending archive

DSpace filters these sections so that only the sections relevant to each user are presented.

5.8.1. View Archived Items Submitted by User

Users can easily view all of the archived items that they submitted from their personalized *My DSpace* page.

5.8.2. View Items being Assembled

Users can access submissions that were interrupted while partially complete (because key information was not available, because all files were not available for upload, or simply because the user was called away for an extended coffee break) from the "Items being Assembled " section of their personalized *My DSpace* page.

5.8.3. View Pending Approval Tasks

Users who are taking part in the approval process for one or more collections within DSpace can view, select, and perform tasks that require their attention from the "Pending Approval Tasks" section of their personalized *My DSpace* page.

6. INFORMATION RETRIEVAL

After submission of digital objects within the collections under the communities and sub-communities, the digital library will be created. It is also mentioned that before creation of Dspace users we have to create the individual as LINUX system user. Any user can use Dspace to search and browse items and collections if we configure the same for global access. Only users who are registered with Dspace can submit items, administer items, collections, or communities or view items that are not globally accessible. After this creation of digital library one can use the library for dissemination of information through searching, browsing, viewing and downloading the items:

1. Searching

DSpace offers users the capability to search DSpace for items of interest.

(a) Query Features: DSpace offers the following search features through its web-based user interface:

* Search all of DSpace
* Bounded search, within all of a specified community's collections.
* Bounded search, within a specified collection
* Simple search
  Searches fields: author, title, keywords
* Case insensitive search
  All searches are case insensitive.
* Truncation, Constraints
  (a) Geo* : Geology, Geography, Geochemistry
  (b) ?ain : rain, gain, main
  (c) +where +dare : Where eagle dare
* Word stemming
  searches for "searched" match any of search, searching, searcher
* Stop words
  common words (e.g. "a", "an", "the") are omitted from the search

(b) Finding Newly Submitted Items: When new items are submitted to DSpace, they can be discovered immediately via search.

(c) Search Results : Once the user specifies a search, DSpace performs the search and produces a result set. DSpace displays the result set, including a terse description for each item in the results. From the terse item description displayed in the search results, the user may select a desired item to view its *Item Overview*

2. Browse

DSpace users may browse the contents of DSpace in the following ways.

(a) Browse Communities and Collections : DSpace administrators organize DSpace items into collections, and include collections in communities. Users can browse the structure of communities and collections, in an outline view. Each outline entry includes text describing the contents and/or purpose of the corresponding community or collection. Users can select an entry from the outline view to access the home page of the selected community or collection, from which further bounded browse or search can be performed.

(b) Browse Items : From the DSpace home page, users can browse all items in DSpace by title, author, or issue date. From a community or collection home page, users can initiate a bounded browse within that community or collection. Dspace supports bounded browse by title, author, or issue date.

(c) New Collections : New collections are displayed in a sidebar on the DSpace home page, and linked to the corresponding collection home page, from where they can be browsed.

(d) Recent Submissions : Recently submitted items to each collection are displayed in a sidebar on each collection's home page.

3. Search, Browse, and Authorization

Search and browse currently display brief descriptions for all items, whether or not the user is authorized to view the item. If the user clicks on the brief description of an item that she is not authorized to view, the system will refuse access to the item overview.

4. View Item Overview

Terse item descriptions in either the search view or browse view are linked to the corresponding item overview. Authorized users can view an item's overview, which displays the item's Dspace core metadata, lists the collection(s) that include it, and provides links to each of the bitstreams that the item comprises.

5. Download Item Bitstream(s)

Users may download each of the bitstream(s) in the item by selecting the bitstream from those listed in the item's item overview.

Bitstreams that:

* have a known bitstream format, that format which
* itself has a corresponding mime-type

CONCLUSIONS

The present study is a unified attempt to describe the basic concepts, capabilities, components and architecture of digital library and also enumerates basic features of repository/institutional repository. Before the description of the creation of digital library by using open source software like Dspace, some core concepts of open source software and Dspace program are discussed.

REFERENCES

1. Das, Subarna and Jana, Sibsankar. "Threats and protections of open sources in the changing context of digital environment: Some issues and observations" National Conference on Initiatives in Libraries and Information Centers in the Digital Era, 8-10th June'06. SALIS, 2006
2. http://eu.conecta.it/paper/brief_history_open_source.html (accessed on 08-01-07)
3. http://en.wikipedia.org/wiki/Digital_library (accessed on 05-01-07)
4. http://www.dspace.org/ (accessed on 06-01-07)
5. http://www.opensource.org/docs/definition.php (accessed on 08-01-07)
6. http://www.webopedia.com/DidYouKnow/Computer_Science/2005/open_source.asp (accessed on 11-01-07)
7. Open Source Software for Digital Repositories: DSpace and Fedorahttp://www.ukoln.ac.uk/metadata/resources/digital-repositories/ (accessed on 06-01-07)
8. Rajashekhar, T.B. Institutional repository software: Features and functionality. http://www.ncsi.iisc.ernet.in/raja/p-dainar/meeting/darpnet-ir-sotware-040408.ppt. (accessed on 08-01-07)

9. Self-Archiving and Institutional Respositories http://www.sparceurope.org/Repositories/ (accessed on 08-01-07)

10. Smith , MacKenzie. Dspace: An Open Source Dynamic Digital Repository. *D-Lib Magazine*. 9 (1), 2003. http://www.dlib.org//dlib/january03/smith/01smith.html

11. Suleman, Hussein and Fox, Edward A. A Framework for Building Open Digital Libraries. *D-Lib Magazine*. 7 (12), 2001. http://www.dlib.org/dlib/december01/suleman/12suleman.html (accessed on 08-01-07)

17

Establishment of Hyderabad-Karnataka Institutional Repository at Gulbarga University Library: A Development Plan

D.B. Patil

Praveenkumar Kumbargoudar

Parameshwar.S

ABSTRACT

The present paper defined the Institutional Repository and examined the development of Institutional Repository. Further, Hyderabad-Karnataka region of Karnataka is assumed as backward region, even though it is having rich historical background, heritage, minerals, folk arts, folk literature, agricultural land and natural resources. For this purpose, there is need to establish an institutional repository covering the subjects pertaining to this region. The paper contained a detailed plan to design an institutional repository using Open Source-DSpace. The Institutional Repository should established using Dublin Core metadata for metadata storing and conversion. The hardware and software requirements and technical details related for establishing Institutional Repository are also discussed.

INTRODUCTION

Over the past few decades, rapid changes in information technology have drastically changed the functions and activities of the libraries. The Information and Communication Technology created a new type of work culture, new forms of information storage, and new means of communication and dissemination of information. The advent of electronic resources and their increased use in libraries has brought about significant changes in Storage and Communication of Information. Further, the changes turned the libraries and information centres to digital libraries and Institutional Repositories (IRs), which made possible the communication of scholarly information throughout the world electronically. Based on the number of institutional repositories established over the past few years, the IR service appears to be quite attractive and compelling to institutions. IRs provide an institution with a mechanism to showcase its scholarly output, centralize and introduce efficiencies to the stewardship of digital documents of value, and respond proactively to the escalating crisis in scholarly communication. Further, it is noted that many of the institutional repositories were established on the basis of the subject disciplines, nature of the parent institutions, nature of the users served etc.

HYDERABAD-KARNATAKA REGION

Based on the historical background, the Karnataka divided into four divisions: Mumbai-Karnataka Region, Madras-Karnataka Region, Hyderabad-Karnataka Region and Old Mysore region. Hyderabad-Karnataka or northeast Karnataka initially comprised three districts of Bidar, Gulbarga and Raichur, which formed part of the princely state of

Hyderabad. The Gazetteer of India gives a vivid account of the famines and scarcity conditions that prevailed in this region from the 17th Century. Today the term, 'Hyderabad-Karnataka' is used to describe the five districts, namely, Gulbarga, Bidar, Raichur, Bellary and Koppal. All these districts have rich historical background, as these were ruled by Rastrakutas, Chalukyas, Vijayanagar empire, Ashoka, Kadamba, Nijams of Hyderabad, etc. Further, this region is having rich religious heritage as many of prophets (Sharanas) of Hinduism have emphasized, Shivaism through their literature. Many places in these regions are having manuscripts and inscriptions about history, culture and social issues related to the region. The region is also rich in Mineral deposits. The Bellary district is having rich collection of Iron Ore and Manganese Ore. Hyderabad-Karnataka region is also popular for different folk arts. To promote higher education in the region, Gulbarga University was established in 1980 by an Act of Karnataka State. Its jurisdiction extends to the five districts of Gulbarga, Bidar, Raichur, Bellary and Koppal of Hyderabad Karnataka. Earlier it was a postgraduate centre of Karnatak University since 1970. The main campus is situated on a 348 hectares of land, 10 kilo meters east of Gulbarga city. It has 35 postgraduate departments and 4 postgraduate centres located at Sandur, Bellary, Raichur and Bidar The University enrolls about 3500 students every year for various post graduate, M.Phil. and Ph.D. programmes in various disciplines. There are about 200 faculty members and about 700 technical and non-technical supporting staff. There are 165 colleges affiliated to this University which enroll approximately 45000 students every year in various graduate/diploma courses in arts, fine Arts, music, social sciences, science & technology, commerce, education and law.

INSTITUTIONAL REPOSITORY:

Institutional repositories are "digital collections that capture and preserve the Intellectual output of a single or multi-university community". While some repositories focus on particular subject domains, an institutional repository stores and makes accessible the educational, research and associated assets of an institution. Although most of the currently established institutional repositories are 'e-prints' repositories, providing open access to the research outputs of a university or research institution, the content does not need to be limited to e-prints, but could potentially include research data, learning material, image collections and many other different types of content[1].

According to Johnson[2], Institutional Repository is 'a digital archive of the intellectual product created by the faculty, research staff, and students of an institution and accessible to end-users both within and outside of the institution with few if any barriers to access'.

The Institutional repositories are created and managed by academic institutions and publishers of the digital materials. According to Lynch[3] "a university-based institutional repository is a set of services that a university offers to the members of its community for the management and dissemination of digital materials created by the institution and its community members. It is most essentially an organizational commitment to the stewardship of these digital materials, including long-term preservation where appropriate, as well as organization and access or distribution."

Universities have traditionally relied upon institutional libraries to manage and preserve scholarly assets. The storage, management and preservation processes for printed materials have been perfected over hundreds of years. These must now be recreated for digital assets. It is incumbent upon university libraries to develop a response to the need to manage and preserve these data. In an educational environment, a digital repository, be it made up of reformatted historic collections, digital learning materials, institute records or newly created digital research materials, will not only be able to capture the increasing amount of material that is being digitised, but it also has the ability to store and preserve this material, to index it and distribute content.

In a university environment most academics now have

research and/or course content held on their computers or local servers. Many may well want it held in a more secure environment. Most lack the time, resources or expertise to ensure preservation of their own scholarly work even in the short term, and clearly cannot do it beyond the life-span of their careers. Universities also need to recognize that a number of academic units curate very large collections of information, measured in tens of terabytes. The preservation of these datasets presents new challenges for institutional repositories, but a solution needs to be found.

INSTITUTIONAL REPOSITORY AT GULBARGA UNIVERSITY LIBRARY: A DEVELOPMENT PLAN

The present repository is planned to store and the reading and research material related to the Hyderabad-Karnataka Region, electronically. The materials include the Inscriptions, ancient Manuscripts, books published by the authors located in the region, books on arts, history, culture, social issues of the region, research reports, theses, dissertations, etc. on the Hyderabad Karnataka region. For this purpose, Open Source Software DSpace is used.

INSTITUTIONAL REPOSITORY DESIGN ARCHITECTURE

Sinha and Bhattarcharjee[4] stated that Institutional repositories may have multi-tier design architecture, which has been divided into three essential components or groups:

Operational Architecture : It is an information management system which represents systems, services and data management layers;

Technical Architecture : It breaks downs operational architecture into functional components and capabilities; and

System Architecture : It shows the technology enablers and their possible inter-relationships.

Institutional Repositories is developed and based on the principles of Designing Digital Library. In digital library architecture, communities can have access to the digital library services locally through campus wide Intranet and globally over Internet. Basically the digital library design architecture has the following important components such as general to specific communities, archives or repositories to serve the needs of the communities, services design as per the requirement of the communities, and scalability and Interoperability to provide seamless access to the university communities. Design of individual services, user interface, display formats, indexing styles, digital preservation, data federation, service federation, web services, security and uniform standards are some other important issues which need attention of the developers of Institutional Repositories.

DSPACE

DSpace is a ground breaking digital institutional repository that captures, stores, indexes, preserves and redistributes the intellectual output of a university's research faculty in digital formats. It manages and distributes digital items, made up of digital files (or bit streams) and allows for the creation, indexing and searching of associated metadata to locate and retrieve the items. DSpace designed and developed by Massachussetts Institute of Technology (MIT) and Hewlett-Packard (HP). DSpace was designed as an open source application that institutions and organizations could run with relatively few resources. It is to support the long-term preservation of the digital material stored in the repository. It is also designed to make submission easy. DSpace supports submission, management and access of digital content[5].

DSpace, therefore, was designed as an open source application that institutions and organizations could run with relatively few resources. The intention to support interoperability (i.e with DSpace implementers at other institutions) led to the adoption of the Open Archives Initiative Protocol for Metadata Harvesting (OAIPMH); the OAI Registry includes DSpace, making its Dublin-Core-formatted metadata available to compatible harvesting code. In addition, DSpace chose to implement CNRI handles as the persistent identifier associated with each item to insure that the system will be able to locate and retrieve documents in the distant future. DSpace was also designed with a batch load submission feature to ease the loading of exiting collection and cut costs[6].

DSpace is open source software designed to make

participation by depositors easy. The system's information model is built around the idea of organizational "Communities"—natural sub-units of an institution that have distinctive information management needs. Each Community can adapt the system to meet its particular needs and manage the submission process itself. Information Model of DSpace is shown as under:

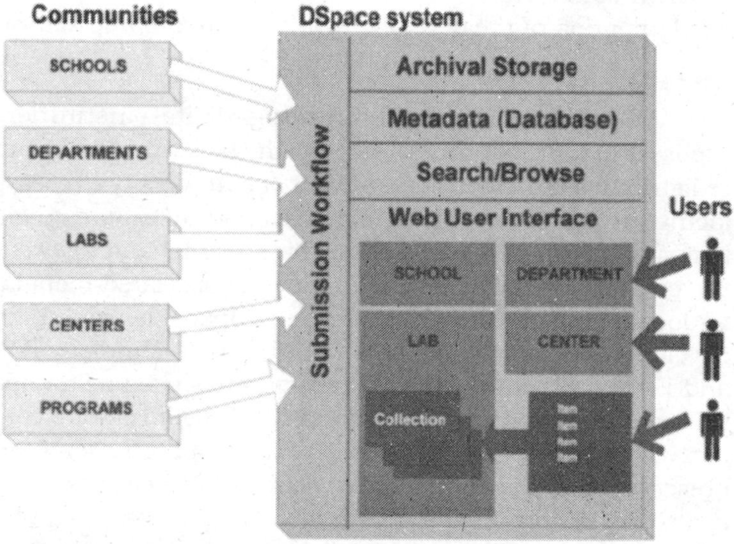

Fig. 1. DSpace Information Model

DSpace uses a qualified Dublin Core metadata standard for describing items intellectually (specifically, the Libraries Working Group Application Profile). Only three fields are required: title, language, and submission date, all other fields are optional. There are additional fields for document abstracts, keywords, technical metadata and rights metadata, among others. This metadata is displayed in the item record in DSpace, and is indexed for browsing and searching the system (within a collection, across collections, or across Communities).

DSpace have web based User Interface. There are several interfaces: one for submitters and others involved in the submission process, one for end-users looking for information, and one for system administrators. The end-user or public interface supports search and retrieval of items by browsing or searching the metadata (all fields for now, and specific fields in the near future).

TECHNOLOGY REQUIREMENTS

DSpace was developed to be open source, and in such a way that institutions and organizations with minimal resources could run it. The system is designed to run on the UNIX like platform, and comprises other open source middleware and tools, and programs written by the DSpace team. All original code is in the Java programming language. Other pieces of the technology stack include a relational database management system (PostgreSQL), a Web server and Java servlet engine (Apache and Tomcat, both from the Apache Foundation), Jena (an RDF toolkit from HP Labs), OAICat from OCLC, and several other useful libraries. All leveraged components and libraries are also open source software. The system is available on Source Forge, linked from both the DSpace informational web site and the HP Labs site.

HARDWARE REQUIREMENTS

For the purpose, storing and communication of the information there is need for Intel Xeon Microprocessor based Dual Core Processors. There must be at least 2MB L2 Cache Memory, with Intel E8500 Chipset. There is need for total 5 hard disk drives each of which have 146 GB capacity. Capture devices such as Scanners and cameras of high capacity are necessary. The other specifications of the Computer systems are with the same as are in Market now. At least 10 Desktop workstations with high speed Local Area Network and high speed Internet Connectivity is required.

SOFTWARE REQUIREMENTS

Many of the Open Source software are available online now. Of which, the present plan aimed to adopt DSpace. There are many other software such as Linux, Windows, Adobe Acrobat Reader, Image software, graphics software, Apache, Unix, Internet Explorer, Optical Character Recognition software, CD/DVD writer software, etc are needed.

MATERIALS INCLUDED

The registered faculty members, research scholars/ research assistant and scientists working at Gulbarga University, Gulbarga may submit their documents to this Repository. At this moment, there is plan to include all the departments/Post graduate centers and administration as individual community. Each community has four distinct class of collection. They are:

* Theses/Dissertations/Research Reports
* Conference/Seminar/Convention Papers
* Faculty Publications such as Books and Journals
* Ancient Materials and Special Collections (Photocopy of Manuscripts, Inscriptions, Maps, Audio-Visual Materials etc)

INTEROPERATIBILITY & OPEN ARCHIVES INITIATIVES PROTOCOL FOR METADATA HARVESTING (OAI-PMH)

Interoperability is the ability of systems, organizations and individuals to operate together to achieve a common goal. According to Caplan[7], Interoperability is 'the ability to perform a search over diverse set of metadata records and obtain meaningful results'.

The Open Archives Initiative Protocol for Metadata Harvesting (OAI-PMH) provides an application-independent interoperability framework based on metadata harvesting that can be used by a variety of Communities, who are engaged in publishing content on the Web. It provides a set of rules that defines the communication between systems (like FTP or HTTP in Internet). The protocol was developed with an objective ensure interoperability between e-prints repositories only, later in version 1.0/1.1 all document like digital objects also brought into its purview and finally the latest version 2.0 supports all kinds of digital resources. The protocol is based on HTTP and XML[8].

Open Archives Initiative Protocol for Metadata Harvesting provides an application independent interoperability framework based on metadata harvesting. OAI-PMH enables automated distribution of any kind of metadata, which may be aggregated into searchable databases by harvesting systems. The Open Archives Initiative evolved out of a need to increase access to scholarly publications by supporting the creation of interoperable digital libraries[9].

CONCLUSION

Hyderabad-Karnataka region have a rich heritage since ancient times. The folk literature, folk arts and fine arts are very popular. Further, the region has rich natural resources like minerals, flora and fauna. The contributions of people of this region to different subject areas are worth to be noted. To disseminate the information this region, there is need for Open Archives covering different aspects of this region.

The present technology provided the benefits of Open Source, Open Access and Open Standards. These have lowered the cost of storage and dissemination of information providing greater accessibility and better prospects for long-term preservation of scholarly literature. Hence there is need for establishment of Institutional repository concerned to Hyderabad-Karnataka region in Gulbarga University Library, Gulbarga. The Institutional repository is beneficial to faculty, research scholars, scientists and students, which provide them an opportunity to access, communicate and publish their research findings online and also develop their career future.

REFERENCES

1. Yu, Helen Hockx: Digital preservation in the context of institutional repositories. Program: Electronic library and Information Systems. Vol. 40. No. 3. 2006. P. 232-243.
2. Johnson, R. (2002), "Institutional repositories: partnering with faculty to enhance Scholarly communication", D-Lib Magazine, Vol. 8 No. 11.
3. Lynch, Clifford. "Institutional Repositories: Essential Infrastructure for Scholarship in the Digital Age." ARL Bimonthly Report, No. 226, February 2003. http://www.arl.org/newsltr/226/ir.html accessed on 25th December 2006.
4. Sinha, Manojkumar and Bhattacharjee, Jayanta: Developing Institutional Repositories: A Case Study of Assam University, Silchar. 4th Convention PLANNER, Aizawl: Inflibnet and Mizoram University, 9-10 November 2006. P. 311- 321.

5. Naik, Umesha and Shivalingaiah, D: Digital Library Open Source Software: A Comparative Study. Proceedings of the 4th International Convention CALIBER. Gulbarga: Gulbarga University, 2-4 February 2006. P. 27-39.
6. Das, Rajesh and Others: Construction of an Information Repository (IR) by DSpace. Proceedings of the National Conference on Information Management in Digital Libraries. Kharagpur: IIT, 2-4 August 2006. P. 325-334.
7. Caplan, Priscilla: Metadata Fundamentals for All Librarians. New York: American Library Association, 2003.
8. Prasad, ARD and Guha, N: Interoperability and the OAI-PMH. Proceedings of the National Conference on Information Management in Digital Libraries (NCIMDiL). Kharagpur: Indian Institute of Technology, 2-4 August 2006. P. 281-290.
9. Sinha, Manoj kumar and Bhattacharjee, Jayanta: Developing Institutional Repositories: A Case Study of Assam University, Silchar. Proceedings of the 4th Convention PLANNER, Aizawl: Mizoram University, 9-10 November 2006. P. 311-321.

18
Digital Libraries Development- Using RFID Methods Information Tools and Techniques

Mahendra Kumar Rawat
Shaliendra K. Rawat

ABSTRACT

Advent of information and communication technologies and their capabilities such as high resolution capture devices, dramatic increase of digital storage media, explosive growth of internet and www, fast processing power and reducing cost of computer, high band width networks and increasing number security system in digital concept. They include infrastructure, acceptability, access, restriction, readability, standardization, authentication, preservation, copyright, user interface etc, At the present time, when libraries of all kinds (public, research, special) are facing economic bard ships the over helming reason for considering new technologies is the potential for cost saving in the operations and the management of material flows. For book identification, for self-

checkout, for anti-theft control, for inventory control, and for sorting and conveying of library books and AV materials. These applications can lead to significant savings in labour costs, enhance customer service, lower book theft and provide a constant record update media collections An automated services library with the support of RFID technology by library personnel RFID technology is helpful in taking inventory, finding missing items and identifying misfiled items. The electronic chips consisting of an integrated circuit and antenna that communicates with a reader by means of a radio frequency signal. Since RFID does not require "line of sight" between the transponder and the reader, it surmounts the limitations of other automatic identification devices. The most important result is that non-proprietary systems can be used for libraries today since the new generations of RFID-chips with the ISO standard 15693 are available. With this technology libraries are not dependent on one company for their lifeline.

INTRODUCTION

Gradual Development of RFID

RFID was introduced in the early 1980s for item tracking and access control applications. Tracking of materials is done using radio frequency based technology combined with microchip technology, hence designated as RFID (Radio Frequency Identification). These contact less and wireless automatic identification data capturing system are highly effective in hostile environments such as industry and logistics, textile and libraries, where barcode labels cannot survive and need for inventory control and waste management. Owing to its ability to track moving objects RFID has been established itself in livestock identification and automated vehicle identification systems, in recent times its use has risen to track books, audio/video tapes and other multimedia collection in a library. After realizing the advantage of RFID technology, libraries are considering it, the more productive tool for low management sooner than barcodes and other identification technologies.

RFID library system was taken from electronic access control equipment. This is a type of door lock security system that only allows access to persons who present a proximity card to an RFID reader located next to a doorframe. In turn this RFID reader is wired to a computer whose software determines access to various parts of a building. Hence "read only" RFID cards were used as a "license plate" type of identification of the person and in a library application the book or other media. Thus a modified electronic access control system was designed to turn the security alarm off and on in a book without library staff intervention or foil date due cards. As the market developed "read/write" RFID labels became competitive in price to the "read only" labels that were used in first generation RFID library systems. This allowed libraries to eliminate the parallel RFID network and additional server that was required for these first generation systems. We will elaborate on this latter in this paper. The actual development of the market, especially in Asia, shows that RFID-Systems are used in about 20 million books. In the USA there are about 60 libraries with approximately 10 million books using this technology or the relevant technical basics of RFID technology will be explained, always pointing out the relevance to libraries. In addition there is a description of RFID library systems down to the most important components. Such a system is taken as an example from a company Bibliotheca Inc., RFID Library Systems. There is a listing of technical criteria, which shall provide a guideline for the evaluation of RFID library systems

How to consume Benefits of RFID for libraries

* Reduce material handling time.
* Do more frequency and accurate inventory to better manage collections
* Improve ergonomics of the repetitive tasks of librarians.
* Improve customer service.

A big advantage of RFID is that its not dependent upon the line –of-sight, since it uses radio –frequency signals. Since

RFID does not require 'line –of-sight' between the transponder and the radar, it surmounts the limitations of other automatic identification devices, such as bar coding RFID systems work effectively in hostile environments where excessive dirt dust moisture and/or poor visibility would normally hinder rapid identification process. One of the most outstanding benefits of RFID is its ability to read through these environments at remarkable speeds responding in less than 100 milliseconds in most cases.

TECHNOLOGY

An RFID-System comprises two units, a transponder and a reader. The transponder is Attached to the object or person to identify; whereas the reader is stationary, in most cases. Both units contain an antenna and a computer chip (chip) to send and receive radio waves and process the information, which is behind the signals The reader unit is connected to a computer and power supply. The signals from the transponder are sent at a frequency of 13.56 MHz. This frequency is approved worldwide for RFID systems. The transponder does not contain a battery – it uses induction to receive energy. This is important to make it useable for a long term application. This feature makes it possible to use it in books and other material.For the use in libraries, the transponder is designed as an RFID-Label, which is comprised of four elements: the chip, the antenna on a foil, the cover paper or plastic label and the silicon liner. Chips for RFID-labels are available from various companies today such as: Philips Semiconductors, Texas Instruments, etc. They vary in capabilities like memory capacity, size, read/write versus read only and the way they are affixed onto the antenna (bonding vs. flip chip). These factors are relevant for the library in terms of performance, usability and of course reliability.

For libraries the reader can have different designs, for example: two stationary antennas with a reading distance of 3 feet between the sensor gates, a paper-sheet size antenna on a desk- top reader with an approx. one foot reading distance. Another design is a hand held unit (wand) with a six-inch reading distance. The readers differ not only in terms of reading distance and size, but also in reading speed and the amount of tags, which can be read simultaneously.

Information is read and the chip programmed to a different status, as being checked out. When these books are carried through the sensor gate at the exit there will be no alarm. The book numbers are stored on the account and a receipt is printed. This receipt also contains the due date for return, the data for late return, and some additional data (e.g. items on hold for the patron, etc.). For those patrons who do not want to use the self-check station they can still go to the circulation desk like they did before. If the Patron goes through the sensor gates with books that are checked out, there will be no alarm. In case the item was not checked out, the alarm will sound and then a signal is transmitted to the information counter and/or a turnstile to block the exit. "Barcode" as well as title and author identify the item. The way the book is tracked using an RFID system. When the book first comes into the library, it will get a library number and be entered into the library data. The RFID label will also bear the number, which is programmed into the chip. The RFID number is then linked to the database. The book will then be put on the shelf and will now be active in the circulation system. The librarian can take inventory by means of a hand held reader (inventory wand). The reader is waved alongside the shelves and picks up all the individual signals from the books. It may also be used to find misplaced books the basic advantages of a modern RFID-System in a library can be summarized as following:

* No lines or greatly reduced lines at the check out counter.
* Less repetitive work (and repetitive stress injuries) for personnel and an increase in interaction with the patrons.
* The use of an RFID system increases the security function in a library
* Reduced material costs and handling (only one label instead of two or three).
* A regular inventory control and update of the database is possible.

* Automation of sorting and conveying functions.
* The easy search for miss-shelved books.

KEY FEATURES OF RFID IN LIBRARIES

The reliability of the system, its ease of operation, and the flexibility of tagging all kinds of media easily, are important criteria in choosing an RFID system. The main aim for today's libraries in adopting RFID is the need to increase efficiency and reduce cost. Automation and self-service can help libraries of all sizes achieve these aims, and RFID has the added advantage that it can also provide security for the range of different media offered in libraries. The technology can also improve circulation and inventory control, which helps allocate human and financial resources. This means that libraries can relieve their professional employees of routine work and operational tasks. All of the tags used in RFID technology for libraries are "passive." The power to read the tags comes from the reader or exit sensor (reader), rather than from a battery within the tag. A few libraries use "smart" card, which is an RFID card with additional encryption, is an alternative to merely adding an RFID tag on staff and user identification cards... Not only does that identify users for issue and return of library materials, but also for access to restricted areas or services. This would make it possible to make it into a "debit" card, with value added upon pre-payment to the library and value subtracted when a user used a photocopier, printer, or other fee-based device, or wished to pay fines or fees.

Advantages over other ID technologies

Designed specifically for libraries, RF labels other the following benefits over traditional barcodes.

1. Combining both material identification and security into one single lag or transponder, thus, saving cost and time.
2. Multiple items can be read at a time, resulting speedy circulation.
3. RFID labels or smart labels can be attached to divergent media, such as CDs, DVDs and other print and non-print media.
4. Tags are read/writ, providing felicity in encoding and decoding.

5. Durable labels i.e. designed to last lifetime of the item they identify.
6. While a laser scanner must read bear codes, RFID emit a radio signal hat can be picked up from a remote site i.e. line – of sight that involved in bar codes in note necessary for capturing the item data.

DISADVANTAGES OF RFID SYSTEMS

High cost : The major disadvantage of RFID technology is its cost. While the readers and gate sensors used to read the information typically cost around $2,000 to $3,500 each; and the tags cost $.40 to $.75 each.

Accessibility to compromiset : It is possible to compromise an RFID system by wrapping the protected material in two to three layers of ordinary household foil to block the radio signal). It is also possible to compromise an RFID system by placing two items against one another so that one tag overlays another. That may cancel out the signals. This requires knowledge of the technology and careful alignment.

Chances of Removal of exposed tags : RFID tags are typically affixed to the inside back cover and are exposed for removal. This means that there would be problems when users become more familiar with the role of the tags. In Indian libraries, it is a major challenge to keep the tags intact.

Exit gate sensor (Reader) problems : While the short-range readers used for circulation charge and discharge and inventorying appear to read the tags 100 percent of the time , the performance of the exit gate sensors is more problematic. They always don't read tags at up to twice the distance of the other readers. There is no library that has done a before and after inventory to determine the loss rate when RFID is used for security.

User Privacy Concerns : Privacy concerns associated with item-level tagging is another significant barrier to library use of RFID tags. The problem with today's library RFID system is that the tags contain static information that can be relatively easily read by unauthorized tag readers. This allows for privacy issues described as "tracking" and "hot listing" Tracking refers to the ability to track the movements of a book (or person carrying the book) by "correlating multiple observations of the book's bar code or RFID tag. Hot listing refers to the process of building a database of books and their associated tag numbers (the hot list) and then using an unauthorized reader to determine who is checking out items in the hot list.

Reader collision : The signal from one reader can interfere with the signal from another where coverage overlaps. This is called reader collision. One way to avoid the problem is to use a technique called time division multiple access, or TDMA. In simple terms, the readers are instructed to read at different times, rather than both trying to read at the same time. This ensures that they don't interfere with each other. But it means any RFID tag in an area where two readers overlap will be read twice .

Tag collision : Another problem readers have is reading a lot of chips in the same field. Tag clash occurs when more than one chip reflects back a signal at the same time, confusing the reader. Different vendors have developed different systems for having the tags respond to the reader one at a time. Since they can be read in milliseconds, it appears that

RFID SYSTEM COMPONENTS

System Components

The RFID Library System consists, as described in section 3, of several components. The most important ones are: the sensor gate(s), the self check unit(s) and the staff station(s). These components are independent of each other and from the main software system (circulation system). Since the components are "intelligent", an additional server is not necessary as with first generation RFID library systems. These components allow for easy addition of components. High reading speed is possible with this concept, which is the transmission of important data directly from the chip. This availability of data in the book/media does not require time-consuming scrolling through the data base server. High reading speed is important for the sensor gate and the inventory wand.

Sensor Gate

The sensor gate was designed for the detection and reading of information from RFID labels, which are carried through a door. The gate supplies the media number that shows which books were stolen.

The reader consi< of two or three antennas, which are parallel to each other , plus housing for the reader electronics. The antennas show a similar design like the sensor gates used in stores for theft control. The aisle width is 90cm (35") with two antennas, and 1, 8 m (70") with three antennas.

Self-Check Unit

After the identification of the patron, this can be done with an RFID ID Card, a typical Barcode library card, magnetic ID Card, or a PIN number, she can put the items (books, CDs, videotapes, etc.) Onto the read surface in front of the self check unit to be Registered under her name and programmed to "check out" The chip will be set on "quiet" mode, so as not to alarm at the exit. It is possible to return books at the self check station. But most libraries prefer to have function to avoid any lines of waiting patrons. So the return function is an optional function as is looking up their account status. Multiple items can be checked out at the same time in a stack. The height of the read range is approximately 25 cm (10"). The thickness of the items, determines the number of items that can be checked out within the read range.

Staff Station

To check out/in books at the staff station is a similar procedure like at the self check unit. There are additional software windows integrated into the LMS which allow other Functions for the staff, plus some controlling functions. The dimensions of the staff station antenna are 240 x 340 x 9 mm (13" x 9" x 0.25"), Which results in a very low profile design? It is connected to a personal computer. The antenna will be set beside the PC or underneath the counter. The Staff Station is modular consisting of the antenna, electronic module and the power supply. Ergonomics ere paramount in the design of the BiblioChip™ Staff Station and Self Check-out Station. This station can also process a stack of materials (to 25 cm,

10" high) and hence, is a great time saver for the staff.

Conversion Station

The conversion station utilizes the same hardware as the staff station and runs under the LMS surface. The difference lies in the BiblioChip software that is written to initialize RFID labels for use in books. The information on the label can by changed with the according update in the database. BiblioChip-Test software can be used for control purposes. The conversion station is normally placed on a table: it comprises a barcode-reader, a PC and the RFID antenna.

Inventory Wand

This device is basically used for various wireless functions: to take inventory, to locate specific types of books or media and to find misplaced items. Another function of this device is to feed data into the main system via a wireless LAN (network). Special library specific software programs can be written and utilized with the inventory wand. The Personal Data Terminal (PDA) utilizes Windows™ CE software.

Book Return Station

Many libraries require a separate book return station. The book will be identified at a RFID reader unit, located inside the book return slot, and then placed in a bin. It will automatically check in books, take them off the patron's library account and reactivate the security function. There are 3 options: The return at a Self Check Station where the return function is activated (Check-Out plus Return or Return only). This can only be used inside the library. Book Return Station without Sorting (inside the building, in a lobby room or at the outside wall for external access)

Book Return Station with Sorting (like above, but with sufficient space for a sorting equipment). For sorting, two or more bins can be used, for sorting books on hold, media groups, etc. In a more sophisticated system the sorting can be expanded to numerous bins with the appropriate conveying equipment. A fully Automatic Book Return Unit with sorting equipment is shown in. In, to the check-in functions mentioned above, it will also print receipts for the patron, as well as interface to conveyor and sorting systems as required

An RFID system comprises of a number of components including a range of transponder handled or stationary radars, data input units, and system software. The transponder or id tags are the backbone of the technology and come in all shapes, sizes and read ranges. A comprehensive RFID system has the following key components. RFID tags that are electronically programmed with unique information. A reader connected to the library information system. An antenna connected to the reader. A server to receive and decode the information and to communicate with the automated library system. Tags also know, as transponders are electronic chips consisting of an integrated circuit and antenna coil that communicate with a means of a radio frequency signal. They have an EAS (Electronic article surveillance) functions to defect thefts. It comes in various shapes and sizes. Tags have three memory components. Item identification i.e. barcode no. Security bit that is tumid off and on as items are checked out and checked in. Variable memory that is of uses in sorting the items. RFID tags are available as labels with adhesive backings and the ability to reel through a label printer. After sticking RFID label on the book, its information's such as Accession number is registered in the chip of the label. This function allows writing such information on chip either from the library database or by scanning existing barcode labels. If any. The tags can be purchased blank when retrospective conversion of bar coded collection is to be taken up or pre-programmed, if automation is at initial stage i.e. libraries, which have collection without barcodes. Reader or interrogator is an electronic device that activates a transponder and retrieves data stored in its IC chip. It is used for communication between RFID tags and a host computer system. A reader generally consists of an RF transmitter and receiver and an antenna for communicated with tags. Communication between the reader and a transponder (tag) via radio waves is a two – step process in the first step a reader through radio waves activates the transponder and in the second step the transponder responds by returning the data on the IC. Reader may be portable and stationary type and with the aid of a processor it decodes the information.

Technical Choice

The choice between low frequency and high frequency depends upon the application. A low - frequency device typically provides slower data transfer and must work at closer distances to an object. Relative speed of tag moving on a production line past an interrogation unit is approximately 20 miles and hour. On the other hand, high frequency devices can work at distance up to 250 feet and at relative speeds greater than 150 miles per hour,. Barring the high fixed costs, high f frequency system is suitable for a smart library. It works when a reader sends a signal to the transponder or ID tag via an antenna. The transponders electronic return the ID code via a modulated signal being continuously reflected off the transponder's antenna. Giving an impressively quick read on the other hand, low frequency systems are more suitable for tracking, monitoring or controlling the workflow of objects used for manufacturing, production, and processes.

HOW DOES IT WORK?

An RFID system consists of a reader, comprising a transmitter and receiver, together with an antenna and integrated circuit transponder tag or "smart labels – microchips attached to the antenna. The transmitter sends out a radio signal on a specific frequency using the antenna/ the tag if within the transformers reading range recognizes this signal. The tag then responds with a signal that is recognized by the receiver. The significance of recent RFID technology is that most tags are battery- less and receive the energy to power the tag form the transmitter signal. This not only make the tags low – cost devices but also saves the environments since most of the application require low –cost and signal use throwaway tags. Smart label or tag (microchip) can be embedded virtually into any object including books and other stock of library individually identifies the book using a unique, unalterable code. The chip communicates with the circulation database of a library so that each item's location, whether on the shelves, checked out or being processed, can be determined with a hand –held reader the clientele and staff members can scan the shelves to find out the misplaced objects by radio pulse. Tagging job can be undertaken either by the library or a book jobber or the publisher at the time of publication. However, most libraries prefer to maintain their own togging and verification station. When RFID tags are passed in front of a reading station, a radio field changes the chip and lets if transmit its data. Thus, the information contained in the microchips affixed to the library materials is "captured" and retrieved using radio frequency technology regardless of its location.

AUTOMATED MATERIAL HANDING

The RFID tag entrenched into each item (books or other media) of the library brings efficiency at all stages of the library management process. The RFID tags communicate to RFID station (a combination of the reader and antenna is an RFID station), which are connected to integrated library software (ILS) and allows instantaneous update of the database.

(a) Barcode number and theft prevention

RFID smart labels or tags reliable and easy to use. Tags are flexible paper – thin with an electronic chip, which are wireless readable and write able. They can be read using radio frequency technology that operates without contact and line of sight. They are designed for lasting to lifetime of the identity and also perform the EAS (Electronic article surveillance) function to detect the thefts. Library users leaving the building pass through a four- lane EAS (Electronic article surveillance) exit gate, which uses RFID to check articles being carried though. Items not authorized for taking away trigger the security system's alarms.

(b) Being converted station and cataloguing

Conversion from barcode to RFID is a combination of programming and the application of the RFID tag.

(c) To maintain Programming

Programming is a single operation that involves of the book ID, encoding of the RFID tag and the activation of the antitheft. The programming of the RFID tag can be done while reading the barcode. A unique number can also be pre-programmed in the RFID tag to link it with the book references.

(d) Applications

Application of RFID tag reduces tine and inconvenience of this repetitive task, since only one label can be applied for both the item ID and antitheft function. And for new items or libraries adopting automation for the first time, the process is even easier, since one just ahs to stick and program one signal label.

OPTIONAL COMPONENTS

Optional RFID system includes the following three components (Bibliotheca 2003):

1. RFID Label Printer
2. Handheld Reader
3. External Book Return
4. RFID label Printer
5. An RFID printer is used to print the labels with an individual barcode, library logo, etc. When the print is applied, it simultaneously programs the data in to the chip. After this process, the RFID label is taken from the printer and applied to the book

1. Circulation desk

Circulation desk where librarians do manual checkout and in of the items, with prolonged queue times is in desperate need of RFID technology, which lessens the cumbersome processes and makes the processes fast and convenient for both patron and the staff. To borrow items users simply identity themselves at self- service and place the items they want to take out on a pad with an antenna. The borrowing station updates the database, assigning the book to the patron and resets the chip to show that the times can be taken from the building. All this is done in one automatic process. Moreover, RFID allows for multiple checks out of books. And if the library utilizes RFID even for patron cards, then the user identification can also be red with the same reader at the time, which benefits the library check in process.

SELF CHECKED OUT

RFID check out system is user friendly, highly intuitive and reduces the question times. At this station, the books to be checked out are placed on the deck and both patron card and stack of books can be read simultaneously i.e. recording the patron's ID, the borrowed items and deactivating the antitheft. All this updating of the library database happens automatically even for multiple items checked out by the same borrower. A receipt confirming the details of borrowed materials and due date is printed out.

CHECK IN

Books can be placed on deck station one without ay intervention by staff. The returned item is instantaneously updated in the ILS and the antitheft is activated. This automated book return gives enhanced benefit to patrons as well as librarians. For patrons it offices great flexibility in returning their material when they want and gives better availability of books as updating the library database is done in real time. Optionally, a receipt is also printed out to confirm the returning of borrowed material.

And for librarians, it saves time by avoiding certain repetitive tasks, since multiple items can be read / write at the same time and at quick pace. It offers reliable book sorting system due to the fact the RFID tags can be read quickly and independent of tag orientation or position.

HIGH SPEED INVENTORY MANAGEMENT

Inventory management becomes possible, fast and accurate, as it is at least 20 times faster than with barcodes. By carrying a handheld inventory reader along the bookshelves to collect the data and do the inventory smart labels inlayed in books can be read in seconds. Up to 64,000 books ID numbers can be stored in the reader memory. It is tremendously time consuming why because instead of handing each book, just walking down a section of a gangway the computer wand reads it, since it's multidirectional. The hand held reader has an audible signal to indicate the misplaced books. This is useful for taking inventory, finding missing items and identifying misfiled items, a common and labor-intensive problem to correct in a library. The collected data is then automatically downloaded to the library database.

SORTING

When book is put on the deck, integrated library software (ILS) harnessing RFID flashes the accession number and shelf number, which facilitate shelving of items. And it provides additional information such as item belonging to other location or if it is a reserved item, etc.

BOOK DROP

When books are returned though the 'Book drop' facility of a library, the smart labels are automatically read and both patron record and library database get update the theft detection system into the smart labels is simultaneously activated. This book drop allows patrons to return items 24 hours a day, 7 days a week. A conveyor sorting system for books that are returned through the books drop can be installed.

ELECTROMAGNETIC SECURITY SYSTEM: CONCEPTS

Bar codes cannot be the signal feed for anti-theft system so the usual combination is to have a combination of bar codes for identification, and some electromagnetic (EM) based anti-theft system. In self service stations the deification system must interact with the anti-theft system so that items have the correct EM state after the circulation transactions, i.e. checked out item must be deactivated, and returned items activated these interaction are still unreliable and lacking in functionality.

As for the single source for the anti –theft system(i.e.)the magnetic strip, able, or rod ,there is a danger of a technology(or system)trap once the magnetic device is attached to the library item it should ideally, not be possible to take it away. This however, marks it difficult to switch to another security system, if the single sources can not be side in the alternative solution .It is also possible that the option of ignoring old magnetic devices

ELECTROMAGNETIC SECURITY

The image shows the main elements of the system: the visitor enters the library through an entrance gate, precedes either directly to the shelf to remove the book or asks for advice at the information counter or goes to the on-line search. He may also want to return some books. The central unit is the self issue Station. At this station books are registered as being checked out together with the visitor's name, they are deactivated in their security function and a receipt is printed. The antenna will give an alarm if an item was not issued properly.

VENDORS

The products of six manufacturers of library RFID systems are available in India through their business associates: Bibliotheca, Checkpoint, ID Systems, 3M, X-ident technology GmbH represented by InfoTech software and systems in India and TAGSYS- the last represented by Tech Logic, Vernon, Libsys in India and VTLS. There are several other companies that provide products that work with RFID, including user self-charging stations and materials handling equipment.

INSTALLATIONS

While there are over 500,000 RFID systems installed in warehouses and retail establishments worldwide, RFID systems are still relatively new in libraries. Fewer than 250 had been installed as of the first quarter of 2004). Most installations are small, primarily in branch libraries. The University of Connecticut Library; University of Nevada/Las Vegas Library, the Vienna Public Library in Austria, the Catholic University of Leuven in Belgium, and the National University of Singapore Library are the only sites that appear to have tagged more than 500,000 items each. So far in India, only two University libraries have adopted the RFID system. First among them is *Jayakar Library of Pune University* and second is *Dhanvantri Library of Jammu University*. The use of RFID throughout Indian libraries will take at least four to five years.

CONCLUSION

It is important to educate library staff and library users about RFID technology before implementing a program. It may be good for librarians to watch developments in RFID until the cost of tags comes down to $.20 or less, the figure which some librarians have determined is the key to their serious consideration of it. While library RFID systems have a great deal in common with one another, including the use of high frequency (13.56 MHz), passive, read-write tags, lack of a standard and compatibility of tags produced by different vendors is a major problem in implementation of RFID in libraries. Current standards (ISO 15693) apply to container-level tagging used in supply chain applications and do not address problems of tracking and hot listing. Next generation tags (ISO 18000) are designed for item level tagging. The newer tags are capable of resolving many of the privacy problems of today's tags. However, no library RFID products are currently available using the new standard. Both cost and equipment may make RFID prohibitive in developing countries at this time.

REFERENCES

1. Boss. R. W. (2003). RFID technology for libraries [Monograph]. *Library Technology Reports* . November-December 2003.
2. Boss. R. W. PLA Tech Notes (May 14, 2004) RFID Technology for libraries.
3. RFID Journal (Online Version 2004) .
4. Koppel, T. (March 2004). Standards in Libraries: What's Ahead: a guide for Library Professional about the Library Standards of Today and the Future? The Library Corporation.
5. Molnar, D., Wagner, D. A. (June 2004). Privacy and security in library RFID: Issues, practices and architectures.
6. Sarma, E. S. Weis, S. A., Engels, D.W. (November 2002). White paper: RFID systems, security & privacy implications. Cambridge, MA: Massachusetts Institute of Technology, AUTO-ID Center.
7. ISO-Standard 15693 (2001): Part 1: Physical characteristics — Part 2: Air interface and initialization, Part 3: Anti-collision and transmission protocol
8. Kern, C.: RFID-Technology – Recent Development and Future Requirements. Proceedings of the European Conference on Circuit Theory and Design, 1999, Vol. 1, Stresa, Italy

19
Library Security: Bar Code, RFID

B.A. Rajeev
S. Jayaprakash

ABSTRACT

The security problems that have plagued the libraries for years, such as theft and other kinds of misbehavior, remain a challenge today. Although some libraries appear well organized in their security programs and policies. Many lack up-to-date written security plans, effective data gathering, and complete inventory procedures. A number of libraries have not taken advantage of the latest developments in security technology—electronic surveillance, barcode, RFID etc.—and remain dependent on more traditional strategy, such as staff monitoring stems.

INTRODUCTION

Security is the condition of being protected against danger or loss. In the general sense, security is a concept similar to safety. The nuance between the two is an added emphasis on being protected from dangers that originate from outside. Individuals or actions that encroach upon the condition of protection are responsible for the breach of security.

New technologies have always been of interest for libraries both for the potential of increasing the quality of service and for improving efficiency of operation.

Bar code is a fundamental technology for library operations and flow management. It provides the coupling between the information system and the physical flow of library materials. The application at the circulation desk, bar code technology has been proven to be robust, reliable and efficient. But bar codes can not be signal feed for anti-theft systems so that usual combination is to have a combination of bar-codes for identification and some electromagnetic (EM) based anti-theft system.

RFID (Radio Frequency Identification) is a technology that enables wireless data capture and transaction processing. It is the latest technology to be used in library theft detection systems. Libraries began using RFID systems to replace their electromagnetic and bar code systems in the late 1990's. RFID based systems moved beyond security to be-come tracking systems that combine security with more efficient tracking of materials throughout the library, including easier and faster charge and discharge, inventorying and materials handling.

LIBRARY SECURITY SURVEY & POLICY

A thorough review of the security of library's collections is an essential first step in developing security strategy. Appoint one member of staff to undertake a fixed term security review (with specific terms of reference) and to produce recommendations. The person appointed must have the confidence of the other staff. (It is preferable that one person rather than a team carry out the survey as a co-ordinated approach is essential).

The survey process can be divided into three stages:

STAGE ONE

SEEKING INFORMATION AND SPECIALIST ADVICE

Internally

Many library staffs are concerned about security. They may have first-hand experience of the problems.

Externally

Discussions with other librarians, especially in libraries known to have good security system.

STAGE TWO

DEFINING THE SITUATION IN LIBRARY

* Who is responsible for security - the librarian, or the staff concerned?
* What is the current budget allocation - indeed, is there any?
* Is there a security policy - if so, have staff seen it?

STAGE THREE

CARRYING OUT DETAILED STUDIES OF THE ,

The buildings and their design:

* How vulnerable is the perimeter?
* How is access controlled?
* Does the design/layout create blind spots?

Storage

* Are storage areas secured?
* Who has access?
* How is rare/valuable material housed?

Book detection systems

* Are they in use?
* Is all material tagged?
* How does the system work?
* Are there operational difficulties?
* How regularly is it inspected?

Exhibition and display

* Are galleries guarded?
* Are cases fitted with alarms?

Loaning items

* What conditions are made for loaning items?

Ownership stamps

* Is all material stamped?
* Are stamps visible?

* Where are stamps placed?

Reporting thefts/exchanging information

* How are thefts reported?
* Does the library share information informally with others?

READERS: Admissions

* What are the entrance criteria?
* What identification is required?
* Are checks made on names/addresses/references etc?

Exclusions

* Is there a policy for excluding readers?
* Is it enforced?
* Is there a blacklist?

Cloakroom facilities

* Are they provided?
* If bags are allowed in the library, are they searched on entry/exit?

Procedures in the study area

* How are items, particularly loose items, issued?
* Are they checked on return?
* Is there a rule that pencils only should be used?

Invigilation

* How well are reading areas invigilated?
* If open-access, do staff patrol stacks regularly?
* Are CCTV, observation mirrors or other security devices in use? Are they effective?

Legal problems

* What are the procedures when a crime has been committed?
* Are staffs familiar with them?

STAFF

Pre-employment

* How closely are references etc checked?

Training and awareness

* Are staffs given any security training? If so, is it adequate?
* How can awareness be raised?

Security staff

* How are they recruited and trained? How are they motivated?

Staff passes

* Are they worn? Are they shown to gain access to staff-only areas?

Searching staff bags

* Is this done? Should it be introduced?

DRAWING UP A SECURITY POLICY

A security policy document need not be lengthy but it should state clearly and authoritatively its aims and objectives.

A security policy should include:

* A firm statement of the library's commitment to protect its collections
* The steps the library is prepared to take to do this: eg maintaining building, providing security staff, controlling entry and departure from its premises, enforcing the wearing of staff passes, providing adequate training for staff, introducing bag searching, installing theft detection systems, calling in the police when necessary
* A clear statement of who has overall responsibility for security - a specially appointed security officer, the librarian, etc
* Details of other staff with security responsibilities. Who is in charge of the warding staff? Who is responsible for the buildings on split sites?
* Emphasis on the responsibility of each member of staff to ensure the security of the library and its collections
* A guarantee that the library will support any member of staff, acting reasonably, in protecting the collections, preventing a crime etc

* Some policy documents also include detailed procedures for staff to follow when problems arise. This can be useful as it reinforces the message and provides all the necessary information in one document. Alternatively, guidelines can be drawn up separately and issued to all members of staff as part of their training process.

The policy document must be circulated to all members of staff. There is no point having a policy if no one knows it exists!

A SAMPLE LIBRARY SECURITY POLICY STATEMENT

* It is the library's policy to take all reasonable measures to protect its collections and other property from loss, destruction or damage and to protect all its buildings from unauthorised intrusion
* Pursuing this policy, the library will ensure that premises are adequately maintained and fitted with suitable technical devices. The library is also committed to an adequate, well-trained security warding staff.
* The library will control the entrance and exit of users. It retains the right to withdraw user facilities when security of the collections cannot be guaranteed.
* The library will ensure that staff at all levels are made aware of their security responsibilities and are property trained to carry out their duties. It will enforce the wearing of staff identity passes.
* The library will prosecute in cases of theft or significant damage. If a member of staff is involved, disciplinary proceedings will be instituted.
* The Head of Library Services is responsible for the overall security policy in the library. The management of warding staff is the direct responsibility of the Site Librarian.

BARCODE

A **barcode** (also **bar code**) is a machine readable representation of information in a visual format on a surface. Originally barcodes stored data in the widths and spacings of printed parallel lines, but today they also come in patterns of dots, concentric circles, and hidden in images. Barcodes can be read by optical scanners called barcode readers or scanned from an image by special software. Barcodes are widely used to implementAuto ID Data Capture (AIDC) systems that improve the speed and accuracy of computer data entry.

Since their invention in the 20th century, barcodes - especially the UPC code - have slowly become an essential part of modern civilization. Their use is widespread, and the technology behind barcodes is constantly improving. Some modern applications of barcodes include:

Practically every item purchased from a grocery store, departmental store, and mass merchandiser has a barcode on it. This greatly helps in keeping track of the large number of items in a store and also reduces instances of shoplifting (since shoplifters could no longer easily switch price tags from a lower-cost item to a higher-priced one). Since the adoption of barcodes, both consumers and retailers have profited from the savings generated.

Rental car companies keep track of their cars by means of barcodes on the car bumper.

Airlines track passenger luggage with barcodes, reducing the chance of loss.

Recently, researchers have placed tiny barcodes on individual bees to track the insects' mating habits.

The movement of nuclear waste can be tracked easily with a bar-code inventory system.

More recently, barcodes have even started appearing on humans. Fashion designers stamp barcodes on their models to help coordinate fashion shows. The codes store information about what outfits each model should be wearing and when they are due on the runway

BAR CODE SYMBOLOGIES

Symbologies are like languages. Unless you're using the correct symbology your bar code may be unreadable. Although each symbology is unique all share common elements such as bars, spaces, quiet zone and human readables.

Some popular bar code symbologies:

Code 39

1234567890

POSTNET

EAN (European Article Number) is the twelve-digit system used throughout the world for bar coding general merchandise.

bars and spaces
quiet zone
quiet zone
human readables
0 12345 67890 5
system digit
manuf. number
product number
check digit

UPC (Universal Product Code), a subset of the EAN system, is used primarily in the US and Canada.

0 12345 67890 5

ISBN and ISSN

ISBN 012345678-9
90000
9 780123 456786

Bar Code Symbology Chart

Below is a chart of the most widely used bar codes and the type of input each requires. For additional information on selecting a symbology, see Selecting Symbology

Codabar Numeric plus-.$/+:

01234567890

Code 128 Full ASCII

01234567890

EAN-128 Full ASCII

01234567890

Code 25 Numeric

01234567890

Code 39 Alphanumeric plus space,-.$/+%

01234567890

EAN-13 Numeric

0 123456 789012 >

EAN-13 + 5 Numeric

12345 >

0 123456 789012

ISBN+EAN-13 Numeric

ISBN 0123-4567-8-9

90000 >

9 780123 456786

ISSN Numeric

ISSN 0123-4560

ISSN+EAN-13 Numeric

EAN-8 Numeric

< 0123 4565 >

EAN-8 + 5 Numeric

< 0123 4565 >

JAN-8 Numeric

< 4901 2347 >

JAN-13 Numeric

4 901234 567894 >

FIM A, FIM B None

FIM C, FIM D None

ISBN Numeric

ISBN 012345678-9

Pharmacode Numeric

POSTNET Numeric

POSTNET 11-digit Numeric

SELECTING A SYMBOLOGY

Each bar code symbology has advantages and disadvantages depending upon the inherent features of the bar code and the demands you place on the bar code. The characters you want encoded, print quality, and the amount of space available for the bar code are some of the factors which may help determine which bar code symbology to use.

Certain needs may make one code more suitable than others. Some needs may only be met by a single bar code symbology. In some cases, industry standards will dictate which bar code symbology must be used. There are times when the end user is left to his own devices to determine which symbology works best.

BENEFITS OF USING BARCODES

In point-of-sale management, the use of barcodes can provide very detailed up-to-date information on key aspects of the business, enabling decisions to be made much quicker and with more confidence. For example:

Fast-selling items can be identified quickly and automatically reordered to meet consumer demand, Slow-selling items can be identified, preventing a build-up of unwanted stock, The effects of repositioning a given product within a store can be monitored, allowing fast-moving more profitable items to occupy the best space, Historical data can be used to predict seasonal fluctuations very accurately.

Bar code scanners are also relatively low costing and extremely accurate – only about 1/100000

RFID

RFID (Radio Frequency Identification) is a technology that enables wireless data capture and transaction processing. It is the latest technology to be used in library theft detection systems. Libraries began using RFID systems to replace their electromagnetic and bar code systems in the late 1990's. RFID based systems moved beyond security to be-come tracking systems that combine security with more efficient tracking of materials throughout the library, including easier and faster charge and discharge, inventorying and materials handling.

RFID is a combination of radio-frequency based technology and microchip technology. The information contained on microchips in tags affixed to the library materials is read using radio-frequency technology regardless of item orientation or alignment (i.e the technology does not require line-of-sight or a fixed plane to read tags as do traditional theft detection systems) and distance from the item is not a critical factor except in the case of extra-wide exit gates. The corridors at the building exit(s) can be as wide as four feet because, the tags can be read at a distance of up to two feet by each of two parallel exit sensors [The devices used for circulating and inventorying are usually called "readers", while the one used at building exits are called "sensors"]

The tags used in RFID systems can replace both EM or RF theft detection targets and bar codes, although the system that 3M introduced in 2000 replaced only barcodes in the belief that EM is superior to RFID for securing. [3M did introduced a comprehensive RFID product that replaces both EM and Barcodes in 2004]

RFID SYSTEM COPONENTS:

An RFID system consists of three components, *the tag, the reader/ sensor and the server/ docking station.*

RFID tags are also known as transponders that are electronically programmed with unique information. Each paper-thin tag contains an antenna and a microchip with a capacity of at least 64 bits. There are three types,

1. Read only 2.WORM 3. Read / Write

Tags are read only; the identification is encoded at the time of manufacture and not rewritable. This type of tags contains nothing more than item identification like serial number or ISBN number. It can be used for item acquired after the initial collections without bar -codes, such tags need not contain more than 96 bits

Tags operate over a range of frequencies. Passive tags can be low- frequency (LF) or high-frequency (HF). LF tags operate at 125 KHz are relatively expensive and have low read range (0.5Mts). HF tags operate at 13.56MHz have a longer range (1Mtr) and are less expensive. Most library applications use HF tags.

WORM (write-once-read- many) tags are programmed by the using organization, but without the ability of rewriting them later. They can be used when a retrospective conversion of a collection that is already bar coded is undertaken. The main advantage of read only tags is that, the information in addition to the identification number can be added. However, it must be information that won't need to be changed.

Read / Write tags which are chosen by most libraries can have information changed or added. For example: A library might add an identification code for each branch. That information could be changed when the holding of the location subsequently changed

Tags can be Active, Passive or Semi-active. Active tags which have their own power supply are substantially larger and more expensive than the tags used in library RFID applications. It is these tags that can be read at a distance of up to ten feet.

All the tags used in RFID technology are 'passive'. The power to read the tags comes from the reader or exit sensor rather than from a battery within the tag. It is important to select a consistent location for book tags (inside the back cover).

A few libraries have placed RFID tags on staff and patron identification cards. Not only does that identify patrons for charging and discharging of library materials, but also for access to restricted areas or services.

The tags used by library RFID vendors are not compatible even when they conform to the same standards because the current standards only seek electronic compatibility between tags and readers. The pattern of encoding information and the software that processes the information differs from vendor to vendor; therefore, a change from one vendor's system to the other would require retagging all items or modifying the software.

Reader: These are radio frequency devices designed to detect and read tags to obtain the information stored thereon. A typical system includes several different kinds of readers, also known as servers when installed at the library exits. The reader powers an antenna to generate RF field When a tag passes through the field; the information stored on the chip in the tag is decoded by the reader and sent to the server which, in turn, communicated with the automated library system. When the RFID system is interfaced with it.

* Readers in the RFID system are used in the following ways;
* Staff workstation at circulation desk used to charging and discharging materials
* Conversion stations, where the library data is written to tag
* Patron self check-out station, where they used to check-out books without staff assistance
* Exit sensors-verify that all books leaving the library have been checked out
* Portable reader-Hand held reader for inventorying and verifying that items are shelved correctly

Server / Docking station /Application : The server is the heart of some comprehensive RFID systems. It is the communication gateway among the various components. It receives the information from one or more of the readers and exchanges information with the circulation database. The server typically includes a transaction database so that reports can be produced. Examples of applications and their uses fall into at least six categories;

* Access control (keyless entry)
* Asset tracking (self check-in and self check-out)
* Asset tagging and identification (inventory and shelving)
* Authentication (counterfeit prevention)
* Point-of-sale (POS) (Fast Track)
* Supply chain management (SCM) (tracking of containers, pallets or individual items from manufacturer to retailer)

RFID STANDARDS

The International organization for standardization (ISO) and EPC global have been very active in developing RFID standards. There are two ISO standards pertinent to library

RFID systems. The current standard ISO 15693 was not designed for the item-level tracking done in libraries. Yet, most library RFID tags follow this standard. ISO 15693 was designed for supply-chain application. It defines the physical characteristics, air interface and communication protocol for RFID cards. The national information standards organization (NISO) convened a "standards development group with the mission of designing a protocol that would encourage interoperability among desperate circulation, inter-library loan, self-service and related allocations. The out come of this group is National Circulation Interchange Protocol (NCIP). It was approved by NISO in 2002

COST OF IMPLEMENTING RFID SYSTEMS IN LIBRARY

The cost of implementing RFID systems for a library with 40,000 items is approximately $70,000 and $166,000 for a library with 100,000 items

The estimate for individual RFID components is as follows:

Exit sensors @ $ 4,000

Portable Scanner @ $ 4,500

Server @ $ 15,000 -20,000

Tags @ $ .85

The most expensive aspect of any RFID system is the cost of the tag and cost of placing the tag on each item. The cost go up when the tags are placed on other media such as CD's, DVD's and tapes ($ 1- 1.50). Customized tags (library logo) increase the cost of each tag further.

LIBRARY PROBLEMS ADDRESSED BY RFID

Libraries are suffering from budget shortfalls with cuts from governments; it is difficult for libraries to keep the library staffed and open. RFID is seen as a way to address the staff shortages. Self-check systems have been very popular with both patrons and staff. RFID self- check systems allow patrons to check-in or check-out several, rather than one books at a time. Self-check systems reduce the number of staff needed at the circulation desk.

With RFID enabled tools, inventory related tasks can be

done in a fraction of time as with bar code readers. A whole shelf of books can be read by the reader with one sweep of the portable reader which then reports that which books are missing or misshelved. For archives handling sensitive materials, the ability to inventory items without handling them is an additional benefit.

Sorting can be accomplished automatically with RFID. As books are dropped into the book drop, the reader reads the tag and uses the automatic sorting system to return the books back to the shelves, the stack or the hold area

Security is another aspect of library operations that may be greatly improved with RFID based security systems. As patron leaves the library, the tags are read to ensure that the item has been checked-out. Librarians also report the loss or hidden items are more easily retrieved using portable readers.

VENDORS

The products of six manufacturers of library RFID systems are available in North America; Bibliotheca, Checkpoint, ID systems, Libramation, 3M and Tagsys

A major supplier of patron self-charging stations used by some of the RFID vendors is 'Optical Solutions', a major supplier of book-drops by 'Birchard' and major supplier of material handling products that work with the systems of all the RFID vendors is by 'Tech Logic', it also sells complete RFID system

ADVANTAGES

Rapid Charging / Discharging

RFID system reduces the amount of time required to perform circulation operations. The most significant time savings are attributable to the facts that information can be read from RFID tags much faster than from barcodes. The system is comprehensive, that combines RFID security and tracking of materials throughout the library.

Self-charging & Discharging

Patrons do not have to carefully place materials with in a designated template and they can charge several items at the same time. Patron self-charging shifts that work from staff to patrons. Staff's are relieved further when 'readers' are installed in book drops

High Reliability

'Readers' are highly reliable. Several vendors of RFID library systems claim an almost 100 percent detection rate using RFID tags. If the material that has not been properly charged is taken past the exit sensors, an immediate alarm is triggered. If the patron card also has an RFID tag, the library will also be able to determine who removed the items without properly charging them

High Speed Inventorying

Its ability to scan books on the shelves without tipping them out or removing them. A hand-held inventory reader can be moved rapidly across shelf books to read all of the unique identification information

Long Tag Life

RFID tags last longer than barcodes because nothing comes into contact with them. Some vendors claim a minimum 100,000 transactions before a tag may need to be replaced.

DISADVANTAGES

High Cost : The major disadvantage of RFID technology is its cost. A reader may cost approximately $2,500-3,500 or more. A server costing as much as $15,000-20,000 and may cost $.60 - .85 each

Vulnerability to Compromise: It is possible to compromise an RFID system by wrapping the protected material in two / three layers of ordinary household foil to block the radio signal.

It is also possible to compromise an RFID system by placing two items against one another so that one tag over lays another that may cancel out the signals

Patron Privacy : There is a perception among some that RFID is a threat to patron privacy that perception is based on two misconceptions.

That the tags contain patron information and that they can be read after some one has taken the materials at home or office

CONCLUSION

It is an unfortunate reality that libraries and archives must be concerned about the security of their collections. It is recommended that all repositories conduct a security survey and draw up a security plan. While there is a place for automated security systems of various types, a repository must not depend solely on these systems to protect its collection. Although some libraries appear well organized in their security programs, many lack up-to-date written security plans, effective data gathering, and complete inventory procedures. A number of libraries have not taken advantage of the latest developments in security technology—electronic surveillance, card keys, etc.—and remain dependent on more traditional strategies, such as staff monitoring and magnetic exit control systems.

Developing effective security systems can, of course, be expensive. Too much emphasis on security can create a negative atmosphere for some library users and, if they are responsible for security enforcement, an intolerable situation for some staff. But nonetheless, every library needs a security program adequate for their situation. This checklist is meant to assist libraries by suggesting inexpensive strategies to improve security. Does your library have:

* an overall statement of your security program purpose?
* a security program plan, with an analysis of current systems and action plans for improving them?
* a schedule for reviewing your security program?
* programs for training library staff and informing staff and users about security issues?
* written security procedures accessible to all staff, including an emergency manual?
* an effective system for reporting security-related incidents and keeping records of such incidents?
* at least a partial inventory system for high-value items?
* good working relations with security personnel in your parent institution?

REFERENCES

1. Chappel,Lee. Conference studies applications and lessons of RFID, Wisconsin Technology Network, June 22, 2005
2. Electronics for you, Vol-37, No. 12, 2005
3. Federal Trade Commission. Radio Frequency Identification: Applications and Implications for consumers, FTC Conference Centre, Washington, June21, 2004
4. Garfinkel, Simson and Rosenberg, Beth(Eds) RFID:Applications, Security and Privacy, Addison-Wesley,2005
5. Klein, Mike. RFID's advantages and challenges, Wisconsin Technology Network, August13, 2005
6. Mc Arthur, Alastair. 'Integrating RFID into library systems-Myths & Realities, IFLA general conference, Berlin, August 2003
7. www.ala.org
8. www.galecia.com/included/does/position-rfid-permission.pdf
9. www.rfidexchange.com
10. www.rfidjournal.com
11. www.librarypreservation.org
12. www.wikipedia
13. www.morovia.com/education
14. www.barcodeindia.com

20

RFID Technology in Library Management: Concept to Completion

Shashikanta Jena
Sanjay Kataria

ABSTRACT

This article provides details about, What is RFID? and how does it work? What are the applications of RFID in Libraries? This paper also aims to clarify each and every aspect of RFI Systems and how does it organize electronic library services.

1. INTRODUCTION

Information Source is the basic source for any academic institution and research & development organization. The thirst of knowledge can't be suppressed by money. Library is a knowledge Center so it is indispensable to carry out effective measures in organizing these knowledge repositories. The inclining trend of information explosion and its significance emphasis a greater responsibility among the Librarians in organizing the knowledge centers. Librarians are marching towards latest technical and technological developments in organizing the library resources. One among them is implementation of RFID (Radio Frequency IDentification) systems to electronically manage the library resources.

2. HISTORY OF RFID TAGS

It has been suggested that the first known device was an espionage tool invented by Léon Theremin for the Soviet government in 1945. This is not quite the case: Theremin's device was a passive covert listening device, not an identification tag. The technology used in RFID has been around since the early 1920's according to one source (although the same source states that RFID systems have been around just since the late 1960s). A similar technology, the IFF transponder, was invented by the British in 1939, and was routinely used by the allies in World War II to identify airplanes as friend or foe.

Another early work exploring RFID is the landmark 1948 paper by Harry Stockman, entitled "Communication by Means of Reflected Power" (Proceedings of the IRE, pp1196-1204, October 1948). Stockman predicted that "...considerable research and development work has to be done before the remaining basic problems in reflected-power communication are solved, and before the field of useful applications is explored." It required thirty years of advances in many different fields before RFID became a reality.

3. RFID TECHNOLOGY

Radio frequency Identification (RFID) It is a generic term for technologies that use radio waves. It is an automatic identification method, relying on storing and retrieving data using electronic tags. Like Bar codes they are used to identify items, But RFID Tags hold more data than Bar Codes.

3.1. How the System works

RFID Tag is a small object, such as an adhesive sticker, that can be attached to or incorporated into a product. RFID Tag contain microchip that is attached to an antenna (the chip and the antenna together called an RFID transponder or an RFID tag) the antenna enables the chip to transmit the identification information to a reader. The reader converts the radio waves reflected bask from the RFID tag, into digital information that can be passed on to computer that an make use of it.

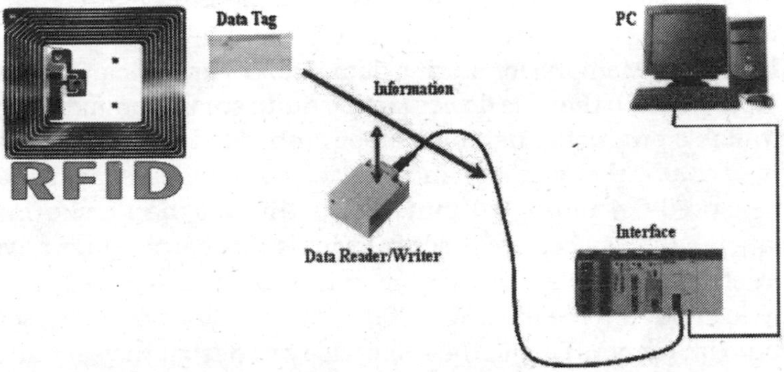

Specimen of RFID Tag and the pictorial representation of the System workflow

3.2. RFID Transponder:

Key Beneeits

* No line of sight needed
* Allows to check-out and check-in several items simultaneously
* Information directly attached to product
* Performing both identification and antitheft in one single operation
* Different shape and sizes available
* Able to tag almost anything
* Accelerate scanning and identifying

3.3. Types of RFID tags:

RFID tags can be active, semi-passive (=semi-active) or passive

Passive RFID tags have no internal power supply. The minute electrical current induced in the antenna by the incoming radio frequency signal provides just enough power for the CMOS integrated circuit (IC) in the tag to power up and transmit a response. Most passive tags signal by backscattering the carrier signal from the reader. This means that the aerial (antenna) has to be designed to both collect powers from the incoming signal and also to transmit the outbound backscatter signal. The response of a passive RFID tag is not just an ID number (GUID): tag chip can contain nonvolatile EEPROM (Electrically Erasable Programmable Read-Only Memory) for storing data. Lack of an onboard power supply means that the device can be quite small: commercially available products exist that can be embedded under the skin. As of 2005, the smallest such device commercially available measured 0.4 mm × 0.4 mm, and is thinner than a sheet of paper; such devices are practically invisible. Passive tags have practical read distances ranging from about 2 mm (ISO 14443) up to about few meters (ISO 18000-6) depending on the chosen radio frequency. Due to their simplicity in design they are also suitable for manufacture with a printing process for the antennae. Development targets are polycarbon semiconductor tags to become entirely printed. Semi-passive RFID tags are very similar to passive tags except for the addition of a small battery. This battery allows the tag IC to be constantly powered. This removes the need for the aerial to be designed to collect power from the incoming signal. Aerials can therefore be optimized for the backscattering signal. Semi-passive RFID tags are faster in response and therefore stronger in reading ratio compared to passive tags. Passive tags are cheaper to manufacture and have no battery; the majority of RFID tags in existence are of the passive variety.

Active RFID tags have an internal power source, which is used to power any ICs and generate the outgoing signal. They may have longer range and larger memories than passive tags, as well as the ability to store additional information sent by the transceiver. To economize power consumption, many beacon concepts operate at fixed intervals. At present, the smallest active tags are about the size of a coin. Many active tags have practical ranges of tens of meters, and a battery life of up to 10 years.

There are four main frequency bands for RFID tags commonly in use. They are categorized by their radio frequency: low frequency tags (125 or 134.2 kHz), high frequency tags (13.56 MHz), UHF tags (868 to 956 MHz) or 433 MHz, and microwave tags (2.45 GHz) or 5.8 GHz).There is a wide variation of transponder devices and contact less chip cards, which deliver similar functions.

4. COMPONENTS OF RFID

4.1. Transponder

The Chip and the antenna embedded together in the RFID Tag are called RFID Transponder. The storage capacity of this chip is of at least 96 Bits. The tags can be permanently activated (programmed during manufacturing) or, at higher complexity and cost, read-write, both. The tags are electronically programmed with unique information. The size of the tag depends on the size of the antenna, which increases with range of tag and decreases with frequency.

4.2. Transceiver

The antenna and the reader together called transceiver. The reader/coupler can send information in two direction: It can read information from a tag and send it to the Server/PC (read mode), or it can read information from the Server and send it to an RFID tag (write mode).

4.3. Server/PC

This provide link between the coupler and your library automation system. The Server /PC is the heart of a comprehensive RFID System. It is the communications gateway among the various components. It receives the information from the antennae and exchanges information with the circulation database. The server typically includes a transaction database.

4.4. RFID Application software

This is to provide a graphical user interface to carry out effective library services which includes Electronic Books drop, Auto shelf detecting System, Electronic security system. This software acts as an interface among all the services mentioned above. This software acts as a front end tool for your circulation database. This provides an interface between the RFID hardware and your library automation software.

5. FUNCTIONS OF THE ELECTRONIC LIBRARY AND INFORMATION SERVICE USING RFID SYSTEMS

5.1. Tagging

This is quit an initiation task in RFID systems. This is nothing but writing information into the chip of the tag. After tagging is successfully completed tag should be fixed into books or other media, they can be read and written to using radio frequency, which operate without contact and line of sight. They have an EAS (Electronic Article Surveillance) function to detect thefts.

5.2. Staff Circulation Station or Multipurpose Station

To be operated by library staff, it enables handling of books and other material having RFID Labels/Tags. It provides for the following functions

5.3. Auto-Checking-out

After establishing the validity of a member card either by barcode reader or by smart card reader, the books to be checked-out of the library are placed on the deck of the station. The corresponding application software function updates the circulation database and the theft detection system into the smart label is deactivated. All this happens automatically when staff is in the process of replacing the existing book by another book being checked-out by the same borrower. A receipt is printed out confirming details of borrowed material and due date.

5.4. ATM Book drop

The books returned by the borrower are put on the deck of the station. The corresponding application software function would calculate the late fine, if any, and would update the circulation database. Simultaneously, the theft detection system into the smart label is automatically activated. Optionally, a receipt is also printed out to confirm returning of borrowed material. Books can be placed on deck station one by one without any intervention by staff.

5.5. Renewal

The books to be renewed are put on the deck of station. The corresponding application software function would check the validity of renewal and accordingly update the circulation database. A receipt is printed out confirming renewal of book and new due date.

5.6. Tag Monitoring

The status of theft detection system into the tag of any book can be found out by placing the same on the deck of the station. Further, the theft detection system can either be activated or deactivated on the Tag. This process is called arming and disarming of books.

5.7. Sorting

When book is put on the deck, RFID Application software flashes collection and shelf no. which facilitates shelving of items. While sorting the checked-in books, the same provides additional information such as item belonging to other location or if it is a reserved item, etc.

5.8. Electronic Security Gate:

The security gates are used to trace any item that has not been checked-out either by staff station or self check-out station. As when the item is issued the electronic security system is activated and the item is being traced by this security gates similarly as and when the item is received by the check in station the security system is deactivated .

5.9. USER Borrowing Station (Touch screen enabled)

This is a self-service station where the books are checked out of the library independently by the borrower using touch screen without any intervention of library staff. It is an interactive station, which prompts the patron to enter his/her library card (either bar coded or smart card as per the configuration of the station). The status of each book as checked-out is automatically updated on the circulation database. The theft detection system of the tag for that book is de-activated to enable smooth passage from the security gate. A receipt is issued to the patron confirming details of borrowed books along with due date.

5.10. Electronic Book Drop:

As books are returned through the Book Drop facility located suitability in a library, the RFID Labels are automatically read and the RFID application software will immediately update both patron record and library database. The theft detection system into the smart labels is simultaneously activated. This enable patrons to drop the book for check-in to library at their own convenience without entering the library since the book drop is placed at the entrance.

6. ADVANTAGES OF RFID

6.1. Rapid charging/discharging:

The use of RFID reduces the amount of time required to perform circulation operations. The most significant time savings are attributable to the facts that information can be read from RFID tags much faster than from barcodes and that several items in a stack can be read at the same time. While initially unreliable, the anti-collision algorithm that allows an entire stack to be charged or discharged now appears to be working well.

The other time savings realized by circulation staff are modest unless the RFID tags replace both the EM security strips or RF tags of older theft detection systems and the barcodes of the automated library system—i.e., the system is a comprehensive RFID system that combines RFID security and the tracking of materials throughout the library; or it is a hybrid system that uses EM for security and RFID for tracking, but handles both simultaneously with a single piece of equipment. [3M has developed readers that can do both concurrently except for videotapes and audiotapes. These have to be desensitized and sensitized in a separate operation]. In either case, there can be as much as a 50 percent increase in throughput. The time savings are less for charging than for discharging because the time required for charging usually is extended by social interaction with patrons.

RFID security and the tracking of materials throughout the library; or it is a hybrid system that uses EM for security and RFID for tracking, but handles both simultaneously with a single piece of equipment. [3M has developed readers that can do both concurrently except for videotapes and audiotapes. These have to be desensitized and sensitized in a separate operation]. In either case, there can be as much as a 50 percent increase in throughput. The time savings are less for charging than for discharging because the time required for charging usually is extended by social interaction with patrons.

6.2. Simplified patron self-charging/discharging

For patrons using self-charging, there is a marked improvement because they do not have to carefully place materials within a designated template and they can charge several items at the same time. Patron self-discharging shifts that work from staff to patrons. Staff is relieved further when readers are installed in bookdrops.

6.3. High reliability

The readers are highly reliable. Several vendors of RFID library systems claim an almost 100 percent detection rate using RFID tags. Anecdotal evidence suggests that is the case whenever a reader is within 12 to 14 inches of the tags, but there appears to be no statistical data to support the claims.

There are fewer false alarms than with older technologies once an RFID system is properly tuned. The libraries contacted that have experience with both EM and RFID security systems, report a 50 to 75 percent reduction.

Some RFID systems have an interface between the exit sensors and the circulation system to identify the items moving out of the library. Were a patron to run out of the library and not be intercepted, the library would at least know what had been stolen. If the patron card also has an RFID tag, the library will also be able to determine who removed the items without properly charging them. However, the author has not been able to identify a library that has implemented this security feature.

Other RFID systems encode the circulation status on the RFID tag. This is done by designating a bit as the "theft" bit and turning it off at time of charge and on at time of discharge. If the material that has not been properly charged is taken past the exit sensors, an immediate alarm is triggered. Another option is to use both the "theft" bit and the online interface to an automated library system, the first to signal an immediate alarm and the second to identify what has been taken.

6.4. High-speed inventorying

A unique advantage of RFID systems is their ability to scan books on the shelves without tipping them out or removing them. A hand-held inventory reader can be moved rapidly across a shelf of books to read all of the unique identification information. Using wireless technology, it is possible not only to update the inventory, but also to identify items which are out of proper order.

6.5. Automated materials handling

Application of RFID technology is automated materials handling. This includes conveyor and sorting systems that can move library materials and sort them by category into separate bins or onto separate carts. This significantly reduces the amount of staff time required to ready materials for reshelving. Given the high cost of the equipment, this application has not been widely used. There were approximately 40 systems in use in North America as of the first quarter of 2004.

6.6. Long tag life

Finally, RFID tags last longer than barcodes because nothing comes into contact with them. Most RFID vendors claim a minimum of 100,000 transactions before a tag may need to be replaced.

6.7. User Friendly

* Light weight
* And allows easy reading of high and low shelves
* Saves time and resources:
* Implementers indicate a 75% reduction inhuman resources required for shelf management activities.

7. KEY BENEFITS

To Librarians:

- Speeds up book check-in / check-out
- Frees staff to better service patrons
- Better space planning
- Increases membership rate

To Patrons

* Easy to use: books can be read in any orientation
* Reduces queuing time
* Provides patron privacy
* Encourages patrons to come back
* The ability to return books during off hours
* Loans for the returned items will be instantaneously cancelled so that patron may immediately borrow again.
* Librarians are able to allocate more time to customer service, as they are free from the labor-intensive loan cancellation activity associated with bar-code system
* Display the return status and printing receipt
* The design of the Book Drops is such that items cannot be retrieved back once deposited.

8. COST INVOLVED

Even though the cost involved is much higher, as the technology is in the initial stages of implementation, taking in to account the benefits it offers, it is advisable to go in for this advancement. Experts predict that the cost is bound to come down shortly, with the growing competition of the vendors.

9. CHALLENGES

The Libraries and Librarians globally as well as locally are facing various challenges due to the implementation of ICT , unprecedented growing in printed and electronic resource, recent trends and developments in teaching learning process. Librarians need to face various LIS IT for providing efficient, effective and personalized value added services and products to the stakeholders. Some of the major challenges faced by librarians are listed below

* Expanding Electronic Information Environment
* Development of Information Infrastructure
* Need for web based Service
* Resource Generation
* Diversified User's Information Thrust
* Explosive growth of Information
* Resource Sharing and Collaboration
* Industrial Interaction
* Need for Quality based Services
* Marketing of Library and Information Products
* Standardization
* E-Collections Building
* Digital Rights Management
* Digital Preservation
* Security in Digital Libraries

CONCLUSION

RFID Technology promises to change our world. It has the capability of making our personal lives and our professional lives more convenient. This technology is exiting in our society for years. It has played a significant role in bringing patron satisfaction, convenience and efficiency in various segment including in libraries. Librarians as Information managers are the leaders in protecting & managing the intellectual freedom and user privacy and it needs to have some responsive and strong determination in implementing this technology.

REFERENCES

1. Napier, Emma(2004). RFID in the livestock industry. Smart Labels Analyst, August 2004. Retrieved August 20, 2004, from http://www.idtechex.com/documents/printview.asp?documentid=195
2. Harris, Ron (2003) SF Library wants to track books with computer chips, Associated Press, Retrieved October 03. 2003, from http://usatoday.com/tech/news/internetprivacy/2003-10-03-sf-library-RFID x.htm
3. Collins, Jonathan (2004). Microsoft pilots RFID. RFID Journal. Retrieved September 02, 2004, from http:// www.RFIDjournal .com/article/articleview/774/1/1/
4. Weinstein, Ron(2005). RFID: A Technical Overview and its Application to the Enterprise. New Technology May I June 200, from http://www.computer.org/join/grades/grades.htm
5. Dr. Harish Chandra (2006) RFID Enhances Digital Library Security and Value Added Library Services: An Implementation Experience, NCIMDiL.
6. Fenkenzeller, Klaus RFID hand Book, edn-2
7. Nirupama Bulusu and Sanjay Jha. Wireless Sensor Network : a system perspective
8. http://www.rfidjournallive.com
9. http://www.rfidtoday.blogspot.com
10. http://www.rfidnews.org/
11. http://www.wam.umd.edu/~sbarraga/RFIDLearn.html
12. http://www.ala.org/ala/pla/plapubs/technotes/rfidtechnology.htm
13. http://www.cenlib.iitm.ac.in
14. http: // http://www.libsys.co.in/lsmart.html
15. http://www.tutorial-reports.com/wireless/rfid/security.php
16. http://www.google.com/image

21
Digital Library

M. Purushothama Gowda

ABSTRACT

This paper introduces the digital library, provides the meaning and definitions, process, key elements distinguish features, advantages and challenges, preservation of digital library materials etc The digital library has the information in electronic form and the electronic media facilitates the access of information available in the digital form at different places. Digital libraries offers new levels of access to broader audiences of users and new opportunities for the library and information field to advance both theory and practice. They contain information collections predominantly in digital or electronic form electronic publications have some special problems of management as compared to printed documents the include infrastructure, acceptability access restrictions, readability, standardization, authentication, preservation, copyright, user interface etc. But still the advantages are more and therefore, the importance of digital libraries has been recognized widely both in the developed and developing countries as well

INTRODUCTION

The term Digital Libraries is the result of information proliferation and technological advances. The revolution in the

Information Technology has changed the basic concept of library, where the print and paper media are the main parts. Digital library is the electronic library in which the access storage and dissemination of information in the digitized form.

Digital images are electronic snapshots taken of a scene or scanned from documents, such as photographs, manuscripts, printed texts, and artwork. The digital image is sampled and mapped as a grid of dots or picture elements (pixels). Each pixel is assigned a tonal value (black, white, shades of gray or color), which is represented in binary code (zeros and ones). The binary digits ("bits") for each pixel are stored in a sequence by a computer and often reduced to a mathematical representation (compressed). The bits are then interpreted and read by the computer to produce an analog version for display or printing.

Digital library is a logical extension of the networked environment and the development triggered thereof and provide the users with coherent access to a very rare, organized repository of information and knowledge. In a sense it is a global virtual library. The library of thousands of networked electronic libraries/databases

WHAT IS DIGITAL LIBRARY?

A digital library is a collection of digital objects that is stored and accessed electronically. The information stored in the library should have a topic common to all the data. For example, a digital library can be designed for computer graphics, operating systems, or networks. The term "Digital Library" has a variety of potential meanings, ranging from a digitized collection of material that one might find in a traditional library through to the collection of all digital information along with the services that make that information useful to all possible users.

The really important point is that a digital library has material stored in a computer system in a form that allows it to be manipulated and delivered in ways that the conventional version of the material cannot be. Digital Libraries are a means to systematically collect, store, and organize information and knowledge in digital form.

DEFINING DIGITAL LIBRARY

The term "digital library" escapes precise definition, often being used interchangeably with "virtual library," or "electronic library". Digital library is an evolving area of research, development and application. Researcher in this area have offered multiple definitions.

In ODLIS (Online Dictionary of Library and Information Science) digital library has been defined as "A library in which a significant proportion of the resources are available in Machine-Readable format, as opposed to print or microform" [1]

Edward Fox has defined the digital library as " the new way of carrying out the functions of libraries encompassing new types of information resources, new approach to acquisition , new methods of storage and preservation , new approaches to classification and cataloguing, intensive use of electronic systems and networks and dramatic shifts in intellectual , organizational and electronic process" [2]

ELEMENTS OF DIGITAL LIBRARY

Donald J. Waters of the US Association of Research Libraries (ARL) identified five elements common to all definitions of the digital library, in 1995

* The digital library is not a single entity
* The digital library requires technology to link the resources
* Linkage between digital libraries and information services are transparent to users
* Universal access to digital libraries is a goal
* Digital library collections are not restricted to document surrogates but include digital artifacts that have no printed equivalent

DIGITIZATION PROCESS

Digitisation requires a basic process, which involve different sets of hardware and software technologies at each step. Determining the appropriate technology is directly linked to the anticipated use and purpose of the material being digitised. For digitizing the text and other material, following methods can be used;

The Basic process of digitization is fairly simple through a wide range of sophisticated techniques and tools may be used. Essentially, a digital image is composed of a grid of pixels (Picture elements) arranged according to a set of rows and columns. Each pixels, presents a very small portion of the image, and is allocated a tonal value; namely black, white or a particular color or shade of the gray. These tonal values are digitally represented in binary code (Zeros and/or ones). So a digital image is actually a grid made up of zeros and ones. The binary digits for each pixel are called bits and are stored in a sequence.

PRESERVATION

Alexander Wilson describes preservation as "The generic term for all activities intended to retain the physical artifacts in libraries or there information content both by direct treatment and by preventive preservation measures".

Some of the issues to be addressed in digital preservation include:

* *Retaining the physical reliability of the image files, accompanying metadata, scripts, and programs*
* *Ensuring continued usability of the digital image collection*
* *Maintaining collection security*

Preservation of digital resources can be possible by three ways,

* Technology preservation
* Technology emulation
* Data migration

DISTINGUISHING FEATURES OF DIGITAL LIBRARIES

* Geographically distributed digital information collection
* Geographically distributed users
* Digital content (audio, video, graphics ,animation, etc.) will gradually increase and content in printed form will increase
* Digital library is not single entity
* Resources of many libraries linked together through appropriate technology and these linkages are transparent to end users

* Supported by specialized staff. Jobs, training and recruitment will be re-profiled
* Seamless access to the users
* Large and diverse collections

OBJECTIVES OF THE DIGITAL LIBRARIES

* to collect ,store, organize and retrieve digital information
* to provide effective and efficient digital information services
* to minimize massive storage and space problem in libraries
* to share the networked information
* to save the time of the library staff as well as users
* to perform various library activities economically
* to contribute to the life long learning opportunities to all people
* to strengthen communication and collaboration between and among the research, business, government and educational communities
* to encourage cooperative efforts which cover the considerable investment in resources, computing , communication and network
* ultimately to satisfy the users requirements

THE BENEFITS OF DIGITIZATION

* immediate access to high demand and frequently used items
* easier access to individual components within items (e.g. articles within journals)
* rapid access to materials held remotely
* the ability to reinstate out of print materials
* the potential to display materials that are in accessible formats, for instance, large volume or maps
* 'virtual reunification 'allowing dispersed collections to be brought together
* the ability to enhance digital images in terms of size, sharpness, colour contrast , noise reduction etc.
* the potential to display to conserve fragile/precious

originals while presenting surrogates in more accessible forms

* the potential for integration into teaching materials
* enhanced search ability , including full text
* integration of different media (images, sounds video etc.)
* the ability to satisfy requests for surrogates (photocopies, photographic prints, slides etc.)
* reducing the burden or cost of delivery
* the potential for presenting a critical mass of materials

THE DIGITAL LIBRARY CHALLENGES

* technological obsolescence will affect the longevity of digital information
* media fragility
* hardware and software compatibility
* periodic transfer of digital material from one hardware/ software configuration to another,
* Legal and organizational issues
* Problems of formats.
* Problem related to security aspects.

THE DIGITAL LIBRARY: OPPORTUNITIES

* The digital library allows access to information to its users as and when they need it from anywhere in the world
* The digital library facilitates improved access to information to providing various sophisticated search and retrieval facilities
* The digital library facilitates for information sharing among users through notification, file sharing and cooperative document preparation.
* The digital library help the users to get the up-to-date information because the time lag is reduced with the help of the web and digital publishing and quick inclusion of digital information in the digital library's collection
* The digital library breaks the barriers of the time, space, language and culture.

* The digital library facilitate improved collaboration among users which was profound impact on the scholarly information life cycle- the process by which researcher and scholars create, use and disseminate information.
* The digital library reduces the gape between nations and people in terms of infrastructure, facilities and resources. Thus, it reduces the digital divide.

CONCLUSION

The digital system intends to provide a new format to library and information services, the professionals must aware of about the its components to accept the challenges within the limitations of the system. The digital library should have the professional skills and knowledge in new environment to meet the diverse needs of the clientele. The issues of digital library, such as scientific, technological, methodological, economic technology are rapidly changing. Development of digital library is the new opportunity to meet the new and diversified challenges of the user community.

REFERENCES

ACM Digital Library: http://www.acm.org/dl/

Arms,W: Digital libraries. Cambridge: MIT Press *Association of Research Libraries*: http://arl.cni.org/

Deegan (Marilyn) and Tanner (Simon): Digital futures: strategies for the information age. Library Association Publishing, London, 2002.

Digital library standards and practices: http://www.diglib.org/standards.htm

Digital Resources from Library of Congress: http://www.loc.gov/loc/ndlf/digital.html

Dlib Magazine: http://www.dlib.org

DSpace: open source Digital Library (DL) system: http://www.dspace.org/

Ganesha: the first web-based digital library software in Indonesia http://gdl.itb.ac.id/

Fox (Edward). Digital Library Source Book (URL: http://vax.wcsu.edu/library/odlis.html)

Fox, E. A.: digital libraries initiatives projects1994-1999. Bulletin of the American society for information science. 26(1): 7-11

Griffin, S. M.: digital libraries initiatives-phase 2:fiscal year1999 awards<http://www.dlib.org/dlibjuly1999/07griffin.html>

ODLIS. Online Dictionary of Library and Information Science.(URL: http://www.dlib.org

Griffin, S. M.: digital libraries initiatives-phase 2:fiscal year1999 awardshttp://www.dlib.org/dlibjuly1999/07griffin.html

Rusbride,C: After eLib, Ariadne,26 , http://wwwariadane.ac.uk/issue26/chris/intro.html>

Greenstone Digital Library: http://www.greenstone.org/english/home.html (Visited 30/10/2003)

IEEE Computer Society Digital Library : http://www.computer.org/publications/dlib/ (Visited 30/10/2003)

Sun Microsystems Digital Library Toolkit: http://www.sun.com/products-n-solutions/edu/libraries/digitaltoolkit.html (Visited 30/10/2003)

WITTEN (IAN H) and BAINBRIDGW (DAVID): How to build a digital library. Morgan Kaufman Publishing, San Francisco, 2003.

22

High-Speed Network Model for HiTech Libraries

Atul M. Gonsai

ABSTRACT

Ever increasing information in digital form and bandwidth-intensive library applications require libraries to build high speed and performance networks that enable the use of the new models for building applications and their implementations. High-speed Ethernet networks are suitable options for large number of users to access voluminous information in a greater variety of ways as well as in desired time frame. This paper presents model for high-speed library networks for the multimedia rich high bandwidth intensive library applications. The paper is divided in three parts describing low-level network setup, middle-level network setup and finally high-speed network setup for the library. Each setup has some functionality, pros and cons for handling and managing library resources with cost and speed elements in consideration.

INTRODUCTION

Digital libraries are fast expanding into the role of independent educational entities that aspire not only to complementing traditional classroom teaching, but also allow open electronic learning for distance and continuing education. These multifaceted roles can be realized only if the course content and the related content management system are versatile enough to be captured into any individual's learning needs. In order to accommodate the digital nature of education, a new modern profile of learning is proposed that allows modular yet efficient transfer of knowledge from the teacher to the learner.

Digital libraries similar to traditional libraries, undertake the tasks of collection, screening, packaging and archiving of educational content for easy development, discovery, delivery, use and reuse (sun micro systems 2000). Collections are developed by acquiring contents through active harvesting and soliciting authors for submissions. To realize the above different components of a digital library in the virtual medium, the hardware and software technologies need to be robust, inter-operable and scalable at all times with support of computer networking. The technologies with specialized hardware and software are used for discovery, storage and archiving of the learning material. They also include specialized databases, high-end multimedia servers (for playing video and audio), and related technologies for handling complex interactions between the learner and the library. These technologies may also include the cables and software that connect the computers in a network, the protocols and standards that help users accurately read information transmitted on the network, and specialized software, such as client-server-database programming languages. These technologies are of special interest to the administrator of the digital library.

To overcome data transfer speed problem of the traditional library network, it is desired to give solution, as high speed data network for libraries for the applications like graphics based network data transmissions and audiovisual data storage and manipulation through various client connected to the central server. This is only possible if the network supports higher bandwidth for data communications. Currently most libraries use Ethernet for their local area networks, which is limited to 10Mbps speed, and only for library campus. Generally, library data are of very high size like video data, tutorials, and large volume of journals and books in digitized form. As the demand for high-speed networks continues to grow, the need for a faster Ethernet technology is apparent.

TRADITIONAL LIBRARY NETWORK SETUP

To date, most digital library projects have focused on replicating and extending the development and delivery of a library collection. Problems associated with digitization and storage of materials, retrieval methods, and delivery of electronic documents has been addressed in various ways including library network setup and its handling. Traditional library network setup was established with Ethernet technology and fewer clients and server machines. Ethernet has become the most commonly used LAN (Local Area Network) technology worldwide. More than 85% of all installed network connections are using Ethernet technology, according to International Data Corporation (IDC, 2000). As a transport protocol, Ethernet operates at 10Mbps data transmission speed and Layers 1 and 2 of the 7-layer OSI networking model, delivering its data packets to any device connected to the network cable (Forouzan 2000).

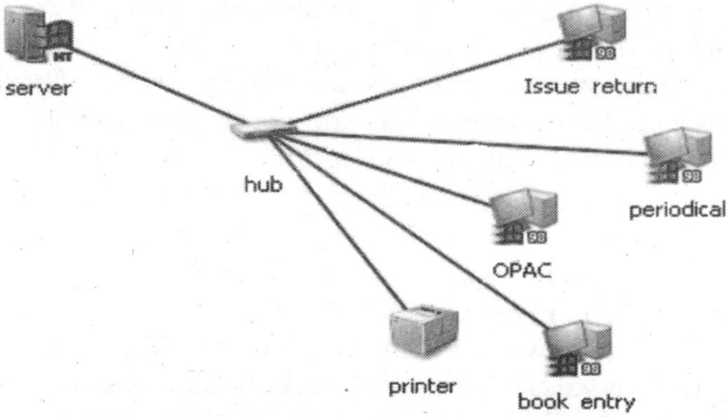

Fig. 1. Traditional library network setup with one server and four client machines

Networking infrastructure involves a number of hardware components including wiring, connectors, racks, network interface cards, client and server workstations, and communications devices such as repeaters, bridges, shared and switched hubs, and routers. It also includes software such as network card drivers, communications protocols, network operating systems and network application tools. The library network setup may include some of the mentioned networking hardware and software as shown in the figure-1.

The most libraries have networks with at least one server and four to five client desktop machines connected together with 10 Mbps Network Interface cards. The server is the main machine with Windows-NT or any other server operating system software installed on it to run library specific applications like SOUL (Software for University Libraries) or any other library management software. While client machine is nothing but each and every time requesting data and information from centrally located server. In short clients are end user desktop.

The data transmission in network setup as shown in figure-1 takes place with Ethernet 10Mbps. Standard Ethernet uses a technology known as Carrier Sense Multiple Access / Collision Detection (CMSA/CD)(Walrand, Varaiya 2000). This is a rather chaotic method of communication sometimes referred to as "Listen before you send". What this means is that when a workstation wishes to send a packet of data, it listens to the network to see if it is busy. If not, it transmits the packet. If at exactly the same time other workstations transmit a packet, a collision is detected, and all transmitting workstations wait a random period of time before trying to re-transmit (Casad New land 2000). On an extremely busy network, these collisions can happen quite often, leading to degradation in network efficiency.

The traditional network setup as shown in figure-1 there are four desktop machines and one server connected to central connectivity device called hub. In this setup server and client Network Interface Cards (NIC) are 10Mbps speed providing user access to OPAC, periodical access and simultaneous transactions like book and magazine issue and return for users. This setup has only one server, which provides library management information, database storing and retrieving, running library software for library with limited support for services.

MIDDLE LEVEL SETUP

Traditional networks operate at 10Mbps speed. At these speed libraries that use extremely large files such as transferring audiovisual contents to desktop, can experience long delays when sending such data across the network. The middle level setup uses the extended version of Ethernet called fast Ethernet, which is simply, an extension of existing Ethernet technology, running 10 times faster. It still uses CSMA/CD for data transmission and supports Ethernet traffic.

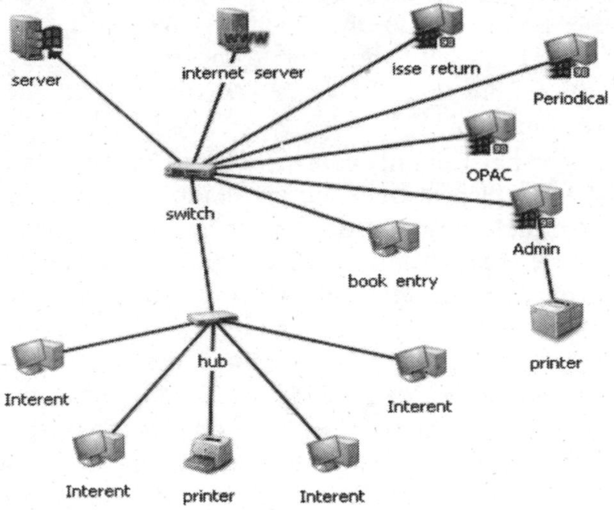

Fig. 2. Middle level network setup with two servers running NT and supporting www services.

The middle level setup for libraries is shown in figure-2. This setup model has two servers one for library applications and the other is for Internet access through remote location. These two servers provide information to switch, which is of 100Mbps. Both the server NIC are of 100Mbps, which is little, bit higher then the traditional network setup. The figure-2 shows four machines like issue return, periodical, OPAC and Admin machine are directly connected to switch with 100Mbps

NIC installed on each machines, giving total bandwidth of 100Mbps.

This middle level setup has internet and www services installed on library network with separated server which provides digital books and journals access through internet to all clients separately connected to hub, which is finally connected to switch as shown in figure-2. The Windows NT server provides user authentication and library management services to the various clients connected to it.

DATA TRANSFER RATE ON SCALABLE NETWORK SETUP – COMPARATIVE LOOK

The table-1 compares the capabilities of typical network configurations in transferring various types of digital media. The transfer rates listed assume the theoretical maximum speed of the various types of Ethernet networks which is shown in traditional model, middle level setup and finally high speed model shown at the end of the paper for library networks. In actual practice, all networks often function below these values.

Table 1. Transfer of Digital Media over Networks

				Network Transfer Rate			
				Ethernet	Fast Ethernet	Gigabit Ethernet	
				10 Mbps	100 Mbps	1000 Mbps	
Media	**Amount**	**Bytes**	**Bits**	**MEDIA TRANSFER RATE**			**Unit**
Text	1 character	1	8	1,250,000	12,500,000	125,000,000	Characters /sec
	1 page (2000 characters)	2,000	16,000	625	6,250	62,500	Pages/sec
Graphics	1 complex line drawing	25,000	200,000	50	500	5000	Graphics/sec
	Bitmap 640x480, 16 million colors	921,600	7,372,800	1.36	14	136	Graphics/sec
Audio	1 sec. music grade audio (sampled 44,100 times/sec. 16 bits/sample, 2 channels)	176,400	1,411,200	7	71	709	*
Video	1 sec. VCR-quality video (640x480 pixels 30 frames/sec. 16 million colors)	6,591,800	52,734,400	0.19	1.90	18.96	*

Audio/Video:

* 1 means network exceeds speed required for instant real-time replay
* 1 means network cannot transmit data fast enough for instant real-time replay

HIGH SPEED NETWORKS - NEED FOR DIGITAL LIBRARY

Backbones & Switch Stacks

A typical network is analogous to the plumbing in house, where many smaller pipes connect to fewer medium sizes pipe, which in turn connect to one large pipe accessing the local water supply. By the same token, if many desktop clients all need to access a server through the same pipe, that pipe should be large enough to carry several times the bandwidth of a desktop clients. Likewise the network backbone must be large enough to support many workgroups or segments (Intel 2003).

With rapid growth of the Internet technologies and applications, and the centralized data center model that developed along with the Internet, more network traffic began to travel across the subnet or workgroup. High-speed network provides a "large pipe" to alleviate congestion in network.

Greater Demand on Servers

Many LANs (Local Area Network) have server network speed bottlenecks due to the addition of new servers to the network and the increased use of applications such as data ware house, data mining, database query, storing and moving audios and videos etc. Today's sever can process larger files and move data faster then ever before, but the network and its server connections must support this performance. Pressure on server performance also comes from ever-increasing desktop speed. The number of PCs are migrating to 100 Mbps speed, so server and network must go for higher speed performance to satisfy desktop needs.

Desktop Revolution

Demand for faster PCs continues to grow as it has in the past. Not long ago if desktop connections and PC processing power were considered more than adequate if the user could simultaneously open MS Word & Excel. Now a days user need and applications use editing video while downloading photographs or exchanging graphics design while talking on Internet phone line.

As application grew more bandwidth the view that 10MBps network was not adequate to suit the desktop & need to change the high-speed network with high bandwidth.

Data Transfer

As shown in table 1 10MBps Ethernet networks are not suitable for transferring VCR Quality Video. To enable emerging desktop centric applications & technologies such as streaming video, mp3 audio & digital image processing & modeling High-speed network is required.

HIGH SPEED NETWORK MODEL

Traditional and middle level setup model operates at 10/100Mbps speed, while high speed network operates at gigabit 1000Mbps speed. Easy and straightforward migration to higher performance level without disruption, low cost of ownership including purchase and support cost and flexibility in network design are prime criteria for the high speed network model. This model is 100 times faster than regular 10 Mbps Ethernet and 10 times faster than 100Mbps fast Ethernet.

The high-speed model as shown in figure-3 shows the server farm to switch connection is of 1000Mbps gigabit Ethernet. This also employs the same CSMA/CD protocol, same frame format and same frame size as its predecessors like 100Mbps fast Ethernet. This model setup has three main server connected to central switch with 1000Mbps gigabit data transmission speed. All three-server has gigabit Ethernet card Installed. The high speed network switch has 1000Mbps network link and distributes network traffic to four hub segments like Internet services, digital content reading room, audiovisual learning and finally library management. Out of four hub segments three are working at 100Mbps speed with 100Mbps fast Ethernet cards installed on each desktop machines. The hub connection has also 100Mbps link support.

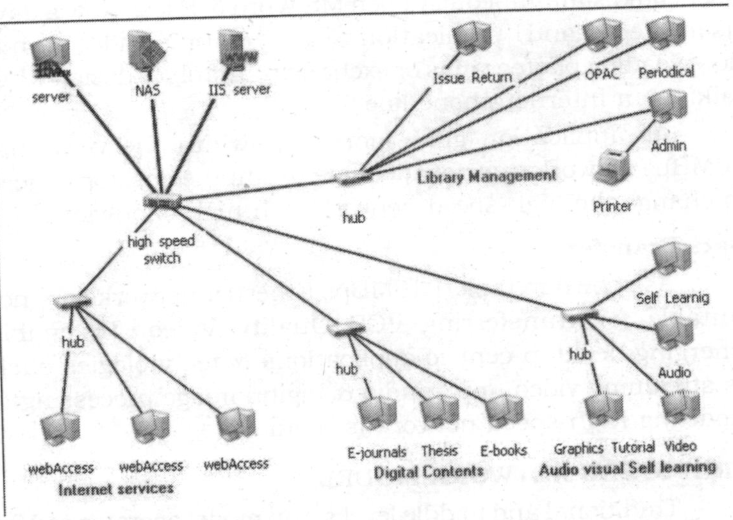

Fig. 3. High speed library network model with three servers and one high speed layer-2 switch supporting four subnets

The fourth segment named audiovisual self-learning as shown in figure-3 needs more than 100Mbps because the data transmission is of high-end audio and video graphics files. Transferring this high bandwidth intensive file on the shared Ethernet makes network busy or low so that this segment must of 1000Mbps.

This high-speed network segment provides simultaneous access to all the clients with streaming audio and video without any hustle form network speed. The high-speed performance is possible because the traffic is segmented. The figure-3 shows library management, user authentication etc. services from windows-NT sever while NAS (Network Attached Storage) server provides database, digital books, thesis, journals audio and video learning material storage (IT professional 2000). The NAS server has very large capacity storage with 1000Mpbs gigabit card installed on it. This server provides automatic storing and transfer of data on network with supporting domain server. IIS server provides Internet access and web services of any other digital library from Internet.

MIGRATING TO HIGH SPEED NETWORKS

A major issue for network administrators is how to get higher bandwidth without disrupting their existing networks. The fact that gigabit Ethernet has the same form, fit and functionality as its 10Mbps and 100Mbps Ethernet, allowing a simple and straightforward migration to high-speed networking. Library segments with unusually heavy bandwidth requirements are the first to be considered for gigabit Ethernet. As per high-speed network model the prime candidates are three servers and audiovisual self-learning room segments. The remaining segment should be of 100Mbps speed for all its desktop machines.

As bandwidth requirements increase for mainstream applications, high-speed connections become more widely deployed. In a common scenario the shift to higher speeds might occur in several phases.

CONCLUSION

A Digital Library service is an assemblage of digital computing, storage and communication machinery together with the software needed to reproduce, emulate and extend the services provided by the conventional libraries. The analysis of depicted models indicates that scalability in the increasing processing capabilities of digital computing of workstations and servers providing services to the clients, larger and larger storage needs and effective management of storage and increasing requirements of network bandwidth and high speed data transfer are the prime issues to the scientists of information technologies. The cost effective solutions are emerging as cluster servers, workstations with high speed processing and data transmission, NAS, SAN (Storage Area Networks), Gigabit Ethernet networks, and VPNs (Virtual Private Networks) are expected to satisfy the communication requirements. The race of networking and internetworking has to emerge as grid-computing infrastructure with high-speed communication technology and fabric attached storage a grid like structure of storage system will be the suitable infrastructure to cater services to a good bit of satisfaction for a longer duration.

REFERENCES

1. Forouzan (2000) 'Data communications and Networking', New Delhi :Tata McGraw-Hill Co. Ltd. Pp 43-57
2. Walrand, V. (2000) 'High-performance communication networks', San Francisco:morgan Kaufmann Publishers, inc. Pp 114-122.
3. Casad, New land (2000) 'MCSE Training Guide Networking Essential', USA: Senior Editors New Riders Publishing Pp 164-170
4. IT professional (2000) 'Microsoft Encyclopedia of Networking', India: Prentice Hall of India Pp 873-875.
5. Sun Micro Systems (2000)The Digital Library Toolkit URL<www.sun.com/products_n_solutions/edu/whitepapers/pdf/digital_library_toolkit.pdf >
6. International Data Corporation (2000) **'The new Ethernet'** URL www.intel.com/network/ethernet/ethernet_r03.pdf (12 November 2002)
7. Intel (2003) Gigabit Ethernet Technology and Solutions URL www.intel.com /../ gigabit_ethernet Technology and Solutions.pdf (21June 2003)

23

Creating Digital Document Archives with Winisis & Genisisweb Software

K Rajasekharan

K M Nafala

1. WINISIS: THE WINDOWS VERSION OF CDS/ISIS

Winisis is a software developed by UNESCO. It is a simple, menu-driven and generalized information storage and retrieval software. The software is designed specifically for creating and managing textual databases. Winisis has capability to create any number of databases with completely different data elements. Winisis application can be used by anyone having a reasonable computer experience.

COMPONENTS OF WINISIS DATABASE

Winisis database comprises of a set of records and each record contains a set of fields. A field in a record is a container of data elements. Winisis database has a *master file* containing all the records of the database. An *inverted file* functions as an index to the *master file* for faster access to any record.

In order to create a Winisis database with any chosen field, you need to define the following components.

Field Definition Table (FDT) : The FDT defines the fields such as Author, Title, Publisher etc. of the records in the database and their characteristics. FDT determines the nature of data entry worksheet.

Data Entry Worksheet(s) : The worksheet is the screen layout used to create and/or update the records of the database. Winisis provides a specially designed editor to create the worksheet.

Print Format (PFT) : The PFT is the format for display or printing of records.

Field Selection Table(s) (FST) : FST defines fields that can be searched in the database. Search is made possible by creating an inverted file of terms indexed from the fields chosen for search.

2. MODE OF INSTALLING WINISIS

Double Click on the **Wisis1.5.exe** to start its installation.

Fig. 1

Then you will get the first screen in the installation process as follows: -

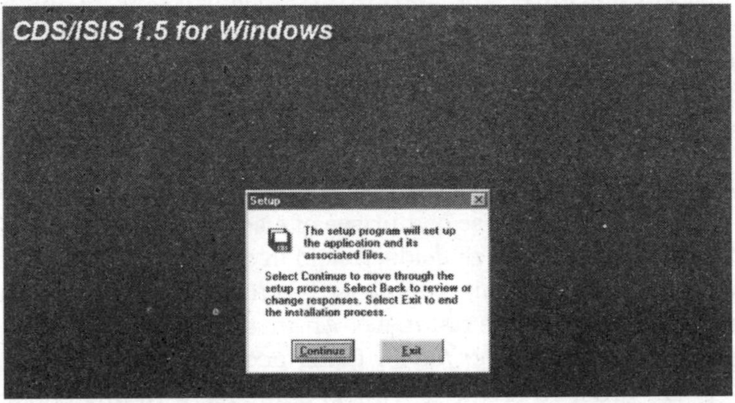

Fig. 2

Click on the **Continue** button and you will get the following window

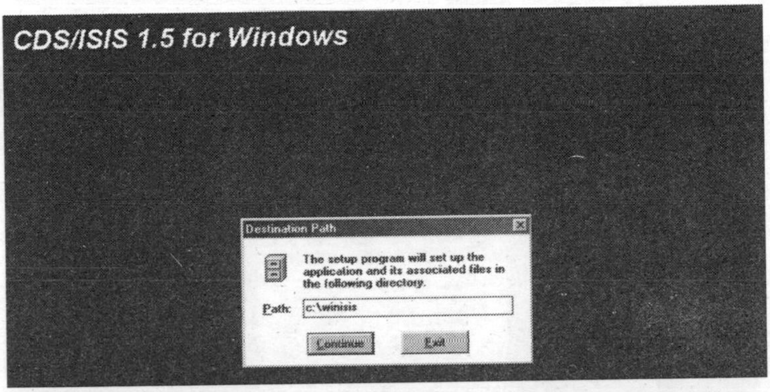

Fig. 3

Click on the **Continue** button.

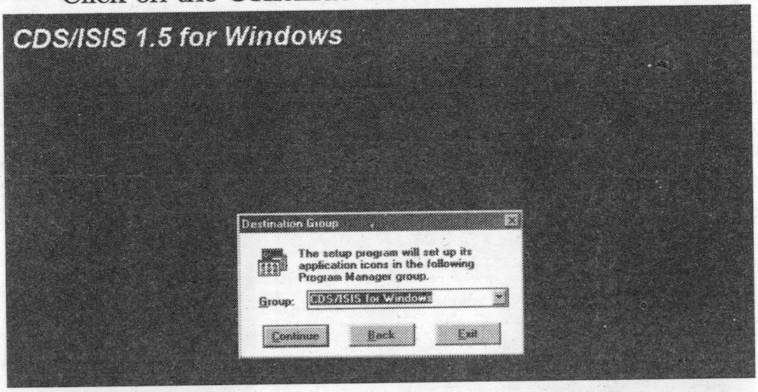

Fig. 4

Click on the **Continue** button

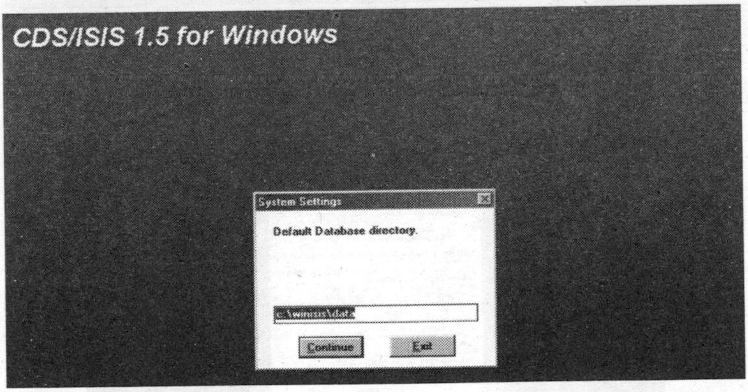

Fig. 5

Click on the **Continue** button

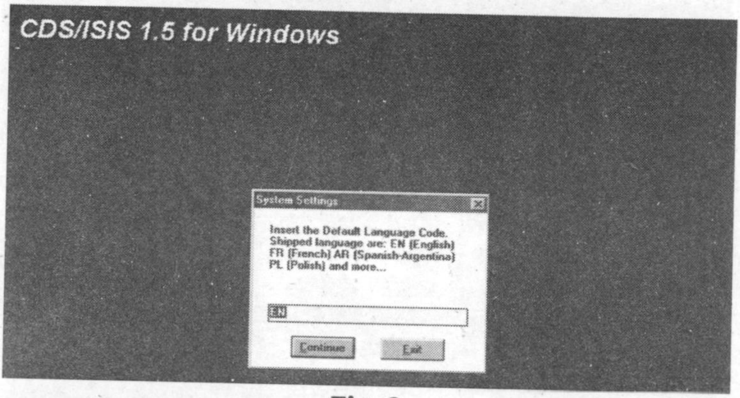

Fig. 6

Click on the **Continue** button

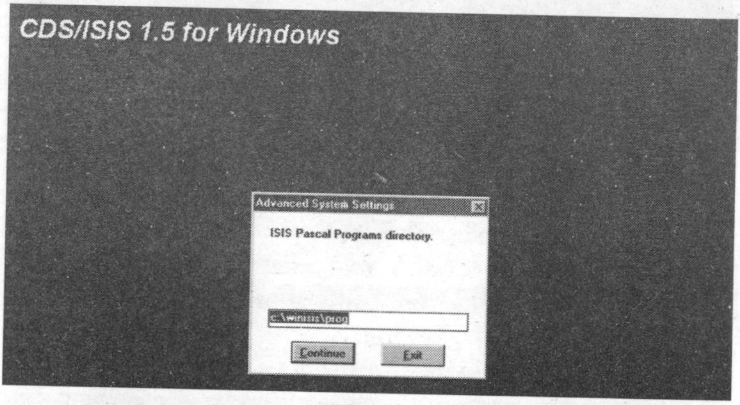

Fig. 7

Click on the **Continue** button

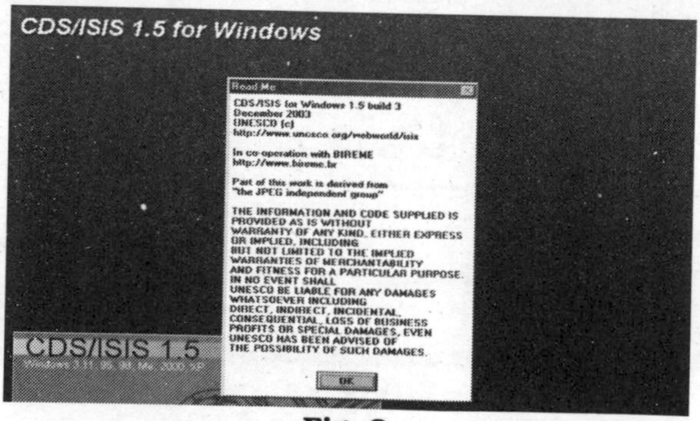

Fig. 8

Click the **OK** button and you will be notified the successful installation of the programme.

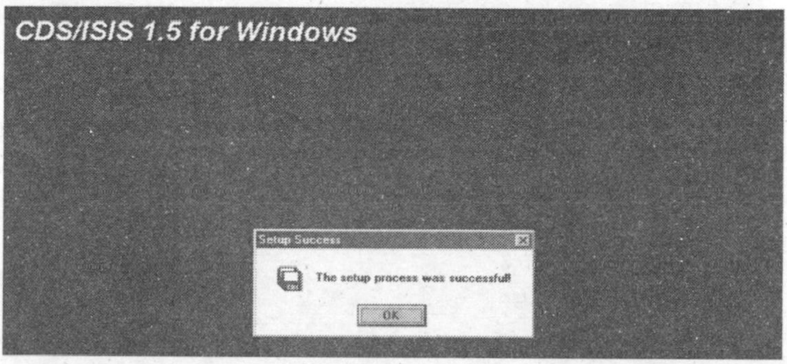

Fig. 9

Click the **OK** button to finalise the installation.

The next step is the creation of database

CREATING THE DATABASE

A **database** is a set of records or pieces of information about entities such as books, journals, articles or conference proceedings. A record is made up of a number of *fields*. Each field contains data about particular facts like author, title, keyword etc.

HOW TO CREATE THE DATABASE OF DIGITAL COLLECTION OF DOCUMENTS, USING WINISIS?

In order to create an archive of digital documents, you need to collect a few full text documents and place them in a folder in your computer. Create a database of the above digital documents in Winisis. Thc database can have any number of fields. But our sample database will have the following tags and fields for convenience.

10 Author

20 Title

30 Keywords

40 Fulltext

(*It is advisable to use an international standard, such as MARC21 or Common Communication Format for Bibliographical Description (CCF/B) for the purpose*)

Creation of database by using Winisis is very easy and automatic.

For creation of database, open the Winisis programme by clicking **CDS_for Windows** under **Start/Program.** Then you will get the following screen: -

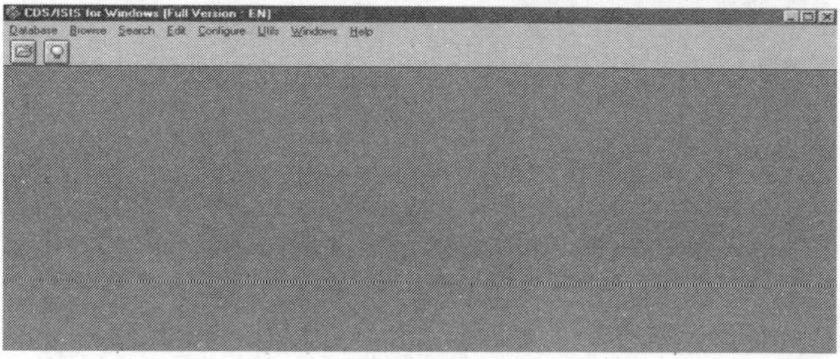

Fig. 10

Click on the **Database** drop down menu and select **New** as follows: -

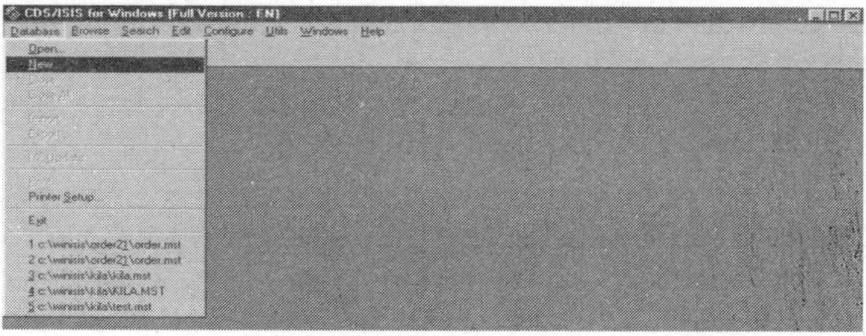

Fig. 11

Now you will be lead to the following screen: -

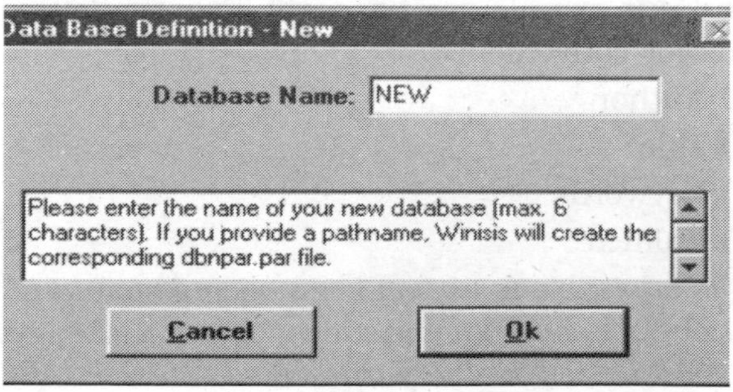

Fig. 12

Give a database name such as **NEW** and click on the **Ok** button. Then you will get the following screen: -

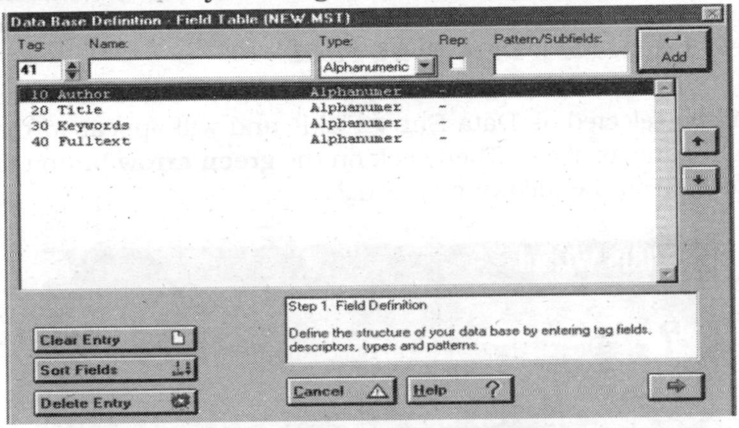

Fig. 13. Field Definition Table

You need to provide the **Tag number** (10, 20, etc) and **Field name** (Author, Title etc) of your choice in the *Name box*. Beginners may choose Alphanumeric under *Type*. Click the check box under *Rep* for multiple occurrence of the field. *Pattern/Subfields* can be ignored, if you are not dividing the field into subfields. Click the **Add** button every time on completion of each entry.

On entering the tag numbers and the name of *fields*, click the **arrow button** at the right bottom corner to move on to the next screen.

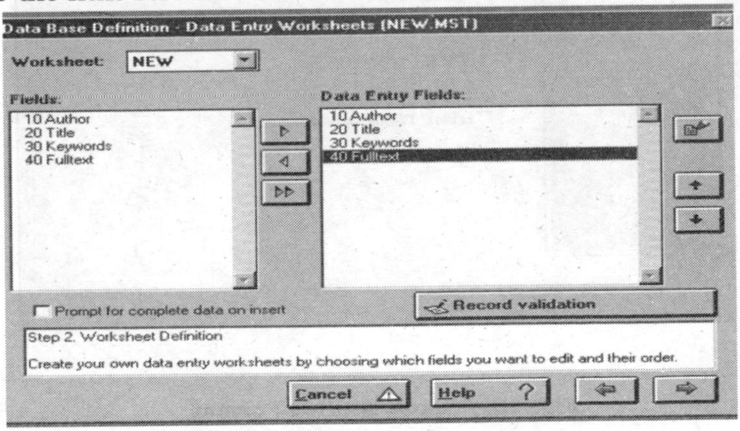

Fig. 14. Data Entry Worksheet

In the above screen, highlight the fields (in the left pane), which you want to include as the ***Data Entry Field*** and click on the **side arrow button** in the middle so as to get the field included as a ***Data Entry Field***.

If you click on the double arrow button above, all fields will be selected as Data Entry Fields and will appear in the right pane as above. Then click on the **green arrow** button to move on to the following screen.

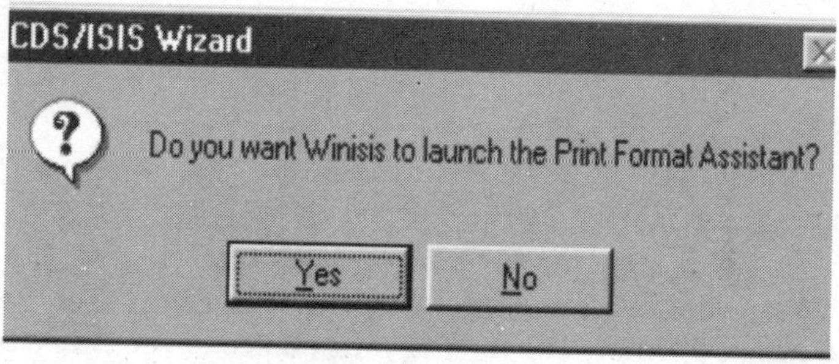

Fig. 15

Click **Yes** to launch the wizard Print Format Assistant

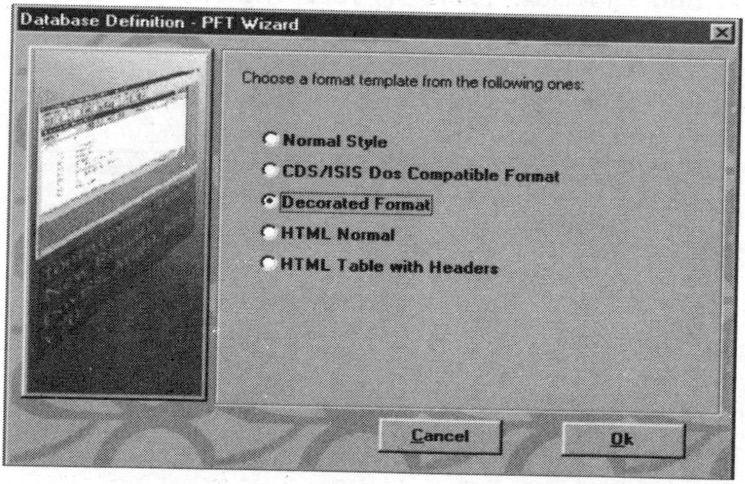

Fig. 16. Choose a Print Format

Select the appropriate print format and click **Ok** button to get the print format screen as in Fig 17.

Decorated format is the preferable choice for the beginners.

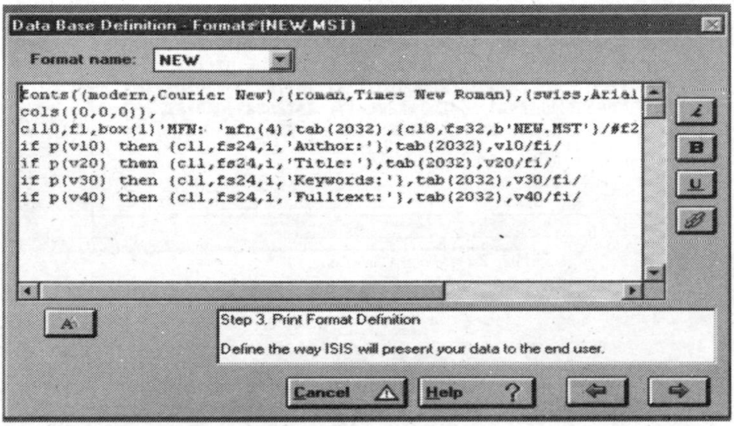

Fig. 17. Print Format

In the print format shown above, you need to add the following format line in order to appear a hypertext link with the words **Click here.** The hyperlink will be cross-linked to the full text document, if the full path of the document is provided in the **tag 40 Full text**

Link (('Click here'), 'OPENFILE ', v40)

Ensure to *provide a space between the OPENFILE command and the single quote,* and the command OPENFILE should be in upper case as shown above.

The meaning of the command is that, when you click on the link **'Click here'**, the click will automatically result in opening the digital document, denoted in the field V40, in a new window.

The resultant print format would appear as in Figure 18.

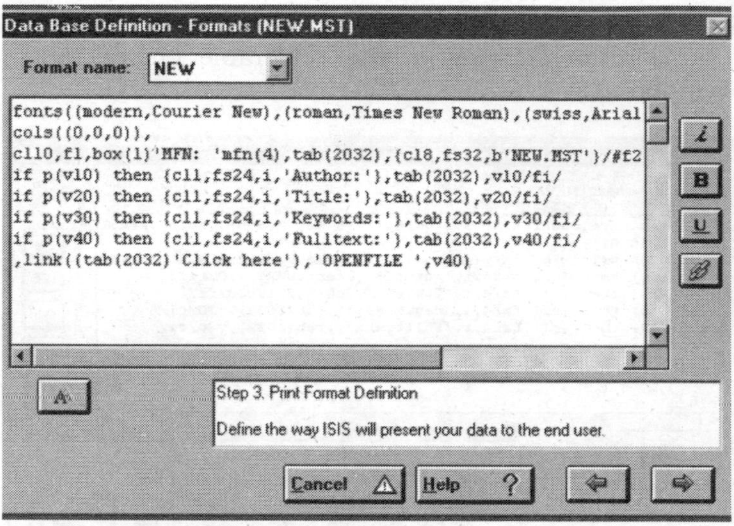

Fig. 18

Click the **Side arrow** button to move ahead and you will be asked whether to launch the Dictionary Assistant. Dictionary Assistant will help you to select the fields for indexing and the indexing technique for creation of *Inverted File Index*.

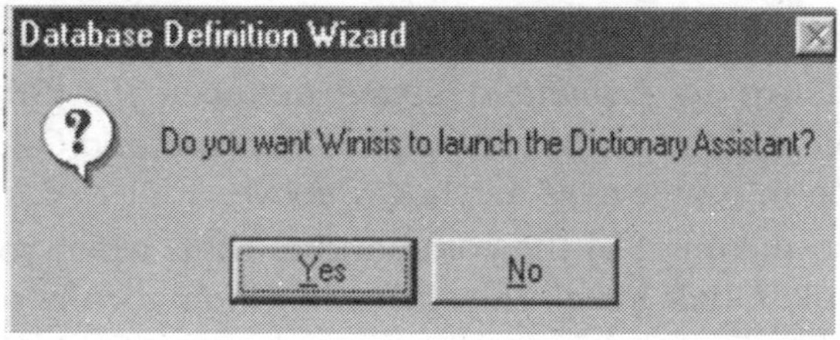

Fig. 19

Click **Yes** to launch the Dictionary Assistant.

You will then get the following screen.

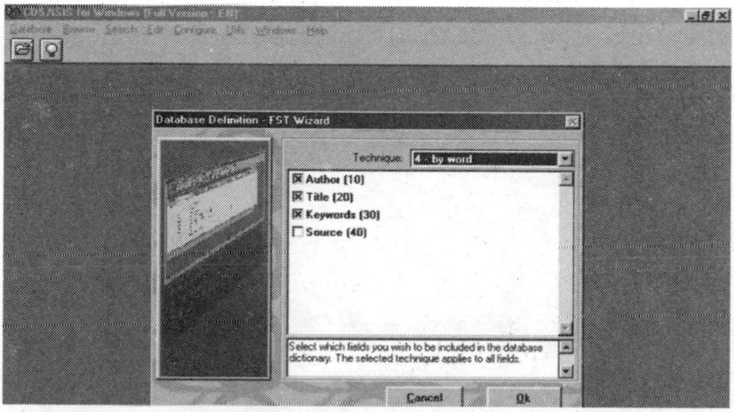

Fig. 20. Field Selection Table

Put **x** mark in the **check boxes** on the left side of the field names and select the appropriate **Technique** for indexing from the dropdown menu at the right top. The most commonly used indexing techniques are *0-by line* and *4-by word*. Select **4-by word** indexing technique in the drop down menu. Then click **Ok** to move on to the next screen.

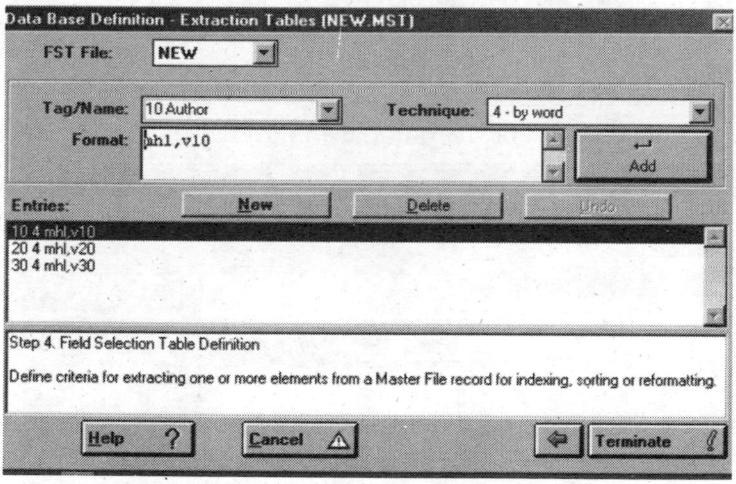

Fig. 21. Field Selection Table-Definition

Here you can change the indexing technique. If you need to correct any entry, just click on the entry in the entry box and that will appear in the edit box shown above. You can edit the text, if needed. Then click the **Terminate** button and you will get the following message.

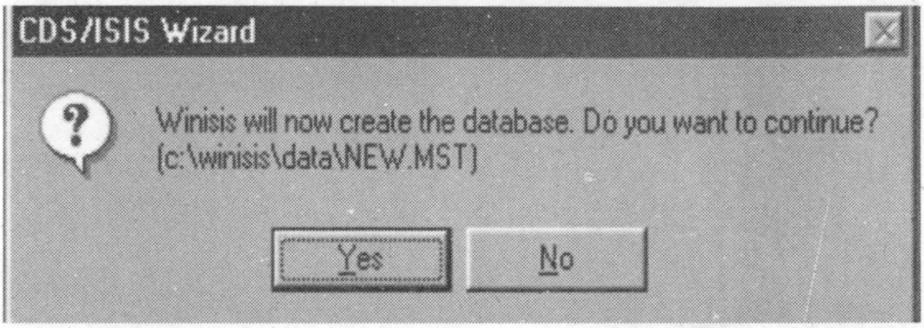

Fig. 22

Then click the **Yes** button for confirmation and you will be notified that the database has been created.

Fig. 23

Click the **OK** button.

Now creation of the database is over.

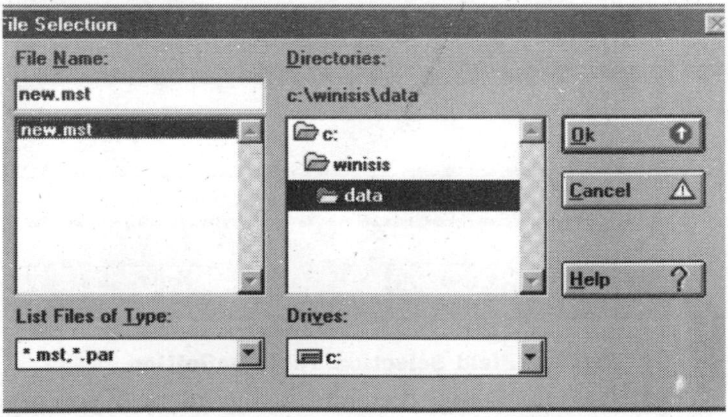

Fig. 24

Then select **.mst** file of the new database (*new.mst* in this example)

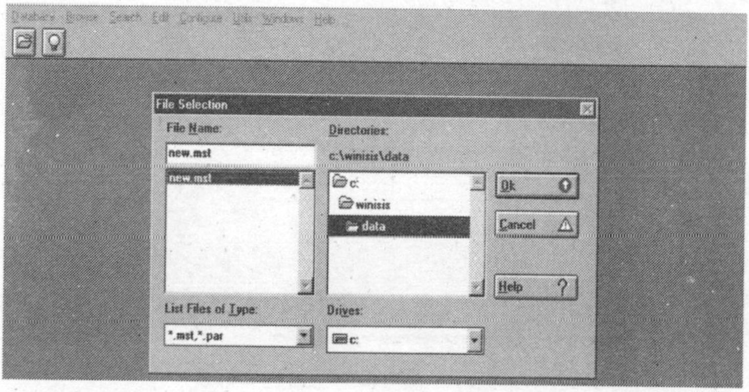

Fig. 25. Opening the Database

Click the **Ok** button to get the following screen.

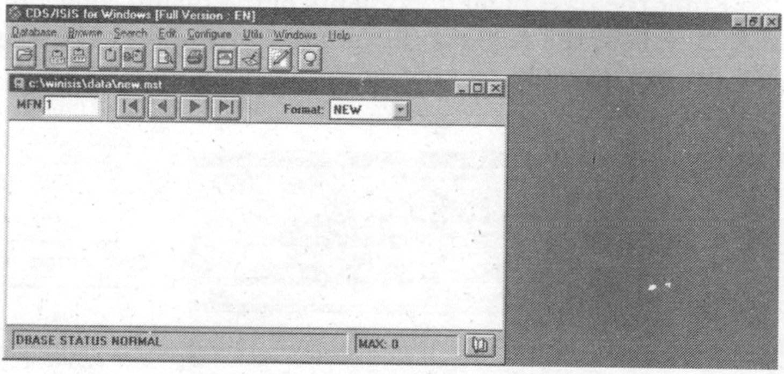

Fig. 26. Database Opened

Database definition process is over and you need to enter the data by opening the Winisis as in Fig 26 and by clicking the **Data entry** under **Edit** menu.

You will then get the following screen in Figure 27.

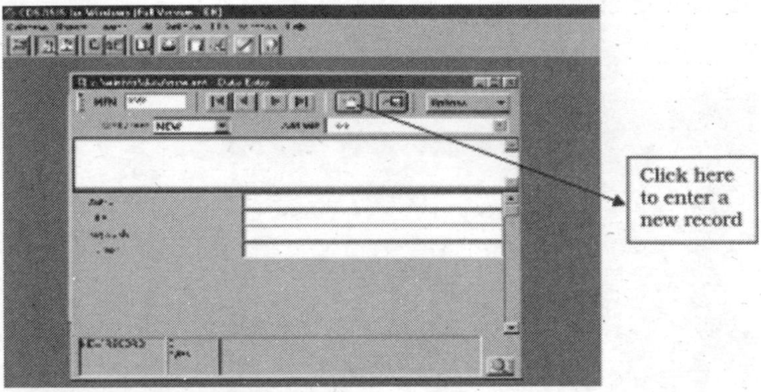

Fig. 27. Data Entry Window

Entering Data in the Database

Enter the data of all documents of the digital collection. The full path of the fulltext documents including extension (.pdf, .doc etc.) should be entered in the **Fulltext** field.

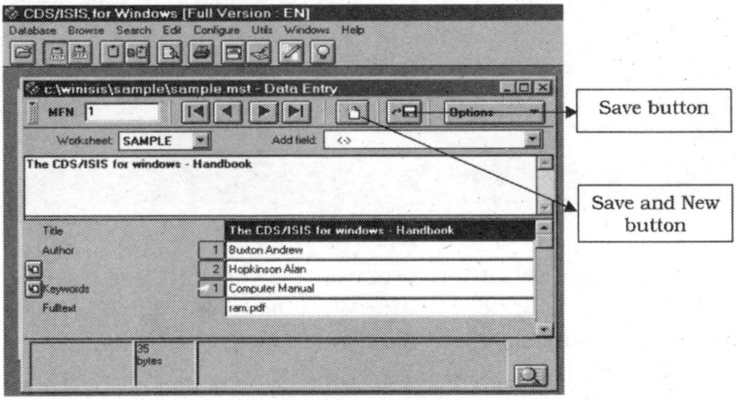

Fig. 28

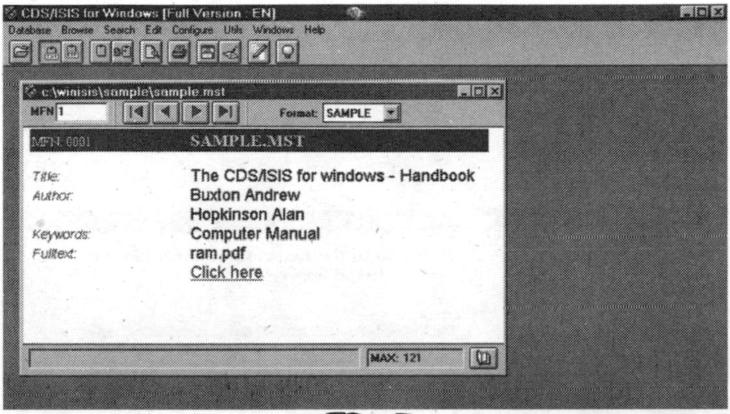

Fig. 29

(If you provide the full path of the documents in the 40 Fulltext field and place the documents in the location mentioned in the field, a click on the link will open the document automatically. The hyperlink with the words 'Click here' serve no purpose in the above case as filename alone is provided. But the link is provided to make the concept clear).

The database creation is over and you can pass on to the phase of creation of web front end.

3. INSTALLATION OF APACHE WEBSERVER

If you want the remote users in your network to access the database stored in your computer, you have to make your computer node a webserver, with a webserver software.

The Winisis database can be made accessible to remote users over a computer network with GenisisWeb front-end, using Apache webserver software.

A webserver software **Apache** and **GenisisWeb** need to be installed, for the purpose.

Apache is a free software used for making any computer, a server in a client-server mode. Apache software is obtainable either from the **Digital Document Archiving Tools & Resources** cd-rom brought out by KILA or from Internet.

Installation process

Double click on the icon and installation of Apache will start

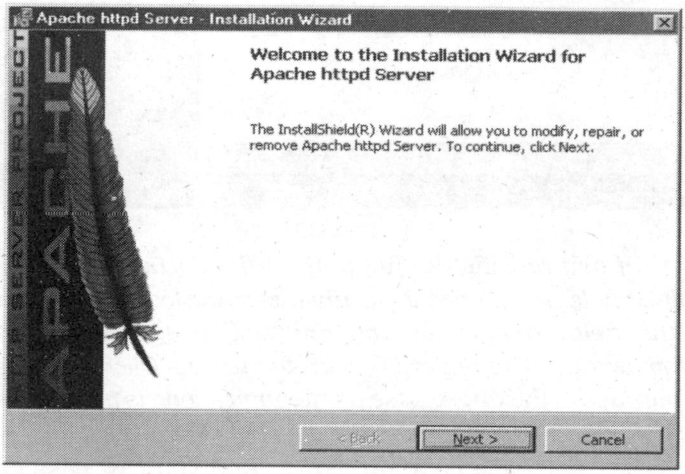

Fig. 30

Click on the **Next** button.

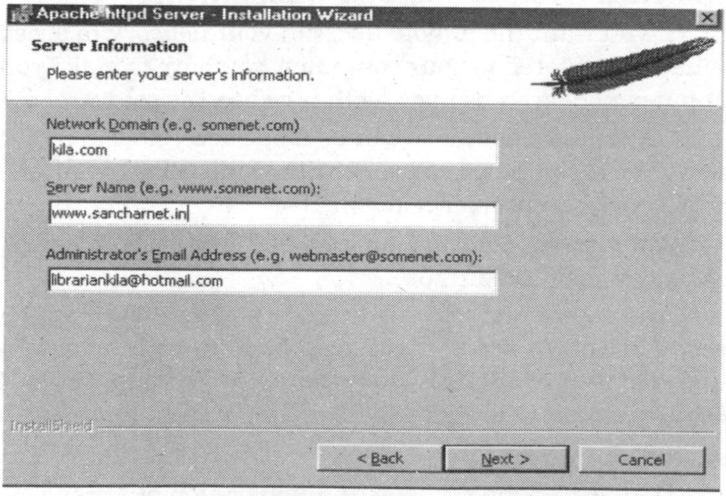

Fig. 31

Here you have to type any domain name, server name and email address. These names need not be real.

Click the **Next** button and the following screen will appear.

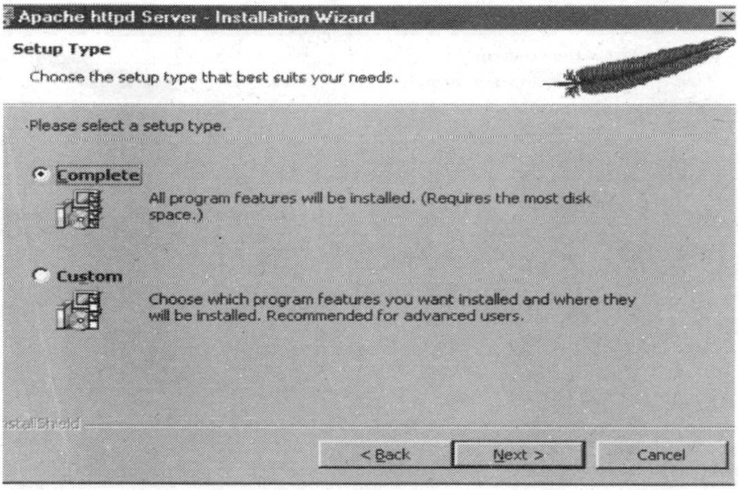

Fig. 32

Select **Complete** (to install all program features) and click the **Next** button.

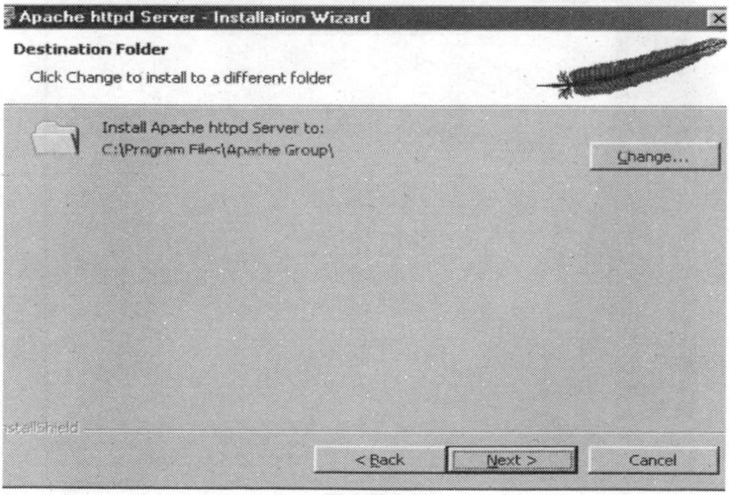

Fig. 33

Click on the **Next** button confirming the suggested path for installation, if you are using the version 1.3.17.

If you are using Apache 2.2.3 version, ensure to change the path to C:\Program Files\ApacheGroup\Apache as destination folder while installing.

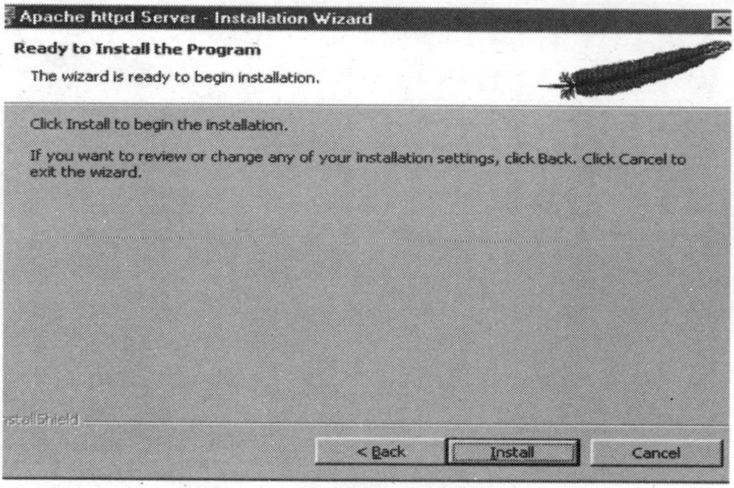

Fig. 34

Click on the **Install** button and you will get the following screen.

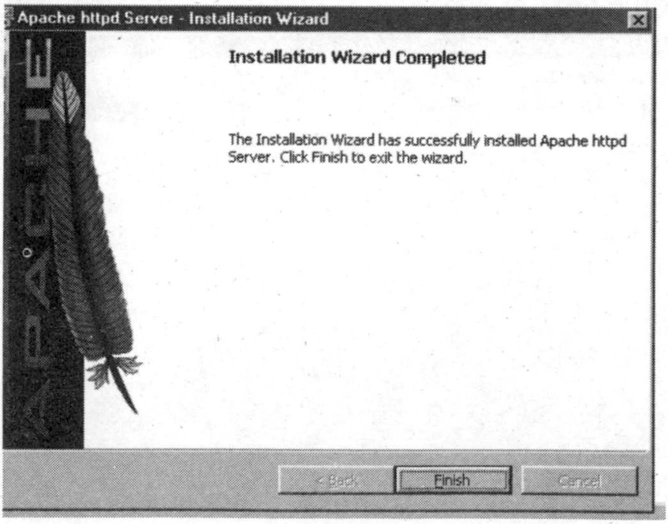

Fig. 35

Click the **Finish** button, when the installation process is completed.

Once Apache is installed, you can start installing GenisisWeb.

4. INSTALLATION OF GENISISWEB

Download the GenisisWeb program from www.scribnet.org website or Unesco website.

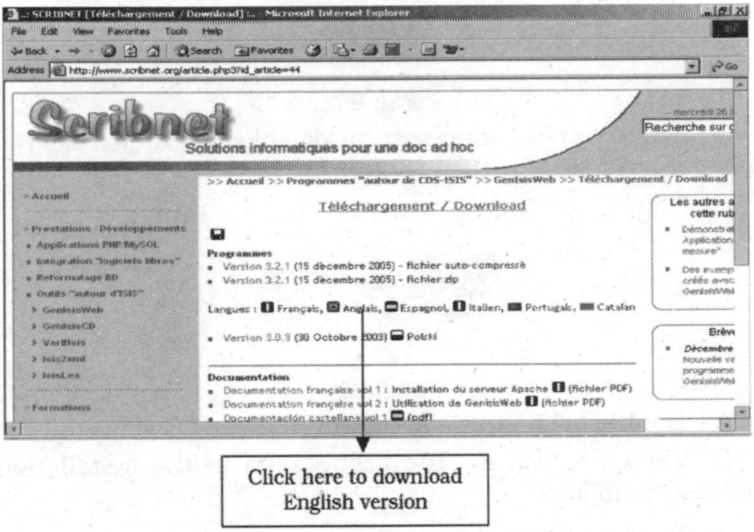

Unzip the downloaded file.

Fig. 36. GenisisWeb zip file

Double click on it and it will show the following screen suggesting a path where you want to copy the files. Give the proper path and click on the **Decompresser** button (Fig.37)

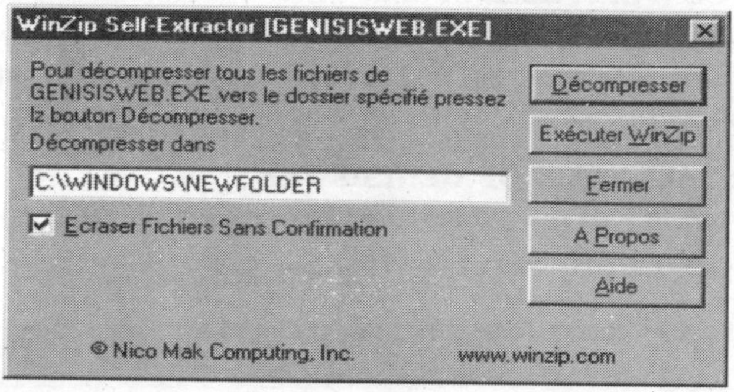

Fig. 37

When you decompresser the downloaded zipped file, you will get the following three files.

Fig. 38

Double click on the setup.exe file shown above

Then you will get the first screen in the installation process as follows: -

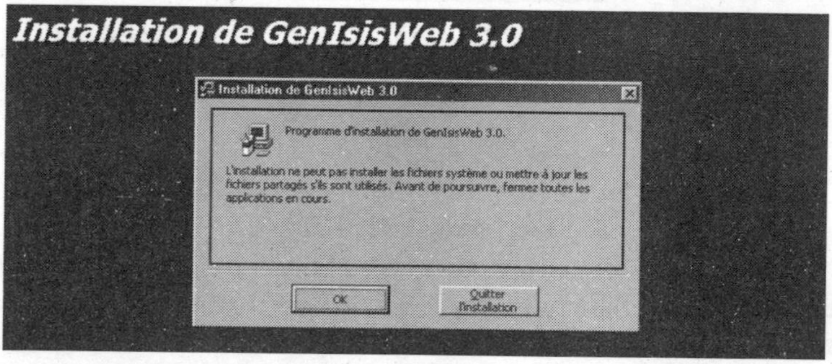

Fig. 39

Click on the **OK** button to get the following screen

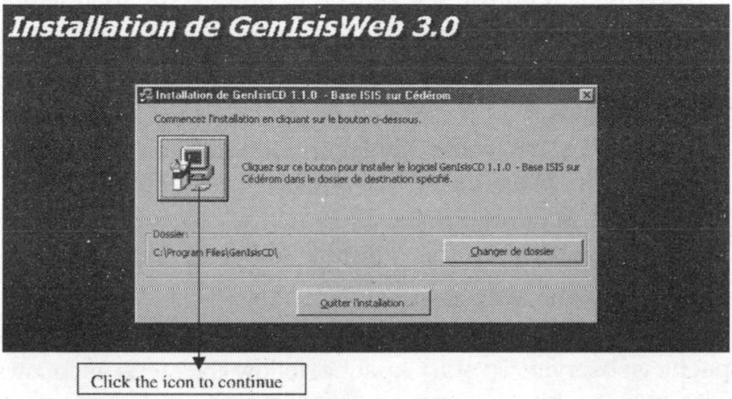

Fig. 40

Click on the **computer icon** on the left side in the above screen.

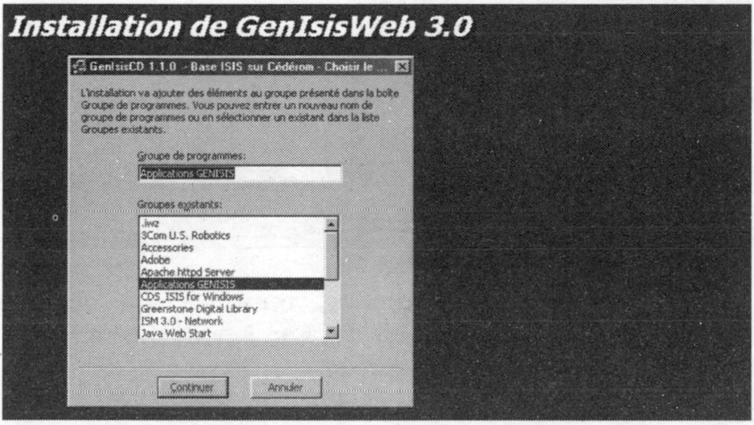

Fig. 41

Click on the **Continuer** button

Fig. 42

Then click on the **OK** button to finalize the installation.

Copy two GenisisWeb files to Apache - A Pre-requisite

Before you start the GenisisWeb for the first time, copy the following files.

1. Copy the "**wwwisis**" folder in **GenisisWeb** to "**htdocs**" folder in "**Apache**".
2. Copy the contents (all files) in the "**bireme**" folder in "**GenisisWeb**" to the "**cgi-bin**" folder in "**Apache**"

Starting Apache Web Server

Before you start GenisisWeb, you have to run the Apache webserver. To start Apache, follow the steps as follows:

Click on Start ⇒ Programs ⇒ Apache httpd Server ⇒ Configure Apache Server ⇒ Start Apache in Console

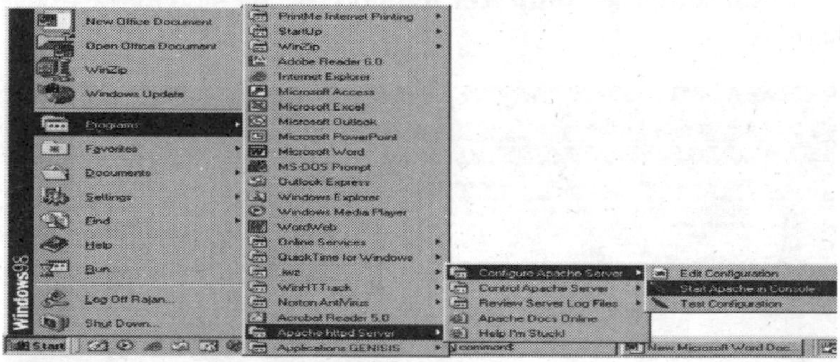

Fig. 43

When Apache starts running, you will get the following window (Fig.44). Then click on the **Esc** key in the computer or **minimize** button on the screen.

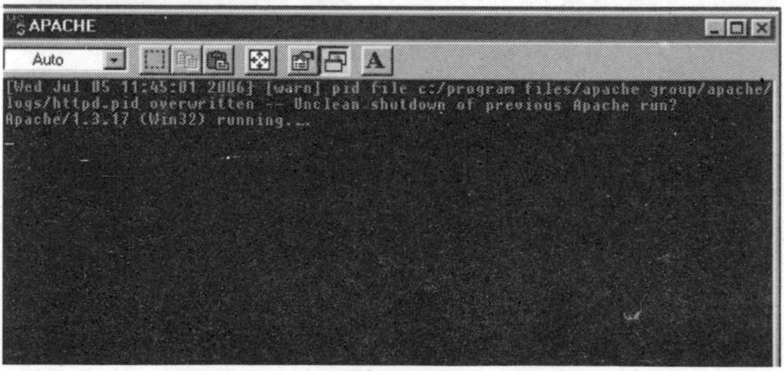

Fig. 44

You can now test to see if Apache is running properly. Open the web browser and type the address "local host" in the address bar and you should get the following screen, if Apache is running. (Fig.16)

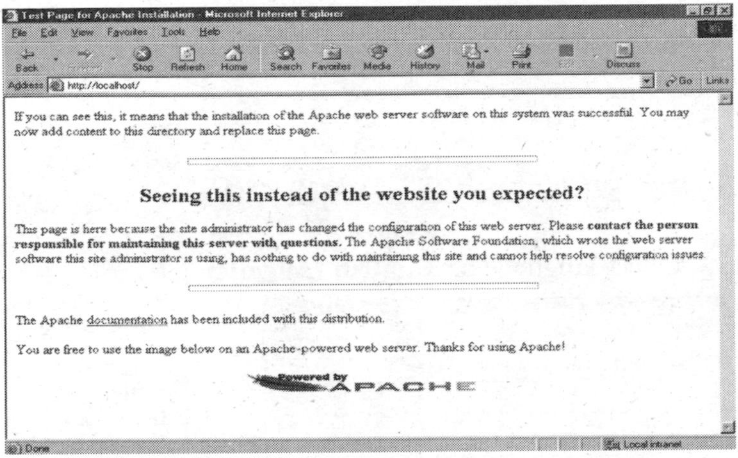

Fig. 45

You can then design your web interface for Winisis with GenisisWeb

Creating the web front-end with GenisisWeb

Starting GenisisWeb

Convert the GenisisWeb in to English version, when you run it for the first time, by following the steps shown below (Fig. 46)

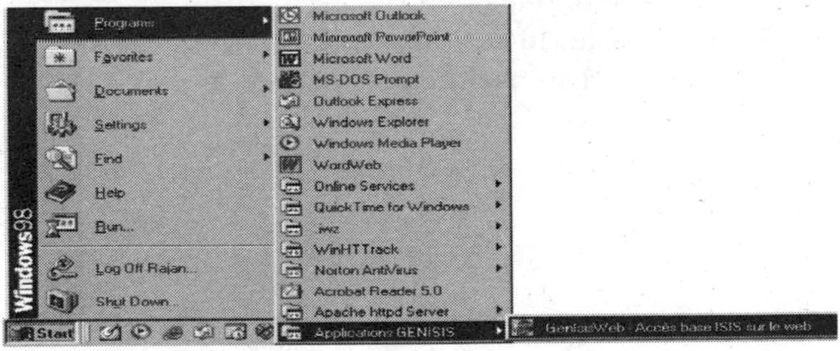

Fig. 46

You will then get the following screen (Fig.47).

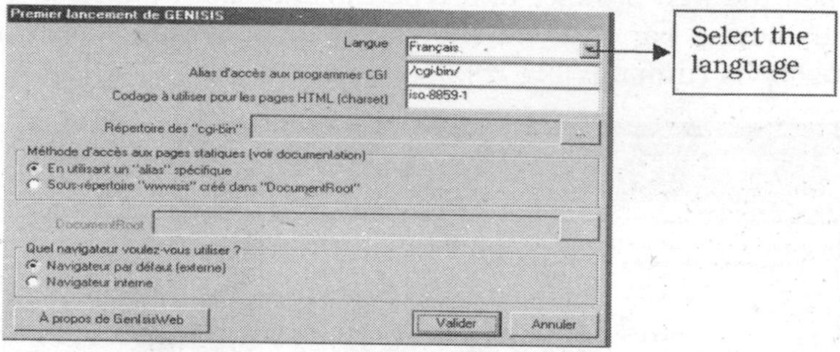

Fig. 47

Select language as **English (Angalis)**

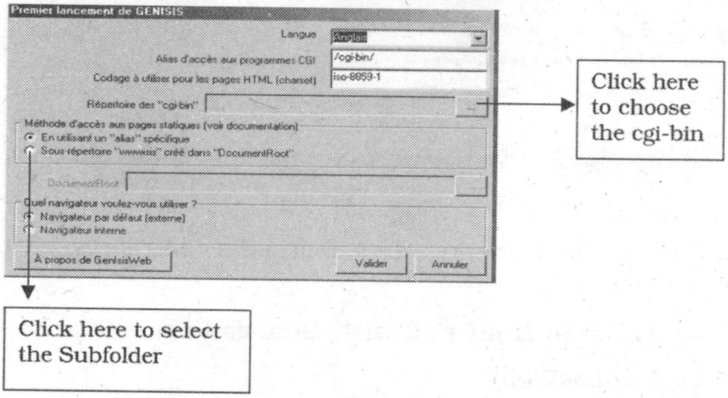

Fig. 48

Select the **Sub-folder "wwwisis" in "Document root"** and click the side button.

Then the following screen with a message in French, asking you whether to use the Apache, will appear.

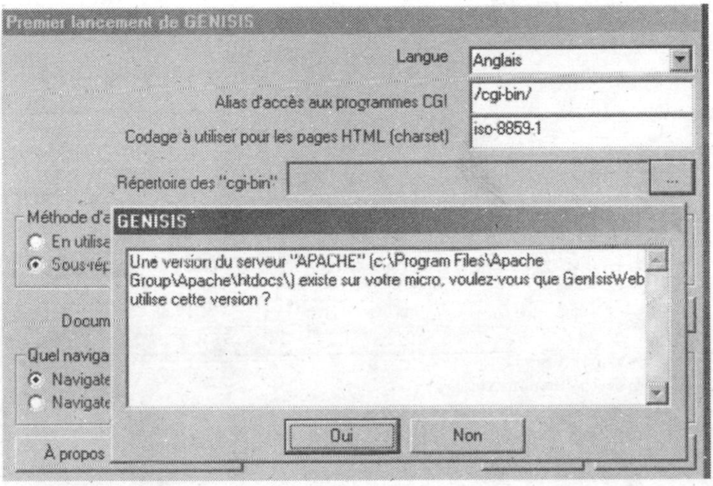

Fig. 49

Click the **Qui** button

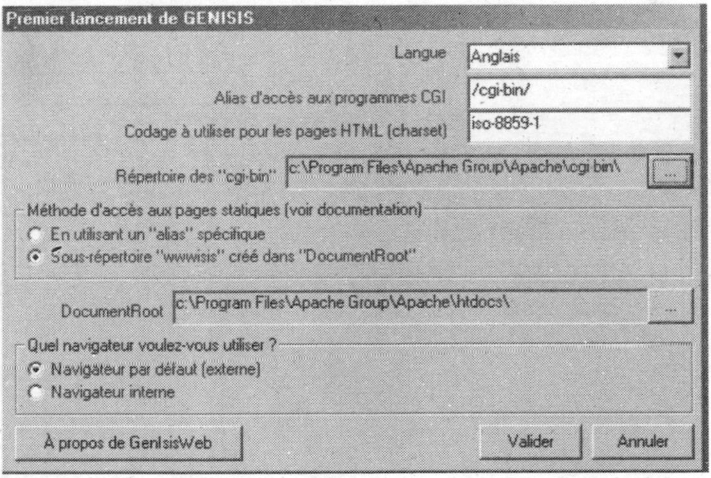

Fig. 50

Click the **Valider** button

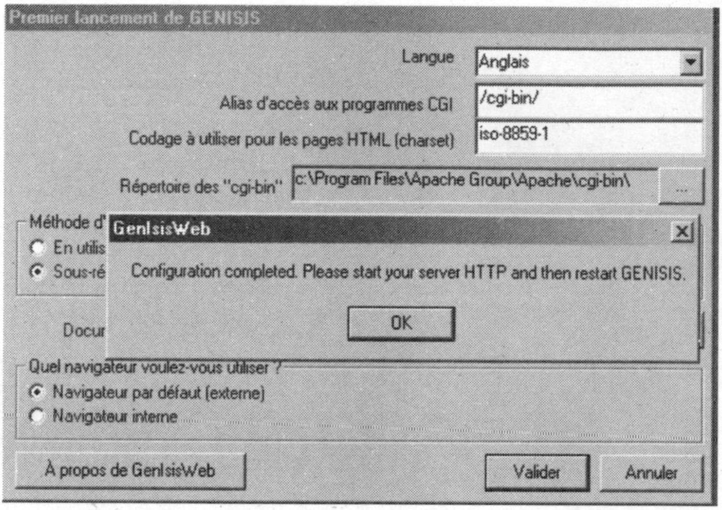

Fig. 51

Click the **Ok** button

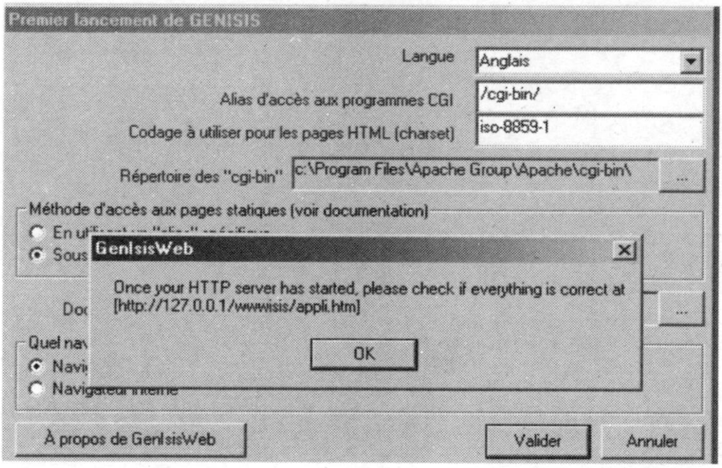

Fig. 52

Click the **Ok** button.

Check whether everything is correct as instructed in the above screen. Now you have to restart GenisisWeb as detailed in the next section.

Creating GenisisWeb application

Open GeinsisWeb by clicking on Start ⇒ Programs ⇒ Application Genisis ⇒ GenisisWeb-Access base ISIS sur le web. Then you will get the following screen (Fig. 53)

Fig. 53

Click on **Application** menu and select New (Fig. 54)

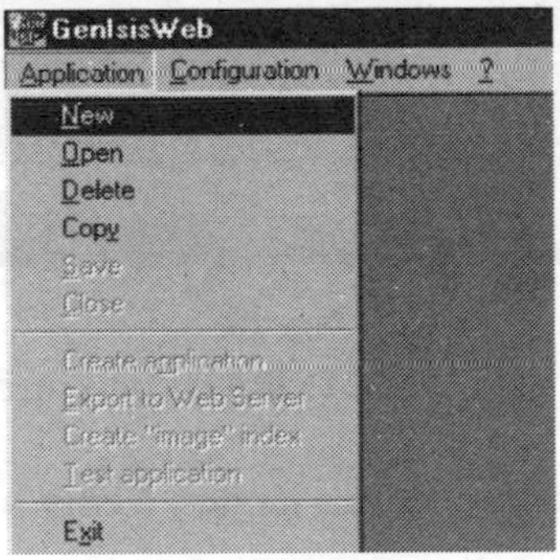

Fig. 54

Then the following screen will appear showing the names of Winisis database available in the computer.

If your Winisis data is in any other folder other than in the default folder (C:\Winisis\Data), choose the **.mst** file from that folder.

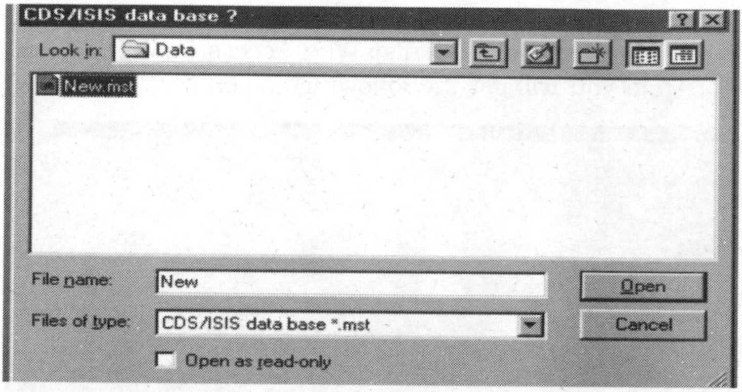

Fig. 55

When you select the database (.mst) and click the **Open** button in the above screen, you will get the following screen.

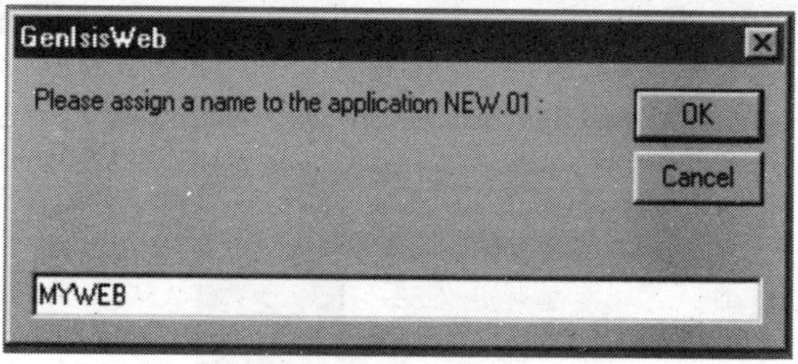

Fig. 56

Give any name like **MYWEB** for your application and click **OK**

You will get three *form design formats* as in Fig.57

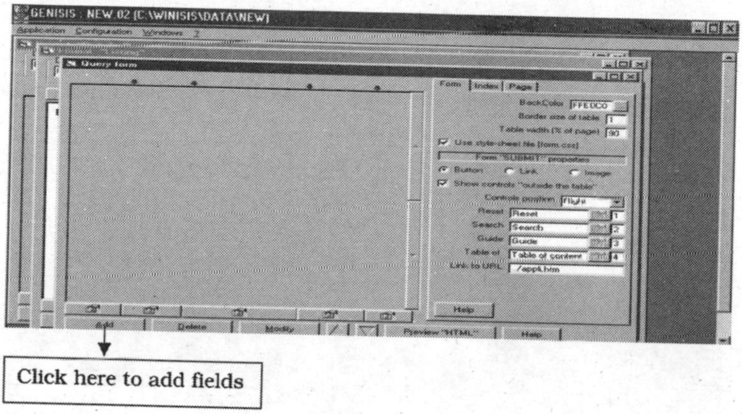

Fig. 57. Form Design Formats

The form design formats are

* Query form
* Format 'listing'
* Format 'details'

Query form : allows you to design the web like *Query Form* - a front-end form for searching the Winisis database.

Format 'listing': allows you to design an *initial display format.*

Format 'details': allows you to design a d*etailed display format.* Since detailed display format is inessential for our purpose we haven't described the creation of Format 'details'.

You have to create the search page with Query form and the display format with *Format'listing'*.

Designing the query form

To design the query form, you have to click the **Add** button in order to add fields. Click the **Add** button at the bottom of the query form and you will get the following screen:

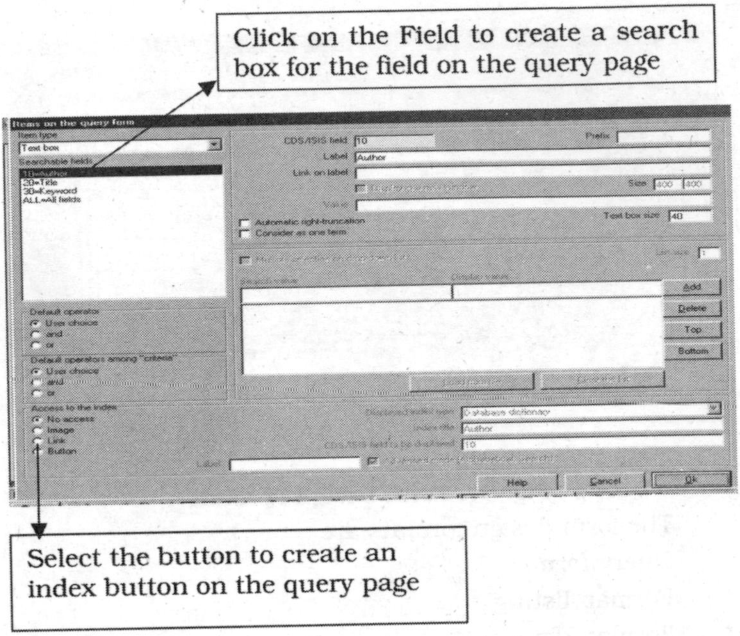

Fig. 58

In the above screen, it is preferable to select **All fields** from the left panel (as it allows search by any term in the inverted file index of the database) and then click **Ok**. This will make the query form very simple.

The items appearing on the left panel are the *fields* you had included in your Winisis database. You may select only one field at a time so as to appear that search box in the Query form and click the **Ok** button every time. If you want to select more fields, you have to click on **Add** button and select fields again and again until you put all those fields.

As well, you can select your option with regard to the search operators and the appearance of the *index button* by clicking the check boxes on the left side of the above screen. Index button would help the users to choose the indexed terms.

Now you will get the following window. The screen below shows that **All fields** alone has been chosen.

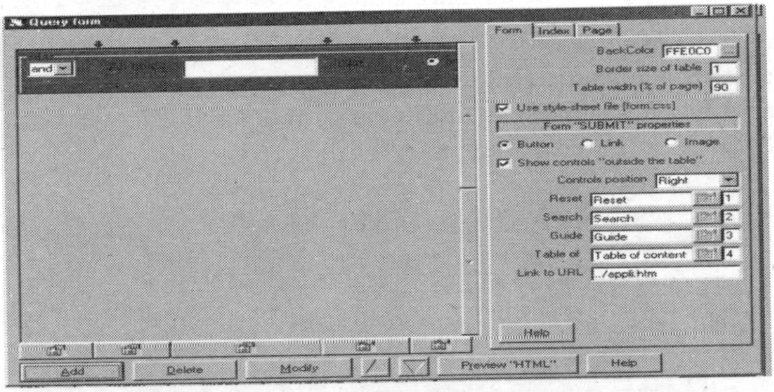

Fig. 59

Select any or all the three tabs **Form**, **Index** and **Page** appearing on the right side of the above screen for appropriately modifying the 'look' of the *Search-box area*, *Index Page* and *Display Area of query form* respectively. You can play with the options in the screen and can choose anything you prefer to have a beautiful look for your web front end. You can change background color and font parameters.

How to change the page display of the query form

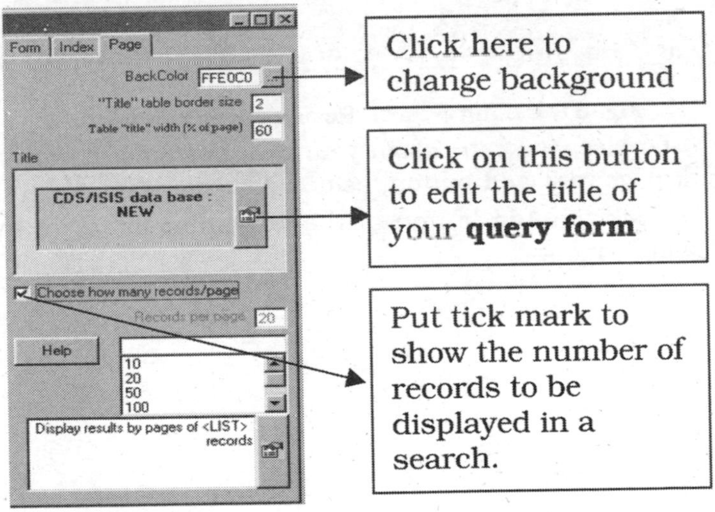

Fig. 60

Designing format 'listing'

Then click on the 'Format-listing' window and you will get the following screen. It will create a default search-result page, which will display all fields contained in the database, if you do not do anything at all.

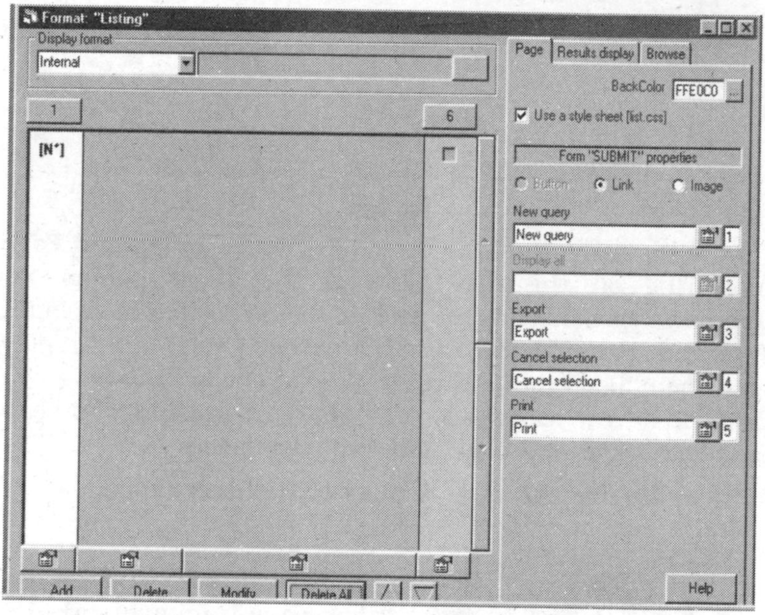

Fig. 61. Default Search-Result Page Definition

Or else, you can design your own customised search-result page with **Add** button, as detailed below: -

Click the **Add** button at the bottom so as to get the following window

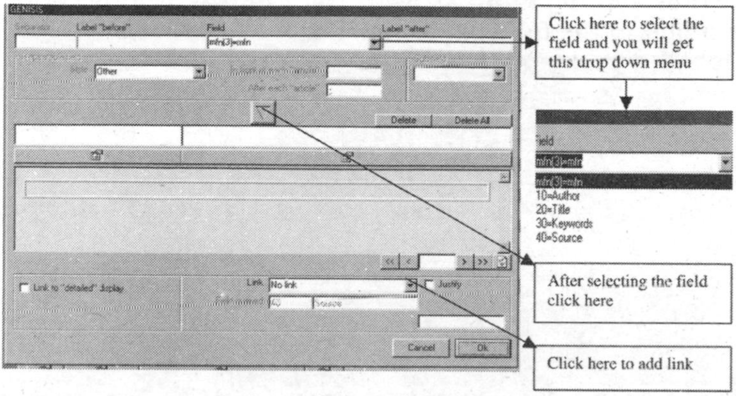

Fig. 62. Create Customised Search-Result Page

In the above screen, select the appropriate **Field** by clicking the drop down menu at the top.

Then click the **down arrow** button at the middle and finally click the **Ok** button.

Now select the next *Field* by clicking **Add** button till all **Fields** except **Fulltext** are selected. *Fulltext* field needs to be provided with links, for opening the fulltext document.

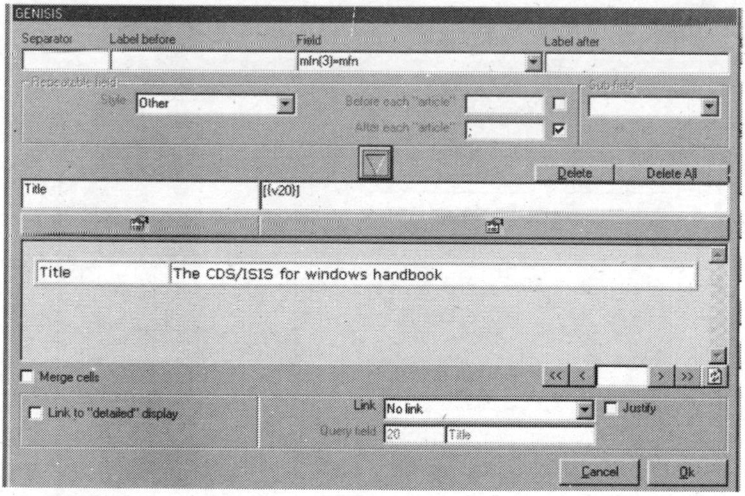

Fig. 63

Now add the **Fulltext** field. The **Fulltext** field need to have a link to the full text documents.

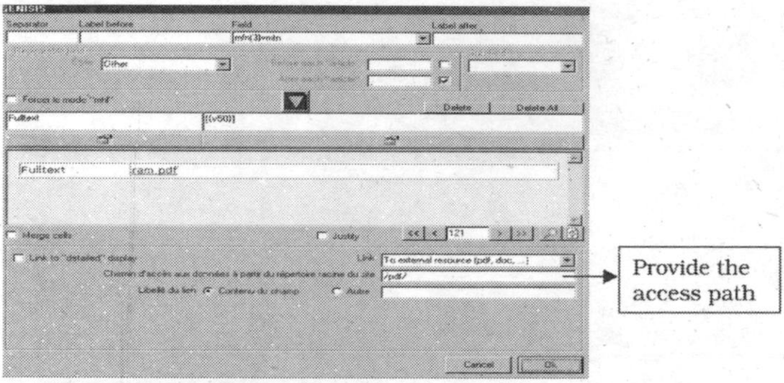

Fig. 64. Providing Link to the Fulltext Documents

Click on the **down arrow** button at the middle as above, so as to display the **Fulltext** file name *ram.pdf.*

Then select the drop down menu appearing against **link** and select **To external resource (pdf, doc...)**, if the full text documents are pdf, doc, html etc.

Then provide the access path to the subfolder where you put the fulltext documents (eg. /pdf/) in *htdocs* ('Document root') as shown in the above figure. Now click **Ok** button to save it.

You may move on to the next screen in Fig 65

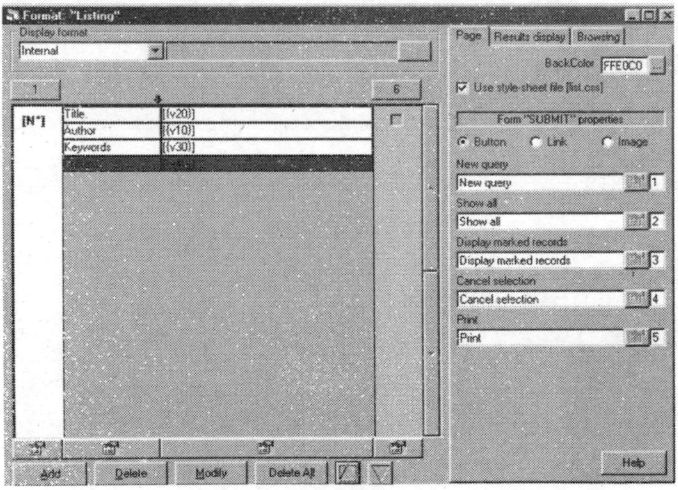

Fig. 65

Designing of two forms (query form & format 'listing') as detailed above are over and you may ignore the **Format 'Details'**.

Create a subfolder (say *pdf*) in **htdocs** and copy all the full-text documents in that folder.

Then click on **Application** drop down menu and select **Create application** as in figure 66

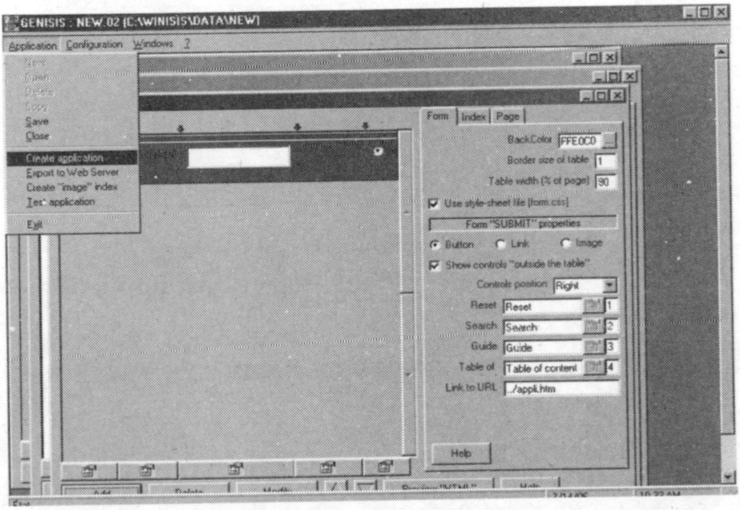

Fig. 66. Create Application

You will be lead to the following message. (Fig.67)

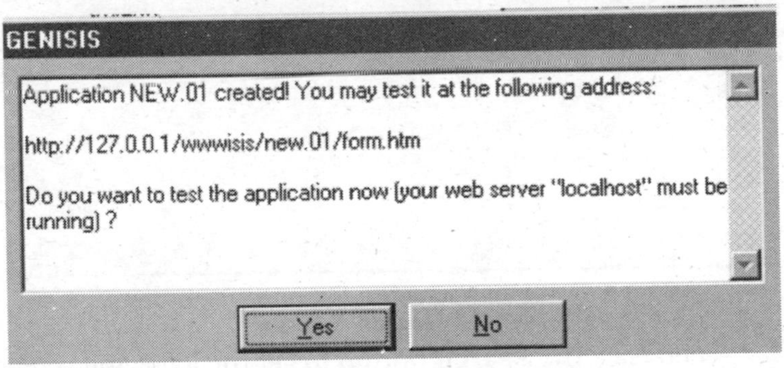

Fig. 67. Test the Application

Click on the **Yes** button and the query form you had created will appear as follows as in Fig 68.

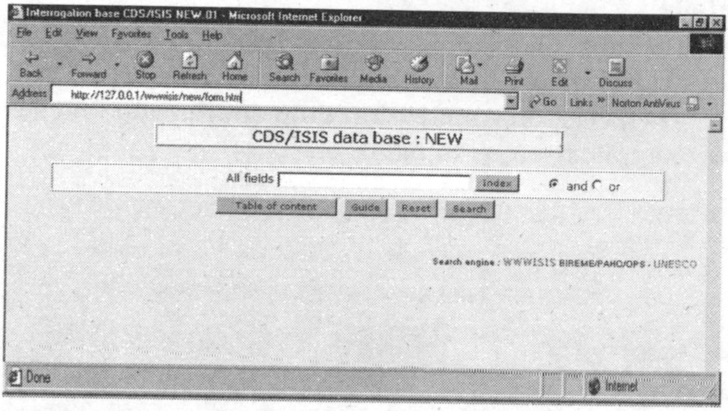

Fig. 68. A Test Window -Query Page

Type any search term in the **Search box** for all fields to make a search.

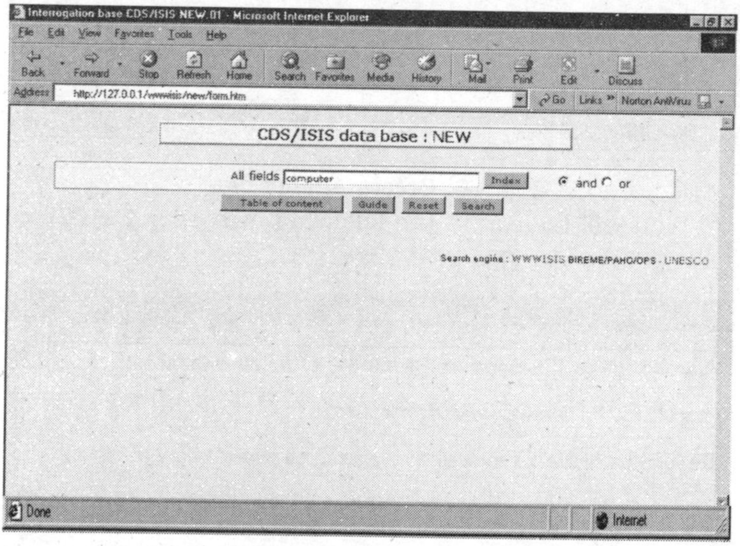

Fig. 69. Search Window

Then click the **Search** button to get the following screen containing the result.

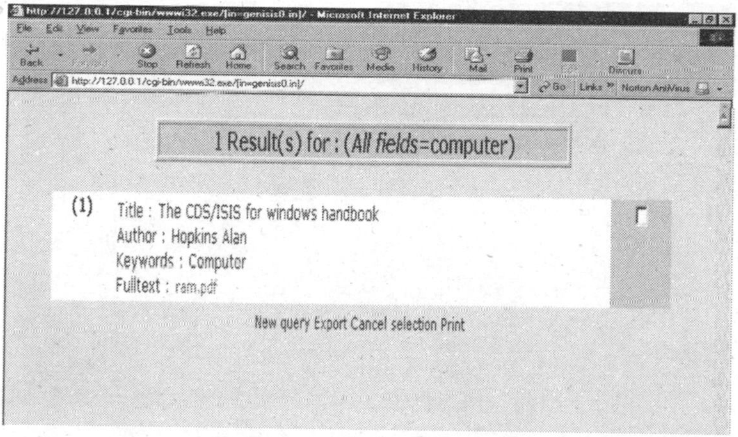

Fig. 70. Search Result Page

If you click on the **link** *(ram.pdf)* against the field **Fulltext** provided above, appropriate document would be opened, automatically as follows:-

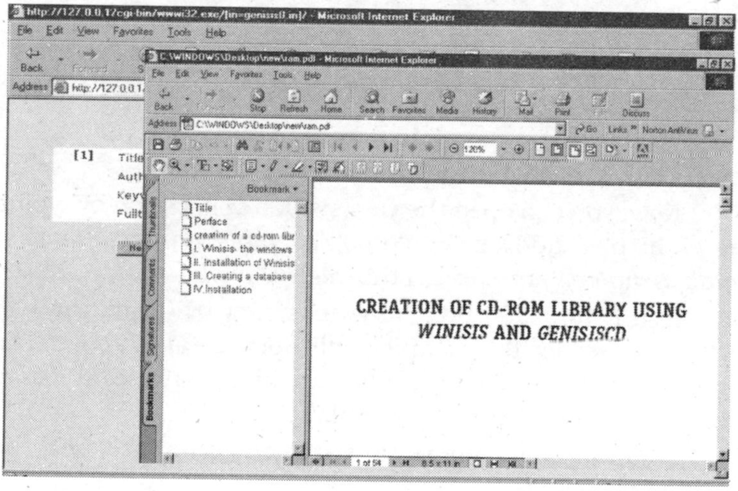

Fig. 71. An Opened Full-text Document

Close the test window and continue as in figure 72

Save the application

Finally *save the application* by clicking the **Save** under **Application** drop down menu as in figure 72.

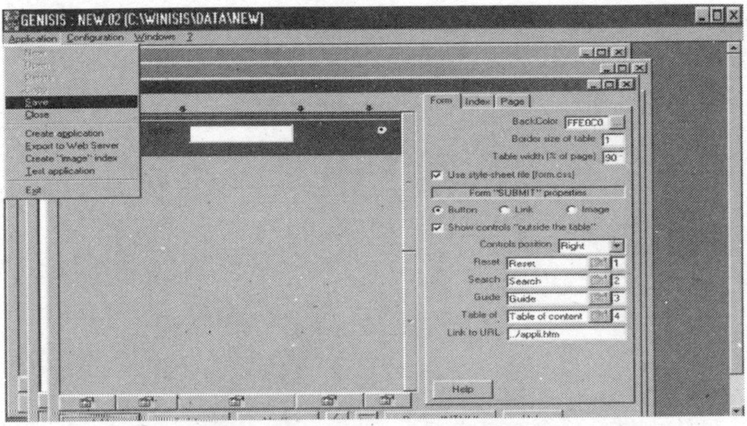

Fig. 72. Save the Application

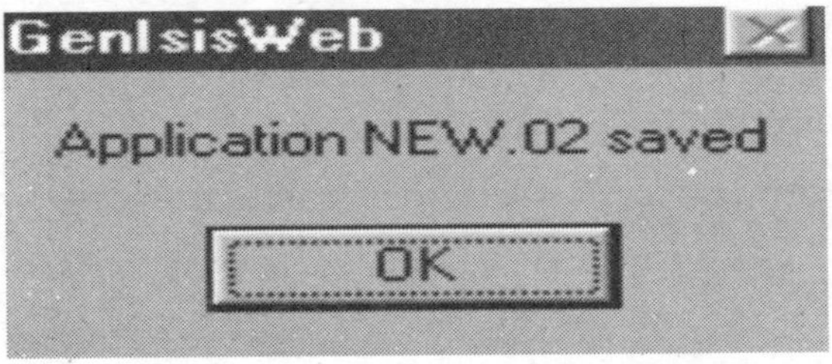

Fig. 73

Click the **OK** button in the above window.

Now, you can open the GenisisWeb application by typing the http address *http://computername/wwwisis/databasename/ form.htm* in the *internet explorer* address bar.

(Eg. http://127.0.0.1/wwwisis/new.01/form.htm will be the address for the sample application created above. The computer will add .01 to the first databasename and .02 to second databasename and so on).

You can allow others to search the database with the above http address.

5. PUBLISHING THE DATABASE IN A WEBSITE

You can publish the Winisis database application created above in a website by export function of the GenisisWeb software.

Exporting the application to the web-server

Open the GenisisWeb application created above.

Click on **Export to web server** under the **Application** drop down menu as in figure 74

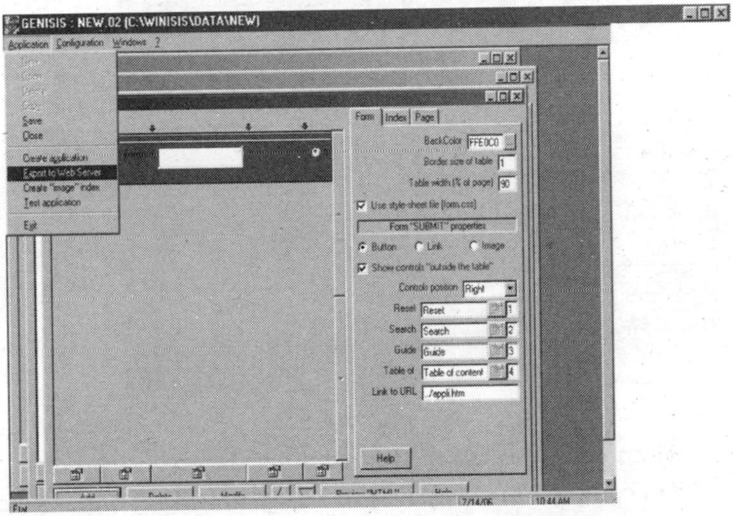

Fig. 74. Exporting to Web-server

Then you will get a dialogue box in Fig.75

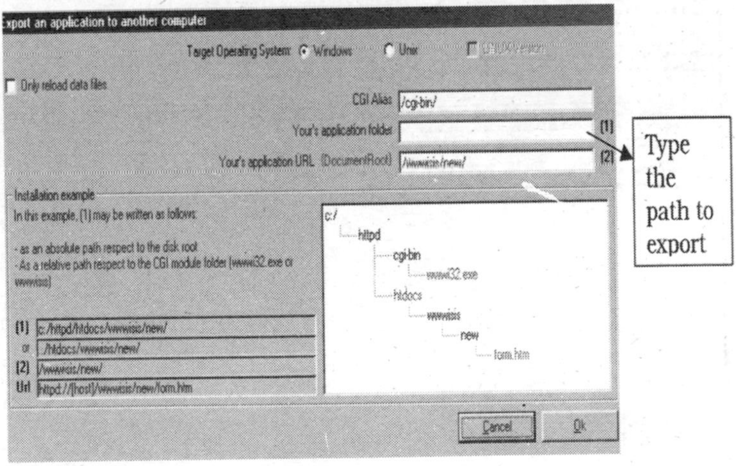

Fig. 75

In the above screen you can choose the operating system **Windows** or **Unix**. Then type a path to export (as shown on left bottom of the screen eg. .../*htdocs/wwwisis/new/*) on the box for **Your's application folder** as above.

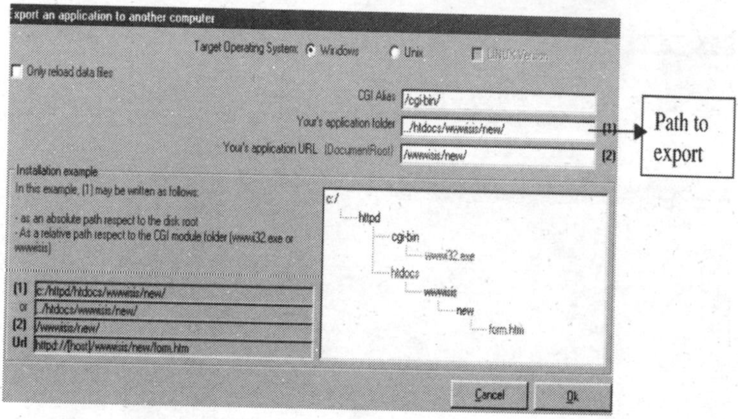

Fig. 76

Then click the **Ok** button to start the export process.

On completion of export process, you will get a message. The message will give you instructions on what to do.

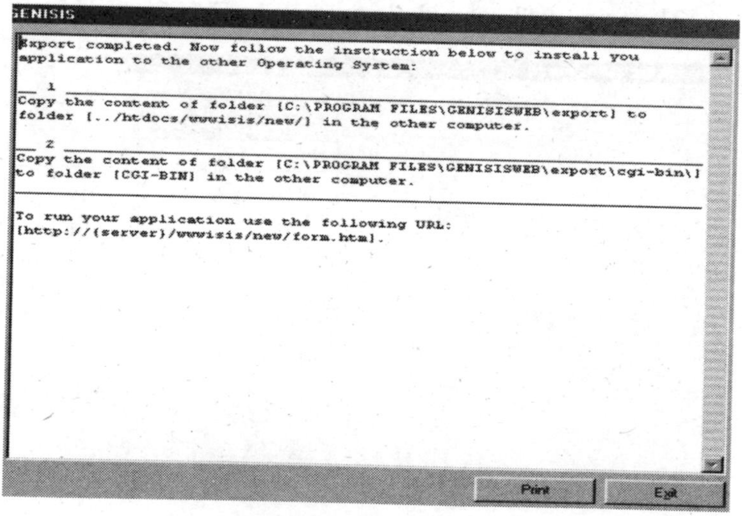

Fig. 77. Instructions

Then follow these steps:-

1. Create a new folder **wwwisis** in the **htdocs** and then create another subfolder namely **new** in **wwwisis** folder of the server computer (..htdocs/wwwisis/new)
2. Copy the contents of the folder **export** (under GenisisWeb) from the first computer to the **new** folder (..htdocs/wwwisis) in the server computer
3. Copy the contents of the **cgi-bin** (of GenisisWeb) to the **cgi-bin** in the server computer (The contents of the *cgi-bin* will be identical files for any database)
4. Create a new folder **pdf** in the **htdocs** of the server and place the full-text documents in that folder
5. When you type **http:/servername/wwwisis/new/ form.htm**, the query form will appear. The query form allows you to search the document collection.

In *Unix*, the instructions will be slightly different.

CONCLUSION

Install the softwares first, then copy the required files as mentioned in the overview at the beginning and then start doing the steps as detailed in the write-up. Even though the description appears much complicated, the steps to be followed are simple and easy-to-do. The application which you create will be stable and useful one.

REFERENCES

1. CDS/ISIS for windows Reference Manual (version 1.3), Paris, UNESCO, 1998.
2. CDS / ISIS for windows – version 1.4 January 2001 : Notes and Format Examples Paris, UNESCO, 2001.
3. Thomas, Jeannine: An abridged Version of CDS / ISIS Reference Manual Version 3.0 Geneva, International Bureau of Education, 1992.
4. Buxton, Andrew and Hopkinson, Alan : The CDS / ISIS for Windows Handbook Paris, UNESCO, 2001.
5. Deepali Talagana : Web Interface for CDS / ISIS GenisisWeb Version 3.0.2 Colombo, Sri Lanka Library Association, 2006.

6. Rajasekharan K and Nafala K H : Manual on Digital Document Archiving Thrissur, Kerala Institute of Local Administration, 2006.
7. Winisis and associated software are obtainable from UNESCO Website *www.unesco.org/isis/files/winisis 15_3.exe*

new inexperienced users are coming to use web resources. In this complex situation, it is very difficult to find precise and relevant information from huge amount of unstructured, randomly scattered information on the Internet. To cope up with this situation computer scientist developed several search devices. Search engine is one of the devices. Search engine is a generic term used for the software that 'searches' the web pages to a specific query. In other way, a search engine is a computer program that searches document on the Internet containing terms being searched by a user. Search engine can be defined as a tool for finding, classifying and storing information on various websites on the Internet.

1. Brief History

The search engine history is not brief in reality, but here some prominent developments are categorized chronologically.

(a) 1990 : The Archie can be considered as the first search engine developed by Alan Emtage, used for indexing and searching file on FTP server.

(b) 1993 : Several developments were being introduced in time period of 1993.

* Veronica (Very Easy Rodent-Oriented Netwide Index to Computerized Archives) was developed at University of Nevada that was used for searching menu items.
* After launching of WWW, the first robot, called World Wide Web wanderer, was introduced by Mathew Gray for effective web search.
* Artijn Koster developed ALIWEB, an Archie-like web-indexing tool where they use their own descriptions and index instead of robot.
* Full-fledged robot based search was started by JumpStation, World Wide Web Worm. They gather information from title and header of web pages and present result in a linear way.
* Repository-Based Software Engineering (RBSE) was introduced where spider uses ranking system for web page presentation.

* First time word relationship was introduced in search engine. But later it was discarded because spider was not enough intelligent to understand the relationship.

(c) 1994 : Some major developments were occurred.

* ElNet Galaxy Web Directory was developed having Gopher and Telnet searching facilities in addition to web search.
* David Filo and Jerry Yang created yahoo search engine.
* Brian Pinkerton of the University of Washington launched the search engine Webcrawler.
* Lycos, Infoseek and OpenText were introduced.

(d) 1995 : AltaVista was developed.

(e) 1996 : Few search engines were developed during 1995. Two names are given below.

* Hotbot search engine developed by The Inktomi Corporation came into operation.
* The LookSmart directory was introduced.

(f) 1997 : Two major things occurred during this period.

* The search engine AskJeeves was launched.
* Excite bought out WebCrawler.

(g) 1998 : Some achievements in this year are:

* It is that year when Google, the most powerful search engine till date was released. Very soon Google has become so popular that even Yahoo have used Google to search their directory.
* MSN search, Open Directory and Direct Hit were launched.

(h) 1999 : Go Network was released by Disney with improved search technology to compete with the Google.

(i) 2000 : Teoma search engine having clustering technique to organize websites by subject-specific popularity was developed.

(j) 2001 : Ask Jeeves bought Teoma to replace the Direct Hit search engine.

(k) 2002 : LookSmart bought WiseNet search engine.

(l) 2003 : Google introduced web semantics in searching.

(m) 2004 : Numerous developments were taken place;

some important phenomena are given below.

* Yahoo dumped Google in favor of its own search engine. Yahoo! launches Local Search Engine
* AltaVista switches to Yahoo! Search
* Lycos Search discontinued
* Google Gmail started free email service
* AlltheWeb switches to Yahoo! Search

(n) 2005 : Some achievements are listed below.

* Google launches Google Local
* IAC/InterActiveCorp acquires AskJeeves
* Google offers free WiFi to San Francisco

(o) 2006 : Google launches Google Mars and Google Video.

2. HOW SEARCH ENGINE WORKS

To know how a search engine works, it is very necessary to understand components, tasks, generic types, and basic mechanism of search engine. A search engine is so designed to help the web users to locate and find right web pages containing relevant information.

2.1. Generic Types of Search Engine

Generically there are three types of search engines in operation.

1. Crawler-based search engine : The search engine having the spider program which crawl or spider for one web page to another and collect information from each web page and make an index is called Crawler-based search engine. During searching this index makes a bridge between users query and web information.

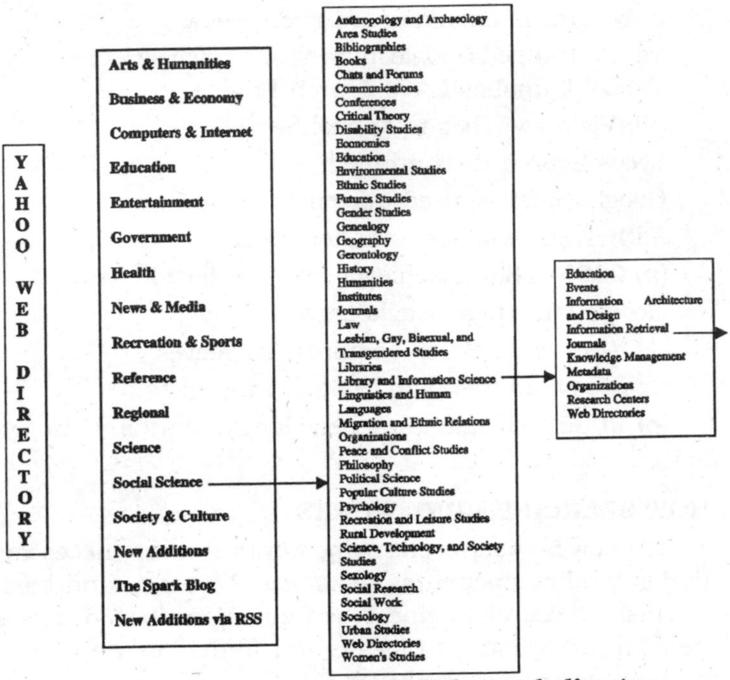

Fig. 1. Subject categories in Yahoo web directory

2. Human-made directory : The human-made web directory is a website that categorizes web pages, so that one can browse links to web pages by pre established topics. It is actually the listing of terms in different categories and sub-categories made by human being (Fig-1). Users require to select a particular category for getting respective web pages. Unlike crawler-based search engine , it maintain hierarchical structure of different categories. The owner of website need to submit short description of subject matter of website to the owner of search engine and only then this website have to be included in the web directory. In this method the users need not to select exact search terms or to follow complex search technique; just select predefined category and get relevant links. But in case of through change of the content of any website, the directory has no mechanism to reflect that change of subject matter of website.

3. Hybrid search engine: It is the combination of crawler and directory. Today most of the search engines use hybrid technique in single user interface.

2.2 Major components of search engine

A typical search engine has the following three components:

1. Robot or spider: Spider is basically a program, used for creating systematic list of words/phrases present in the websites. Actually this program travel through the hyper-linked web pages and simultaneously construct index of these words/phrases.

2. The database : It is the database of index terms collected from the web pages by spider program. The database is the systematic storehouse of million of web pages and forms the index that is searched by the users. The database will have to update frequently to keep pace with the introduction of new websites and modifications of existing websites.

3. User interface: It is a search engine program that search and locate the words/phrases in the pre existing index database and refer information according to the ranking on the basis of relevancy.

2.3. Basic tasks performed by search engine

Any search engine, given below, performs four basic tasks:

(i) Searching of WWW one the basis of predefined set of criteria.

(ii) Keeping index of words frequencies and locations on the web pages.

(iii) Updating/rebuild index database by visiting websites at regular interval.

(iv) Allowing web users to search by using query terms.

2.4 Core mechanism of search engine

As mentioned earlier, there are three components in search engine. The integrated and inter-connected operation of three components give raises the core mechanism. It will be effective to discuss in three phases (Fig-2):

1. Phase I : In the first phase robot or spider program automatically move one web page to another of an website by using hyperlinks present in the web pages. In each page, spider automatically read out the content and collects information about the contents and links. Unlike computer virus, spider program does not physically move from one computer to another; rather it just visits web pages of websites. In regular interval the spider will visit the web pages to collect changed or modified information if any. Each search engine has its own algorithm or technique about ways and frequency of visiting web pages. Besides web pages, some search engines are highly comprehensive in coverage; collecting information about all kinds of digital resources present in the Internet like newsgroup, discussion forum, gopher, listservs and FTP sites etc. Search engines are unable to acquire information from the database-driven sites, which are referred to as hidden web or invisible web. Again the spider program of search engine by policy does not collect information and links from some websites like adult-oriented pornographic sites.

2. Phase II : The robot or spider program developed an index database by systematically arranging the URLs, terms, titles, headers, and other relevant information collected from different web pages of different websites by using complex ranking algorithm taking into consideration the following parameters:

* Text within the title tag
* Domain name
* URL directories and file names
* HTML tags: headings, emphasized (<em>) and strongly emphasized (<strong>) text
* Term frequency, both in the document and globally, often misunderstood and mistakenly referred to as Keyword density
* Keyword proximity
* Keyword adjacency
* Keyword sequence
* Alt attributes for images
* Text within NOFRAMES tags
* Content development

In case of insertion of new website or modification of existing website the spider frequently wandering to the cyberspace through web pages and collect information and readjust the index database of search engine accordingly.

3. Phase III : In phase III, the search engine agent software program plays an important role. Actually it is a user interface, which accepts any search query from users through input devices and then sent it millions of web pages of search engine. The agent program helps to match the user query to index and present links according to the relevancy. Virtually instantaneously, the search engine will sort through the millions of web pages and present to the users screens on a given topic and arranged according to the relevant ranking. It is noticed that in many times a number of non-relevant pages may also come out, still search engine instantly do an amazing job.

For the determination of relevancy of the web pages, search engine follows a set of rules, called 'algorithm'. Most of the search engines follow some general rules given below:

(a) Location and frequency : It is the main rule in a ranking algorithm. It encompasses three things

* Pages with the search word/phrase appearing in the HTML title tag are often assumed to be more relevant than others to the topic.
* Search keywords appear near the top of a web page (headings or in the first few paragraphs of text), by assumption that any page relevant to the topic will mention those words right from the beginning.
* A search engine will analyze how often keywords appear in relation to other words in a web page, by assumption that words having higher frequency are often deemed more relevant than others.

(b) Number and frequency of web page indexing : This rule is basically the corollary of location/frequency rule. It may include:

* Different search engines add different amount of spice to the location/frequency method. Some search engines index more web pages than others.
* Frequencies of web page indexing are different in different search engine. Some search engines index web pages more often than others.

* In case of "spamming" search engines may penalize pages or exclude them from the index. Spamming is the process of repeating a word, hundreds of times on a web page, to increase the word frequency for higher ranking in the listings.

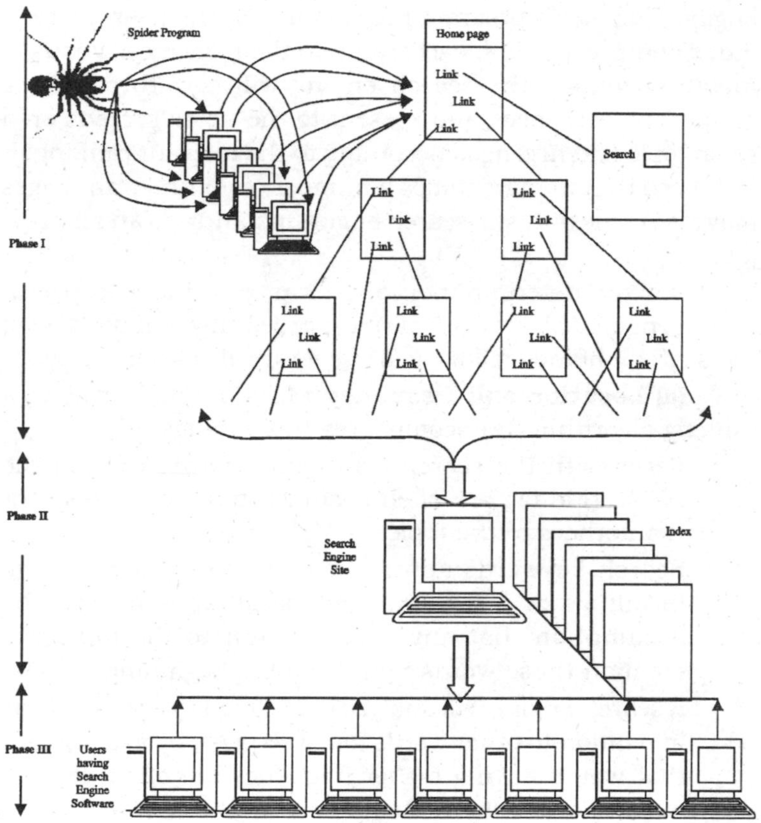

Fig. 2. Mechanism of search engine (Adapted from Ref. 1, 4)

(c) Off the page ranking : All major search engines use "off the page" ranking criteria. Crawler-based search engines have plenty of experience now with webmasters who constantly rewrite their web pages in an attempt to gain better rankings. It includes:

* Link analysis criteria to know how pages link to each

other and from this analysis search engine can asses the subject matter of the page and lists ranking accordingly. In addition, sophisticated techniques are used to screen out attempts by webmasters to build "artificial" links designed to boost their rankings.

* Clickthrough measurement technique means that a search engine may watch what results someone selects for a particular search, then eventually drop high-ranking pages that aren't attracting clicks, while promoting lower-ranking pages that do pull in visitors. As with link analysis, systems are used to compensate for artificial links generated by eager webmasters.

3. MECHANISM OF COMPLEX LARGE-SCALE HYPERTEXTUAL WEB SEARCH ENGINE

In the above section a general mechanism of search engine is explained. In the present section, I shall give a high level overview of how a complex web search engine works. Most of the large and popular web search engine works in very complex mechanism. Again each and every popular search engine has some how different functioning mechanism. In practical, we noticed that searching through same search term give rise different numbers of ranked pages. For example a search was conducted on 12-08-06 by the term 'digital library' through some popular web search engine produce following numbers of web pages.

* Google – 474000000
* Yahoo – 781000000
* MSN – 42038341
* Ask.com – 15020000

Here it is being tried to describe in a very simplified way, the mechanism of very much popular web search engine 'Google'. In Google, there are several components in the search engine. The interacting functions of these components, actually give rise the embedded mechanism of the Google search engine (Fig-3). The components and their functions are cyclically enumerated below:

1. **Crawlers:** In Google, several distributed crawlers do

the web crawling i.e. downloading of web pages.

2. URLserver: There is a URLserver that sends lists of URLs to be fetched to the crawlers.

3. Store server: The store server holds the fetched web pages. The store server then compresses and stores the web pages into a repository.

4. Repository: The repository contains the full HTML of each and every web page. Every web page has an associated ID number called a docID, which is assigned whenever a new URL is parsed out of a web page. Here documents are stored one after another and are prefixed by docID, length and URL.

5. Indexer: The indexer performs a number of functions. It reads the repository, uncompresses the documents, and parses them. Each document is converted into a set of word occurrences called hits. The hits record the word, position in document, an approximation of font size, and capitalization. The indexer distributes these hits into a set of "barrels", creating a partially sorted forward index. The indexer performs another important function. It parses out all the links in every web page and stores important information about them in an anchors file. This file contains enough information to determine where each link points from and to, and the text of the link.

6. Barrels: After parsing of each document, it is encoded into a number of barrels. The indexer distributes these hits into a set of "barrels", creating a partially sorted forward index.

7. Sorter: the indexer and the sorter perform the indexing function. The sorter takes the barrels, which are sorted by docID and resorts them by wordID to generate the inverted index. This is done in place so that little temporary space is needed for this operation. The sorter also produces a list of wordIDs and offsets into the inverted index.

8. Anchor file: This file contains enough information to determine where each link points from and to, and the text of the link.

9. URLresolver: The URLresolver reads the anchors file and converts relative URLs into absolute URLs and in turn into docIDs. It puts the anchor text into the forward index, associated with the docID that the anchor points to. It also generates a database of links that are pairs of docIDs. The links database is used to compute PageRanks for all the documents.

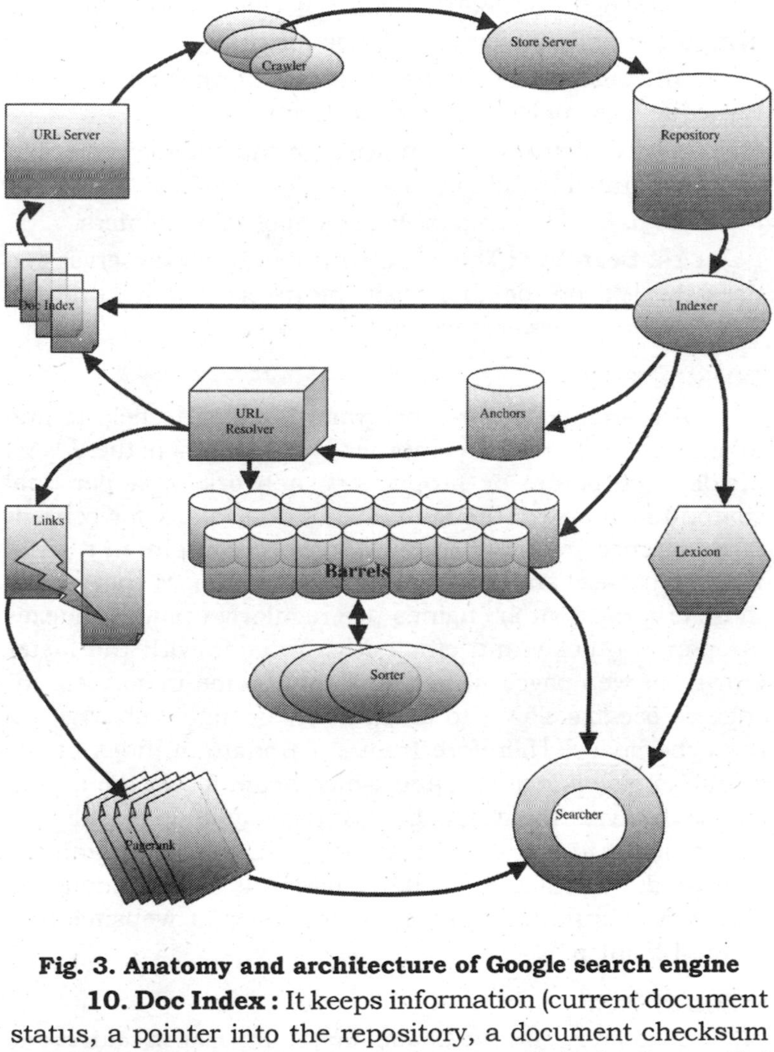

Fig. 3. Anatomy and architecture of Google search engine

10. Doc Index : It keeps information (current document status, a pointer into the repository, a document checksum and other statistics) about each document in Index Sequential Access Mode. In addition, there is a file, which is used to converts URLs into docIDs.

11. Link : It parses out all the links in every web page and stores important information about them in an anchors file.

12. PageRanks : It also generates a database of links, which are pairs of docIDs. The links database is used to compute PageRanks for all the documents.

13. Lexicon : It is the collection of millions of words. Basically it is implemented in two sections:

* *A list of the words* : Words are concatenated together but separated by nulls.
* *A hash table* : This table is composed of pointers.

14. Searcher : The searcher is run by a web server and uses the lexicon together with the inverted index and the PageRanks to answer queries.

CONCLUSION

A search engine is a program designed to help to find information stored on a computer system such as the WWW, inside a corporate or proprietary network or a personal computer. The search engine allows one to ask for content meeting specific criteria (typically those containing a given word or phrase) and retrieves a list of references that match those criteria. Search engines use regularly updated indexes to operate quickly and efficiently. To cope with the faster growth of web pages, it is noted that, some major search-engines became slower to index newly coming Web pages in the cyberspace. Therefore frequent update of index of the search engine is required and which again forces the search engine to revisit the web pages periodically. Side by side it is very difficult to index invisible web, which are dynamically generated. But still search engine performs a tremandous job in a very minute time to retrive the relevant websites in a ordered fashion.

REFERENCES

1. Chaudhury, G.G and Chaudhury, S. Information sources and searching on the world wide web. London, Library Association Publishing, 2001. Pp. 15-47
2. Cohen, Laura. Second generation searching on the web. http:/

/library.albany.edu/internet/second.html (accessed on 12-08-2006)

3. http://en.wikipedia.org/wiki/Search_engineb (accessed on 12-08-2006)
4. IGNOU MLIS course material. Information communication technologies: Applications. Part II. New Delhi, IGNOU, 2005. Pp. 337-378.
5. TakuyaMurata. The Mechanism of the Search Engine. http://c2.com/cgi/wiki?MechanismOfSearchEngine (accessed on 02-09-2006)
6. Webcrafters, Florida. Optimized websites. http://www.optimizedwebsites.com/search_engine_ranking.html (accessed on 22-08-2006)

26

Evaluation of University Websites Targeting English Speaking Users: A Comparative Analysis of Selected Sites in Developed and Developing Countries

Raymond Wafula Ongus

T. D. Kemparaju

Constantine Matoke Nyamboga

ABSTRACT

In the world of the 21st century, librarians and indeed all information professionals are compelled not merely to adapt change, but to prepare for it, facilitate it and shape it. With the rapid development and increasingly popular usage of the Internet through the World Wide Web (WWW), information professionals have been offered a very lucrative opportunity to assert themselves as information gatekeepers and gateways, respectively. Through systematic evaluation procedures on information resources such as Websites, proper guidance may be offered to targeted end-users in order to facilitate much more efficient retrieval of information and hopefully, better utilization of the same. This paper looks at several selected university Websites designed in English, all of which were subjected to a uniform set of criteria for the purposes of evaluating the Website design and content coverage. Following its classification into developing and developed countries of origin, the data collected was comparatively analyzed and subsequent inferences together with recommendations proffered in line with the set objectives.

INTRODUCTION

Libraries all over the world are charged with fundamental responsibilities that constitute their raison d'etre within their respective user communities. The tasks include selection, acquisition, processing, dissemination, maintenance, evaluation, promotion and preservation of information resource materials in a variety of formats. All this is expected to be proactively carried out as per the specific information needs of the library clientele, to facilitate proper decision-making. Contemporary libraries maintain various combinations of recorded knowledge in their stock, including print-based, electronic and other emerging media.

In conjunction with computer technology, libraries are increasingly being equipped with information infrastructure (i.e. *infostructure*), which enables their users to rapidly access information from outside the libraries' "four walls". This mainly occurs by means of Websites on the Internet.

Systematic evaluation of all information resources at regular intervals ensures the sustenance of desirable and internationally acceptable standards, in terms of timeliness of content, appropriateness, validity, relevance, accuracy and so on. Users can therefore be suitably guided to use information resources of highest quality and which are likely to be greatly beneficial.

Thus, in the digital age, one can effectively declare that new roles are emerging for the librarian to serve in the global network environment. These roles comprise the following:

1. information navigators;
2. educators on information seeking skills;
3. publishers of required information;
4. intermediaries (end-user surrogates);
5. information marketers;
6. information organizers and disseminators;
7. planners and policy makers; and finally, perhaps most importantly
8. information evaluators

WHY EVALUATE WEBSITES?

A Website, as per the definition forwarded by Gray (2004), is a set of related pages of information that are meaningfully linked together electronically on the Internet. The general rule of thumb is to consider all electronic documents on the Web with addresses beginning with a unique hostname as belonging to one Website. In order to locate and access a Website, one needs to enter its file address or uniform resource locator (URL) into the appropriate space provided for by the browser. The URL is the standard for specifying an object on the Internet. Supposing one enters a hypothetical URL such as *http://www.assessingsites.com/info/education.html* in a given Web browser, no matter where in the world one may be or wherever that Website may be hosted, the same page should pop up on the screen. What actually happens behind the scene is that the Internet browser divides the URL into four parts as follows:

1. The protocol/ access method used (i.e. hypertext protocol (*http*))
2. The server/ host name (*www.assessingsites.com*)
3. The folder name (*info*)
4. The file name and extension (*education.html*)

In general, the two slashes in the URL after the colon indicate a machine name (Boutell, 1996). The information on the remote server is located and broken up into small packets.

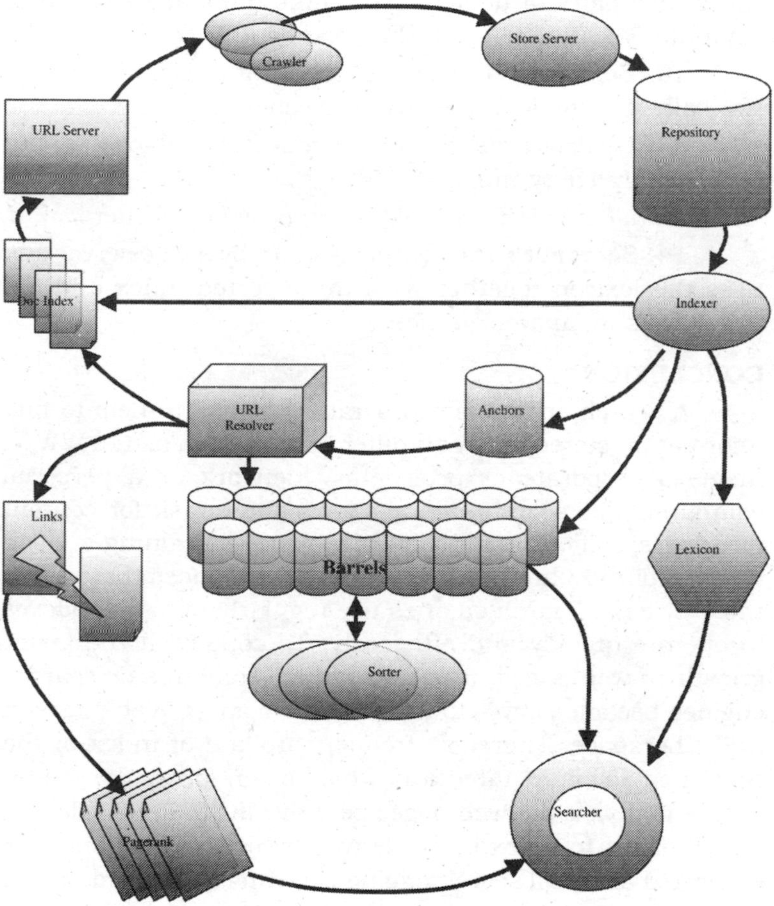

The packets are rapidly sent over the telecommunication medium, often using different routes and reassembled in a logical and meaningful sequence on the user's computer, according to the way the markup language instructs the Internet browser. Of course, there are more intricate technical details to this process of information transfer, but they fall beyond the scope and purpose of this paper.

Website evaluation is a necessary process to enable planners and developers to keep up with the increasingly diverse nature of sites that are posted on the Internet. It is also imperative to evaluate Websites for the purposes of quality control, given the fact that anyone and any organization can publish anything on the Internet at any chosen time. Furthermore, most of the Internet is not reviewed or "filtered". In other words, unlike the more traditional information media (books, magazines, videos and so on), which pass through an editor, the content of a Web page does not have to be approved by anyone before it is made public. Seldom is there a reviewing process conducted by peers or an authority, or checking by a publication or editor or selection by a librarian during collection development. Conversely, anyone is capable of selecting and using anything on the Internet. Unfortunately, in many cases gullible clients often believe: "If it is on the Internet, it must be true". This kind of view is typically accepted without checking the credibility of the Websites consulted. That attitude does not necessarily portray sincerity, which is why a deliberate attempt to evaluate and classify Website qualities is crucial. Just as the Websites are dynamic in nature, their evaluation has to be a continuous process for effective results to be obtained.

OBJECTIVES OF THE STUDY

The main intentions of this study are to evaluate and compare educational Websites that are hosted in different parts of the world. The specific objectives of the study were therefore stated as follows:

(i) To compare the accessibility and user-friendliness of the respective Websites

(ii) To determine whether the Websites indicate ownership

and also whether they are regularly maintained.

(iii) To evaluate the quality of information content covered by the respective Websites

(iv) To assess the quality of citations in the Websites in terms of availability of bibliographies and/or useful links to other related sites.

(v) To investigate whether Web design quality affects the quality of Web content among the selected sites.

(vi) To establish ways in which university Websites from developing countries differ from those of the developing world.

TSCOPE AND LIMITATIONS

This study was strictly confined to university Websites, indicative of the background of the paper's authors. Other types of educational Websites were excluded due to constraints of time and costs associated with the work involved. English language was focused on because it is the language in which all the authors are mutually well versed and hence could effectively work with. Although English language is claimed to carry the majority (approximately 60%) of Websites on the Internet, it was a limiting factor because many Websites in other languages had to be overlooked in order to carry out the investigation.

METHODOLOGY

In total, it is estimated that Websites of universities worldwide possibly number about 7,000. However in this study, a total of 318 university websites in English language were purposively selected for the study. They were drawn from 119 countries around the world. Both public as well as private universities were considered equally in the sampling frame. After selection, the Websites were classified into seven (7) homogenous groups pertaining to the following regions:

1. Africa
2. Asia
3. Europe
4. Latin America/Caribbean
5. Middle East

6. North America
7. Oceania

In the 1960s to the early1970s, both the United Nations Organization (UN) as well as the Organization for Economic Cooperation and Development (OECD) established that some countries were not quite up to the mark in terms of economic development (Hacche: 1970 & Todaro: 1994). For the purposes of this paper, the loosest possible delineation was employed in defining the aforementioned regions. The developing world was taken to collectively mean Africa, Asia, Middle East and Latin America/Caribbean, whereas the developed world was collectively taken to mean Europe, North America and Oceania.

All the university Websites used in this survey, were located by means of Web-based databases, identified by the following URLs: *http://univ.cc/*, *http://www.google.com*, *http://www.usc.edu/dept/overseas/ipww.html* and *http://www.lmu.edu/globaled/wwcu*.

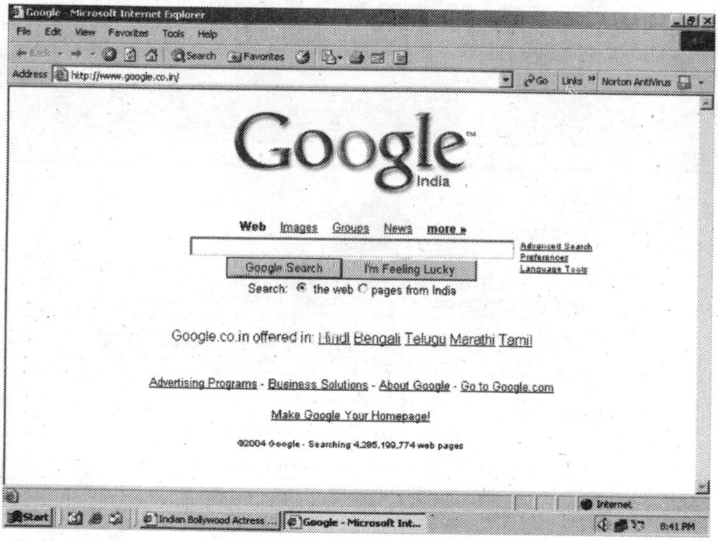

Fig. 1. The Google Website used to confirm URLs of university Websites

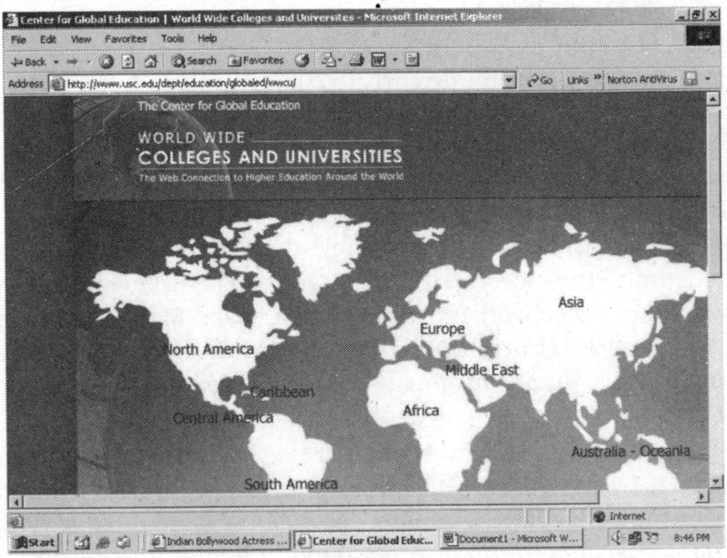

Fig. 2. A Website of worldwide universities and colleges with Websites

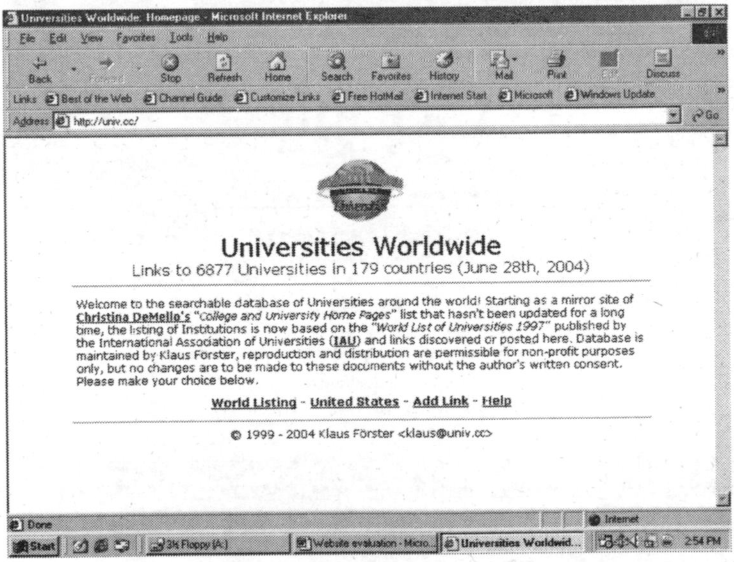

Fig. 3. An alternative Website listing worldwide universities with Websites

The principal tools used for the capturing of data from the Websites were checklists and rating scales, to capture data in paired ways (see Appendices I and II respectively). Karen McLachlan developed this form of Website evaluation in 1996, as a means of introducing the World Wide Web to novice users (McLachlan: 2002). The same method was adapted for this research because of its suitability in the context of this particular study. The evaluation forms were categorized as follows:

(i) Checklist for evaluating the quality of attributes comprising the Website's design, namely:

* Downloading speed
* Homepage design
* Ease of navigation
* Use of multimedia
* Browser compatibility
* Manner of presentation
* Maintenance
* Availability of further information

Based on the number of "*Yes*" (1mark) and "*No*" (0 mark) answers to each of the Web design attributes, the Websites were rated according to the following schema:

(24 –16 Marks) : Very well designed Website, easy to use

(15 -11 Marks) : Website design needs to be improved but site is usable

(10 – 0 Marks) : Poorly designed Website, difficult to use

(ii) Checklist for evaluating the quality of attributes comprising the Website's contents, namely:

* Efficiency of the Website
* Information providers
* Information currency
* Information quality

Similarly, based on the number of "*Yes*" (1 mark) and "*No*" (0 mark) answers to each of the Web content attributes, the Websites were further rated according to the following schema:

(24 –16 Marks) : Very useful Website for users' information needs

(15 -11 Marks) : Website worth bookmarking for future reference

(10 – 0 Marks) : Website not worth coming back to

ANALYSIS OF COLLECTED DATA

The analysis involved the application of both descriptive and inferential statistics carried out by means of SPSS for Windows (Version 7.5.1) software.

The data revealed that the Websites were used by the respective parent institutions as dynamic promotional tools, accessible by a large population of users at any given time. The targeted audience was perceived to comprise the following: students (99.1%), staff (72.9%), researchers (53.8%), alumni (36.9%), corporations (9.4%), parents (4.1%) and so on.

This study therefore attempted to assess how well the university Websites were designed and also proceeded to examine how well the corresponding contents were presented to the targeted end-users. In all cases, comparisons were made between developing countries and developed countries.

(i) Evaluation tables for Website design:

Table 1. General comparison of Web design for selected university Websites in the regions under study

	Africa	*Asia*	*Europe*	*Latin America & Caribbean*	*Middle East*	*North America*	*Oceania*	*Total No. of observations in Developing Countries (& corresponding percentages)*	*Total No. of observations in Developed Countries (& corresponding percentages)*	*Grand Total No. of observations (& corresponding percentages)*
No. of countries represented in the study	*24*	*21*	*29*	*19*	*14*	*3*	*9*	78	41	119
No. of university Websites selected	***42***	***46***	***55***	***31***	***40***	***48***	***56***	**159**(100%)	**159**(100%)	**318**(100%)
Average time (in Seconds) for Websites to fully download using 56Kbps modem	46.45	56.37	37.38	34.77	52.28	37.88	35.36	**48.51** (Avg. time)	**36.81**(Avg. time)	**42.66**(Avg. time)
No. of Websites downloading in the given cut-off time (20 seconds)	11	12	12	13	3	13	23	**39**(24.5%)	**48**(30.2%)	**87**(27.4%)
Very well designed Websites	20	21	34	11	17	39	45	**69**(43.4%)	**118**(74.2%)	**187**(58.8%)
Websites needing										

	Africa	*Asia*	*Europe*	*Latin America & Caribbean*	*Middle East*	*North America*	*Oceania*	*Total No. of observations in Developing Countries (& corresponding percentages)*	*Total No. of observations in Developed Countries (& corresponding percentages)*	*Grand Total No. of observations (& corresponding percentages)*
improvement but are usable for now	14	16	14	14	18	4	10	**62**(39%)	**28**(17.6%)	**90**(28.3%)
Poorly designed Websites	8	9	7	6	5	5	1	**28** (17.6%)	**13**(8.2%)	**41**(12.9%)

NOTE: Data indicates that only a small proportion (27.36%) of the university Websites considered could download within the cut-off time of 20 seconds, using a standard 56Kbps modem. Apparently, the average downloading time of Websites in developed countries was generally closer to the ideal timing. Further, the data is indicative of the fact that the poorly designed Websites were not as commonly incident as the very well designed and the barely functional ones, combined. This was found to be more strongly evident in the developed countries than in the developing countries.

Table 2. Comparison of detailed design aspects of selected university Websites in the regions under study

	Africa	*Asia*	*Europe*	*Latin America & Caribbean*	*Middle East*	*North America*	*Oceania*	*Total No. of observations in Developing Countries (& corresponding percentages)*	*Total No. of observations in Developed Countries (& corresponding percentages)*	*Grand Total No. of observations (& corresponding percentages)*
Websites with good homepage design (At least 4 out of 6 Pts)	29	36	45	22	28	41	43	**115**(72.3%)	**129**(81.1%)	**244**(76.7%)
Websites with good navigation mechanisms (At least 3 out of 5 Pts)	20	28	36	15	29	44	47	**92**(57.9%)	**127**(79.9%)	**219**(68.9%)
Websites with good use of multimedia (2 out of 2 Pts)	18	15	23	13	16	29	24	**62**(39%)	**76**(47.8%)	**138**(43.4%)
Websites with browser compatibility (1 out of 1 Pt)	35	40	52	30	35	45	53	**140**(88.1%)	**150**(94.3%)	**290**(91.2%)
Websites with good manner of presentation (At least 3 out of 5 Pts)	27	28	41	23	29	41	53	**107**(67.3%)	**135**(84.9%)	**242**(76.1%)
Websites with good										

	Africa	*Asia*	*Europe*	*Latin America & Caribbean*	*Middle East*	*North America*	*Oceania*	*Total No. of observations in Developing Countries (& corresponding percentages)*	*Total No. of observations in Developed Countries (& corresponding percentages)*	*Grand Total No. of observations (& corresponding percentages)*
maintenance (2 out of 2 Pts)	7	5	14	7	4	18	23	**23**(14.5%)	**55**(34.6%)	**78**(24.5%)
Websites with good links for further information (2 out of 2 Pts)	21	17	39	15	13	39	36	**66**(41.5%)	**114**(71.7%)	**180**(56.6%)

NOTE: Data indicates that the majority of the universities' Websites did not employ multimedia/graphics appropriately for optimum results. Moreover, most of the Websites were found to be inadequately maintained, particularly those in the developing countries. The sites in the developing countries could also do with better links for further information. Otherwise, the rest of the investigated aspects pertaining to the Website design appeared to be above average, with the developed countries posting higher percentages in most areas.

(ii) Evaluation tables for Web content

Table 3. General comparison of Web content qualities for the selected university Websites in the regions under study

	Africa	*Asia*	*Europe*	*Latin America & Caribbean*	*Middle East*	*North America*	*Oceania*	*Total No. of observations in Developing Countries (& corresponding percentages)*	*Total No. of observations in Developed Countries (& corresponding percentages)*	*Grand Total No. of observations (& corresponding percentages)*
No. of countries represented in study	*24*	*21*	29	*19*	*14*	*3*	*9*	78	41	119
No. of university Websites selected	***42***	***46***	***55***	***31***	***40***	***48***	***56***	**159**(100%)	**159**(100%)	**318**(100%)
Very useful Websites	16	16	24	13	12	35	37	**57**(35.8%)	**96**(60.4%)	**153**(48.1%)
Websites worth book marking for future reference	18	16	19	10	13	7	15	**57**(35.8%)	**41**(25.8%)	**98**(30.8%)
Websites not worth revisiting	8	14	12	8	15	6	7	**45**(28.3%)	**25**(15.7%)	**70**(22.0%)

NOTE: Data indicates that the very unhelpful websites are not as commonly incident as the very useful ones and the ones worth bookmarking, combined. This situation was more remarkable in the developed countries than in the developing ones. On comparing percentages, it was found that the developed countries appeared to have a greater proportion of useful Websites than the developing countries. Thus, there were much fewer Websites not worth visiting in the developed countries than in the developing countries.

Table 4. Comparison of particular Web content aspects of selected university Websites in the regions under study

	Africa	*Asia*	*Europe*	*Latin America & Caribbean*	*Middle East*	*North America*	*Oceania*	*Total No. of observations in Developing Countries (& corresponding percentages)*	*Total No. of observations in Developed Countries (& corresponding percentages)*	*Grand Total No. of observations (& corresponding percentages)*
Websites with good efficiency (At least 1 out of 2 Pts)	37	41	48	28	31	45	52	137(86.2%)	145(91.2%)	282(88.7%)
Websites with good information providers (At least 3 out of 5 Pts)	28	26	30	17	21	32	35	92(57.9%)	97(61.0%)	189(59.4%)
Websites with good information currency (At least 3 out of 4 Pts)	13	9	18	10	8	28	38	40(25.2%)	84(52.8%)	124(38.9%)
Websites with good information quality (7 out of 11 Pts)	33	32	42	22	22	43	49	109(68.6%)	134(84.3%)	243(76.4%)

NOTE: Although the data depicts Web content development traits that are generally above average, a large majority of the Websites particularly in the developing countries did not appear to contain current information. The Websites in the developed countries surveyed posted relatively higher percentages for virtually all the Web content attributes under study.

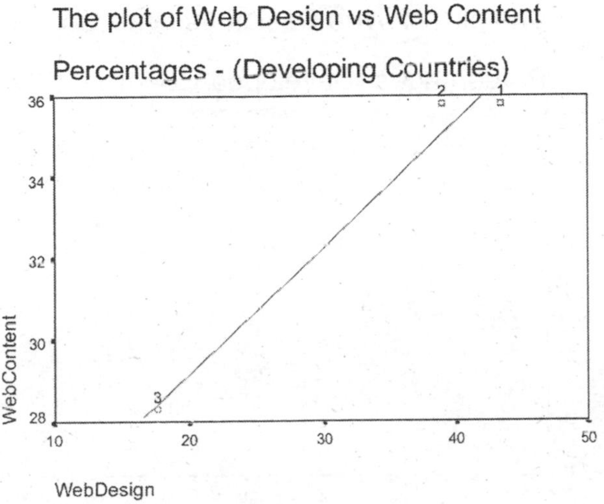

Legend:

	Percentage of Websites with given type of design quality	*Percentage of Websites with type of content quality*
V. Good (1)	43.4%	35.8%
Medium (2)	39.0%	35.8%
Poor (3)	17.6%	28.3%

Fig. 4. A scatter plot of Web design percentages against Web content percentages observed in the developing countries

NOTE: Karl Pearson's product moment coefficient of correlation 'r' from the above data was calculated, and established to be 0.988. This indicated a very high positive association between Web design quality and Web content quality for the Websites considered in this study. Further, by conducting a 2-tailed, paired samples t test with ± = 0.025 (95% confidence interval) and 2 degrees of freedom, the calculated t statistic was found to be 0.06. This value is less than the conventional critical value of 4.303. This implied that the positive relationship between Web design and Web content was statistically insignificant.

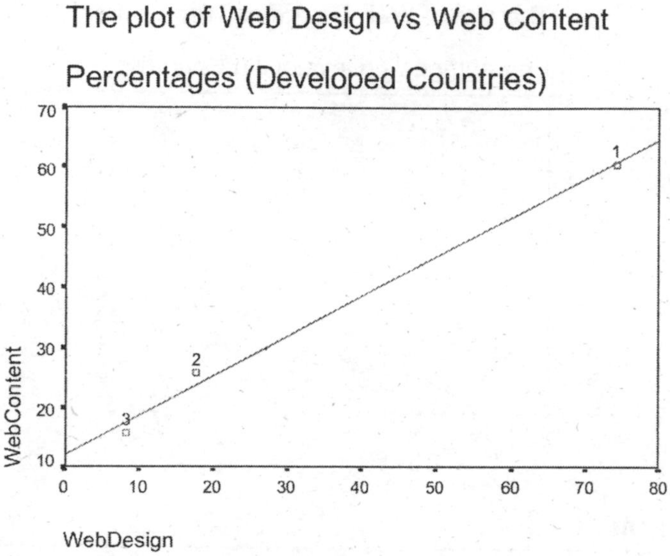

Legend:

	Percentage of Websites with given type of design quality	*Percentage of Websites with type of content quality*
V. Good (1)	74.2%	60.4%
Medium (2)	17.6%	25.8%
Poor (3)	8.2%	15.7%

Fig. 5. A scatter plot of Web design percentages against Web content percentages observed in the developed countries

NOTE: Karl Pearson's product moment coefficient of correlation 'r' from the above data was calculated, and established to be 0.996. This indicated a very high positive association between Web design quality and Web content quality for the Websites considered in this study. By conducting a 2-tailed, paired samples t test with ± = 0.025 (95% confidence interval) and 2 degrees of freedom, the calculated t statistic was found to be -0.88. This value is less than the critical value of 4.303. This implied that the positive relationship observed between Web design and Web content was also statistically insignificant.

RESULTS AND DISCUSSIONS

From the study it is apparent that the quality of university Website design does not universally have a meaningful effect on Web content quality, even though the two seemed to be strongly correlated in this study. It is advisable, therefore, for users to prudently use the websites and where necessary, consult well-trained librarians and other knowledgeable information professionals.

University Website designs in developing and developed countries should adhere to globally accepted norms of Website construction, in order to achieve optimum results. The W3C (*http://www.w3.org*) has long advocated for the design of sites for maximum accessibility. With this in perspective, the following points are recommended:

1. Speed should be emphasized on, by invoking minimal design techniques. Designers should concentrate on the quality of the message being conveyed rather than unnecessarily overloading a site with flashy multimedia effects. The snazzy graphics can be saved for the subsequent pages, which can be opened after having committed oneself to the Website. Home pages particularly, should be kept simple yet as welcoming as possible with only the most effective graphics/effects carefully selected for use.
2. Web designers should employ established Website design norms preferably after thorough acquaintance with Web and graphic user interface (GUI) conventions. The positions and actions of links, buttons and so on should not be changed unnecessarily because if consistency is maintained, the user has to learn it only once. Some users may get frustrated with an ever-changing Web interface.
3. Web designers should conduct proper research of facts, update the Website content regularly and have the updating date as well as authors' details clearly displayed for the purposes of authentication.

4. Web designers should minimize mouse travel around the screen and keystrokes to be entered because it would give users unnecessary work. Successive buttons and/or hyperlinks should be conspicuously availed close by. Moreover, it is advisable to provide multiple ways of doing the same thing.
5. Users should always be informed of what is happening within the Website in order to reduce disorientation. They should be provided with a mechanism of informing them where they are, how they can proceed to another page, how to go back to where they previously were, how to save, how to print, how seek for help and so on.
6. University Website designers and content developers should ensure that they research about the most suitable and useful external links to be availed to the Website visitors. This would help to expand the limits of the Website so that users would easily be able to access reliable information that is of value outside the given boundaries.
7. Information professionals within universities should be adequately trained in Website design techniques and Web content development/management. This is the only way they would be able to soundly advise the designers of their university Websites to generate the best products within the accessible budget.
8. The top-level managers of universities particularly those in the developing countries need to be sensitized on the importance of the Websites. In this manner, enough funds would be allotted for setting up and properly maintaining the sites at much more regular intervals, while adhering to internationally acceptable standards.

Following this study, it is suggested that the following areas of interest be investigated at a higher level:

(i) Whether similar results are manifested when studying university Websites in alternative languages other than English Language.
(ii) Whether similar results are evident in Websites of other spheres of modern life other than the tertiary education sector.

(iii) Whether the quality of university Websites has any relationship with the quantity of funds allocated by their respective parent institutions.

CONCLUSION

The study has attempted to demonstrate the application of a prototype Website evaluation process, which information professionals may employ. Perhaps with certain modifications, this procedure may be applicable to varied circumstances. Information professionals empowered with the basic systematic skills of objectively distinguishing the quality of information services would be a real asset to the Internet user. The clientele would be the beneficiaries in that they would be able to access the Websites that best satisfy individual as well as corporate information needs. The authors opine that if the ensuing information is appropriately used and assimilated, then such clients would have a competitive edge over those without access to such value-added services.

REFERENCES

Boutell, Thomas. 1996. *World Wide Web FAQ: What is a URL?*. URL: http://www.unimelb.edu.au/public/www-faq/url.htm

Gray, Matthew K. 2004. *Websites, Hostnames and IP Addresses, Oh My*. URL: http://www.mit.edu/people/mkgray/net

Hacche, John. 1970. *Economics of Money and Income*. London: Heinemann Educational Books Ltd, 342-343.

McLachlan, Karen. 2002. *Adventures of Cyberbee: Web Evaluation*. URL: http://www.cyberbee.com/guides.html

Todaro, Michael P. 1994. *Economic Development*. 5th ed. New York: Longman, 28-31.

W3C. 1994 – 2004. *W3C (World Wide Web Consortium): Leading the Web to Full Potential...*" URL: http://www.w3.org

APPENDIX I

CHECKLIST AND RATING SCALE FOR WEBSITE DESIGN

Geographical region to which the Website is affiliated:

Site Title: Subject:

URL:

Audience: Website Developer:

Evaluate the Website's design according to the criteria described below. Circle "Y" = Yes (1 Mark) and "N" = No (0 Mark)

1. Downloading speed

(a) The Homepage downloads efficiently (takes at most 20 seconds with 56 Kbps modem) Y N

2. Homepage design

(a) The Homepage is attractive, has strong eye appeal Y N

(b) You can tell where you are immediately (clear title, description, image captions etc.) Y N

(c) There is an index, table of contents or some other clear indicator of the contents of the site Y N

(d) Site sponsor/provider is clearly identified Y N

(e) Information/method for contacting sponsor/provider is readily available Y N

(f) Copyright date or date site was established is easy to determine Y N

3. Ease of navigation

(a) User is able to move around within the site with ease Y N

(b) Directions for using the site are provided if necessary Y N

(c) Directions are clear and easy to follow Y N

(d) The links to other pages within the site are helpful and appropriate Y N

(e) Internal and external links are working properly (no dead ends, no incorrect links, etc.) Y N

4. Use of multimedia

(a) Each graphic, audio file, video file, etc. serves a clear purpose Y N

(b) The graphics, animations, sound clips, etc. make a significant contribution to the site Y N

5. Browser compatibility

(a) Site is equally effective with a variety of browsers such as Netscape and Internet Explorer Y N

6. Manner of presentation

(a) There is sufficient information to make the site worth visiting Y N

(b) The information is clearly labeled and organized Y N

(c) The same basic format is used consistently throughout the site Y N

(d) Information is easy to find (in no more than three clicks for example) Y N

(e) Lists of links are well organized and easy to use Y N

7. Maintenance

(a) The date of the last revision is clearly labeled Y N

(b) Out-dated material has been removed Y N

8. Availability of further information

(a) A working link is provided to a contact person or address for further information Y N

(b) Links to other useful Websites are providedY N

9. Sub-totals

10. Grand Total

11. Rating scale

Based on the total of "Yes" and "No" answers, give this site your overall rating (tick only one option):(a). 24 – 16 Marks: Very well designed Website, easy to use(b). 15 – 11 Marks: Website design needs to be improved but site is usable(c). 10 – 0 Marks: Poorly designed Website, difficult to use

APPENDIX II

CHECKLIST AND RATING SCALE FOR CONTENT EVALUATION

Geographical region to which the Website is affiliated:

Site Title: Subject:

URL:

Audience: Purposes of the site:

Evaluate the Website content following the criteria described below. Circle "Y" = Yes (1 Mark) and "N" = No (0 Mark)

1. Efficiency of the Website

(a) The Homepage downloads efficiently Y N

(b) User is able to determine the intended audience of the site Y N

2. Information providers

(a) The author(s) of the material on the site are clearly identified Y N

(b) Information about the author(s) is availableY N

(c) According to the info given, author(s) appears qualified to present information on this topic Y N

(d) The sponsor of the site is clearly identifiedY N

(e) A contact person or address is available so the user can ask questions or verify information Y N

3. Information currency

(a) Latest revision date is provided Y N

(b) Latest revision date appropriate to materialY N

(c) Content is updated frequently Y N

(d) Links to other sites are current and working properly Y N

4. Information quality

(a) The purpose of this site is clear Y N

(b) The content achieves this intended purpose effectively Y N

(c) The content appears to be complete (no "under construction" signs) Y N

(d) The content of the site is well organized Y N

(e) The information in this site is easy to understand Y N

(f) The site offers sufficient information related to the needs of its user(s) Y N

(g) The content is free of bias, or the bias can be easily detected Y N

(h) This site provides interactivity that increases its value Y N

(i) The information appears to be accurate based on the user's experience Y N

(j) The information is consistent with similar information in other sources Y N

(k) Grammar and spelling are correct Y N

5. External linkage

(a) There are working links to other sites that are related to the users' needs/purposes Y N

(b) The content to the linked sites is worthwhile and appropriate to the users' needs/purposes Y N

6. Sub-totals

7. Grand Total

8. Rating scale

Based on the total of "Yes" and "No" answers, give this site your overall rating (tick only one option):

(a) 24 – 16 Marks: Very useful Website for users' information needs

(b) 15 – 11 Marks: Website worth book marking for future reference

(c) 10 – 0 Marks: Website not worth coming back to

27

Development of Virtual Libraries in India: Problems and Prospects

Mamata Mestri
K. Praveenkumar
S. Parameshwar

ABSTRACT

The paper explains about the development of the Virtual libraries. The developed countries all over the world are developing virtual libraries faster and compared to the different countries, there is slow development in Information and Communication Technology applications in India. This is mainly because of growing population, illiteracy, low standard of living, less importance to telecommunication facilities, shortage in supply of Energy Sources, lower number of computer and Internet users. These problems become obstacle for the development of the Virtual libraries in India causing a Digital Divide. To improve the use of Information Technology applications and to fill the Digital Divide gap, the Government of India and different state government already initiated certain policies and projects. The paper also discussed the policies and projects of Central and different State

Governments to increase the use of Information Technology applications in administration.

INTRODUCTION

The developments in Information and Communication Technology applications transformed the Libraries into Electronic Library, Digital Library, Hybrid Library and Virtual Library. Depending on the level of ICT applications in the libraries these libraries were classified. Virtual Reality technology transformed the libraries into Virtual Libraries.

Sangam and Kulkarni[1] stated that the terms Virtual Library, Electronic Library and Digital Library are used synonymously. But there is difference between these terms as under:

Electronic Library is a library that has use of computers and such other activities as online databases and automated record keeping and computer based decision making. Digital Libraries are libraries in which all information exists in digital format. The information itself may however reside on different storage media such as electronic memory magnetic or optical disks, but user will not necessarily perceive any difference between them. Virtual Libraries use the technologies of Virtual Reality (VR). This is known as tele-presence in its simplest form. In a Virtual environment, one would be able to browse without having to physically go to it. Using Virtual Reality equipment and facilities one would be able to enter virtual library, browse around its rooms and shelves, use index or catalogue, select a book (by pointing to it and touching it).

Virtual Reality is an oxymoron, where Virtual means the existing or resulting in essence or effect though not in actual fact, form or name and Reality means the quality or state being actual or true. i.e. both these are self-contradictory words. The term Virtual Reality refers to an environment or object simulated by computer hardware and software in such a way that the viewer experience the environment or object as though it were real.

The virtual library exists independently of the amount or nature of the electronic information to which it provides access. There are no limits on the size, content or value of data in a virtual library. Its definition is shaped by individual or organizational need[2].

LIBRARIES AND VIRTUAL TECHNOLOGY

A number of different definitions have been developed in recent literature, a result of which is the need to distinguish between[3]:

* The library as we know it, which enables users to search for needed information from sources worldwide; to browse and retrieve selected information and request help at any point in the process.
* The library without walls- the virtual library, which facilitates these tasks instantly from users' own network-connected computers, any time, any where and
* The virtual reality library.

Virtual library may be defined as "a library with little or no physical collection of books, periodicals, reading space or support staff, but one that disseminates selective information directly to distributed library, usually electronically"[4].

Virtual library is a library without walls, spread across the globe from where one is able to retrieve the whole world of information through a properly networked workstation. Here the user gets impression as if he is moving through a large library though library does not physically exist, yet the user is able to retrieve the information needed by him[5].

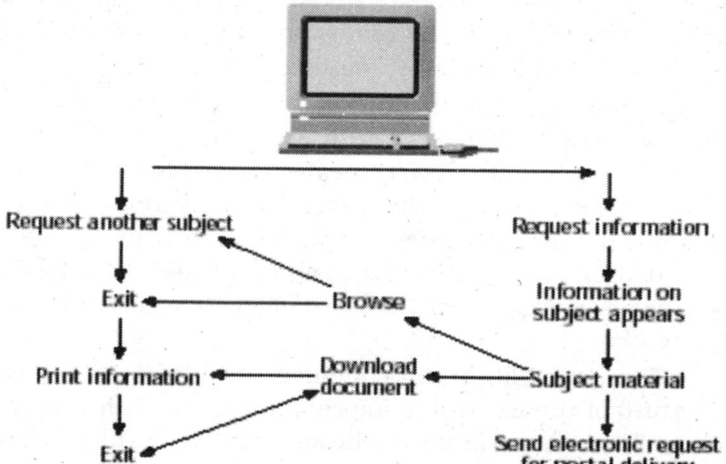

Of course, every developed country transforming their libraries into Virtual Libraries. To use the Virtual library, the user population must be literate, preferably well knowledge with the Web and Virtual Reality Technology. Further, there are adequate resources such as Electricity power generation in the country, higher standard of living, proper telecommunication facilities etc. Due to the developments in ICT applications and the nature and problems of the people in India, there is threat of digital divide, which became major obstacle for developing the Virtual Libraries in India. The different problems are discussed as under:

PROBLEMS

Of Course any of the nations in the world, is not completely free from its own problems like unemployment, Poverty, Illiteracy, Crime etc. In other words, every nation is having its own problems like-wise; India is also having certain problems. These problems are the hindrance to the development of the digital libraries in India. They are discussed as under:

1. Growing Population and Illiteracy

India is the second largest country in growing population. Approximately $1/3^{rd}$ of the population is illiterate and uneducated. The following table shows the population and literacy rate of different Countries in the world.

Table 1. Table showing Geographical Area, Population and Literacy of the different countries

Sl. No	*Country*	*Geographical Area (Sq.kms)*	*Population (In Millions)*	*Literacy Rate (In %age)/ Year*
1	China	95,96,960	1295.0	86 (2002)
2	India	32,87,590	1049.0	65.38 (2001)
3	Germany	3,56,910	82.4	99 (2002)
4	Japan	3,77,835	127.5	99 (2002)
5	Russia	1,70,75,200	144.1	100 (2002)
6	United Kingdom	2,44,820	59.1	99 (2002)
7	United States of America	96,29,091	291.0	97.9 (1991)

Source: Competition Success Review Year book 2005.

It is noted that the virtual libraries become reality, only if the complete population of the respective country is literate. In this case, it is observed from the above table that literacy rate is higher in Russia, Japan, Germany, UK, USA AND China. But in India, the literacy rate is still 65.38% and it is a problem for the development of the virtual libraries.

2. STANDARD OF LIVING AND TELECOMMUNICATION FACILITIES

Growing population has caused unemployment and poverty in India. Consequently there is a lower standard of living and lower GDP per capita. Due to these factors, there is slow development in telecommunication facilities. The following table showed the GDP Per capita, number of fixed telephone links and Mobile Cellular available for people in different countries.

Table 2. Table showing GDP Per Capita ($), Telephone facilities and Cellular Phones in different countries.

Sl. No	*Country*	*GDP Per capita $*	*No. of Telephone Connections (In Thousands)*	*No. of Cellular Phones (In Thousands)*
1	China	4700	135000	65000
2	India	2540	27700	2930
3	Germany	24051	53720	60043
4	Japan	31407	60381	56000
5	Russia	8900	35500	17608.8
6	United Kingdom	26150	34878	43500
7	United States of America	36300	194000	127000

Source: (i) Competition Success Review Year book 2005.
(ii) Career and Competition Monthly Chronicle: India 2005: A Handy Compendium of Statistics

It is noted that India is having lowest GDP per capita and there are lower number of Telephone and Cellular Phone users. For the development of the virtual libraries, there is need to develop the standard of living and improve telecommunication facilities for the people.

3. DEMAND AND SUPPLY OF POWER

It is noted that the electricity is the basic and main source of power for working of any electrical and electronic equipment. Adequate Production and supply of Electricity helps the population to enable the use of telecommunication facilities and computers. As per the Census of India 2001, of the total 191963935 households in India, only 107209054 (55.84%) households are having electricity and the remaining 84754881 (44.16%) households are powered with alternative energy sources such as Kerosene, solar power and others.

Further, the Energy and Power Supply in India in the years 2002-03, 2001-02 and 2000-01 are as under:

Table 3. Table showing the Demand and Supply of Power and Energy in India in selected years.

Energy (MU)	*2002-03*	*2001-02*	*2000-01*
Requirement	458777	522537	507216
Availability	417090	483350	467400
Shortage (%)	9.1	7.5	7.8
Power (MW)			
Peak Demand	81492	78441	78037
Peak Demand met	71520	69189	67880
Shortage (%)	12.2	11.8	13.0

Source: The Penguin India Yearbook 2005.

From the above data, it is clear that there is shortage in power supply and about half of the households in India are not using Electric power till now. Hence there is need to develop power sector in India, for the development of the virtual libraries.

4. COMPUTER, INTERNET AND VIRTUAL TECHNOLOGY USERS

The awareness about the Information Technology, Computers and Internet is essential for the development of Virtual library. Hence for the development of virtual libraries, the majority of the population must be able to use the computers, internet and Virtual Technology. The following Table shows the statistics about the Computer users in different countries in 2002 and 2005.

Table 4. Table showing Number of Computer Users in different countries in 2002 and 2005.

Sl.No.	Country	2002 (%)	2005 (%)
1	China	35	35
2	India	6	21
3	Germany	63	67
4	Russia	19	35
5	Canada	75	79
6	United Kingdom	59	76
7	United States of America	74	76

Source: http://yaleglobal.yale.edu/display.article?id=7031

The Internet is popularly used media for communication in virtual libraries. Hence, to access digital and virtual libraries, the internet usage is also a most important factor. The following table shows the Statistics about the Internet users in different countries in 2002 and 2005.

Table 5. Table showing Number of Internet Users in different countries in 2002 and 2005.

Sl.No.	Country	2002 (%)	2005 (%)
1	China	24	33
2	India	3	14
3	Germany	47	60
4	Russia	7	15
5	Canada	68	71
6	United Kingdom	47	71
7	United States of America	64	70

Source: http://yaleglobal.yale.edu/display.article?id=7031

It is noted from the above table that only 21% of the population know about the Computers and only 14 % of the population use Internet in India. For operating and accessing virtual libraries, the majority of the population must be able to use computers and able to search Internet. When compared to other countries, the majority of Indian population is unaware of these technologies. Hence it is a major obstacle for the development of virtual libraries in India.

5. STATUS OF LIBRARY AND ITS PROFESSIONALS:

It is noted that when compared to developed countries,

the development of the Libraries is slow in India. Even after 59 years of Independence, many of the State Governments have not enacted Public Library Legislations so as to provide public library facilities to common public. In many colleges, the Library professionals are still considered non-teaching and supporting staff. A few academic libraries are managed by non-library professionals. Even though Dr. Ranganathan emphasized Open Access system for the libraries, many academic libraries are working with closed access system for their collection.

6. DIGITAL DIVIDE

The "information and technology gap" or "digital divide", to refer to the gap between those who can effectively use new information and communication tools, such as the internet, and those who cannot. This definition, however, is disappointing, as it is rather too simplistic. It is true that the most dramatic kind of digital divide is the global divide: some countries can use the internet, and others cannot, because of the simple fact that the indispensable technological infrastructure is missing[6].

As the digital divide focuses on the higher end of ICTs involving the electronic transfer of information using digital formats which may themselves be replaced by new technologies such as virtual systems within the next decade. It assumes that the benefits of these technologies and access to the world of information that is contained within them is a benefit that no citizen in the twenty-first century should be without, certainly not at least in the developed world.

The digital divide is usually referred to as the "inequality of access to the Internet." The digital divide is the gap between those people and communities who can access and make effective use of information technology and those who cannot. Simply, A common euphemism that describes the haves and have not of the information age, usually urban versus rural communities. The digital divide is the socio-economic/ technological difference between communities in their access to computers and the Internet. The term also refers to gaps between groups in their ability to use ICTs (Information and

Communications Technologies) effectively, due to differing literacy and technical skills, and the gap in availability of quality, useful digital content. The divide is seen as a national/social/political problem. It became an issue among concerned parties, such as governments, scholars, policy makers, and advocacy groups, in the late1990s[7].

Cullen[8] stated that 'A number of research and policy papers addressing the issue of the digital divide identify specific groups of people as being especially disadvantaged in their uptake of ICTs. These include people on low incomes, people with few educational qualifications or with low literacy levels, the unemployed, elderly people, people in isolated or rural areas, people with disabilities, sole parents, elderly people, women and girls. Because they are often already disadvantaged in terms of education, income and wealth status, and also because of their profound cultural different from the dominant Western culture of the developed world, many indigenous people, and some migrant and ethnic minority groups are identified as having a very low uptake of ICTs. In the USA therefore Afro-Americans, Latinos, as well as North American, Indian Nations are identified as needing targeted programmes to increase their participation in the digital economy'. The digital divide is always described in terms of the difference in the number of telephones, internet users or computers per head between rich and poor countries[9].

Prospects and Developments

The Government of India, Union Territories and State Governments already, formulated and executed various plans and policies to curb the growth rate of population, Literacy programmes, increase in standard of living, to achieve full employment, developing Agriculture and industrial sector, Improvement in Power Production and Supply, to increase the exports, etc. due to such efforts, India is developing in all respects.

Even though many of social, political and economic problems proved to be obstacles and problems for the development of the digital libraries in India, the Government of India and different state governments initiated Information

Technology projects to develop the application of Information Technology in administration and planned to educate the people. Of course, it is not possible to discuss all the measures and policies undertaken by the Government of India for encouraging use of ICT and web in India. Following are a few policies of the Government of India and developmental trends in promoting use and development of the Information and Communication Technology, electronic media and Information Sector. The policies and trends undertaken by the various state governments and Union Territories are discussed by Shashi Prabha Singh[10].

The Prime Minister of India constituted a National Task Force on Information Technology and Software Development in May 1998 with the purpose of formulating a long term National IT Policy to convert India into an IT software superpower. As it is not possible to mention all the developments, the developments stated in the following paragraphs are the only a few achievements made in different departments and sections of the Central Government:

* A Land Information System has already started using Geographic Information System (GIS) and remote sensing to help the farmers to plan their activities and facilitate decision making and planning at the local level. Government is also planned for a System known as "Agriculture Online" for the exchange of Ideas and Information between farmers, Agricultural Scientists, traders and exporters.
* The higher education institutions consisting of 310 Universities and academic institutions 16,000 affiliated colleges were networked with the help of INFLIBNET, an Inter-University Centre of UGC. In 28th December 2003, UGC-INFONET Electronic Journal Consortia was started by INFLIBNET and at present it is providing 4000+ Research Journals to 100+ Universities in India Online. The INFLIBNET is conducting regular training programmes in different applications of ICT to the information professionals. Now a days, every Indian University is using internet for its activities such as Admissions, Exams, Results etc.

* Postal Department got computerized and several new services based on Internet were introduced. E-Post is a new service available at 204 Post Offices at present in a few states – Andhra Pradesh, Gujarat, Goa, Kerala, and Maharastra to cater the postal service to the persons who do not have a PC or internet facilities. E-Bill post is a multipurpose web based facility for paying telephone bills, mobile phone bills, Electricity bills etc, online. Speed Net is another internet based tracking and tracing service for the customer at Speed Post Counters. The computerization and VSAT connectivity for the postal service is under progress.
* India has the fifth largest telecom network in the world comprising of 61.09 million telephone connections (basic and mobile) and over 1.48 million public call offices. There are over 16 million cellular subscribers in the country, growing at the rate of about 1 million per month. The number of digital electronic exchanges was around 300 increased to 36,772 in July 2003.
* The software and IT industry has grown significantly during 2003-04 by emerging as one of the fastest growing sectors with a growth rate of over 30.5% and an export value of US$12.5 billion. According to the National Association of Software and Services Companies (NASSCOM) estimate in 2002-03, the total revenue from the India IT market was Rs. 317 billion against Rs. 291 billion in 2001-02. The Indian IT and electronics industry recorded a production of Rs. 80,884 Crore during 2001-02 as compared to Rs. 68,450 Crore during 2000-01 showing a growth of 18 percent. Software export alone has jumped by approximately 10 percent to Rs. 36,500 crores during 2001-02 from Rs. 3,700 Crore during 1996-97 with a compound annual growth of about 60 percent.
* The Government of India computerized different departments under E-Governance programme. The departments are Customs and Excise department, Banks, Railways, Air Transport, Income Tax and Telecommunications etc. so as to facilitate Online

Transactions. Similarly the Electronic Voting Machines were introduced in Elections.

* Government also taken up development programmes in Mass Media, such as Television, Radio, Newspapers and Magazines. Electronic Media developed in such a way that the actual situations at various polling booths in Loksabha Elections 2004 were telecasted live through Video-Conferencing.
* The Collections of many of the Academic Libraries and Special Libraries were digitized already and can be accessible through the networks. Several Information Systems and Networks are developed connecting libraries. NISSAT developed several Metropolitan Area Networks such as ADINET, BONET, CALIBNET, DELNET, etc. The Other networks are INFLIBNET, ERNET, SIRNET, etc. Through networking of the Libraries, many libraries are sharing their resources online.
* On September 20, 2004 Geo-Synchronous Satellite Launch Vehicle (GSLV) is launched from Sriharikota and put EDUSAT, the educational Satellite. The EDUSAT is set to bring about revolutionary changes in distance education, converting homes into virtual classrooms. Through EDUSAT, a teacher from a television studio can simultaneously address hundreds of students in different schools and colleges in the various parts of the country if the educational institutions have a terminal to receive the programme. The EDUSAT has 12 transponders, which are capable of generating regional beams covering different parts of India. It is estimated that programmes from EDUSAT can reach 1,000 class rooms and 50,000 students.
* According to Essential Science Indicators (ESI) during 1997-2001, India produced 76,970 papers as against 1, 14,894 by China. The Number of Scientific papers is just one measure of state of research in the country.
* India has joined a select club of six advanced countries with the Pune-based Centre for Development of Advanced Computing (C-DAC) developing the country's

Super computer. C-DAC developed 'Param Padam' a super computer which promises the creation of a seamless computing platform for supercomputing at an affordable price in the international market.

* Digital Mobile Library Project: The Govt. of India with the collaboration of C-DAC aimed at bringing about one million books of digital library at the doorsteps of common citizens. Internet enabled mobile Digital Library is brought for the use of common citizen for promoting literacy. It makes use of mobile van with satellite connection for connectivity of internet. The van is fitted with printer, scanner and cutter and binding machine for providing bound books to the end users.
* NGO's Initiatives: According to estimates, around one million NGOs are functioning in India, majority of which are working for the poor and the downtrodden. Some of the NGOs have taken initiative in setting up information disseminating centers in rural areas. A few such schemes include Drishtee Project, Gyandoot Scheme, The Sustainable Access in Rural India (SARI) Network, General Resources and Information Dissemination (GRID) Center, etc.
* Corporate Initiatives: The motive of increasing market base has prompted several corporate houses to take up projects aimed at setting up information kiosks in rural areas in different parts of the country. In most cases such kiosks provide various information required by the rural people, besides information relating to the products and service offered by the respective corporate houses. Such developments include Amul's Disk Net, Hindustan Lever's i-Shakti, Ogilvy and Mather's Param Project, Parry's India Agriline, ITC group's e-chaupal project etc.
* India also ahead in production and export of the electronic products, as disclosed in the following table:

Table 6. Table showing Electronic Exports from India

Sl.No	Items	1999-00	2000-01	2001-02	2002-03
1	Electronic Hardware	1,400	4,788	5,800	5,600
2	Computer Software	17,150	28,350	36,500	47,500
	Total	18,550	33,138	42,300	53,100

Source: Chronicle Year book 2005.

CONCLUSION

Change, transformation and development are the essence of human life and society. Major changes occur due to technological developments. With the change in technology, the society is also transforming along the line of the latest technology. The Libraries are not exception to the same. From the above discussion it is clear that India is developing in all respects so as to overcome technological backwardness and digital divide between poor and rich, rural and urban population, illiterate and literates. But it is noted that growth of Indian economy is slower compared to other countries. For the all round development, the digital and virtual library must be able to serve the masses rather than only a few. On the other hand the mass people of India must be able to know and use the virtual and digital technologies for their development. Computer education to the masses and application of information and communication technology in all the areas is emphasized in this respect for India. The efforts of the governments also appreciable in this regard. To overcome the digital divide still few more efforts such as compulsory computer education, developing awareness of the ICT applications, etc are required to achieve a 'developed country' status.

It is also essential for the working library professionals, library science students and teachers, to know about the latest technology applications such as Virtual reality, so as to design and develop the future virtual libraries. For this purpose, there is also need for the training and manpower development activities from various Universities and professional institutes.

REFERENCES

1. Sangam, SL and Kulkarni, SR: Concept of Virtual Library. ILA Seminar Papers 47th All India Library Conference. Warangal, 20-23 December 2001. P. 681-695.
2. Pacifici, Sabrina I: Virtual Library: Mythor Reality. http://www.llrx.com/features/virtual.htm accessed on 07th November 2006.
3. Stella Neal: The Virtual Library: a Market Perspective. The Bottom Line: Managing Library Finances. Vol. 10. No. 3. 1997. P. 100-106.
4. Powell, Alan: Management Models and Measurements in the Virtual Library. Special Library. Vol. 185. No. 4. Fall 1994. P. 260.
5. Murthy, SS: Library and Information Service in the Electronic Information era. Journal of Library and Information Science. Vol. No. 1. January 1999. P. 68-69.
6. Hubregtse, Sjaak: The digital divide within the European Union. *New Library World.* Vol. 106. No. 1210/1211. 2005. P. 164-172.
7. Subhendu Kar and Pralay Sarma: Bridging the Digital Divide through Digital Libraries: A Proposed Solution. *Proceedings of the National Conference on Information Management in Digital Libraries.* Kharagpur: Indian Institute of Technology, 2006.
8. Cullen, Rowena: The digital divide: a global and national call to action. *The Electronic Library.* Vol. 21. No.3. 2003. P. 247-257.
9. Mutula, Stephen M: Bridging the digital divide through e-governance: A proposal for Africa's libraries and information centres. *The Electronic Library.* Vol. 23. No. 5. 2005. P. 591-602.
10. Singh, Shashi Prabha: The role of technology in the emergence of the information society in India. *The Electronic Library.* Vol. 23 No.6. 2005. P. 678-690.
11. Bright, PS, Ed: Competition Refresher Book of the Year 2005. New Delhi: Bright Careers Institute, 2005.
12. Chronicle Year book 2005. New Delhi: Chronicle Books,2005.
13. Gulati, Anjali: Use of Information and Communication Technology in Libraries and Information Centres: An Indian Scenario. *The Electronic Library.* Vol. 22. No.4. 2004.
13. O'Brien, Derek, Ed: The Penguin India Reference Yearbook 2005. New Delhi: Penguin Book, 2005.

14. Rajaram, Kalpana: Spectrum's Handbook of General Studies 2005. New Delhi: Spectrum Books, 2005.
15. Sachdeva, SK, Ed: Competition Success Review Year book 2005. New Delhi: Competition Success Review, 2005.
16. Subburaj, VVK, Ed: Sura's Yearbook 2005. Chennai: Sura College of Competition, 2005.
17. Tara Chand, Ed (2005): Tata Mc Graw Hill's General Studies 2005. New Delhi: TMH, 2005.

28

Expert Systems: Impact on Library Services

K. Praveenkumar.

D.B. Patil

S. Parameshwar

ABSTRACT

Basically the paper explained about information management techniques using emerging Information Communication Technology (ICT) and Artificial Intelligence (AI). Artificial Intelligence is emerging technological discipline which included advanced applications such as Natural Language Processing, Automatic Programming, Robotics, Expert Systems and such other advanced mechanized applications. The present paper explained about the structure of an Expert System which included Knowledge Base, Knowledge Acquisition, Inference Engine, User Interface, Explanation Facility and External Interface. It highlighted the use and application of expert systems in providing different library services such as Library Cataloguing, Subject Indexing, Database Search Service, Reference Service and Collection Development. It concluded with remarks that how technology plays an important role in providing specialized library services to the users.

INTRODUCTION

Information Management deals with the development of the information and its effective utilization. The information to be managed includes both explicit, documentary information and subjective information and information management includes all the processes associated with the identification, retrieval, collection, storage, organization, sharing and communication of the information. To be successful information management requires systems for the management of information repositories and to cultivate and facilitate the sharing of information and organizational learning.

The Information and Communication Technologies, web technologies and database techniques have compelled library and information centers to use these technologies effectively to render services. With the increasing in the number of Electronic resources, it has become imperative for information providers to redefine their role in disseminating information to the users.

Now the Artificial Intelligence techniques are developed and applied to many subjects. These are computer programmes developed to perform intelligent tasks such as diagnoses of diseases in Medical Science, solving differential equations in symbolic forms in Mathematics, automatic translation in Linguistics, analyze and design electronic circuits in Electronics etc.

ARTIFICIAL INTELLIGENCE

According to Patterson, Artificial Intelligence is a "branch of computer science with the study and creation of computer systems that exhibits some form of intelligence, system that can learn new concepts and tasks, systems that reasons and draw useful conclusions about the world around us, systems that can understand a natural language or perceive, comprehend a visual scene and systems that perform other types of facts that require human types of intelligence".[1]

Artificial Intelligence techniques are attempting to create machines that can replace manual as well as mental power and intelligence of human beings. Artificial Intelligence has more success at intellectual tasks such as multilingual computing, game playing and theorem proving. The Artificial techniques included Natural Language Processing, Multilingual computing, Intelligent Retrieval from Databases, theorem proving, Expert Systems, Automatic Programming and Robotics. The present paper explained the development of Expert Systems and its application to Library operations.

EXPERT SYSTEMS

Expert System is a branch of Artificial Intelligence. It was developed by researchers during 1970s and applied commercially throughout the 1980s. Expert System is a computer program that emulates the decision making of a human expert in narrow domain of expertise such as diagnosing a heart disease, predicting a stock in the stock market etc. Expert System reasons by heuristics or approximate methods. It explains and justifies solutions in user-friendly terms[2].

Expert System regarded as "the embodiment within a computer of knowledge based component from an expert skill in such a form that the system can offer intelligent advice or take an intelligent decision about a processing function. A desirable additional characteristic, which many would consider fundamental, is the capability of the systems on demand, to justify its own line of reasoning in a manner directly intelligible to the enquirer. The style adopted to attain these characteristics is "rule based programming".

In simple terms, an expert system stores large amount of data and disseminate it in a systematic way as required by the users. Expert system represents one of the most advanced facets of information technology. That is they help the users in some of the most complex and least understood human information handling tasks like decision making, problem solving, diagnoses and learning. They perform it by storing a large amount of factual information on a subject area with lines of reasoning employed by human experts in that area.

Building an expert system is known as knowledge engineering and its practitioners are called knowledge engineers. The knowledge engineer must make sure that the computer has all the knowledge needed to solve a problem[3].

Most of this material is supplied to the program at the time, it is written, but also has facilities for adding to this base of information as it is applied in new situations. The subject expertise is provided initially by interviews, observations of successful practitioners on the subject.

STRUCTURE OF THE EXPERT SYSTEM

Generally structure of an expert system consists of the Facts and Heuristics. The following are the basic components of an expert system.

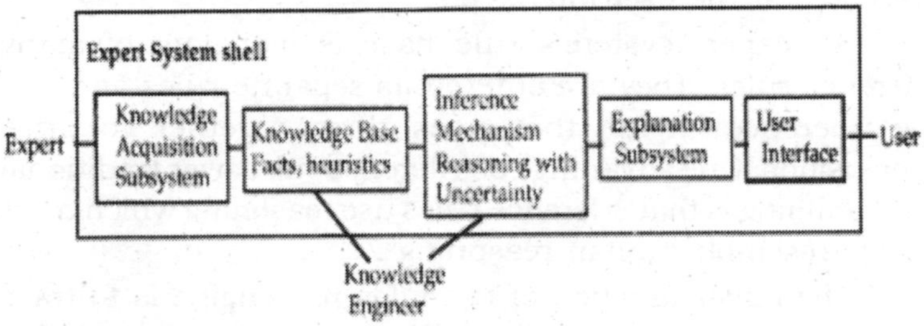

Fig. 1. Basic Components of Expert System Tools[4]

1. Knowledge Base

The core module of an expert system is Knowledge Base. It stores large amount of data relating to specific discipline. It represents knowledge through logic, reasoning, scripts, binary tables, semantic networks and on conceptual dependency.

2. Knowledge Acquisition

The Knowledge represented in the Knowledge Base has to be acquired and organized from the subject experts. Subject experts make decisions based on qualitative and quantitative information. The subject expert has to translate the standard procedures and more difficult experience based heuristics into a suitable form for the expert system.

The knowledge acquisition process, which started in the specification phase, continues into the development phase. The developer must extract knowledge from the previous case discussions. The types of knowledge the developer looks for can be grouped into three categories: Strategic, judgemental and factual. Strategic knowledge is used to help create a flow chart of the system. Judgemental knowledge usually helps define the inference process and describes the reasoning process used by the expert. Finally, factual knowledge describes the characteristics and important attributes of objects in the system[5].

3. Inference Engine

It is also called "Rule Interpreter". The inference engine is that part of the program which reasons and determines how to apply the knowledge in the knowledge base to the queries presented at the user interface.

An expert system's rule base is made up of many inference rules. They are entered as separate rules and it is the inference engine that uses them together to draw conclusions. One advantage of inference rules over traditional programming is that inference rules use reasoning which more closely resemble human reasoning[6].

The major function of the inference engine is to trace its way through a set of rules to arrive at a conclusion. The engine will trace the conclusion by logical searching through key terms. It reaches conclusion on the basis of programmed rules.

4. User Interface

It provides the user to communicate and interact with the system. Users normally interact with the system either for getting information as per his/her need or for getting detailed explanations to specific queries.

5. Explanation Facility

Getting answers to specific queries forms the explanation mechanism of an expert system. Explanation facility is actually a part of User Interface. It helps the user in the following ways:

* If the User is an expert, it helps in identifying what additional
* knowledge he is needed;
* Enhances the user's confidence in the system;

* Serves as a tutor in sharing the system's knowledge with the user.

6. External Interface

External Interface provides the communication link between the expert system and the external environment. When there is a formal consultation, it is done through the user interface. The external interface with its sensors gets the minute by minute information about the situation and acts accordingly.

The Communication subsystem, that is a part of the external interface, permits the system to communicate with a global database for its operation. The facts that have been inferred by the inference procedure are recorded in the global database called blackboard. Black board system consists of:

* A global database from which different knowledge sources acquire data.
* A variety of knowledge sources.
* A scheduler to control and co-ordinate the activity.

With the information in the Blackboard, different knowledge sources, which are in the production rule format, get activated. The scheduler controls the sequence of execution of rules and every time rule is triggered, the result is saved in the blackboard.

In this way, system proceeds to function. For performing these activities the system should have a good communication facility.

Another important constituent of the external interface is the Database Management System (DBMS). The DBMS serves as an archive for all the consultations, the system had with the user. The records of consultations will help in determining the scope of the information needed and disseminate the same.

IMPACT OF EXPERT SYSTEMS ON LIBRARY SERVICES:

Following are the various applications of expert systems to the different operations of the library.

1. Library Cataloguing

Basically cataloguing in a library is rule based. As an

expert system works on logic and reasoning based on some rules, Library cataloguing work is systematically maintained through expert systems.

2. Subject Indexing

The assignment of approach terms to the documents, to represent the subjects dealt with is another activity that might benefit from the expert system. An interactive program, MedIndEx, has been developed at the National Library Medicine, using expert system principles, to assist the indexer in using Medical Subject Headings to represent the subject matter of biomedical articles. The system can perform two major tasks (i) prompt the indexer to assign a particular term or type of term and (ii) correct the indexer when a term is used inappropriately.

Other approaches to automatic indexing or computer aided indexing, also claim to use expert system techniques.

3. Database Searching

Much work has been done on the development of "intelligent front-ends" or "intelligent interfaces", which help for the searching of databases through online networks. Denning and Smith presented some general design principles to guide the implementation of intelligent interfaces. Further, explained about a model prototype, ELSA (Electronic Library Search Assistant) [7].

4. Reference Service

The Survey of Association of Research Libraries regarding the use of expert system in research libraries indicated that Reference Service is the area that has received most attention. The question answering in reference service is an obvious application of expert system approaches, because similar questions are repeated time to time again and many of the libraries record questions received and answers provided and if it is an expert system the records are created in its Knowledge Base.

Bailey and Myers stated about a general expert system-Reference Expert (RE) developed at the University of Houston. The database of Reference Expert is much smaller- 340 reference sources in printed and CD-ROM form; almost 150 are indexes and the remaining are other types of reference sources. Reference Expert is intended to help the users to find sources to answer their reference questions when library professionals are not available. Menus lead a user down to an appropriate level of subject heading, then offer the user various possible answers to the questions[8].

5. Collection Development

The expert systems also developed for acquiring different kinds of documents and collection development in libraries. Hawks described about an expert system capable of recommending a source to order and acquire documents such as reports, monographs, government publications and others. The systems are able to rank the potential sources to reflect probability of success in acquisition and collection on the basis of information content[9].

The benefits of expert systems are:

1. Make Scarce expertise more widely available, thereby helping non-experts achieve expert like results.
2. Free some of the time of human experts for other activities.
3. Promote Standardization and Consistency in relatively unstructured tasks.
4. Provide incentives for creating a database of knowledge in a permanent form (e.g. not dependent on the availability of particular individuals).
5. Perform at a consistently high level (e.g. not influenced by fatigue or lack of concentration).

CONCLUSION

The Knowledge and Rule based expert systems will be of a great value to the library profession when applied to highly specialized activities that are now accomplished through the significant time, money and energy of the human experts. The future library will be able to deliver effective services to its users within a few seconds, if expert systems are developed. There is one question whether the expert system replace the librarians and librarianship. Even though expert systems designed there is need to frame rules on which expert systems work. For this purpose, subject experts that are library professionals are essential. But in future, the librarianship must be more technology oriented.

REFERENCES

1. Patterson, DW: Introduction to Artificial Intelligence and Expert Systems. Delhi: Prentice Hall of India, 1992. P.5.
2. Ojha, AC and Shah, Pinesh: Expert System using JESS. The ICFAI Journal of Information Technology. Vol. 2. No.1. March 2006. P.29.-35.
3. Engelmore, Robert S and Feigenbaum, Edward: Expert Systems and Artificial Intelligence: Introduction. http://www.wtec.org/loyola/kb/c1s1.htm accessed on 25th June 2006.
4. Expert Systems Building Tools: Definitions http://www.wtec.org/loyola/kb/c3s2.htm Accessed on 25th June 2006.
5. Expert System Tutorial. http://www.carlisle.army.mil/usacsl/divisions/std/branches/keg/expert/build.htm Accessed on 25th June 2006.
6. Expert System. Wikipedia, the free Encyclopedia. http://en.wikipedia.org/ExpertSystem accessed on 25th June 2006.
7. Denning, R and Smith, PJ: Interface design concepts in the development of ELSA, an intelligent Electronic Library Search Assistant. *Information Technology and Libraries.* Vol. 13. 1994. P. 133-147.
8. Bailey, CW and Myers, JE, Ed: Expert Systems in ARL Libraries. Washington DC: Association of Research Libraries, 1991. Spec Kit P.174.
9. Hawks, CP: Expert Systems in Technical Services and Collection Management. *Information Technology and Libraries.* Vol. 13. 1994. P. 203-212.
10. 10. Patil,D.B: Expert system: an overview. In Inf, Comm, Lib and Community development. ed by B Ramesh Babu and S Gopalkrishnana. Delhi: B R Pub, 2004.pp. 663-675.

29

Emerging Libraries

Chinmayee N. Bhange

ABSTRACT

The new technological developments, which had occurred during these few decades, have drastically influenced the functions and services of the library. They have also affected the attitude of library users. The libraries have now begun to transfer from manual operations to an automated system. The impact of these technologies on the libraries will depend on the technologies involved; and the extent to which they are being utilized for library operations. Bearing these two factors in mind, this paper describes four basic scenarios for the future development of library systems. Four basic types of library systems are discussed: polymedia libraries; electronic libraries; digital libraries; and virtual libraries.

INTRODUCTION

The library adopted technological changes into three stages. In the first stage, technology is used to do the same things, but more quickly than before. Library used computer applications to speed up its functions of acquisition, cataloguing and circulation. This stage brings computers in the internal operations of the library.

In the second stage, technology is used for new applications and to do new things. Libraries began to enter in this stage with technological advances such as online catalogs, which have greater search capacities than traditional card catalogs, and this new database searching permits searchers to search materials electronically which has broadened their search process.

In stage three, technology is used in ways that create fundamental changes within libraries. Now libraries are moving towards this stage, which pictures the virtual end of the library where users' information needs are satisfied entirely by electronic information available in homes or offices. (Morris, 1989). This stage may reduce the image of the library as a physical place; however it cannot completely demolish the role of the librarian or the printed materials in the library, they will still exist in the future.

The new technological developments, which had occurred during these few decades, have drastically influenced the functions and services of the library. They have also affected the attitude of library users. The libraries have now begun to transfer from manual operations to electronic system (Akeroyd, 2001).

The impact that these technologies will have will depends on two main factors: the technologies involved; and the extent to which they are taken up. Bearing these two factors in mind, this paper describes four basic scenarios for the future development of library systems (Barker, 1999). Four basic types of library systems are discussed: *polymedia libraries; electronic libraries; digital libraries; and virtual libraries.*

POLYMEDIA LIBRARIES

The term 'polymedia' is used to denote the use of several different independent media for the storage of information and knowledge. For example, paper, microfilm and compact disk each represent a different physically distinct storage technology. However, taken together they would constitute an example of a polymedia storage facility. Bearing this in mind, *polymedia libraries* will therefore be institutions that store information and knowledge using a wide variety of different media types. Essentially, such libraries will be very similar to conventional library systems, as we know them today. They will therefore contain conventional books along with information that is held on videos, audio tape, CDs, microfilm, video discs, computer software, and so on.

The management and organisational processes within *polymedia libraries* will be much the same as they are at present within conventional libraries, that is, basically manual. The information retrieval processes used in these libraries will also be of a manual nature - based upon the use of card indexes, microfilm, microfiche, and so on. Although such libraries will contain computers (for use by users) this technology will not be used for the realisation of any form of library automation.

Because of the absence of automated processes, an important aspect of polymedia library systems will be the access they provide to human librarians. The library staff will therefore act as a rich source of expertise with respect to library matters and the retrieval of information using the various mechanisms that a particular library makes available.

ELECTRONIC LIBRARIES

The expression 'electronic library' is one which has a range of different meanings associated with it. E-libraries might consist of Web-based or Web-adapted resources, which have been "collected" with a particular client group in mind. Physically, such a collection usually appears as a Web site or compilation of links published on a Web server to which – depending on the content or other aspects of the library – there may be access from the global Internet (Kovacs, 2000). Obviously, the most important way in which this is likely to be achieved is through the widespread use of computers and the various facilities that they are able to make available - such as, on-line indexes, full-text searching and retrieval facilities, automated record keeping, computer-based decision-making, and so on.

Barker (1999) further adds that, one important 'hallmark' of an electronic library will be the conscious movement towards the more widespread use of electronic media for the storage, retrieval and delivery of information. This will often mean that libraries of this sort will usually be involved in an active and extensive book computerization programme. Although there will be extensive use of electronic media within these libraries, conventional books will still coexist alongside the electronic publications.

Within *electronic libraries* it will still be possible to gain access to librarians in order to seek help and assistance relating to library matters. However, attempts will often be made to computerize some of the more routine queries that librarians have to handle. This will be achieved through the use of interactive software that embeds rule sets that enable it to emulate human expertise within particular areas.

DIGITAL LIBRARIES

A current focus for many libraries is to digitize information and make it available online. Hawkins feels that the concept of the digital library violates some traditional assumptions about libraries and collections. He believes that there should be a move away from the concept of the library as a physical place, and that libraries and collections are about much more than books. The concept of the digital library defines it as a repository of all kinds of information, which is not subject to limitations of format or physical space.

LIBRARY IN THE DIGITAL WORLD

A library is often associated with large buildings filled with massive roes of storage racks for printed books and journals. A conventional library is gauged by the number of titles that it holds and by the number of titles that it subscribes.

In contrast, the modern digital library will be a sleek array of computer-based information systems. This library will be gauged by the number of accesses made rather than by the number of titles it holds (Balakrishnan, 1996).

The term "digital" is actually somewhat a misnomer. Digital libraries basically store materials in an electronic format and manipulate large collections of those materials effectively (Rathore, 2000).

For many years, librarians have drawn attention to the rapid explosion of published information and to the difficulties it posts for libraries and information services attempting to provide ordered access to the world's information for their users. The advent of digital information, together with the development of worldwide information and communication networks, has brought a new order of magnitude to this problem. While in the past, the library's role may have been defined in terms of collection that it brought together and that largely satisfy its clientele, the modern library as we have seen, is more likely to act as an access interface to the global wealth of information, the "information universe". It includes the books held by the worlds' libraries, all current and past journal issues, newspapers, databases of various types, the resources of the world wide web, report literature, ephemera such as handbills, patents, recorded visual images whether still, video, audio, realia such as artistic and museum objects, representations in virtual reality and so on (Brophy, 2001).

VIRTUAL LIBRARY

The characteristics that make interactive multimedia attractive for teaching purposes and reference tools are also what help to make them accessible and easy to use by a variety of users. Virtual libraries rely on interactivity to allow patrons to explore sites and to use resources. While the terms 'virtual library' and 'digital library' are frequently used interchangeably, they are in fact not the same thing. A digital library consists of a networked collection of multimedia information typically available in one location, while a virtual library comprises a set of links to various resources on the Internet, such as documents, software or databases. The links in a virtual library are transparent to users and it provides them with one interface to information (Fecko, 1997)

Virtual library systems depend for their existence upon a rapidly maturing area of technology known as virtual reality or 'VR'. VR has often been described as the 'ultimate multimedia experience' - the simplest form of which is known as telepresence. Such experiences depend upon the ability of a computer (and its associated interaction peripherals) to create highly realistic simulations and surrogations in which users can become 'totally immersed'. VR technology has been used in many successful ways to create virtual landscapes, cities, buildings and offices. The technology has also been applied to the fabrication of virtual classrooms, laboratories and instrumentation.

THE UNIVERSAL LIBRARY

Digital library is really a transitory phase towards The Universal Library – a vast distributed information and active advice repository accessible from anywhere with an increasing improved indexing, extraction and summarization techniques. It will be a library without walls or national boundaries.

The "universal library", an amalgamation of all recorded human knowledge, searchable from your personal computer, sounds like a fantasy. But the elements are now under development.

CYBERSPACE

"Cyberspace" is a term coined by William Gibson referring to the interconnected web of databases, telecommunications links and computer networks which perpetually seem to constitute a new space for human communication and action.

"Cybernetics" is a related but older term coined by Norbert Wiener to describe the science of control and communications in animals and machines.

Both terms stem from the cognate "Cyber" which is derived from the Greek Kubernetes ("Steersman"). Cybernetics is concerned with the study of any system – it is sometimes referred to as systems theory – not simply computer systems. While as science it has yielded a wide range of insights, its major practical impact has been in engineering and in the design of large, complex computer systems.

In popular usage, the prefix "cyber" has tended to be used very loosely to mean something related to computers (Kawatra, 2000).

CONCLUSION

The co-existence of print and digital documents presents problems for libraries. Decisions should be made regarding, which resources should be converted to digital format, and guidelines are needed to reach these decisions. The types of information that are digitized range from course reserves to rare documents.

Hawkins describes the digital library concept as 'specifically both a solution to the economic problems facing libraries and a vehicle for a new functionality that promises to transform scholarship and bring the cultural, social and economic benefits of information to the many.'

Collection development is still a concern for digital libraries. Graham (1995) further asserts that with experience, libraries will realize that there is still a responsibility for collection development and management with digital libraries. He states:

"It is sometimes loosely proposed (not by librarians) that libraries need not acquire electronic information, for it will be available somewhere on the network. Such proposals ignore the obvious truth that some institution must still, in the end, take responsibility for the information."

REFERENCES

1. Akeroyd, John. (2001). The future of academic libraries. *Aslib proceedings*.53 (3): 79-84.
2. Balakrishnan, N. (1996). *Impact of Information Technology on Library Science.* In: Malwad, N.M.; Rajashekhar, T. B.; Ravichandra Rao, I.K.; Satyanarayana, N.V. (Eds.) *Digital libraries: dynamic storehouse of digitized information.* New Delhi: New Age International, 192-206.
3. Barker, Philip. (1999). Electronic Libraries of the Future. Retrieved November 30, 2002, from *http://web.singnet.com.sg/~abanerji/sect5.htm*
4. Brophy, Peter. (2001). The Library in the 21st. Century: New Services for the Information Age. London: Library Association
5. Fecko, Mary Beth. (1997). *Electronic Resources: Access and Issues.* London: Bowker-Saur. 148p.
6. Graham, P. (1995). Requirements for the digital research library. College and Research Libraries. 56(4): 331-339.
7. Kawatra, P. S. (2000). Textbook of Information Science. New Delhi: A.P.H. Publishing Corporation. (Chapter 13: The Universal Library 275-304)

8. Kovacs, Diane K.; Elkordy, Angela. (2000). Collection Development in Cyberspace. *Library Hi Tech*. 2000; 18(4): 335-339.
9. Morris, Dilys E. (1989). Electronic information and technology: impact and potential for academic libraries. *College and research libraries*. 50(1): 56-64.
10. Rathore, R.S. (2000). Digital Libraries: a Boon For Resource Sharing. In: T, Ashok Babu [et al]. Vision of Future Library and Information Systems. New Delhi: Viva Books. 200 – 208.

Index